60 Years of Journalism
Edited and with introductions by Roy Hoopes

The late James M. Cain was a newspaperman, playwright and novelist. Cain is best known for his controversial novels: *The Postman Always Rings Twice, Double Indemnity, Mildred Pierce, Serenade, The Butterfly* and *Past All Dishonor*. The first three novels were made into back-to-back blockbuster movies in the mid-1940s.

Cain always considered himself a journalist, a "newspaperman who wrote yarns on the side." Cain had a distinguished 60-year career as a journalist. He began his newspaper career on *The Baltimore American* in 1917. He then worked for *The Sun,* Baltimore, before enlisting in the Army in 1918. After the war Cain wrote editorials for *The New York World*. He also wrote for: *The New York Sun, The American Mercury, The Atlantic Monthly, The Nation, Vanity Fair, McCall's, Redbook, Liberty,* and *The Ladies Home Journal.*

When he was in his eighties he began writing articles for *The Washington Post* and literally spent his last living hours at his typewriter.

The book is fascinating reading and includes some of Cain's best articles and essays. The material is sometimes serious, sometimes humorous and provides a unique look at 60 years of history.

H.L. Mencken and Walter Lippman, two journalistic legends and Cain's editors, had nothing but praise for Cain. Mencken said Cain was "the most competent writer the country ever produced" and he never wrote a bad article.

60 Years of Journalism

60 Years of Journalism
by James M. Cain

Edited and with Introductions by
Roy Hoopes

Bowling Green State University Popular Press
Bowling Green, Ohio 43403

Acknowledgements

"The Widow's Mite-Or Queen of the Rancho" first appeared in *Vanity Fair* and is reprinted with permission. Copyright © 1933 (renewed 1966) by the Conde Nast Publications, Inc.

"Preface-Who's Who in America" by James M. Caine is reprinted with the permission of Marquis Who's Who, Inc.

"Mr. Mencken and the Multitudes" first appeared in *The New York Times*. Copyright ©1950 by The New York Times Company. Reprinted by permission.

"Walter Lippman has style," "Silent Night-1918," "Hot Hollywood," "Charles Laughton A Reminiscence of a Revelation," "The Gentle Side of W.C. Fields," "Things I Should Have Done I Did Not Do-Dammit," "American My Foot," first appeared in *The Washington Post* and are reprinted with permission. Copyright ©1974, 1975, 1976, 1977 by The Washington Post.

Contents

James M. Cain:
Newspaperman, Playwright and Novelist—In That Order
Introduction

The late James M. Cain is, of course, best known for his controversial novels—*The Postman Always Rings Twice, Double Indemnity, Mildred Pierce, Serenade, The Butterfly, Past All Dishonor*, the first three of which were made into back-to-back blockbuster movies in the mid-1940s and all of which continue to be published and read regularly around the world. He also was quite well known as a Hollywood screenwriter in the 1930s and '40s, due primarily to the success of his three big movies, rather than his own talents as a scriptwriter. He did, however, make a small fortune during his 17 years in Hollywood and enjoyed a glamorous career in the gossip-columns. But the fact is, Cain was never a screenwriter and he knew it. His famous movies were turned into screenplays by other writers, and he only earned three B-Picture credits writing for the movies. He also suspected that he was not really a novelist: "I am not a novelist at all," he once said, "but a playwright who casts his plays in novel form."

He spent a life-time pursuing his ambition to write plays, but his achievements as a playwright were not much greater than his screen credits— "Crashing the Gate," which was written in the 1920s, staged in New England, but never reached Broadway; a Broadway version of *The Postman* that closed after 72 performances in 1936; "7-11," which played one week in summer stock in Cohasset in 1938; "The Guest in Room 701," written in the early 1950s, but never produced; and a 1953 roadshow revival of *The Postman*, starring Tom Neal and Barbara Payton, about which *The Chicago Tribune* said this "crude dramatization suggests that if the theater isn't dead, someone ought to arrange a mercy killing." He also wrote for *The American Mercury* several "dialogues" which were essentially one-act plays that have been produced over the years.

However, the real James M. Cain, by his own admission, was a journalist, a "newspaperman who wrote yarns on the side," as he liked to phrase it. And despite the fame and fortune he earned in Hollywood and with his best-selling novels, he always insisted in his *Who's Who in America* resume that he be classified as a "newspaperman," rather than a "novelist." He had a distinguished 60-year career as a journalists and a remarkably high percentage of his non-fiction prose is as durable as his fiction. When *Vanity Fair* resumed publication (with much fanfare in the spring of 1983), its first issue included an article by Cain that had appeared in the magazine in August of 1933. *Time* said that the Cain article (on Malibu Beach, see page 178) was the best thing in the new magazine.

The relationship between Cain's fiction and his journalism has been

1

explored by many critics and reviewers beginning with the publication of *The Postman.* William Rose Benet in reviewing Cain's first novel noted his now-famous style and said that newspaper journalism teaches compact writing—and "Mr. Cain has learned it." Whether or not Cain's style grew out of his newspaper writing or the basic fundamentals he learned during the years he taught English, grammar and journalism is debatable. In fact, Cain may have actually taught newspapermen more than he learned from them. Benet was more to the point when he said that "this novel derives from the sensationalism of America fostered by the daily press." *The Postman* had, in fact, evolved from a story that had been widely covered in the 1920s press. One day in 1933, Cain and Vincent Lawrence, a Hollywood screenwriter who helped Cain in his Hollywood career in much the same way Mencken and Lippmann encouraged his journalism, were talking about the Ruth Snyder-Judd Gray murder case, which had dominated the newspapers in 1927. Albert Snyder was a mild little Long Islander and art editor of *Motor Boating* magazine. His wife, Ruth, and her lover, Judd Gray, a corset salesman, conspired to murder Snyder, then turned on each other after the murder. Lawrence said: "I heard that when Ruth Snyder packed Gray off to Syracuse where he was to stay the night she murdered her husband, she gave him a bottle of wine which he desperately wanted on the train, but he had no corkscrew with him and dared not ask the porter for one, for fear it would be the one thing he'd remember him by. When the police lab analyzed it, they found enough arsenic to kill a regiment of men. "Did you ever hear that, Cain?"

Cain had not, but he said to Lawrence: "That jells the idea I've had for just such a story. A couple of jerks discover that murder, though dreadful enough morally, can be a love story, too, but then wake up to discover that once they've pulled the thing off no two people can share this terrible secret and live on the same earth. They turn against each other, as Judd and Ruth did."

Edmund Wilson was also aware of the impact of daily journalism on Cain's writing. In his classic, "The Boys in the Backroom" (the boys included Cain, John O'Hara, William Saroyan and John Steinbeck), Wilson calls them "poets of the tabloid murder" who are "ingenious in tracing from their first beginnings the tangles that gradually tighten around the necks of the people involved in those bizarre and brutal crimes that figure in the American papers." And David Madden, in his excellent study, *James M. Cain,* says: "Cain is in the tradition of the American journalist turned writer. Like Twain and Hemingway, he reported from the scene; like Ambrose Bierce and Mencken, he wrote essays on public affairs and manners." Madden also noted that "none of his heroes are newspapermen," which is true enough, and there was a good reason.

Cain was a superb journalist, perhaps coming as close to being a poet of the press as anyone writing in New York between the wars. The two main thrusts of Cain's journalism career occurred while he was writing articles for *The American Mercury* and editorials for *The New York World* in the 1920s and, without qualification, he attributes his success as a journalist to the encouragement he received from his two editors—H.L. Mencken and Walter Lippmann. They, in turn, had nothing but praise for their protege: Mencken called Cain "the most competent writer the country ever produced" who never wrote a bad article. And Lippmann once answered a reader, who had complained of an editorial by Cain: "He is...our expert on stuffed shirts and clay feet and this brief treatise contains a staggering amount of the most horrible truth."

Cain was born in Annapolis in 1892, but grew up across the Chesapeake Bay in Chestertown, here his father moved in 1903 to take over the presidency of little Washington College. Cain was a precocious child and with encouragement and help from his father, entered Washington College early and came out at the age—18—when most kids are just finishing high school. All during his college years he felt like a "midget among giants" and he quite literally did not know what to do when he graduated. He tried a series of odd jobs in Baltimore and around the Eastern and Western shores before finally deciding "out of the blue" (while sitting on a bench in Lafayette Park across from the White House in 1914) to become a writer.

This took him home to Chestertown, where his father gave him a job teaching English and grammar at the College's prep school. The most significant result of this experience was that Cain became a walking encyclopedia of grammar and punctuation, which he maintained until the end of his life was the only thing you could teach a writer—except for typing.

And in his spare time he learned to write: "I played the typewriter on which I was becoming a virtuoso," he said, "writing short stories in secret, sending them off to magazines, and getting all of them back. In a year or more of trying, I didn't make one sale, until the thing became ridiculous."

Cain's father did not give much support to his son's aspiration to become a writer, but his mother was very encouraging. She had been appalled the year before when Jamie, as everyone called him in Chestertown, came home to announce that he wanted to be an opera singer. Rose Cain was something of an opera singer herself, having studied for years in New Haven and given up a promising career to marry James W. Cain. She knew Jamie did not have a grand opera voice nor the temperament to become a singer. But she saw promise in his writing, and when he was not able to sell his short stories, she encouraged him to go up to Baltimore and try to find a job on a newspaper. That, everyone agreed, would be a good place for a writer to start.

Cain began his newspaper career on *The Baltimore American* in 1917.

Then he worked briefly for the *Sun,* before going to Europe with the American Expeditionary Force in 1918. In the Army he made something of a name for himself as the editor of *The Lorraine Cross,* the newspaper published by the 79th Division. He returned to his old job as a reporter on *The Sun* in 1920 and gained national recognition covering the trial of William Blizzard, a young West Virginia coal miner who was being tried for his role in leading an armed band of coal miners in an attack against the hired guns of the coal operators, who were also sworn deputies of the West Virginia State Police. The state called it treason, but Cain disagreed, and his reporting of the trial caught the eye of *Sun* editor and columnist, H. L. Mencken, whom Cain had met by now. It also caught the eyes of the editors of *The Atlantic Monthly* and *The Nation.* In 1922 and 1923, Cain wrote three magazine articles, one for *The Atlantic,* two for *The Nation,* which signalled the literary world that a talented young stylist was developing, as this opening paragraph of his second *Nation* piece suggests:

Rough mountains rise all about, beautiful in their bleak ugliness. They are hard and barren, save for a scrubby, whiskery growth of trees that only half conceal the hard rock beneath. Yet they have their moods. On gray days they lie heavy and sullen, but on sunny mornings they are dizzy with color; flat canvases painted in gaudy hues; here and there tiny soft black pines showing against a cool, blue sky. At night, if the moon shines through a haze, they hang far above you, dim outlines of smoke; you could throw a stone right through them. They are gashed everywhere with water courses, roaring rivers, a bubbling creek. Along these you plod, a crawling midge, while ever the towering mountains shut you in. Now and then you top a ridge and look about. Miles and miles of billowing peaks, miles and miles of color softly melting into color. Bright yellows and reds give way to greens and misty grays, until they all fade into faint lavender and horizon blue.... A setting for a Nibelungen epic, revealing instead a sordid melodrama.

The success of his Blizzard trial reporting, the magazine articles and the encouragement of Mencken, all helped give Cain the feeling that the time had come for greater things. The greater thing, of course, had to be the Great American Novel, which every reporter worth his salt in the 1920s was presumed to be contemplating, if not writing. In fact, the Great American Novel was discussed so often in the literary columns then that Franklin P. Adams, in "The Conning Towers," appearing in *The New York World,* had come to calling it "The G.A.N." Cain's G.A.N., he decided, would be based on his experience in the West Virginia coal mines.

He took a leave of absence from *The Sun* to go back down to West Virginia to gather more "dope," as Cain always called his background research. But first he wanted to talk with Mencken about his novel, and although he and Mencken would eventually become friends, this first meeting was a disappointment, with Mencken brushing off the aspiring novelist with what Cain called "No. 5 of his acts for young writers." In Cain's estimation, the conversation was useless and he decided Mencken had no idea how to write a novel. "Two years out of a man's life—that's a novel," was the gist of Mencken's counsel.

The disappointing meeting with Mencken did not discourage Cain and he went down to West Virginia, spent a month or so gathering dope, came back to Baltimore and devoted two months to trying to write his G.A.N. The novel evolved around a daring concept for 1922, one that was taboo in literature—incest! And it owed, something in its approach, he said, to John Dos Passos' *The Soldiers*, which had just been published: "My man was to be a radical union organizer, in the mine fields of the 1920s, winding up as part of the march of 1921, his mind on the destruction of a system he felt was constrictive like a chain around the men. My whole novel was to highlight his compulsion to break things apart, and his final discovery that he couldn't. At that point he was to be alone in a woods above the mines between two trees, that in futile rage he kept trying to push apart, apparently thinking they might fall, as he had seen the temple fall when the hero toppled the pillars, in the opera Samson and Delilah. But nothing happened—the trees just stood there."

And so did Cain's novel—it would not move. He wrote one draft, but disliked it. He wrote a second and threw it in the waste basket. Then he wrote a third, but decided that it was still bad and threw it in the waste basket. Cain had discovered the hard way what thousands of journalists have learned and what Mencken did not tell him—that an ability to write good newspaper stories and magazine articles does not necessarily make you a novelist. So he had "to go slinking back to work," ashamed to admit to his colleagues—especially Mencken—that the Great American Novel still had not been written.

His first attempt to write a novel had convinced Cain that he was not a novelist; and in his discouragement, he also decided he was not a reporter: "I could never quite believe," he said later, "that it mattered a damn whether the public learned the full name and address of the fireman injured at the blaze." So, by the summer of 1923, Cain was ready to leave *The Sun*, but he did not really know what to do next. Then suddenly an opportunity developed on one of his visits to his parents' home in Roland Park. The senior Cain, after being fired as president of Washington College in 1918, had taken a job as vice president of the United States Fidelity Guaranty Company in Baltimore and was doing quite well. At Roland Park, Cain met Enoch Garey, an ex-West Point football star, who the senior Cain was pushing as President of St. John's College in Annapolis. Garey surprised both Cains by telling them he would take the job if the young Cain would come down to St. John's as a teacher of English and journalism and also help him with other chores connected with the presidency.

By this time, Cain had married his college sweetheart, Mary Clough, who was teaching in the Baltimore school system. He discussed the job offer with Mary, then decided to accept it and the Cains moved to Annapolis for what started out to be a very pleasant experience—but which ended with Cain at the lowest point in his career. In less than a year, his marriage had come apart, he had lost his job in a dispute with the president of St. John's over the dismissal of four football players and was confined to a tuberculosis sanitarium in Sabillasville, Maryland. The only bright spot in his two semesters at St. John's was the response to the articles he wrote for Mencken's new magazine, *The American Mercury*, which will be discussed in the next section.

Cain was released from the sanitarium in the Fall of 1924, but was warned by his doctor that he should avoid strenuous work. So he went to New York, armed with a letter of introduction to Arthur Krock, who was working on *The New York World*. The letter was glowing with praise for Cain, "one of Henry's rare understatements," Krock said.

By 1924, the legendary gold-domed *World* building, at the north corner of Park Row, had passed its prime. When it was dedicated in 1890—sixteen stories, towering 310 feet—it was the tallest building in the city, and incredulous visitors from the hinterlands (as well as sophisticated New Yorkers) paid to visit its domed top, from where the view was spectacular and the climate—intellectual as well as atmospheric—heady. But now the building had deteriorated. For one thing it was drafty, and when a *World* reporter died of influenza in 1922, the paper's flamboyant editor, Herbert Bayard Swope, complained to owner Ralph Pulitzer that he was probably done in by the foul atmosphere on the twelfth floor.

Swope's office, known as the "lion's den," or, as Lincoln Schuster called it, the "swope-filled room," was also on the twelfth floor, as were the offices of the *Evening World*. One floor below was the Sunday department, and one floor above, the restaurant. The condition of the restaurant had reached the point where it was said that the only good thing ever to come out of it was *What Price Glory?*, the new Broadway smash *World* writers Maxwell Anderson and Laurence Stallings had conceived over lunch in its seedy confines.

At the top of the building, in the rarefied atmosphere of the fourteenth floor, was the talented corps of editorial writers who worked for the recently hired Walter Lippmann—Anderson, Charles Merz, Allan Nevins, John Heston, and W. O. Scroggs. Between assignments, as Pulitzer's right-hand man, Arthur Krock also contributed an occasional editorial.

Cain arrived at a critical time in the declining days of the *World*. Its rise to journalistic glory had begun in 1883, when Joseph Pulitzer, the publishing genius who had built the *St. Louis Post-Dispatch*, purchased the paper from New York financier Jay Gould. Within two weeks, the front page had been transformed from the sedate print-dominated format of the traditional nineteenth-century newspaper to an attractive, lively page featuring a large photograph, engaging headlines and well-written news stories. *The World* had begun its crusade to lead the American press into a new era of journalism. Unlike most papers of its time, it supported the Democratic party and the workingman against the entrenched Establishment and prided itself on hardhitting stories exposing political and economic corruption.

Since 1920, the paper had been under Swope's direction as executive editor. This dynamic journalist had been one of the *World's* star crime reporters in the early years; then its war correspondent in France. But despite his energetic leadership, the *World's* distinctive reporting began to decline after World War I. "By 1923," Morris Markey later wrote, "the reaching out, the sharp and arresting miracle of zeal" was gone. "Somewhere in those years, so subtly that a moment cannot be fixed with any certainty at all, the rude vigor, the yowling boisterous assurance of the Pulitzer tradition died. The times were changing. The *World* was changing. With every politician a grafter, why bellow at one? With an aura of sad futility drooping over the earth's evils, why explode to the echo of a single evil? Why snarl at a President of the United States?"

If the *World*'s reporting had declined, however, the editorial section had gradually emerged as the paper's most distinctive feature. It was intelligent and well written, and its lead items were sometimes brilliant. Although the op-ed page did not have articles by outsiders, it did have columns, including the already famous "Conning Tower" by Franklin P. Adams, Heywood Broun's "It Seems to Me," Laurence Stallings's book review, "The First Reader," and a regular column from Washington by Charley Michelson (who would one day be President Franklin D. Roosevelt's press secretary). The Sunday "Metropolitan Section" also ran a regular feature by Will Rogers. It was the quality of these sections that prompted *The New Yorker*, soon after its birth in 1925, to proclaim it intended to be a weekly comparable in intelligence, good taste, honesty, courage, news sense, and interest to the *New York World*. And "the Page Opposite Editorial, rather than the front page," wrote Markey, "became the goal of every dreamy cub in the land."

At thirty-two James M. Cain was hardly a cub, but it was the *World's* Page Opposite that lured him that day late in September, 1924, when he sought out Arthur Krock in the upper reaches of the Pulitzer Building. And what Cain did not know was that one of the editorials that day, headed "The Insatiable Telegraph," was to be the last editorial written for the *World* by Maxwell Anderson. The blossoming playwright had specialized in what editors call human-interest editorials, little essays, sometimes light and breezy, on subjects of interest to everyone—food, transportation, human relations, animals, holidays, sports, music, etc. But now, after the success of *What Price Glory?* Anderson was ready to devote full time to writing plays and Lippmann desperately needed a human-interest editorial writer to replace him. The result was that Cain was hired as an editorial writer rather than an op-ed page editor, as he had hoped.

This was the beginning of a distinguished New York journalistic career, which lasted until the *World* folded in 1931. In six years, his work on the *World*, combined with the writing he was doing at the same time for Mencken, resulted in James M. Cain's emergence as one of the most prominent journalists in the country. John Lee Mahin, a script writer who later met Cain in Hollywood, recalls that when he was on *The New York Sun* in the 20s and became interested in editorial writing, someone told him: "If you want to learn about editorials, there's a guy over on the *World* who writes them." He was referring to Cain, so Mahin began reading some of his editorials and said: "They were masterpieces."

Perhaps the most significant aspect of his job on the *World* was that he had found another mentor who, along with Mencken, would help him develop as a writer. Cain's admiration for Walter Lippmann, as a man, a writer and, most important, literary stylist, at times bordered on hero worship.

While writing his editorials and, eventually, a regular bylined column for the Sunday *World*, Cain was also contributing to *The American Mercury*. And his first contributions were vintage Mencken iconoclasm. But gradually, in the mid-1920s, he began writing satiric dialogues, which attracted considerable attention, not only in New York but in Hollywood.

His reputation as a writer and editor were also known to Harold Ross, so that when the *World* folded in 1931, Cain was hired by *The New Yorker* to become the 26th Jesus, which was *New Yorker* parlance for managing editor. He replaced a charming young fellow named Ogden Nash, who everyone agreed was a better poet than administrator. And in a remarkably short time, it was also agreed that James M. Cain was a better writer than he was managing editor. There has probably never been a more obvious journalistic example of a square peg in a round hole than Cain's brief career working for Harold Ross.

Cain would eventually become very close to H.L. Mencken and had almost immediately developed a rapport with Walter Lippmann. But he never did understand Harold Ross and was completely unable to establish a working relationship with the *New Yorker* editor. Cain's appraisal of Ross is somewhat ambiguous. For example, he told one ex-*New Yorker* hand that he thought that beginning with Ralph Ingersoll, the "Jesuses" really ran the magazine and that Ross was just "a problem child in the office perpetually creating the chaos he wanted to cure." He also thought not enough credit was given to Raol Fleischmann and Katherine White for their contributions to building the *New Yorker*. He felt that Ross did not discover talent, that he, in fact, discouraged talent and was responsible for losing more good writers than he kept. And he noted that when Ross died, the *New Yorker* went right on running, as the *Saturday Evening Post* did after George Horace Lorimer's death. In other words, the *New Yorker* succeeded in spite of Ross.

On the other hand, Cain said "I have a prodigious admiration for Ross." He gave him credit for discovering, or at least giving them their first real show window, a great many writers who went on to become famous. "He illustrated the principle that an editor must spark contributors. He was marvelous to talk to, and the effect he had on writers, artists, and such people was electrical. He had an original mind, with enough naivete about it to go questing for fundamentals, sometimes the fundamental everyone takes for granted."

As for Ross' presumed wackiness, like not running a piece after he had paid for it and his inability to articulate what was wrong with it, Cain said he had all the more respect for his decisions because of that. "Whether in magazine editing, playwrighting, screenwriting or whatever, the creative process in most of its stages is intuitive, with explanations thought up after the fact, not considered in advance of it. The article Ross rejected, you would usually find, had its own adequate disqualifications, even if Ross would be somewhat inarticulate as to what they were .... I think most who knew him well would say there was a bit of a gap between what went on in his mind and what came out of his mouth."

After only nine months on the *New Yorker*, Cain accepted a job offer in California, which was easily the most significant development in his literary career. Paramount Studios had offered him $400 a week, compared to the $200 he had been making at the *New Yorker*. But more important: "I'd been gradually coming to the conclusion," he said, "that if I was to write anything of the kind I'd been dreaming about for so long, it could not be based in New York .... Those killingly funny drivers of New York cabs, secretaries, bellhops, and clerks behind the counters were completely sterile soil." However, the country bumpkin dialogues he had been writing for Mencken in *The Mercury* were different. He took pride in them. They were a colloquial "down home idiom of Anywhere USA—Anywhere but New York."

Success in California, however, was elusive. The job at Paramount lasted six months and his contract was not renewed. He had flopped in his first attempt at screenwriting—"hit the deck like a watermelon that has rolled off the stevedore's truck." The failure hurt. The successful journalist "who had usually been the white-haired boy of editors," as he put it, "found there was one kind of writing I was not good at. I couldn't write for pictures"—which did not prevent him from spending the next 16 years trying.

But he could still write and he immediately became what every unemployed writer becomes—a free lancer. He began producing short stories and then articles for *The Mercury, Vanity Fair, McCall's, Redbook, Liberty* and *The Ladies Home Journal*. Then, encouraged by Alfred A. Knopf, he decided to try another novel—this one about a California drifter and the wife of a Greek who owned a gas station-restaurant, who conspire to murder the Greek to get his business. He called it *Bar-B-Que*, sent it off to Knopf, not expecting it to sell more than 500 copies, even if Knopf accepted it.

With both Mencken and Lippmann praising the manuscript, Knopf accepted it. They agreed to a new title—*The Postman Always Rings Twice*—and the novel was scheduled for publication in the Spring of 1934. Meanwhile, Cain was approached by B.A. Bergman, who had succeeded Cain at the *New Yorker* and was now working for the Hearst syndicate. Bergman wanted Cain to write a regular column for $85-a-week, which Cain eagerly agreed to do after being assured by Bergman he could write about anything he wanted to—except politics. This restriction did not concern Cain, who considered politics the least interesting subject on earth. His favorite "subject of subjects" was Man and his relation to his fellow men—and women.

Meanwhile, a friend who worked in one of the movie studios and to whom Cain had given a carbon of *The Postman*, called him one morning and said: "Jim, I called up about that book. I make a confession to you. When I went to bed last night, I took it with me, expecting to read 20 pages to know what it's about in case I ran into you—and perhaps finish it some other time. I put that book down at three o'clock in the morning, having read every last page. And what I called to say is I think when that book comes out, you're going to wake up famous."

Cain did wake up famous when *Postman* was published. It was that rare combination—a widely acclaimed literary success and a phenomenal bestseller. And Cain spent most of the rest of his life trying to live up to it. He was in great demand now from book and magazine publishers, but for fiction rather than articles on non-fiction.

By 1935, Hearst also decided he did not like James M. Cain and forced Bergman to discontinue his column—which meant, essentially, that Cain's career as a journalist was over. However, late in his life, when he was in his 80s, he started writing articles again for *The Washington Post* and he quite literally spent his last hours on earth where he preferred to be—at his typewriter. Despite the success of his novels and his permanent place in American literature, he insisted to the end that he was a newspaperman who wrote yarns on the side. And perhaps the most significant comment he ever made about his career came in a remark he once made to me, discussing his fiction: "I never write about newspapermen," he said. "It would be transparent that I am writing about myself."

Roy Hoopes
Bethesda, Maryland
August 1985

I. Mencken and the Mercury—1920s Iconoclasm

Introduction

One of the most intriguing aspects of James M. Cain's early career is that despite the fact he grew up in Chestertown, Maryland, on the Eastern Shore, where *The Baltimore Sun* was available, and he worked for *The American* and *The Sun* in Baltimore before he enlisted in the Army in 1918, he had never really paid much attention to H.L. Mencken, easily the most dominant intellectual figure in Baltimore, if not the entire Eastern Seaboard. Cain said he knew of Mencken and his column but never read him, assuming he was just "a hick celebrity of the kind Baltimore produced."

What first attracted Cain to Mencken was a *Sun* column headed "The Clowns March In," written early in 1920, by which time Cain had returned from France and was working for the *Sun* again. The clowns were the candidates for the presidential nomination—Leonard Wood, Hiram Johnson, Charles Evans Hughes, James M. Cox. Somewhat contemptuously, Cain started to read it but by the time he had reached the point where Mencken called Wood "a pompous old dodo with delusions of persecution," he knew he had discovered something new and exciting. Mencken's style almost intoxicated Cain. He quickly went out and bought a copy of the *Smart Set*, which he knew Mencken edited with George Jean Nathan, and a handful of Mencken's books. After reading as much of Mencken as he could lay his hands on, Cain knew his writing would never be the same. Even 40 years later, he could recall Mencken's columns; for example, the one in which, after covering the Dempsey-Carpentier fight, Mencken tore into the legend of Carpentier's prowess. Admitting that Carpentier did land a pretty good blow on Dempsey, Cain recalled that Mencken said Dempsey "shuffled amiably" and then came in for the kill. Cain always thought "shuffled amiably" was the perfect description, way "beyond the capacity of any sports writer."

In 1922, when he was preparing to take a leave of absence from *The Sun* to go down to West Virginia to gather "dope" for his first attempt at a novel, Cain called Mencken, saying he wanted some advice. Much to his surprise, the great man showed up at his desk on "the rim" (where the editors read copy) in the *Sun* City Room and the two writers chatted about novels for 10 to 15 minutes. This first meeting was a disappointment to Cain, but the two men would eventually become friends. Cain was a tall, hulking six-footer with a heavy frame, pockmarked face, unruly black hair and was gradually acquiring the habit of speaking out of the side of his mouth feigning the tough talking newspaper man, but usually with perfect grammar. Mencken was about 5'10" and a little stocky and stodgy in appearance. At that time, he always wore single-breasted blue serge suits, with stubby, well-polished black shoes, and his hair parted in the middle. It was sandy, or perhaps reddish, straight and not very thick. His face was clear and pink and his whole

11

appearance was "well-scrubbed," as Cain put it. His eyes were blue, rather large and opened very wide, especially when he talked, which was most of the time. They had a sort of surprised look, as though the whole human race constantly astonished him. "But when he laughed," said Cain, "they crinkled up in a strangely Mephisthophelean way—but not Satanic.

Mencken's speech both enthralled and baffled Cain, because he could not quite place its origin. He finally decided it was pure Baltimorese, but as spoken by a Baltimorean who used perfect grammar and pronounced every word clearly and without slur. It was a rich voice, overlaid with a city editor's bark, "a bit facetious, terse and syntactically complete. It was pitched a bit high, as though talking to someone upstairs. It had a slight fade-away drop at sentence end, as though giving you a chance to cut in if you wanted to, and there was a bit of truculence in it, an amiably humorous kind."

Their eventual friendship came as no great surprise. Not only did the two men share a love for writing, they also had a passion for music, grammar and language. Mencken's sentences exploded like rockets with outlandish, idol-busting, myth-shattering thoughts expressed in words and phrases that made you sit up and slap your leg: "pap," "slobber," "hocus-pocus," "sissy," "boobus Americanus," the "booboisie," "homo boobiens," "oafish faiths in imbecile enthusiasm," "incredible absurdities" and, one of his favorites, "bilge of idealism." Like Mark Twain, Mencken thought the human race was absurd, but he loved people—at least some of them, especially writers, musicians and those who liked to sit around and talk (meaning mostly listen), drink beer and make music. What he did not like was the phonies—the academicians, politicians, bureaucrats, lawyers, preachers, editorial writers, corrupt businessmen, pompous literary men, the "Comstocks," in other words, the leaders of the institutions that were beginning to dominate the shallow American culture of the roaring 1920s. The times were ready for an iconoclast and Mencken was the man. And the voice of iconoclasm would be the new magazine which he was planning to launch in January of 1924 and for which, in late 1923, he was looking for contributors.

One of the first writers Mencken sought out was the young Cain, who by now was at St. John's College in Annapolis, teaching English and journalism—James M. Cain style. Two of Cain's favorite pieces of writing were the Lord's Prayer and The Sermon on the Mount, which he often read to his classes to demonstrate how much you could express in terse writing. He repeatedly told his students: "Boil it down. Boil it down." He also expressed Dr. Johnson's famous dictum that "no one but a blockhead ever wrote except for money." And Cain knew his markets. One student, unable to complete an assignment, copied a story out of the popular magazine, *Youth's Companion*, turned it in and after Cain read it, he yelled out the name of the boy in class. But instead of giving him hell for copying, Cain held up the boy's paper and said: "Send it to *Youth's Companion*. They'll buy it."

Cain had hardly begun teaching at St. John's when he received a letter from Mencken inviting him to have lunch at Marconi's in Baltimore, one of Mencken's favorite restaurants. Cain arrived promptly at 12:30 and was seated by Mr. Brooks at the table in the rear where Mencken usually assembled his luncheon gatherings (and later according to Mr. Brooks, courted Sarah Haart, whom he eventually married). When Mencken arrived, it quickly became apparent that in inviting Cain to lunch, he was doing what any editor of a new magazine does—trying to persuade all available, talented writers to write articles for him. The new magazine, which Mencken, George Jean Nathan and a young New York publisher named Alfred A. Knopf, were planning to launch in January, 1924, was to be called *The American Mercury*—a title Cain did not think much of because it reminded him of *The London Mercury*. But Mencken did not ask his opinion. What he wanted to know was whether Cain had any article ideas for the first issue. Cain was flattered, and it did not take him long to come up with the idea of a profile of a union labor leader, based on the material he had amassed on his trips to West Virginia. Mencken was excited about the proposal and it was agreed that Cain would write it. The article was scheduled for the first issue and would launch a regular *Mercury* series to be called "American Portraits."

With the business at hand out of the way, Cain and Mencken settled into a long conversation, as Mr. Brooks brought coffee, more coffee and more coffee. They talked about books and music and authors and ideas, with Mencken offering his usual Olympian comments. The lunch lasted until 4:30 or 5 in the afternoon, well beyond Mencken's allotted time for a business lunch. And Cain was flattered that the great man had spent so much time with him and he never forgot the excitement of this first prolonged conversation. Mencken sat with his chair tilted back against the wall and talked continuously, with Cain enchanted. "I felt exactly like a boy who had had his baseball autographed by Babe Ruth," said Cain, "and Babe Ruth could inspire the small boy to be a lot better ball player than he might have been without the autographed ball to reassure him, and that's how it was in some part with Mencken. His effect on you sitting there in Marconi's was impossible to comprehend."

Mencken's enthusiasm, ideas and especially his interest in Cain encouraged the young writer, who was still depressed by his failure to write his novel. After the luncheon at Marconi's, Cain rushed home exhilarated and ready to work on his article about the labor leader. He finished it soon after arriving at St. John's and was paid $60 by Mencken. Then Mencken invited Cain up to 1524 Hollins Street to discuss what he might write next, and after an evening of tapping Mencken's basement liquor supply (this was during Prohibition), which at one time was so well stocked that the floor tinkled when you walked across it, they hit on another American "type" to attack—

the editorial writer. The uninspired, pro-Establishment prose appearing on most of the country's editorial pages was one of Mencken's pet peeves. Cain shared his disapproval, and although it was not known who suggested the subject, Cain left Baltimore with another assignment and buoyed by Mencken's interest in him. But as the weeks slipped by, he was concerned that he had not received an advance copy of the inaugural issue of the *Mercury* with his labor leader profile in it.

Then Cain received one of the greatest disappointments of his life. The first issue of the *American Mercury* came out in January 1924, amid much fanfare and acclaim, but when Cain rushed down to the newsstand to buy it, he realized why Mencken had not sent him an advance copy: *His article was not in it!* He knew Mencken liked the article and that it was scheduled for that issue, and his disappointment was not relieved by Mencken's explanation. It seems that the union printers at the press Knopf had picked to print the magazine had refused to set his article in type because Cain's portrait of a labor leader was not 100% flattering, although Cain steadfastly supported the union cause. Mencken, Nathan and Knopf at once decided to find another printer "as we couldn't have them dictating to us what we would publish," Mencken explained. "But in case we had to sue them, we had to show some tangible injury the brawl had caused us, and so we held the article out. It'll appear next month"—and it did. But Cain knew that the first issue of any magazine was the one to be in, the one everyone saved.

Today any one of the early green-covered issues of the *American Mercury* is a collector's item, but Cain was right about the first issue—not only was it the one most people saved, but it hit the country's newsstands like a string of exploding firecrackers. The world suffered from at least a score of painful diseases, Mencken and Nathan proclaimed, "all of them chronic and incurable." And it was evident that the magazine was not going to confine itself simply to pointing out the ills of the world of literature and theater. Mencken, at least, had broadened his range of interests and was now ready to attack any American institution he thought needed reforming. He looked on the new magazine as a conduit for his ideas in all areas of human endeavor. The Enemies included: the Ku Klux Klan, the Anti-Saloon League, William Jennings Bryan, Billy Sunday, lodge joiners, Methodists, Socialists, censors, capitalists, Greenwich Village, pedants, Prohibition, and the South, particularly southern cooking. That would do for a start.

The first issue contained a gentle debunking of Abraham Lincoln, a critical article on Senator Hiram Johnson of California, an expose of the teaching of American history, essays by Mencken and Nathan, and a regular feature called "Americana," in which the magazine reported on ludicrous events and items from around the forty-eight states. Cain's labor leader article would have blended perfectly into the issue, which also featured an incendiary article by Ernest Boyd called "Aesthete: Model 1924."

Cain's article, as Mencken promised, was in the second issue, and he was traveling in good company—a play by Eugene O'Neill ("All God's Chillun Got Wings") and a short story by Sherwood Anderson ("Caught"). In addition, there were articles by Morris Fishbein, Gerald W. Johnson, Carleton Beals and Carl Van Doren, most of them in the debunking spirit Mencken preferred. And at least one of Mencken's literary entourage, disappointed in the January issue, had nothing but praise for Cain's February contribution. Sinclair Lewis, in London revising his manuscript of *Arrowsmith*, read Cain's portrait of the labor leader and wrote Mencken: "Christ, that was a lovely article by Mr. James Cain."

Cain's association with the *Mercury* was a dramatic and major leap forward in his writing career, the beginning of his reputation as a major magazine writer. His portrait of the typical labor leader is etched in the tough language of the mines and is dominated by a cynical mocking tone. And it is easy to see why the union printers refused to set it.

Cain finished his article on editorial writers, which, considering that within two years Cain would be one of the country's leading editorialists, was ironically critical. Then he set his sights on another of Mencken's favorite targets—the arrogant see-both-sides-of-the-question intellectual most often found sheltered in one of the nation's universities. Cain had met several of these pedants in his father's world as well as in his own brief teaching career. In fact, he wrote Mencken from St. John's that "there is a bird here who is the perfect type." The result was "Pedagogue: Old Style," which may go a long way toward explaining why Cain was never popular among the college professors of the 1920s and '30s.

Before he could start his fourth article, Cain's marriage broke up, he was out of a job and in a TB sanitarium. While "chasing the cure" for tuberculosis, as the saying went, he wrote two more articles for Mencken—on male and female politicians, which continued to enhance his reputation as an iconoclast.

However, his *Mercury* articles also prompted some to consider him primarily a Mencken clone and when he went to work on *The New York World*, a job which Mencken helped him land, one of the paper's stars—Franklin P. Adams—said that Cain "wrote with no thought in mind but what Henry Mencken would think." (Later FPA would change his mind in an enraptured *New York Tribune* review of *The Postman*, which would help launch the novel to bestsellerdom.) In New York, Cain continued writing for *The Mercury* and, for a while at least, spread his iconoclasm in the form of journalistic essays. After the indictment of politicians came a scathing attack on "the typical American man of God," which appeared two years before Sinclair Lewis's *Elmer Gantry*. The "Sage of Potato Hill"—E.W.

Howe, editor of his widely quoted *Monthly*, published in Atkinson, Kansas—commented that "in a literary style not excelled by the best magazine at home or abroad, Mr. Cain calmly says pastors are not only useless, but a nuisance." Howe said he did not think such a statement was possible in the United States and that he was not accepting Mr. Cain's opinion—"only wondering at his boldness."

It was a remarkably bold piece and must have had an impact on Lewis, who was a good friend of Mencken's. By this time, Cain had already become a drinking buddy of Lewis's and it was difficult to imagine the two writers not discussing Cain's article about the pastor.

In his last iconoclastic article for Mencken, "The Pathology of Service," Cain attacked do-gooders and do-gooding in a pseudo-scholarly piece, laced with impressive footnotes and quotations. However, by now he had found a new outlet for his social and political criticism and his iconoclastic period was over. In the April 1925 issue of *The Mercury*, he published a fictional dialogue called "Servants of the People" based on an actual incident in Maryland: several Seventh Day Adventists had died in a poorhouse and they were cremated. Then relatives of one showed up protesting that the deceased would have objected to being cremated because it would have made it difficult for him to rise up from the dead on Judgment Day. The crisis is resolved (and the Seventh Day Adventists vote saved) when the county commissioner agrees that the county will pay for a Christian burial.

The piece was every bit as scathing in its criticism of our political insititutions, but instead of being written in his usual tightly-knit stylized prose, Cain presented it as a dialogue, a one-act play. Between 1925 and 1929 he wrote eight of these little plays helping to establish his reputation as a master of dialogue on a par with Sinclair Lewis and John O'Hara. The success of the dialogues also encouraged him to pursue his goal of becoming a playwright—and once again, Mencken offered a helping hand. He introduced Cain to Philip Goodman, a former advertising man, who had become a successful producer, his recent successes including "The Old Sock," written by *N.Y. Tribune* columnist Don Marquis, and "Poppy," starring a young comedian named Bill Fields, later known as W.C. Fields. Goodman had been particularly impressed by Cain's dialogues and before long Goodman was producing a play by Cain entitled "Crashing the Gates," which opened in Stamford—and closed in Worcester.

Although Cain had now failed as a novelist and playwright, Mencken still had faith in him and continued to push his career. He began to talk with him about book possibilities and wrote Blanche Knopf, wife of the publisher, inviting her to meet Cain at his house. Mencken had been encouraging Cain to write some additional dialogues—enough to make up a book. He did and this eventually led to Cain's *Our Government*, published in 1930 by Knopf. It produced some marvelous reviews, but did not sell very well, which puzzled

Mencken. Thirteen years later he still could not understand why it did not "create a sensation ... there was capital stuff in it," he wrote Cain.

In the late 1920s and early '30s, Mencken also played a part in another important development in Cain's career. In 1928 he published his favorite short story, "Pastorale," in *The Mercury*. The theme was Cain's favorite—the problems lovers face when they conspire to commit murder. Now, after having decided that he could not write long fiction in the third person, he found he could write short fiction in the first person, especially when he put his story in the mouth of an Eastern Shore yokel. He followed "Pastorale" with two other short stories in 1929 and 1933—"The Taking of Montfaucon," based on a World War I experience, and "The Baby in the Icebox," his first attempt to write about the California drifter, which sold to Paramount for his first movie.* Mencken especially liked "Baby," calling it the best thing he had ever done, and the response to these three *Mercury* stories gave Cain the confidence to try long fiction again—which lead to the writing of *The Postman Always Rings Twice.*

Cain wrote one more article for *The Mercury*, "Tribute to a Hero" (see Section III) and it was obvious that his iconoclasm days were over. Although he did have a few unkind things to say about his days at Washington College, the piece was an unabashed 4th-of-July tribute to his college football hero, John Garfield Moore, and it caused quite a bit of comment in intellectual circles back East. However, by now most of the attention was focused on *The Mercury* itself (which had financial problems) and Mencken, who, it seemed to many (including *Mercury* publisher Alfred A. Knopf) to be too kindly disposed to Adolph Hitler and too harshly critical of Franklin D. Roosevelt. Finally, both Knopf and Mencken agreed that a new editor was needed and Mencken resigned, which, says Cain, "knocked me for a loop." Although he was no fan of Hitler's and would later become critical of Mencken's red-baiting in his column, Cain was deeply appreciative of the encouragement Mencken had given him in his career and knew that *The Mercury* was something special in American journalism. It was the "only place," he wrote Mencken, "I ever got the curious excitement that one ought to get when he has something in print."

Cain wrote more than 20 articles, some short stories and dialogues during Mencken's tenure as editor of *The Mercury* and HLM considered him his star contributor, "the only author I ever knew who never wrote a bad article," he told Ward Morehouse; "I never turned down a piece by him."

At one point, Cain considered writing a book about Mencken. He

---

*"She Made Her Bed," starring Richard Arlen, Robert Armstrong and Sally Eilers (1934).

thought most biographers started out with the idea that Mencken's insolence was a joke, but were shocked to learn that he was indeed the anarchist he claimed to be. "They always take him at his own evaluation," he said, "iconoclast, mocker, the heaver of dead cats into the sanctuary." That's the way he put it one time and he was certainly all of those things. "But a man who writes novels," Cain once told me, "knows that there comes a point where you have got to ask: What is this guy for, what's he in favor of? And the way he tells it is that he's in favor of liberty. And he was—a certain kind of liberty. He was in favor of literary liberty. But I don't think Mencken would have lifted a finger to defend the right of some colored man in Baltimore to get up and make a speech against the white society. To him, that would just have been funny."

Cain never did write his book about Mencken, but he helped many Mencken biographers by sending them long sketches or profiles of the Sage and he wrote several reviews of Mencken biographies, one of which is included at the end of this section. Cain started out approaching Mencken as a Babe Ruth who had autographed his ball. But he said, "the small boy is never really close friends with an idol like Ruth," and Cain could never overcome his hero worship. Gradually, however, he outgrew Mencken, although he never lost his fascination for him and the respect for his genius which, in itself, he said, made friendship awkward. And he was forever grateful for Mencken's encouraging him to write his *Mercury* sketches, which led to his first book and helped establish his reputation as a writer of dialogues. But he was leery of getting too close to Mencken, aware of his habit of turning against his friends. Cain did not want to be included in that group. So, on those Sunday morning train trips to New York, he said, "I listened, enchanted as always with the brilliance of his talk, but when he would begin sliding toward a greater intimacy, perhaps with some anecdote about romance, of the kind that only close friends discuss with each other, I would become fascinated by the New Jersey road outside, and not quite hear what he said."

He felt Mencken preferred it that way, that he liked people to keep their distance. But "I often thought," said Cain, "his gay, rolicsome manner was partly a screen, we could even say a mask. Back of it was a moody, introspective nature that often felt very bitter as his times, as one of his friends put it, 'began passing him by'."

When Mencken died in 1956, it was a heavy blow to Cain. The funeral was unceremonious and Spartan, following Mencken's wishes that only a few old friends should be present to see him off on his last journey. Cain's reaction to the starkness of the occasion was summed up in a letter to Arthur Krock: "We could have remembered, I thought, that though he disbelieved he was entering the next world, he was at least taking leave of this one, and permitted some sort of rites that would have served as a memorial to what he did, which was considerable. Somehow, we were made to subserve a gag, and the effect wasn't so much bleak as blank. The minute of silence didn't quite say it."

In later years, Cain would say that he was not proud of his *Mercury* pieces, that they were written while he was too much under the spell of Mencken's iconoclasm. They may have been, but the relationship between the two men did inspire some classic journalistic essays, which are reprinted here. Not only do they reveal an authentic voice of the 1920s revolt, they are typical of the kind of journalism and writing that made *The Mercury* the most influential American magazine from 1924 until the Great Depression. And despite Cain's reservations about Mencken's intellectual positions, he told many interviewers over the years that it was Mencken primarily, "who liberated me from the village pump."

As for Mencken, when he resigned his editorship of *The Mercury* in 1933, he wrote Cain: "I tell you the literal fact when I say that [your contributions] were among the best things I printed, if not actually better than any other."

R.H.

The Labor Leader
(February, 1924)

He is recruited from people of the sort that nice ladies call common. Such people are mostly out of sight in the cities. The streets they inhabit are remote from the boulevards; their doings are too sordid and trivial for newspapers notice, save when the police are called in. In the small towns they are more openly on view, to the horror of the old families. Bug city or small town, they are all alike. They are of the sort that mop up the plate with bread. That have 6 x 8 porches on their homes, and wash flapping on the clotheslines. That take a bath every Saturday night, and slosh blue, soapy water down the gutters. That own a $25 phonograph and these four records: "In the Shade of the Old Apple Tree," "Barney Google," "Walking with Jesus" (Orpheus Quartet), and "Cohen on the Telephone." That join the Heptasophs, the Junior Order, and (if getting up in the world), the Odd Fellows. Whose women-folk grow fat and rock on the porches wearing blue check dresses. Whose men-folk are laid up with elusive ailments related to the stummock. Whose female children know gross names for the anatomical parts and harass other children by yelling:

> I dare you like a dare dog,
>   I treat you like a hound;
> I sell you to the rag man,
>   Two cents a pound!

And whose male children sing:

> There she goes, sweet as a rose,
> All dressed up in her best Sunday clo'es!

Who say Mom and Pap, I'll Thank You for the Beans, Ain't No Use to Hisself, Yes'm, See You Later, Lick That Kid, Make Him Shut Up ....

Cockney or yokel, that is where he starts. He is of the same clay as this grotesque company, and sees nothing queer about it. The village blacksmith, who whispers to a lot of boys about the bank president's daughter, he considers a very sharp and well-informed man. He believes the plumber's wife who swears she saw a ghost in the graveyard, and hunches close to her while she jibbers .... The boy who follered 'em and seen 'em; women muttering over backyard fences; the Grand Exalted Keeper of Records and Seals, dusting off the regalia; the party that went to the morgue to see the razor-slashed body of the woman in the big mystery murder; the wife who says the Mister ain't home when his growlings are plainly audible; the man who knowed the feller didn't kill hisself, the man who says there are some funny things a-going on, I'm a-telling you; the preacher who says Prepare to Meet Thy God, the End of the World is at Hand .... All these sisters and brothers he accepts without question. Doesn't he see ghosts himself, sometimes? Wasn't he thinking about that very suicide case? Didn't he go to the morgue himself and hold that kid's perspiring hand while she gasped? What is out of the way in all this? What else would you? Suspicion, credulity, secrecy, hog meat, cabbage, fat: all perfectly natural, all part of the zest of life.

II

Given sufficient numbers of them and a *casus belli*, it is very easy to organize such people in to Labor unions. Why they organize has been explained by labor economists from Karl Marx down, with many abstruse theories involving algebra, the Sermon on the Mount, and the law of diminishing returns; but it is commonly overlooked that it is part of their nature to pack into a hall and hearken to a speaker from state headquarters, to cheer a resolution "that a committee be appointed to notify McCabe that we want a straight 40 cents an hour or they needn't blow the whistle Monday morning," and then to forget to take a vote. For the lady recording secretary to bounce up from her notebooks and announce that all she wants to say is that there's two spies in the hall and everybody knows who they are and they can go back and tell everything they seen and heard and make it twice as strong if they want to. For a gentleman to say there's another thing he wants to know, and that is why do they pay them truck drivers $15 a day when they wouldn't give their own men the 55 cents an hour they asked for, which it was only fair and reasonable, and besides no more'n they was promised the first of the year. For a gentleman in the rear to shout "How about McCabe?"—and for the rest to hiss. For the temporary chairman to say, "Well, the way I git it is we ain't going to work Monday unless we git 40 cents an hour straight, and if ever'body is agreeable, we'll adjourn until Sunday afternoon—oh, there's one more thing, I got to name that there committee . . . . Now, remember, Sunday afternoon, and ever'body come.''

Organization usually takes one afternoon, with constitution and by-laws to be mailed down from state headquarters, charter to follow. There is a temporary chairman who does not count. After preliminary details, the chief business of the local is the election of permanent officers. Automatically every member becomes a candidate for office—openly or secretly, mostly openly as follows:

For President: Every man, woman, and child in the local.

For Vice-President: The incumbent temporary chairman.

For Recording Secretary: Every female, with active members of the Rebekah Lodge to the fore.

For Corresponding Secretary: Every female, with active members of the Rebekah Lodge to the fore.

For Treasurer: Every man, woman, and child in the local.

For members of the Executive Committee: The woman who bawled out the foreman that time he got fresh, together with nine crafty males now hope to impress the management with their cleverness, and thereby get company jobs.

If it is a new local, and particularly a local in a weakling union, like the textile workers', electioneering will be heated but not serious. Most of the candidates will go around saying it seems to them the main thing is to get a good president, a union ain't no good unless them that runs it has some git up and git; that they had ought to be careful about the man they pick for treasurer, and make him put up a bond; that this here committee is an important thing, now, and they had better git some fellers that know what they are doing and that none of this no-account element that is trying all the time to run things to suit theirself and don't know what they want, nohow . . . . But if it is a well-established local with a fat treasury, and particularly if it is a local in a big national union, with good jobs farther up the line, then electioneering is fast, furious, and to the death. Down in West Virginia, for example, where there are 80,000 miners, an election by the United Mineworkers of America causes more excitement than the election of a governor, and is fraught, I believe, with greater public consequences. There are numerous fat jobs—president, vice-president, and secretary-treasurer of districts and subdistricts; all sorts of committeemen who draw $10 *per diem* and traveling expenses, beside offices in local unions. The candidates scurry about in their flivvers, handing out cards bearing their likenesses and their qualifications for office, and buttonholing everybody. The election is held under strict rules and every effort is made to get out a big vote. There are watchers, judges, challengers, now and then a recount, good lusty fights.

All this is pretty much like a county election, and it has similar results. That is, the fellow who gets elected proves that he is adept at vote-getting, but otherwise is as much like those who elected him as a member of the State Assembly is like those who elected *him*. But there are differences. The county vote-getter has mainly to possess craftiness and a talent for petty intrigue. The union vote-getter must possess these too, but even more he must possess youth, physical courage, and heavy-hitting fists. When a gentleman in the rear arises and demands to know of the president of the local what became of that money that was voted for strike relief over in Croxton yards and never a nickel of it was spent there, as he knows from a fellow that was over there the whole time the strike was on; and when the president of the local replies that anybody who puts out a report that there was anything wrong with the way that money was spent is a dirty liar and he can prove it,—when this situation arises, and it is, so to speak, a standard, conventional situation, why the one that wins the fight is going to be the next president of the local. If the president can hold his spurs, all right; if not, he steps down. The fight settles the minor issue of the money, and the winner is elected by acclamation. These people are all for the fellow who is on top, who can prove himself Some Man. Particularly the women, if it is a mixed local, are for the brawny lads, with loud voices and a good front.

III

He is a youngish, big, powerful man, with a thick red neck and a suit wrinkled at elbow and knee by bulging muscles; a man with wary, catlike physical poise; a man with a head shaped a little like a prize fighter's. He presides at local meetings, pounds his gavel, and announces that it has been moved and seconded. He lays the charge of dirty liar and proves it. He goes through a strike or two, and finds out that a strike has its compensations. There are fine whisperings and plottings, unaccustomed and elevating intimacy with the women. He goes to state conventions, expenses paid, and maybe to a national convention. After two or three years, if he is an exceptionally good slugger and even ordinarily crafty, he becomes a state committeeman, a national committeeman, finally, International Representative. By now his cap is full. A good salary, traveling expenses (and plenty of travel), hardly any work, a lot of authority, all conferred by the constitution, Page 17, article 5.

Now he maintains an office. A labor headquarters is a curious place. Usually it is tucked away up some dark stairway, and the doors, dimly visible, bear all sorts of long-winded legends: International Seaman's Union of America; International Brotherhood of Locomotive Engineers; International Association of Longshoremen; United Mineworkers of America;

International Brotherhood of Railway and Steamship Clerks; Freight Handlers and Station Employes. Two thirds of the doors bear the additional legend, Keep Out. Inside, these offices carry unmistakeably the flavor of the old front stoop. The furniture is expensive enough, but the wrong color. There is no rug, only bare boards. The mural decoration usually consists of the American Federation of Labor chart calendar, setting a goal of 4,000,000 members by January 1 next. Spittoons, typewriters, one or two filing cases. But the invariable and inevitable piece of furniture is a great black safe . . . . The lady employes suggest somehow the laundry and shoe factory, although two-thirds of them are pretty, for your labor leader has a sports taste in women. They are hostile and mysterious. They can't give out any information on that; you'll have to see the International Representative. No, he isn't in today. They don't know when he'll be in. You may think I exaggerate. Once out of curiosity I made a round of one of the floors of the American Federation of Labor Building in Washington. Half the doors were locked, although it was not a holiday. In the rest of the offices every legislative representative was out, and not a single stenographer could tell where one of them was or when he would be in . . . . Eventually, after you go out and call the International Representative over the telephone, you will find out that he was in all the time. He informs you, when you finally get to him, that if he had known it was you it would have been all right, but they've been watching him so close here lately he has to be careful as the devil.

They've been watching us! This is the ever-recurrent *motif* in the whole American labor turmoil. Probably no strike has ever been called that this note was not sounded in it. In the mines, buildings trades, print shops, clothing factories, railroads, everywhere; let a strike be called, and "they're watching us." But they don't catch us asleep, not by a long shot! We're watching them, too. We got information out there in that safe that's going to wake this old town up one of these days, all this stuff they've been pulling. We ain't quite ready with it yet, but when our people send in some more confidential reports it'll be something tremenjous. You wouldn't hardly believe it, sitting right there in that chair, if I was to tell you, but it's a fact, and we can prove it, that he didn't kill hisself, and she did have a nigger baby last summer . . . . The Blow from Behind, or The Mystery of the Stolen Papers, by Old Sleuth.

IV

After you finally get into his office, you perceive that certain changes have come over the International Representative. He is still boorish: he doesn't rise when you enter; he has his feet on the desk; he keeps his hat on. But he has developed a bit since the time he slugged his way into the presidency of the local. For one thing, he slings the English language in a more free and easy fashion. As the American business man has come to the point where everything, from the advent of his first born to the death of his best beloved, is a Proposition, so the International Representative has come to the point where everything is a Matter. "This Matter you speak of, now, I don't want to be quoted in it, see? but if there's anything going in I want it to go in like it is, the truth about it, I mean, and not no pack of dam lies like the papers generally prints. What I say, now, don't you put it in like it come from me, because I don't know nothing about it, except what I read in the papers, not being notified in no official way, see? Besides, it's a matter which you might say is going to have a question of jurisdiction to it, and I don't want to have nobody make no charges against me for interference in no matter which it ain't strickly a point where I got authority. But I can give you a idea about it and you can fix it up so's them that reads the paper can figger out their own conclusion on how we stand in the matter."

He is also up in a worldly way. He has a car now and a tin garage back of his home. The porch has a canvas swing in it. The old $25 phonograph is gone, and in its place is a nice $350 machine, with Japanese birds on the door, and these records: "In the Shade of the Old Apple Tree," "Calvary" (Homer Rodeheaver), "Barney Google," "Yes, We Have No Bananas," "Rock of Ages" (Shannon Quartet), "Walking With Jesus" (Orpheus Quartet), "Cohen on the Telephone," and "Mose Brown's Suicide" (Comedy Monologue). The old chromos that once adorned the walls are gone also, and in their place are prints like "Love's Coronation," in nifty gilt frames. His wife wears bungalow aprons and the favorite toy of his child—his kid—is a cap pistol. He doesn't take his wife and kid to conventions, however. Nix; convention ain't no place for a woman! "Say, you look like you know how to keep something to yourself: tell you something funny happened up to our last convention. Believe me, that was some gang there, too. Them guys had money every color there was, and all on the table, too. I seen $3,000 in one pot in one game there .... Well, anyhow, was a feller there from Indianapolis had his wife with him. Said it was his wife, I don't know, I reckon it was. Anyhow she was some cute baby. I seen her in the lobby one night and she give me a smile, so I says to myself, 'Me for you, kid.' So I gets the guy and takes him to a near-beer s'loon and we gets soused, see? Anyhow, he gets soused and I takes ginger ale. Then they give him the bum's rush and I has to take him back up to his room at the hotel. She is there waiting for him, like I figgered, and her and me puts him to bed and he passes out. Then her and me goes down and has some real likker .... Some baby, believe me!"

So this is he who, according to the newspapers, takes matters under advisement, studies questions, delivers ultimatums, directs strike activities, makes counter proposals, signs tentative agreements. He who, according to the Liberal weeklies, is a burning idealist, with lofty brow and glistering eye, panting to deliver the Oppressed, abolish the Sweatshop, and realize the Brotherhood of Man; something between a ritualist revolutionary, a jail poet, and a mountain preacher. The newspaper picture puzzles him a little, for he doesn't understand all the words, and he is suspicious of newspapers, anyhow: he associates them with police courts and injunctions. The Liberal picture doesn't bother him a whit, for he never sees it. Most of the Liberal weeklies he has never heard of, those he has heard of he usually confuses with something else (as witness the recent excoriation of the *Nation* by Sam Gompers) . . . . The picture he has of himself is of a powerful, crafty fellow, a fellow of infinite brawn and terrifying jaw, a fellow of big shoulders and unfoolable shrewdness; in short, a sort of combination of Jack Dempsey and William John Burns.

V

Well, all good men come to an end some time. So with the International Representative. Sooner or later somebody with a louder voice and harder fist will push him out.

"What will you do then?" I once asked a miners' official.

"Who, me?" he replied. "Why, man, I can go back to the mines any time. I haven't forgot my trade."

I looked at the big blue Stutz, the sporty clothes, the pretty wife, and smiled. He laughed.

"Well, hell," he said, "I can always sell out to the operators. They got a good job waiting for me whenever this blows up."

The Editorial Writer
(April, 1924)

You are, I shall suppose, a cub reporter on a newspaper. Life is a bleary maze of thick green pencils, skew-cut copy paper, busted typewriters, round sergeants, coroners, near-beer saloons, corpses, patrol wagons, and three-alarm fires, with a cacaphonous accompaniment of whoops from Saturday night drunks, the *clack-clack* of telegraph instruments, the rumbling of presses, *cop-e-e-e!*—and over all the majestic chant of the city editor: Gimme a new lead on it . . . . Better get on that right away . . . . Cut it to two sticks . . . . Work it up from that angle . . . . Smoke him out, make him come clean . . . . Well, it's worth a feature, anyway . . . . Get the low-down on it . . . . Hell, we should worry if he wants it in or not . . . !

It's all terribly confusing, and your head aches: it is so hard to tell appearance from reality. For instance, the old gent frowning so portentously in the swivel chair, the one you thought it would pay to stand in with, is nothing but the head copy boy; and the kid chewing tobacco with his feet on the desk, that you thought was the janitor, is the news editor, with authority to tell even the city editor where to head in. There doesn't seem to be any way of going by looks. They all mooch about in waistcoats, without coats, all have prematurely gray hair, all have the same funny look about the eyes.

You start in your chair. There is that man again, over by the city editor. Who is he, anyway? You have seen him around a lot, and intended to ask about him. But—*is* he the same man? They all look so much alike, and this one in particular looks like a synthetic portrait of everybody in the shop, from the make-up man to the anemic copy reader who sits on the other side of the copy slot. It must be the same man, though. He always wears a green eye-shade, and his shirt makes a little soft pillow where it rolls out from under his waistcoat over his belt. Yes, it is the same man. Come to think of it, his face has lurked in the background all through these first awful days. Who is he, anyhow? You prepare to make covert inquiries.

Well, well, save your breath. Pull up your chair and I shall tell you who he is. The man is a Priest. He is Keeper of the Soul of the American People. He sits alone in his office, high above the maddening crowd, and as he sits, soft voices rise from below. When he hears them, he passes into a long, long dream, and as he dreams, his hand (which holds a pencil) begins to write and write and write . . . . The voices are so soft that few could hear them at all, but the man hears them because hearing them is his trade. They are the Voices of the People, the Voice of God. And they go into his ear while he dreams, and in his head they become thoughts. Not ugly, naughty thoughts such as you and I have, but thoughts that Nobody Will Deny—Beautiful Thoughts that the People think, about Rights of the Taxpayer; Do Your Duty, Mr. Mayor; Our Grand Old Man, the New Parking Plan, Five years of Peace, and Mr. Tchitcherin's Latest Treachery. And as the thoughts pass out again, through his hand, they become renewed, purified, transmogrified, until they become the very soul of the American people . . . . In brief, this fellow in the green eye-shade is the man who writes the editorials.

Like yourself, he started as a cub. He too had a terrible time finding his way around, and he too soon developed that weary wisdom, that precocious wisdom about life—Well, hardly that. But a veneer of wisdom, a posture of cynicism. On $22 a week, cynicism was about the only luxury he could afford. It helped a lot when he had to eat in one-arm haricotieries . . . . He had his derivitive names for some of the certified prominent citizens. For instance, Mr. Littleton Thomas Titscomb, president of the Second National Bank, who made 942 four-minute speeches during the war, he called Little Tom Tit, and boasted that he never had to go hear Tom Tit's speech, for he already knew it by heart. Mrs. Bertha Willoughby, of the School Board, he called Bertha Krupp. His Excellency, Oglesby A. Adams, governor of the State, he called Old Up-And-At-'Em. Sometimes his wisdom reached lyrical heights as he argued with his fellows: he made glib references to the City Hall Crowd, and cynical predictions about things: They're not going to let Nick Beal walk off with that nomination. Don't fall for that stuff. They know who they're going to put in there, and when it gets too late for anybody else to file, they'll put him up, see? Hell, all this talk about Nick Beal just hands me a laugh.

So his early years. He passed through the stage where he said: Ain't this a hell of a life for a white man? Where he called the telephone girl Sweetie. Where he said: They got a hot way of running things around this joint; *I'll* say they have. Where he called the theatre managers by their first names, ordered gin by telephone, clapped the mayor on the back, corresponded for *Variety*. He saw the staff change completely as the men came, saw, and got the gate. He held his job, though. After a few years the city editor called him by his first name and relied on him whenever a *big* story broke, such as a suicide, love-nest, or murder, or a bad wreck up on the P.B. & R. Oh, he had come to know the business, all right. According to the life line in his palm, a Great Big Change was just about due in his life.

II

And sure enough, it came. He had been covering the big McGinnis murder case, wherein the bandits jumped out of the car, shot the bank messenger, and scuttled off with $5426 in good hard cash—BANDITS SLAY RUNNER, GET $5426 LOOT, ESCAPE IN AUTO. The case had been on for two days, and not a trace of the jolly *banditti* had been found. He had been up two nights on the story, and came down the next afternoon ready for more heavy work. But a surprise was in store. He was called into the managing editor's office.

After a preliminary compliment about the story, the managing editor got down to business:

"You know, I think it's about time we went aboard the police department in this town and went aboard them right. This is the eleventh murder this year where they haven't even made an arrest. Gosh, that's rotten! . . . . But we don't want to be unjust, and that's what I wanted to see you about. You're in pretty close touch over there. Do you think we're justified in jumping on them with both feet?"

Is Our Hero flattered? He is. Consulted by the managing editor! On a question of *editorial policy!*.

Indeed, his mental processes at this point give the whole key to his subsequent development, and throw a bright white light on the whole business of writing about public affairs in these United States. First, about his cynicism (by now he doesn't think of himself as cynical—simply hard-boiled). Does he come out and tell the managing editor that all this crusade stuff is the bunk and the police department will go on running the same old way until the end of time, crusade or no crusade? He does not. His cynicism

evaporates faster than the clouds in the last verse of "Anchored." Cynicism!
Why, you dumbbell, how do you get that way? The managing editor doesn't
want to know his *personal* feeling about the police department. So far as that
goes, a lot of those boys over there are friends of his;—no better bunch in the
world—and he and Sweeney, captain in the Eleventh Precinct (where the
murder was done) are right down buddies. No, nothing like that. What the
managing editor wants to know is whether the police department need
reorganization (shake-up) for the public good. When a crime like this is
committed, it concerns the whole community ....

So he looks solemn and tells the managing editor he has been wondering
why the paper didn't take up that angle. Of course, he's no authority on police
systems, but it stands to reason when their Bertillon bureau is away out of
date, and they haven't any system for keeping track of suspicious characters,
and they have no men available for special assignment, no "flying squad" ...
"You've said enough," says the managing editor. "Now let's handle it this
way." So the upshot is that he is sent off on a trip to New York, Philadelphia,
Baltimore, Pittsburgh, and Cleveland, and makes a study of police systems in
those cities. He draws $250 expense money (feeling pretty important), stays
away a week, and writes a series of articles under the caption: HOW OTHER
CITIES COPE WITH CRIME. For the first time since he has been on the
paper he sees his name signed to what he writes .... And Sweeney loses his
job.

It has been a turning point in his life. As a result of his articles, he gets a
$10 raise. He is frequently consulted by the managing editor. He finds it pays
better to be Constructive than Cynical, or even Hard-Boiled. Oh, the devil; he
hates to think what a fool he was once. So he begins to orient things with a
view to the Public Interest involved. He takes them seriously. The police
department gets into the limelight again, and he is asked to write an editorial
about it. By now he is a real expert on all public matters: the taxable basis, the
City Hall crowd, the school situation, the police department, the merit
system, vice, the health department, the city Federation of Labor, the flying
squad of the Prohibition enforcement bureau, the State police, the situation
in the counties, the attitude of the women voters, and the date of the birthday
of Rufus P. Higgins (president of the Consolidated Foundry Company and
Our Grand Old Man).... So he gradually comes into his own. One day the
editor dies unexpectedly, the assistant editor is promoted to be editor, and Our
Hero is made assistant editor. At last he is an Editorial Writer. He is to write
the local editorials (and foreign editorials too on Tuesday, the new editor's
day off).

So the next day he shows up at 9 A.M. instead of 2 P.M., hangs his coat in
the editor's office, and sits down to work. He has quite a day ahead of him.
There are two columns of editorials to get out, and editorials don't grow on

trees. Then a dozen or so of breezy sayings must be composed, to sandwich between the editorials and relieve the tedium a bit. Then other papers, magazines, etc., must be clipped for novel tid-bits, and these must be captioned (But, Sir, If You Were Governor, Would You Compel All Dry Law Violators To Drink Prussic Acid, As You Propose?) Then most likely a number of people will be in, to see about something or other . . . . Well, to work, to work!

First off the bat: What to write an editorial about, heigh-ho, heigh-ho? He skims through the paper. The first story he spies is this: MAYOR PLAYS HORSE—FOR KIDS AT NEW-PLAYGROUND OPENING. Well, well, well! This surely must have an editorial. So he hitches up to the typewriter.

But mark you: In the old days, when he was a cynic, his own honest reaction to this story would have run about like this:

"Say, that there is a hot sketch, ain't it? Playground for the kiddies. You heard about that playground, didn't you? Nick Beal had three acres out there he couldn't sell to the P.B. & R. and dam if he didn't wish it off on the city. 'S a fact. Say, what do you know about Nick riding them toties around on his back? How does he get that way? Does this town hire that fat mope for a mayor or a mule, I'd like to know."

Not exactly lofty, but incisive, in its way, and possessed no doubt of a certain interest to the public, if published. But does it occur to him to write it? Or to paraphrase it into more orthodox prose? Or to ignore the whole performance, on the ground that such monkeyshines are not worth writing about? Not on your life!

Great guns, no! Of course, everybody knows about Nick and the P.B. & R. deal, but nobody has ever brought any charges against him, and if you went on putting things like that into the paper you would have the worst libel suit on your hands you ever saw in your life. As for Nick putting in his whole time at the City Hall, why it has come to a pretty pass when the mayor of this town can't spend a few hours at a playground opening that cost the city $75,000 and he got half of that! As for not writing anything about it, why, man, remember that a whole lot of people are interested in that playground. There were 5000 children out there, and everyone of them has a father and a mother, or most of them have, anyhow. Besides, it's a community affair, and it's up to the paper to take an interest in everything of that sort.

So—to the editorial. He captions it: "The New Playground." The first paragraph:

> Every resident of the city must rejoice at the opening of the Evergreen Park Playground. Coming as it does at the beginning of the warm weather, it means that thousands of little tots will have the opportunity for fresh air and play all through the Summer. Wholesome frolic in such surroundings means that when school opens in the Fall, thousands of sturdy, sun-burned scholars will be on hand to take up the more serious business of life with renewed vigor.

And so on. A paragraph on the need for sturdy bodies. A paragraph on fresh air as the best Road to Wellville. A paragraph on the hitherto inadequate playground facilities of the city. Then to His Honor, the Mayor:

> Happy the official who can spare an hour or two during a busy day to romp with the kiddies at a time like this *Parva leves capiunt animus*. It is well so, and it would be well for us all to realize it more often. We salute you, Mr. Mayor, as one who has not forgotten the happy days of childhood. And we freely confess that our salutation is slightly colored with envy.

This graceful tribute out of the way, he picks up the paper again. The next story he spies is: MERCURY SETS MAY 14 RECORD. To the machine again. Does he pull down the side of his mouth and say: "Well, hell, it's supposed to be hot in May, ain't it?" Nay, nay. He hops off this way: "At the wedding feast men may be seated according to high or low estate, but before Old Sol all men are equal." On to the next story: CITIZENSHIP SCHOOL—GRADUATES 31 ALIENS. He writes: "One reads with a sense of civic pride of the work which the Citizenship School of the Chamber of Commerce is doing toward qualifying aliens for the complex duties that will confront them after they become citizens." On to the next: TO PUSH CONSTRUCTION—ON SCHOOL NO. 78. He writes: "The School Board is to be congratulated on its determination to lose no time in the completion of School No. 78; and if its action comes rather late, the patrons in that section, served so poorly by the present structure, at least have the satisfaction of knowing that it has been taken at last." And so on and so on. Next Tuesday, when the editor is off, he will write: "The decision of M. Poincare to make drastic cuts in expenditures in order that the budget can be balanced and the downward course of the franc arrested, will be read with satisfaction by all who realize the far-reaching implications of the present fiscal situation in France." And on June 22, birthday of Rufus P. Higgins, he will write, under the caption "Our Grand Old Man":

> How chastened and humble most of us must have felt yesterday when we learned that Rufus P. Higgins had passed the seventy-fifth milestone of his life. Serene and untroubled as the years march slowly by, this Grand Old Man of industry and public affairs spent the day at his desk as usual, a simple private soldier in the ranks of productive effort.

And so on, and so on, and so on. Day after day, week after week, month after month, year after year. Take up any provincial paper in the land and turn to the editorial page. If you find a single editorial that rises above this general level cut it out and paste it in your hat. You won't find it again.

III

Why is such stuff written? Why is its tone so uniform, from Portland to Portland, and so feeble? I think its hollowness is the hollowness of an echo; it is *not* the genuine thought of the man who writes it. Certainly he never talks any such ponderous blatter. Mostly his conversation consists of long anecdotes about what Bill Murphy said up at the State convention back in 1912 .... Rather it is his notion of what the great multitudes of plain men think. Often, of course, he gets as low as plain fawning, and that may be because he is afraid if he doesn't stay on the right side of Bill Murphy he will lose that place on the Board of Police Examiners that has been promised him for next year, after Pete Humphreys gets out. But even if he is of comparatively high spirit, he soon comes to regard himself as a sort of tribune of the people, rather than as one speaking in his own right.

Thus he becomes an inverted horn, a recording instrument, tuned to catch the slightest murmur from that great throng milling about below. In very few instances does he write what he himself thinks. He takes a sort of pride in having voted the Republican ticket for 22 years, all the while writing Democratic editorials; and a sort of pride by inversion in his paper, that was so broadminded it never even thought of discharging him from it .... He writes what the upper end of that great horn tells him to write—what the people think. Often he erects what the people think into transcendental verity: "The opinion of so eminent an artist as Mr. Jan Humperdinck as to the location of the Robert E. Lee statue should be weighed carefully before a decision is made; *yet in the face of so overwhelming a popular demand*" .... So, his writings attain their unbelievable flatulence and blowisness; they are permeated throughout with the greasy smell of voting booths and assessors' notebooks, for it is these things that the people are primarily concerned with.

But, you say, sometimes he does get really heated up—assails the mayor and police department, wages crusades, demands complete and searching investigations. Yes, but always within the compass of the horn. If he writes for a Democratic paper, he assails a Republican mayor bitterly; but he says only what all Democrats think about the mayor, and what all Republicans would think of a Democratic mayor. He never calls attention to the odd fact that all mayors somehow contrive to look alike. That is an octave above the range of the horn. He subscribes, by the rules he imposes on himself, to all the notions that the people hold: that it is a civic duty to vote (he may not have voted for 20 years himself); that foreigners ought to become naturalized (his own mother may be a citizen of the Irish Free State); that girls ought not to use paint (his own daughter may put it on with a feather duster). The sum total of these notions makes a fairly definite philosophy, a stew in which all ideas must be dissolved before they may be promulgated—and any idea not therein soluble is ruled out of the paper . . . .

The characteristic flavor of this *potage mondain*, I believe, is supplied by the moral judgement, the judgment that includes an ought or ought-not, that assesses blame or credit: The mayor ought to take action . . . . The police department is to be praised for its efficiency . . . . The dancer should not be permitted to land . . . . All good citizens of the community must have been shocked to hear . . . . No man is more truly entitled to the epitaph, *Requiescat in Pace* . . . . A complete investigation of the scandal should be demanded by Congress . . . . All of us might learn a lesson from the example of the girl who . . . . The warmest co-operation should be extended the Health Department in its effort to . . . . The action of the City College trustees will meet the approval of all who . . . . The deficit in the State budget is a matter that should be explained and explained at once . . . . Before Germany presents this plan formally to England and the United States she must first convince the world she is really at work . . . . Most thoughtful citizens will condemn these trips on the *Mayflower*, feeling that the President of the United States might better occupy his time than by courting the favor of politicians . . . . Nicholas R. Beal is an official who, most thinking citizens will agree, should be supported for re-election . . . . It does seem, however, that the Weather Man, after giving us 16 rainy days in succession, might vary his repertoire a bit . . . .

If, as an editorial writer, you hoist the *fasces*, you will dissolve your ideas in the soup willy-nilly, no matter how brilliant you may be, and write just such silly stuff as this. There are many men on the big Eastern papers who are vastly informed in their fields; they are perambulating encyclopedias on foreign affairs, on city, State, and national government, on labor questions— not all of them got their posts by the same route as Our Hero, who is the Average Case. But do their writings show any vitality? Would you re-read their editorials? Hardly ever. They succumb to the limitations of their depressing trade. It would seem, indeed, that *any* man must succumb. The minute EDITORIAL appears over what he writes, that minute what he writes ceases to be worth reading. Composing in his own right, his tempo may be sizzling fast, but his editorials will move at a decorous *andantino*. Composing in his own right, he may thrust sharply at the truth, scale high pinnacles of fancy, unloose flashing wit—but not in his editorials. Do the people thrust at truth? Scale pinnacles? Wax witty? Then neither does he. He has become a Spokesman. His writing is the writing of the Committee on Resolutions.

IV

This seems to be a story without a moral. I have racked my brains for one, and the only one I can think of is not original, but I give it:

When he dies the Press Club buries him.

Pedagogue—Old Style
(May, 1924)

His appearance suggests the esoteric purity of the cloister. Particularly the eyes, which have the liquid depth of clear opals. They are lambent, melting, fine. They have none of the cold penetration of a banker's eyes, nor the craftiness of a trasdesman's, nor the heavy-lidded dreaminess of a musician's, nor the suspicious squint of a proletarian's. They are not masculine eyes, nor yet feminine: their sexless glow is like the look you associate with adolescent girls, or maiden ladies of forty-five. They are monastic, upturned eyes, which sometime, maybe years ago, maybe yesterday, have glimpsed the word Excelsior.

His face harmonizes. It is not the face of this vulgar day, but calls up, by style of eyeglass or parting of hair, memories of yesteryear. Whether young or old, it is fresh and ruddy. If here and there are wrinkles, then they are not deep cruel seams, but fine, lightly traced lines. If there are gray hairs, then they are not the streaks of soul-wracking years, but an even, rich powdering. A face finely chiselled, young at twenty-five, youngish at thirty-five, at fifty, at seventy; boyish at eighty, its owner *emeritus* for a decade. A face habitually relaxed in a sunny half-smile. A face that Time has laid on a special shelf and taken great pains with, has etched carefully and stained delicately, burning in one pigment at a time. A face clear, mellow, and serene, like a meerschaum pipe.

When you meet him, you find him charming. His welcome is sunny and genial, like his smile. He plays golf, and will invite you into a foursome. He plays billiards and will take you to his club, set you up to a rickey, trim you neatly, and console you like a gentleman. He canoes, and always has a place in the boat. He is ready at your whim: he never has any special dressing to do. In the Summer he idles in flannels and soft shirt. In the Autumn he wears the trick breeches prescribed for golf. Other seasons he wears rough, comfortable, collegy-Englishy looking clothes. He is always ready for play, and delighted you have come. Delighted as a nice mannered boy is delighted when another nice-mannered boy has moved into the block—another boy to play with, and while the time away.

He is cultured. If you are a scientist, he knows something about science, and has a new magazine he would like to show you. If you like music, he has been to concerts, and will tell you about them; possibly he will confess humorously that he plays the violin or clarinet himself, though not as a professional, simply for his own amusement. History, politics, art; he likes to talk of such things. About some of them, he admits, he doesn't know much, but he believes that every intelligent man ought to take an interest in them, if for no other reason than that they affect us all vitally, and besides, a man can't very well afford to ignore any great field of human thought, as he often tells his classes. Your discussion, you will find, will always end on a resolved chord, though you might prefer a dissonance. You will argue at length, about it and about, and admitting for the sake of argument Kant's great postulates concerning Space and Time. Then you will find yourself warped slightly out of your original position by way of doing justice to the concept of the French Realists, and you will see him edge slightly toward your side, as he will have to admit that there is some measure of validity in the Renaissance idea; in turn you will point to the basic theory of constitutional government. Then, *Presto!* Three chords from the full brass choir and the argument is over. He discovers that you both have essentially the same point in mind, but have approached it from different angles. If you grant him his attitude (you nod gracefully), his view of the question is precisely the same as your own, and you are back where you started . . . . After he has brought the canoe to port and put it to bed he thanks you for a stimulating afternoon and hopes the discussion can be continued some time in the future. As you mumble a pleasantry you stare at him incredulously. His eyes give off a glow of unusual brightness: obviously he means every word he says. He did enjoy it, and devoutly hopes you will go out with him again. You go your way puzzled. You have a vague feeling of dissatisfaction; you don't think he got your point at all clearly. Yet when you think of the staggering amount of dialectic involved in restating it, you are glad you didn't try. Beside, you have a curious impression that it doesn't matter much, anyhow. You inhale deeply, blow a cobwebby sensation from your nose and cheeks, and pray that you may meet some ribald lout who will hie with you to the bootlegger's and tell you in plain language, without syllogisms, that you are full of flees.

II

If you seek his society often, the cobwebs thicken and a feeling of weariness overtakes you. In spite of his humorous quips, you feel you are being wrapped in strange, stifling folds. These, were it not for his eyes, which perpetually haunt you, and the discourtesy involved, you would like to rip off, and dance naked in the wind, at grips once more with reality. For you see, if you grant the premise that there is a Creator, and hardly any sane man would deny that, you immediately posit a purpose, since it is inconceivable that a creator would have made the Universe without having some purpose in mind. This brings you directly to the common problems of Ethics, Science, and Religion. The next question, of course, is what purpose . . . . In vain you wave your arms and kick your feet, recalling that the whole point at issue is whether or not there is a Creator: you are a paralyzed bird, drowning in the python's spittle. In vain you think hotly to yourself that the Creator may have had no purpose whatever, beyond possibly diverting a bored Creatoress from an afternoon of Eternity. In vain you wonder querelously in what hell are the problems of Ethics, and who pays to have them solved. You are caught, and struggle as you may, you are held. You have granted his premise, and out of this seed he has reared a stately bean-stalk of logic and irrefutable conclusions. The oppressive folds, you perceive, are made of bright green leaves, and willy-nilly you try to chew your way out. On the bright green leaves you chew and chaw, and your belly tells you there is no sustenance in them; but why can't you chew your way out?

If your hobby is literature or aesthetic things, no doubt you hailed him as a boon companion after that first genial, delightful five minutes. As you mentioned Poe or Kipling or Nietzsche or Tolstoy his face lighted up and he besought you to come around, since those who have heard of such writers are all too few .... But after accepting his invitation you are as oppressed as though you had discussed less interesting things. Poe, he will tell you, he feels is really the greatest of all American writers, particularly in the realm of poetry. He is aware that Poe's fame is well established as a critic and short-story writer, but not so well as his fame as a poet, which he feels is a pity, since so far as he knows Poe is the only poet who was ever able to give any account of how he did it, and of course this is scarcely less important than the ability to write it. Maupaussant, he thinks, is the greatest of French writers, since his stories are such marvels of technique. Of the modern Americans he does not think much. Of course, Cabell has a very charming style, whatever that counts for, but any student of medieval legends knows that two thirds of the allusions in his stories have no historical justification whatever. As for Lewis, if you grant that the aim of the artist is to make a photograph, why then you have to concede that Lewis is a great artist. But if you grant that he must instill some spiritual quality into his books, that rules Lewis out of court, absolutely. Beside, Lewis has never demonstrated that he has mastered the novelist's technique, and with so many poor novels crowding the catalogues at present, that much at least ought to be insisted on.

So, repeatedly, lured by his fine eyes and delightful sunniness, you quest eagerly into him, and at each seeking you find only stalky green leaves and bright shining shells with no kernels in them. He quickly becomes a sort of problem wiht you, even more absorbing than the problems of Ethics. Why is he such a disappointment? Why does he blight every subject with his mouldy, cobwebby logic? Why so much dialectic and so little sense?

III

Possibly I presume in diagnosing his trouble, but I think it is his incurable hankering for the posture of wisdom. Sometimes he would be a stern, impressive wise man. He stands up before his defenseless classes and lectures them on the necessity for doing their thinking by Rational Processes. He spouts much foggy gas about the World Ground, the implications of Free Volition, the Categories of Consciousness, the difference between the Mathematical Conception of Solids and our ordinary conceptions, about *a priori* and *a posteriori* methods, the successive steps in Scientific Investigation, the fundamental distinction between Economic and Statutory Law, the nature and principles of Physical Phenomena. He is insistent on exact definitions, and is impatient when his students cannot prove that when two variables each approach a limit they are at the shortest distances between two given points. He is sharp, and hard to fool. The boys are stupid and poorly prepared. Or else, granting the boys are above average, the subject must be uncommonly deep, and the man who understands all about it must be uncommonly sagacious . . . .

More often, however, he is humorously, tolerantly, whimsically wise. When he catches one sophomore whispering the translation to another sophomore, he deposes that the blind are leading the blind, and gets quite a hand from the rest of the class. If he is among his colleagues, he recalls that many students have received their diplomas by the grace of God and the faculty, and on the whole it hasn't been his experience that such students have reflected discredit on the institution. Many of them, indeed, have turned out to be fine young men, and beside, he feels that if a student spends four years at college and applies himself reasonably well, he is entitled to a diploma, particularly when you consider it from the point of view of his parents. So, gentlemen, this student was not one of those who were born great, and certainly he has not achieved greatness, nor is he likely to. The question is, do we want to thrust upon him such measure of greatness as goes with the Bachelor of Arts degree . . . . I think this player ought to be made to understand that in the general scheme of things there is a distinct superiority of mind over matter, and to that end he should be kept in his studies . . . . Well, on the whole, I don't think we are making a mistake. Justice should be tempered with mercy, and I suppose this is one of those cases where the poor in spirit shall inherit the Kingdom of Heaven and they that mourn shall be conforted.

Thus the early stages of the Faculty Meeting. But it is in the later stages that wisdom blossoms into full efflorescence. A thick haze of cigarette smoke, an atmosphere of mellowness, of quips, whimsies, and salty proverbs. Then, out of the haze a buzz of talk, and out of the talk a recurring *Leitmotif*, sounding over and over in the many keys: On the other hand, I very often feel . . . . In thinking the matter over, though, I can see . . . . It has been my experience, however . . . . Well, of course, I suppose I shall have to concede you that . . . . I have often thought of that particular point myself . . . . But hasn't it been your observation . . . . I believe, however, in a case of that kind

. . . . But I often tell myself, looking at it from that point of view . . . . Well, I can certainly go with you that far . . . . After years of observation of students in that subject . . . . As I see it, it comes down very much to this . . . . I had rather err, of course, on one side or the other . . . . Well, if we are going to demand that, then I think we should insist . . . . But do you feel, considering it from that angle . . . . I should sum up the whole question by saying . . . . But you must remember . . . . To put the whole thing into a nutshell . . . . Well, I confess I have often wondered whether . . . .

The very quintessential distillate of wisdom: the judicial review! The delicate balancing of one side against the other side! That delicious, teetering moment before it becomes apparent that both sides (in the last analysis) are right!

IV

But *a quoi bon?*—all this wisdom that always hangs on dead centres, this profundity that never adds to the sum of human knowledge, this culture that never produces anything? If you except the slight service it does in ramming information into the heads of the young, it is doubtful whether it is of any use whatever. *Has* wisdom of any heft ever stopped at the balancing point? *Can* there be real profundity that adds nothing to the sum of human knowledge, but only defines and classifies what other men have thought? *Is* there such a thing as pure, non-productive culture? I doubt it. Even men of real culture who are non-productive have a fierce sort of partisanship about it. It matters deeply to them. They may not write music, but they get sozzle-eyed drunk and go to hear Wagner, drenching themselves in beer, whisky, and the music of "Tristan" and "Die Meistersinger." They may not write essays, but they roll Schopenhauer under their tongues. They may have no theory of art, but they roar at "Babbitt," and care not a whit whether Lewis is a photographer or a sign-painter, or whether he has mastered the novelist's technique. They know little of the World Ground, and less of Metaphysics, but they have sense enough to know there is no such thing as a Science of Ethics. The culture of such men is lopsided, incomplete, and far from pure. But it has life and blood in it, so far as it goes; it is no wan and ghostly cellar-plant of postulates, premises, and conclusions.

So, as I say, I doubt whether all this pother of logic and erudition has much substance behind it. But there the gentleman is, in any college or university of the land. Having, by four years of servitude, come into possession of his Ph.D., he sits back and allows nature to take its course, his face growing pinker and fresher, his hair grayer and grayer and whiter and whiter, and his commencement robes more gorgeous, as D.C.L.'s and Litt.D's and LL.D.'s descend gently upon him, like manna from Heaven. Sometimes he writes a book, whereof the opening sentence is "Literature is self-expression through words." And as he lectures and smiles and rebukes contumely and memorizes bright quips out of Latin grammars and the Gospel of St. Mark, so his eyes glow brighter and brighter, at the thought of what a wise man goes there, and after all, it *is* worth while.. . .

Politician—Female
(November, 1924)

The course of events since the ratification of the Nineteenth Amendment seems to give ribald amusement to many ill-mannered persons. Woman suffrage, it is alleged by these scoffers, has failed absolutely to produce any of the results predicted for it by its advocates; its present effect upon the political scene in the Republic is utterly negative; it has, alackaday, even bitten the hand that fed and reared it, until the militant owner of that battle-scarred member is now almost as forgotten as Whittlesey and his Lost Battalion.

Of these things—of the purely political results of the extension of the suffrage, that is—I cannot speak. I am congenitally unable to get the point in politics. I never seem to see what difference it makes whether the bill passes or not. But if I am thus incompetent to appraise the *intrinsic* results of suffrage, I can at least appraise certain of its *extrinsic* aspects and consequences. In other words, though I can't comprehend what good a woman politician accomplishes, I am thoroughly sensitive to how she looks while she goes about her business; if I am blind to her as a public force, I nevertheless vibrate to her every glance and posture as a mime in the great American drama. It is this glancing and posturing that I wish to discuss—not the inner phenomena, but the outer.

My point of view, of course, is perhaps somewhat un-American. It is the nation's habit to shut its eyes to the outer seeming, provided the inner reality be found pleasing in the sight of God . . . . And it may seem that I go out of my way to find an inconsequential and inappropriate angle of approach, one having no sensible bearing on the subject. But is this really true? Is it entirely logical to judge the lady only on the basis of her yeas and nays, her attendance at committee meetings, the content of Good, True and Beautiful in her speeches? I don't think so. To do so would be to fall in with the national habit of taking everybody seriously, of giving credit if the heart is in the right place, of you-kid-me-I'll-kid-you. The thing to do is to get under the hide of the lady herself, to get clearly in mind what she is primarily concerned with. And what is this? Why, clearly, the distinction and homage that will accrue to her, the figure she will cut, the *gloire* she will amass and enjoy. That is to say, her mind is not on her humble and contrite heart at all, but on her trappings and outer show, as every other sane person's mind is. Well, this outer show is precisely what I want to inquire into.

II

In the course of my examination of such exteriors, I came some time ago to the conclusion that there is only one situation in which a woman can be completely ridiculous: that one in which her husband and her lover shake hands, fill glasses and pledge each other's health. I am still convinced that this theory is sound, but of late I have become sharply aware that there are situations a-plenty in which women in the mass , as opposed to woman the individual, can be ridiculous. Woman, indeed, like the harmonica, shines best as a solo instrument. When she attempts to play *ensemble* the result is often disastrous. The reason therefore is simple. Her appeal to the imagination, when she does appeal to the imagination, must carry something of the sinister with it. No woman was ever remembered for smug, tame little attributes, but only for terrifying, primeval qualities. If her charm is beauty, there must be a suggestion of snakes, skulls and fatal elixirs about it, else she suffers from a doll-like vapidness. If her charm is intellect, there must be a menace in it: mystery, guile, the capacity to inspire fear, else she is merely that most banal of God's creatures, an Interesting Conversationalist. So with all her other charms. If they are not deadly, then they are flat, tepid, uninteresting.

This suggestion of the sinister, for some reason, inheres only in one woman at a time. The moment the concept is made plural all its values change: the common denominator is oppressively trivial. One shrinks from a shrillness, a jangling, above all, from a pettiness, which in one woman are usually out of sight. A gossoon, when he finds his beloved calling on his sisters, is surprised to find how usual she seems. A nun, in the singular, is full of romance: one thinks of a broken heart, rosaries, and long hours alone with misty dreams. But when a bevy of nuns issue from a convent, one is conscious only of clacking tongues, flapping gowns and shiny faces. Have you ever noticed the sisterish ineffectuality of the three Rhine maidens in the first act of "Das Reingold"? How much better if Alberich had circumvented only *one* guardian of the gold! ... If you have any doubts on this general point, try to imagine certain divine ones playing *ensemble*: Garden singing in the chorus, Fannie Brice as a harem girl, Pavlowa third from the end in a pony ballet . . . .

At the outset of her career in public the lady politician faces the handicap resulting from this principle. She must cooperate: she must go to meetings, engage in shrill debates, have her picture taken in groups of fifty on the White House lawn. Acting willy-nilly against this background, she succumbs to its implications. She does all those things which no woman should do: she bustles, she talks loud, she gets into excited verbal sparring matches. Her whole utterance becomes banal: Madame President, don't you think we ought to have a committee on publicity, too? ... If I am to have such things said to me right to my face, I am going to resign from the club!... Don't you think women have a great deal to *learn* about politics?... I must say I can't understand what the Governor is *thinking* about, to make such an appointment .... We women must remember it's *organization* that counts ....

We *women*! What a hideous phrase! How it reeks of church suppers, charity card parties, culture clubs, treble clef choirs! Of fat arms, creaking corsets, quaking hips! No breath of elusive perfume hangs about it, no memory of a sidelong glance, a delicately curling cigarette, a tremulous, *andante* languor .... Females in wholesale lots!

III

In other directions the way of the Lady Bryan is blocked, too. "Woman's place," says the man in the street, "is the home." The savage rebuttals levelled at this simple proposition invite inquiry, to see if there may not be a kernel of truth in it. The hastiest reflection shows that there is. It sums up briefly the instinctive perception that there is something wrong with the role of a woman posturing on a stump. Whenever a woman is completely effective, it is always in a role related to what we vaguely associate with the worn-out but excellent word home. That is, a role related to the business of living itself, not to the business of providing the means and bulwarks of living. With a man, of course, the opposite is true. The part he plays in living *per se* is so trivial that he must bolster it up by participation in outside affairs—by, in one way or another, conquering the world. The moment he allows the emphasis to swing the other way he becomes a sit-by-the-fire, a cockerel, a drone, a henpeck.

A woman steps into this man's sphere at her peril. I think the reason is that her natural role is so much more brilliant than the best a man can make out of his that she suffers a come-down by the change. I suppose it requires more brains to run a railroad than it does to run a suburban cottage and bring young into the world, but in drama the voltage arises, apparently, not from the proved intelligence quotient involved in an undertaking, but from what it costs you to do it .... However that may be, as soon as a woman steps in the male motley, her dignity begins to vanish .... Certain apparent exceptions, of course, spring to mind. There is the woman who makes her own living, often gallantly enough. There were certain queens, Cleopatra, Elizabeth, Catherine, who are surely among the most romantic of their sex. But these exceptions are largely illusory. The lady underwear buyer, when she is alluring, is alluring not because of her skill in selecting underwear, although human comfort may be greatly augmented thereby, but because of herself, *i.e.*, she has her roots in living, not in buying underwear. So with the queens. They compelled attention and admiration, not because of the legislation they fostered, or the wars they won, or the tax-rates they reduced, but by the peculiarly superb quality of the womanhood that was in them, thrown into brilliant relief against the times in which they lived.

The lady politician disregards all these basic principles. Since changing economic conditions have forced many women to work, she idiotically assumes that a day of feminism has arrived—that it is time to cast off certain "shackles" and take her place beside men, the heroic. She does not see that her employed sisters work only because they have to, and there is a complete disjunction between their hearts and their vocations. She must put her soul into her own job, acquire a *Weltschmertz*. She will shine, not as a woman, but as a public figure . . . . Well, it simply won't work. Once floundering about in an alien scene, she gets into difficulties that multiply by geometric and hyper-geometric progressions. It seems impossible for her to clinch her talons on the only variety of politics which is really impressive: where cold, sordid gain is the stake, and the game is played by intrigue, counter-intrigue, and every known kind of sweaty, shifty-eyed artifice. This seems to be beyond her. Clutching blindly for something to justify her presence, she identifies herself with pale, wan issues, out of which no dollars will be made, wherein there will be no double-crossing, no throat-slitting, no weeping, wailing and gnashing of teeth, no grand, drunken celebrations: mothers' bills, children's bills, better babies' bills, health bills, school bills, sex-equality bills, hospitality bills, honest-weight bills. Out of politeness the men usually pass the whole proposed crop at every session, and that leaves the ladies worse off than before. For, despite the warnings of an alarmed press, which sees in these bills only more and more jobs, there are only so many of them that can be thought up, and the business of whooping them up, therefore, finds itself with progressively less and less to feed on. The steam, screeching the pop-valve so magnificently in 1920, now hardly stirs the needle; in a few short years, no doubt, it will die out altogether and leave the grand old Rainbow Limited stalled on a dead centre at the bottom of the grade.

It may very well be that these bills advocated by the fair are all excellent measures; that we shall all be happier, fatter and healthier in every way as a result of them. I have never read any of them, and cannot say. But, dramatically speaking, they are impossible. The glamor of their sponsors, already jeopardized when hauled out of the twilight of boudoirs on to the hustings, simply fades out altogether in the midst of such peewee activities. The thing becomes ridiculous. Is this, then, the end of all the fighting, hair-pulling, cake-baking and posing for pictures?—that the Governor is authorized and herein and hereby directed to appoint in each of the several counties a nurse, whose duty it shall be to determine the weight of all children born in the said county not later than ten days after birth and at intervals of three months thereafter, and to enter the said weight on suitable records and forms, to be furnished by the State Department of Health, as provided in 30-A of this section? ... The King of France, with twice ten thousand men, couldn't make this seem important. It may make for better babies, but it completely and irretrievably wrecks the lady politician.

IV

So far it is possible that I proceed too confidently, with too many *a priori* assumptions. I shall now try to prove my point. In Washington, that great city, there lives a lady whose career has a direct bearing on what I have said. I prefer not to name her, but I shall make it easy for you to guess who she is: her father was of the highest eminence, and her husband is and has been for a number of years a member of the Congress of the United States, and is somewhat bald, and, strangely for a Congressman, a gentleman.

I do not know this lady, but I have seen her, and I hear now and then of her doings. She is completely effective dramatically. She is what every lady politician in the country would like to be. She is well-dressed, she has an air, she is charming; her general effect, as they say, is that of a knock-out. She is reputed to control large affairs, to bend public men to her will, to make them listen to her with respect, and sometimes with a little fear. She is skillful, adroit, subtle. The things she is interested in are the things men are interested in: the cold, clammy things that really matter in politics. She, as the phrase has it, puts them across. She is a power. In the literal sense of the word, she is a politician.

But—does she cooperate, organize clubs, talk about "we women"? She does not. She plays a solo game. Does she run for office, sport Feminism, seek out all the frayed apostlettes of the movement, so easily accessible in Washington? No. She knows what a woman's sphere is, and stays in it. She has no illusions about the uplift. She is what the politicians call a twenty-minute egg. She is a brilliant success, shedding more lustre in a minute than all the rest of her de-shackled sisters do in a year.... She completely illustrates my point.

High Dignitaries of State
(December, 1924)

One is struck by a curious blowziness in American public men. I have no reference to their usefulness; for all I know, they are wise and competent, and add to human happiness. I am speaking of the cut of their jibs, the way they look and sound, their effectiveness as dramatic figures. It may be that to the student of government they are models, and offer material for thick books; but to the connoisseur of a show there is undoubtedly something lacking about them.

Set down the great figures of American history beside the great figures of other scenes and times, and the former always appear at a disadvantage, despite the fact they were probably more useful men. Washington, Jefferson, Lincoln, Lee, Wilson,—these names surely do not carry the glamor that goes with Alexander, Caesar, Constantine, Charlemagne, William, Cromwell, Louis, Peter, Frederick, Napoleon, and Bismarck. About that old-world galaxy, granted, there is a smell of the sordid: these men were in habitual contact with greeds, lusts, and hatreds from which fine natures recoil. They were adventurers. There was not one of them who did not, at one time or another, shoot the bones for the whole pile. There was more than a suggestion of the sinister about them: they were in unusually close touch with brute reality: they faced the fact of a cruel, senseless world without being oppressed, without needing balm in Gilead: they were unfettered by the timidity, the "morals" that give ordinary men pause. It was not so much that they were unscrupulous as that they were cynics, magnificent cynics, cynics on a heroic and shocking scale. When, to boot, their evil ventures prospered, there was a flavor of black blasphemy about them, of unholy alliance with Satan, so that some of them were hailed as children of the gods, and one at least as the Man of Destiny.... A fine set of bozos surely, a pirate's guard, the ermine never quite concealing dirk and dice-box. Yet what a glitter, what a hypnotic lure!

Now turn to our Americans. Unquestionably, they accomplished much: it is agreed the world is better for their having lived in it. In the popular picture of any of them the brow is always drawn with care, with sorrow, with pain; they all travelled the Valley of the Shadow and stalked through Gethsemane. Yet as actors in the play they cannot stand comparison with the least of those I have named from across the water. Ask the average man whether he had rather be Lincoln or Napoleon. If he tells the truth he will say Napoleon. Lincoln stands for all his national *mores* stand for: a cheer for him in some vague way is always a cheer for God, Moses, and the Eighteenth Amendment. Napoleon stands for all *his* national *mores* stand *against*: a cheer for him is a cheer for the devil and the Masque of the Red Death. Yet—the average man can no more resist the appeal of that dizzy career than he can resist spitting off the end of a dock. Lincoln, the man his acquired philosophy tells him he *ought* to be like, remains a prosaic figure in rusty black and a half-gallon hat. Napoleon, the man his deeper self tells him he would *like* to be like, is a figure of fabulous romance.

If the greatest of American statesmen are thus dramatically weak, the general run are dramatically impossible. If Washington, Lincoln, and Lee have an appeal, it has its source in their great *scenes a faire*, the moments when they made great decisions, rewrote history, changed the map of the world. Subtract this from them and there is nothing but a pother of phrases, most of them pretty stuffy. The present-day American statesman is simply Washington and Lincoln with the great moments left out, an imitator of what has gone before, conforming to a set mold as unchangeably as a bond salesman, a mouther of set phrases, a wearer of pot hats and undertaker clothes. From Maine to California he is exactly the same; his every phrase and gesture can be forecast as accurately as those of Civitas, Veritas, and Pro Bono Publico. He exudes a characteristic aroma, a dregsy reek.... Of what? It is rather elusive. I have been after it for some time now, and I am not sure that I have got it, but I shall try and get down what I think it is.

II

The source of all dramatic appeal in public men, I think, is power. It is this that makes us envy a statesman, when we do envy him. Again, it is a requirement of drama that the appeal of the protagonist be susceptible of indefinite expansion and contraction. That is, it must be possible for him to scale greater heights than the rest of us, and to come crashing down for a greater fall. Power alone enables the statesman to do this. Power is capable of indefinite expansion; it feeds a lust that grows until it seems greater than the human frame can endure. Had Napoleon's appeal rested on other things, there would have been the same Napoleon afterward as before. But his appeal lay in his power, and the excitement for the audience lay in watching his diabolical expertness in holding and swelling it. He was astride two horses, three horses, five, ten, ten thousand, and still he held his feet and galloped on. Finally, in this mad race between the man and his fate, the man lost and was crushed to pulp—a climax as perfect as was ever recorded. After his fall he was not the same Napoleon. He was Napoleon shorn of his power, the visible symbol of his greatness, the one thing that gave him his glamor in his heyday, the one thing that could be cut from under him to bring him to earth.... So with every other great dramatic figure in history. There can be no real magnificence without a foot on somebody's neck.

But in America power is the one thing that is denied the statesman,—power and all the trappings and symbols of power. I do not mean that the American statesman does not *have* power. What I mean is that the nation cannot tolerate power on public view. It is a corollary to the Declaration of Independence that no man ought to hold dominion over other men. The American statesman, therefore, must pretend that he hasn't any power, that he only holds in trust certain powers delegated to him, that he is not even remotely interested in arrogating them to himself personally. He asks "respect for the office, not the man." He is therefore under the necessity of making his bid for fame on other grounds.

Well, what other grounds are there? In the American scheme of things only one service to his fellow-men, or as it has come to be called, Service. I am unable to think of any other claim he can make. I have been examining the standing of a number of American heroes, not their real doings exactly, but the reason posterity has placed its seal of eminence upon them, and in every instance I find them measured by their contribution to the national weal—their "records," as the newspapers say. Nay, I uncover a still more lamentable circumstance. I find many a captivating man condemned by posterity because he did *not* make a perceptible contribution to the national weal. But of that more in a moment.

Now, it must be very apparent that this Service, as an ingredient of drama, is very defective. It may reduce the tax rate and improve Conditions, but it does not add anything to the candidate's heroic lustre. For one thing, opportunities for Service are very spotty, a fact which accounts for certain phenomena very puzzling to our better-informed newspaper writers. Let us suppose that a citizen, having taken counsel with himself, decides to enter public life, and in the proper manner files his papers for nomination and election to the State Legislature. It is impossible, considering the state of public prejudice, for him to address his prospective constituency thus: "Ladies and gentleman, I hereby solicit your support for this office because if I get it I shall be pretty important, with power to name three doorkeepers, a page, and a filing clerk in the next Legislature, all of which I promise to choose from deserving voters in this district. Vote for me. I want the job."

That would lay him open to all sorts of accusations: playing politics, corruption, and the like. What he must do, first, is to pretend he is not at all interested in the power and glory that go with being a delegate. His friends must write letters to the newspapers demanding that he run. Then he will be able to hatch a cock and bull story beginning: "Upon the earnest solicitation of a large number of voters in this district, and at great personal sacrifice, I have decided to enter my name." Then he must cast around for some way to perform Service; in popular parlance, he must find an "issue." But it quite often happens that there isn't any issue to find. That is to say, his prospective constituency is employed, has money in the bank, and doesn't give a damn who is elected.

Nevertheless, an issue must be found. So he addresses his first meeting thus: "Ladies and gentlemen, I come before you tonight to speak on a subject which I know is next to all of our hearts. Before I begin I want to say I didn't go after this office, it has like you might say come to me, that is if I get it, anyway I never had no intention of running for office until some of my friends come to me and showed me how it was my duty I should run. But what I want to say is this: We about had enough of Smithism in this district, and if I get elected all I got to say is the laboring man is going to get looked after like he ain't been looked after since this Smith ring got into office, and I say it's time somebody looked after the laboring man. Folks, I'm a plain business man, I am, but nobody can't say I ain't been fair to organized labor, and nobody never heard no complaints in *my* shop. Way I see it, the issue in this campaign is, Is the laboring man going to get a square deal, or are they going along giving him the little end of the stick like they done last time and like they're going to do so long as they have Smithism in this district? Now you take this here full-crew law: they got a paper going around says it ought to be repealed, but what I say is them as is trying to get this very fine law repealed had better look out, or the laboring man is going to rise up and demand what is coming to him, and that ain't no more'n right...."

If he is a candidate for Vice-President of the United States, the way he sees it is that the Reds are trying to land in the White House, and if he is a candidate for President of the United States, the way he sees it is that there is a deliberate and iniquitous plot afoot to destroy the Supreme Court, and that way leads to Revolution.

It takes no more than a glance at these "issues" to see that there is a distressing suggestion of unreality about them. One feels that if a cigarette were held against them they would go *pop* like a toy balloon. We should then be as well off as before, so far as I can see: it would take a wise man to say what difference it makes who gets elected, and on what issue.... But what I am trying to get at is simply the flabbiness of these issues as dramatic themes. Drama, indeed, is an inexorable Muse: she feeds on reality: there is no fooling her with shoddy stuff, and it makes little difference whether she is staged in theatre or parliament hall.

III

I hereby state the general, common-sense objection to the thematic material with which the American statesman is provided. There are others more technical. Assaying human merit on the basis of Service somehow implies that the servitor, in some way, is of better stuff, more pleasing in the sight of God, than the rest of us. But there is a well-marked limit, and it is quickly reached, to the capacity of one human being for conceding finer soul-texture to another human being. It affronts the ego to concede intrinsic superiority to another—or much superiority. Thus Service is bogged on a score I have already mentioned: it is inelastic: it does not permit the protagonist to soar far above us and plunge far below us. It is one of those blind themes that lead nowhere: it won't develop: it won't orchestrate. The public man who relies on it for bedazzling his fellows suddenly finds that its pedestal is only 2 1/2 inches above the level on which the multitude stands and can't be jacked any higher. Then he usually steps down from the pedestal altogether and pretends he had rather be with the crowd. This, I believe, accounts in part for the insistence with which our public men proclaim that they are nothing but plain men of the people, and have their pictures taken running threshing machines on a Vermont farm, or lighting pipes, or cussing in plain he-man fashion.

Finally, there is the unescapable fact that Service can be effective dramatically only when it costs something to perform it. The soldier, for example, always has an appeal. His part in the slaughter may be ludicrously small. But in doing it he may get bumped off, and actually he does often get bumped off. So as long as he goes marching off to war there will be crowds to cheer him on the way. But how about the $1-a-year man? A few times, perhaps, he performed some sort of Service. But is he a hero? He is not. He is a pretty sorry joke. His Service, no matter how valuable, cost him nothing to perform, and he must yield place to every yokel who shouldered a gun and went where the shells were whickering. And how about, say, a senator, at $7,500 a year, with no war going on? The thing becomes ludicrous ....

The point involved is obvious, and the public, I think, is always aware of it. Else why does it always seek to make martyrs of its favorite public men? Lincoln, Wilson, and Harding are good examples. In the case of Lincoln, the relation between his death and his Service is hard to see; in the case of Wilson it is still harder to see, and in the case of Harding it is almost impossible to see. Yet the public leaped at the chance to write *Pro Patria* over their tombs. So, in lesser degree, with other heroes. They are not lucky enough to get shot, but they can at least look haggard and ill, and this a great many have proceeded to do, to their great advantage. But how about the Bill Tafts who look fat and contented? ... Well, what kind of hero was Bill Taft? Thus doth a good digestion make clowns of us all. A gunny sack around his foot and a crutch, and he might have been reelected.

Thus, it is clear that politics under democracy, on its visible levels, is an impossible trade for heroes. The man who seeks romance there is doomed to disappointment. Fortunately, there are other levels, where no record is kept, and where the connoisseur of drama may refresh a jaded palate. I refer to those greasy dives where the game is played under cover, where wan and ghostly issues fade out and are no more, where reality is the thing, riches for some, bare life for others, where titans snarl and bite, wrestling savagely—for what? For power, the one thing that can put an edge on politics. Here is glamor, a pure incandescent glow. Policemen, contractors, newspaper reporters, whitewings, prostitutes, mayors, minor privilege holders, bootleggers, senators, firemen, councilmen, judges of elections, garbage men—what a lovely motley! How brightly does the ideal of Service burn in these patriotic breasts? ... All playing in dead earnest, raking in their chips with claw-like fingers; all pawns, pushed about by the Boss.

The Boss! There is dark fascination about him, without a doubt. He is the one romantic figure in American politics. Tweed, Croker, Hanna, Gorman, Murphy, Penrose—these names stir the imagination. Most 100 per cent Americans would rather have known one of them well than to have known every President since James A. Garfield. What did they accomplish? Why-nothing! What did Napoleon accomplish? ... It is the irony of drama that such men, who think nothing of Humanity and only of themselves, should have such an incomparable appeal. Or is it indeed irony? Possibly it is only inexorable logic. For after all, just how genuine is this Service? As a philosophy, an abstract idea, something evolved from dialectic, it is a pretty thing to play with, I grant. But hardly to be put into practise. It implies that a man habitually thinks more of others than of himself;—not tangible, concrete things, like his family, but shadowy, never-seen others, swarming by myriads;—such an implication passes credence. Actually, no man *does* put others before himself, and to cast him in a role which avers that he does so is to cast him in a role palpably false at the outset, and foreordained to be perpetually and irremediably ridiculous.

Be this speculation as it may, it is a curious commentary on the national mind that the political figures I have named, men whom any student of human beings would pick out as among the most interesting we have ever produced, should be condemned by a sort of conspiracy of silence to ultimate oblivion. Who will say that Penrose was not as much of a man as Wilson? That he was not essentially as honest a man? Yet who will say that he will be remembered after fifty years? ... No, the picture drawn for posterity in the United States is not true to life. It is like those moving pictures made so that certain colors which show in the set do not show on the screen. In our political scene all those rich, vibrant colors of the game as it is actually played, with its sordidness, its intrigue, its excitement, are blanked out; even the newspapers do not display them from day to day: the picture that actually shows is a wishy-washy thing of false moustachios, false whiskers, and false circles under the eyes .... Tweed, Croker, Hanna, Gorman, Cannon, Murphy, Penrose, and a regiment of their prototypes in every city in the country, all irresistibly picturesque figures, virtuosi of human passion, makers and busters of Presidents; and all are sleeping under the hill ....

And Harding has a Memorial!

The Pastor
(May, 1925)

Of all the roles in which man may be cast, the one least likely to be ridiculous is that of divine service. The holy man has in him a spark that sets him apart from all his fellows. Whether he be monk, rabbi, dervish, fakir, yogi, or shaman, he moves us to doff our hat; we see something in him that most of us have long since sold for our mess of pottage, almost forgotten. Perhaps it is the touch of poetry that all males are born with, that moony sighing for the stars which practical men learn to put behind them. Perhaps it is something else; I don't know. Whatever it is, we yield it a sneaking respect. A novice clad in flapping cassock, thumbing a clacking string of beads while he meditates in a stone courtyard, moves us curiously and profoundly. Catching him unawares, we instinctively turn our backs, as we would on coming upon a girl swimming naked in a pool: we recognize something eternal, something that has always been a part of the universe and always will be. It makes little difference whether the man as individual is dignified or not. That part of him which is consecrated to the divine mysteries commands our veneration, whether the rest of him be knave, craven, or clown; the role itself is dramatically solemn and moving.

Wherefore, it is all the more surprising that the typical American man of God in these our days is so loathsome, such a low, greasy buffo, so utterly beneath ridicule, so fit only for contempt. I refer, of course, to the evangelical brother. He is the only authentic American product; all the other priests and friars among us are exotic species, not germane to the discussion. His condition, if you ponder it, is remarkable. He numbers in his ranks many a man who as individual is undoubtedly admirable, who cherishes his friends and is kind to his family, who goes about in the world doing laborious and often demonstrable good. Yet, as regards his vocation, the observation made above must be reversed: it makes little difference how admirable he is as individual, that part of him which is preacher inspires our contempt, and his role is therefore dramatically impossible. Why?

Before trying to answer this, let us have a look at his origin. In the beginning he too was a holy man. But then something happened. Along in the Sixteenth Century he began gibbering and squeaking to himself and presently was demanding a reformation. What was the significance of this? I don't mean the ecclesiastical significance. I mean the subjective significance. Remember, he didn't stop at halting the gay life of Rome. He demanded other things, and presently he got them. He did away with what he called idolatry and popery: surplices, incense, and Latin. He did away with beautiful churches, and foregathered in mean meeting-houses. He did away with beautiful music, and began yowling mean hymns. In short, he did a wholesale trading of beauty for ugliness, and I think some thing is to be deduced from that fact.

Although I am no authority on the Middle Ages, I think there must have been some lyric spirit in those times, with their cathedrals, their chivalry and their pious looting trips to Jerusalem, and that this lyric spirit is what froze up in him. With the first settling of the whirling human motley into set forms, this lyricism, this poetry that accounts alike for monastery and feudal castle, began to disappear. Here and there, of course, it remained, or at least the tradition of it remained; but with the less imaginative kind of men it was lost, and with it went the poetic conception of religion. Such men began demanding religion with common sense in it, religion you didn't have to fast all night to understand. Well, that is the kind of religion they got. In England, France, Germany, all over Europe, those clods huddled where they could and did their coarse shouting, and formed themsevles into godly battalions, and fought wars, and perfected the thumbscrew.

II

This was the condition of our man of God when he migrated to America and began passing laws against witchcraft. But his development was not complete. The New England Puritan of the Seventeenth Century was still a far different animal from the revival whooper of today. His nearest surviving relative is the Dunkard or Mennonite elder, a narrow, repellent block of flint, but still retaining more than a shred of respectability. What made the finished product we know today? Here, I must say, come threads I can't trace back to their beginnings. But mainly, I believe, even more than the Asbury influence, there was the influence of the national philosophy itself. That is, a gradual osmosis took place. There seeped into him the flabby, pointless urbanity of the American hawker and salesman, the man of trade. The original Puritan preacher, with his belief that sin was abominable and that sin was the flesh, learned to relax his sour face; he learned the jargon of the advertising man, the go-getter; he learned to laugh the har-har-har of the town booster, to clap his lay brother on the back. He learned efficiency. He stuck electric lights in the steeple cross.

Profound changes, then, have taken place within him since the day when he was a holy man. I think we may say that he is no longer a holy man today. Nay, I falter and stammer too politely: he *is* no longer a holy man: the fact sticks out like the grease on his coat collar. No more conclusive proof of it is needed than his revised attitude toward himself, his flock, and his God. Your holy man, pure and simple, is one who has consecrated *himself* to God. He espouses celibacy, he lives in a stone dungeon, he grows a beard, he shaves his head, he dons a cassock, in token of his retirement from the world. And he essays some kind of pious service: he teaches the young, ministers to the sick, or illuminates manuscripts; or if he is especially pious, he makes Benedictine or Chartreuse. He may even conduct the holy ritual or interpret a gospel, but always the emphasis is on himself: his own life is the offering he has brought to Jahweh, the jealous. In this circumstance, I believe, is to be found part of his dramatic appeal: he casts in with his poetry all that he has on this earth; he can do no more. We perceive it to be silly; but it implies a stout spirit, and as I say, we doff our hats.

But with the American ecclesiastic of today the emphasis is the other way around. He doesn't offer himself to God; he offers others to God. He doesn't measure his piety by the number of paternosters he has mumbled in the day, or by the healing draughts he has brought to the sick, or by what he has taught the young, or by the wine he has bottled, or by the fasting he has done, or by the floggings he has endured, but by the number of souls he has induced to hit the trail. Here, I submit, is his fundamental dramatic weakness. For him to be dramatically effective, of course, it is not necessary that he have an eye to beauty. As I have pointed out, the Dunkard elder is as unaesthetic a clod as one can well imagine, yet he remains dramatically passable. I once risked my neck and nearly lost my life attending a convention of most of the Dunkard elders in the United States, and I know a little whereof I speak. The Dunkard will explain at length his belief that the stage is vile, the reason for his own singular clothes and the hideous dresses he puts on his womenfolk, his general belief that all beauty is the work of the devil. But when he is done he purses his craggy lips and shuts up. He is perfectly willing to let you go to hell in your own way. We may regard him as queer, but he is willing to live out his queerness and let us live out ours. We and he are at peace; we can salute him as we pass with honest good feeling.

But when a man becomes his brother's keeper, he at once loses all charm and becomes simply a stinking nuisance. Why is this? Let us transpose the question out of religion, where our prepossessions are so troublesome, and see if we can apply it somewhere else, and possibly get a helpful answer to it. Let us go, say, to the field of economics. Suppose a man believes in the Single Tax. Well, there is nothing offensive about that. Suppose, being a taxpayer and therefore an interested party, he undertakes to convince us that we should all be better off under the Single Tax. There can be no objection to that. Society is always in a state of flux, and there is a set on the left for the man with a stake in the game who wants to change it. But suppose, having not a nickel's worth of property, our enthusiast suddenly conceives that Henry George was divinely inspired, and that for some occult reason the rest of us *ought* to and *must* have the Single Tax. At once it appears that there is no seat in the hall for this fellow. He is an offensive busybody, fit only to be locked up. Suppose now, still having no property, he hires out to a Single Tax society to annoy the rest of us with his twaddle. Again, and doubly, he is seen to be impossible. He is a hireling mouthpiece, speaking only because he is paid. He not only has no seat in the hall, he is specifically ruled off the floor as a lobbyist.

Let us return now to our evangelist, and see if we can apply what we have learned. In the first place, there is no view you can take which makes him an interested party to the doings of my soul. It is simply none of his damned business what happens to my soul. In the second place, he is paid by the year and sometimes by the conversion to tell me what is good for my soul. He gets so much in cash, so much in kind: ham, cabbage, chicken, and Maryland biscuit—and so much in a parsonage. He is no celibate, but has a wife, usually a pretty eyeful. To spade the garden he has sons, and to bring his slippers he has daughters, who mostly take after their mother. In short, he is not in the service of God at all, but a hireling of a very earthy association. In fact, he has forgotten that he ever was in the service of God. He is making a living like an honest man; and the way he makes a living is to save souls, and the way he saves souls is to yell at them and scare them to death, and make them see it is good business—for them, and, above all, for him.

III

I come now to his worst offense, one I cannot forgive him: he has degraded God to the level of a cackling Methodist Bishop, has dragged Him in the muck of his own shoddy soul, until He is only a dirty travesty. I wish to dwell on this a bit, for it has direct bearing on the capacity of the American clergy for arousing our rage; it explains in part not only why he is so loathsome, but the peculiar quality of his loathsomeness.

As to whether there is a God or not, I have no means of knowing and cannot say. But this much I know: if we are to believe in God, the only concept of Him acceptable to imaginative men is a God of the most exalted sublimity, a God of thunder and ocean, of the hushed forest; a God of great cathedrals and beautiful chalices, a God of exquisitely wrought poetry, painting, and music; a God of David, Ambrose, Gregory, da Vinci, Palestrina, Mozart, and Bach. Such a God we may conceive without impiety, and having conceived Him so, we have conceived something as near the divine essence as is possible to the puny mind of man.

But having so conceived Him, it must be obvious there is only one thing left for us to do: fall down on our faces and worship Him. But to stand before the temple, beat a tom-tom, and seek to lead a rabble inside—how about that? No. The man who does that merely shows he has no conception of the awfulness of what he is talking about. Yet that is just what the evangelical pastor does. Clearly, it would be impossible for him, even if he felt it, to convey to the cattle before him a tithe of the divine significance. He doesn't try. Like all artists of persuasion, he simply offers inducements. He makes God a sodden thing that sodden men can understand. He chats with Him familiarly, waxing occasionally jocose; he extols Him with cheap hymns, that have a shouting chorus; he bellows "amen," and I judge he thinks God is pleased with all this commotion. He does more. He makes God a party to all sorts of absurd notions: he makes God abhor the Catholics, the Jews, and the Negroes; he makes God a Prohibitionist, a Nordic Blond, a patriot, a cad.

To "sell" God this way, of course, was exactly suited to the special American lack of taste. A proceeding already disgusting by its very nature became doubly so when efficiency was introduced into it. In addition to the electrically lighted cross, there came all sorts of innovations. The church was made a community center, and such sanctity as it held was chased out, so that sheik and flapper could pet in the corner and anybody could come in and warm his feet—provided he were not a Catholic, a Jew, or a Negro. Schools were opened for the training of Sunday-school teachers. Bible classes vied with each other to see which could get the most members; canvassers went forth wearing blue and red buttons, and when the votes were counted, one side accused the other of cheating. Intrigue got into the annual conference, and pastors pulled wires to get fat charges. Congregations turned thumbs down on the poor oaf who mistakenly supposed that religion was something more than pep, a $100,000 edifice, and membership. Energetic district superintendents kept a weather eye peeled, and presently landed jobs with the Anti-Saloon League. Then the whole gabbling crew descended upon us, and jammed Prohibition down our throats. How much, think you, does God concern Himself in all this poppycock?

The net result, as I say, is to inspire those of us who have any surviving respect for God with an unspeakable loathing. We gaze on all this traffic and, without knowing exactly why, we feel a sick, nauseated revulsion. We feel as we felt when we were children, and had a bright glamorous picture of Santa Claus, with his fat little belly and fairy reindeer, and then suddenly came on a vile old loafer ringing a bell over an iron pot. It seems a blasphemous mockery that men can preach such vulgar nonsense, call it religion, and then belabor the rest of us for not being washed in the blood of the Lamb.

IV

There remains the pastor's greasiness. I must direct your attention to the fact that the popular picture of him, looking like a cartoonist's drawing of a Prohibitionist, is at considerable variance with the actuality. He is no lantern-jawed fellow with flapping coat-tails and a stove-pipe hat. He is usually large and fat, and except for a white necktie, he dresses much as the rest of us dress. His peculiar mark is oleageneity; he looks as though he would smell sweaty, as though his hand would be moist, as though he would paw you over: something tells you to stand at a distance and keep edging away. In short, he looks as though there were something wrong with him, as though he were not the person to have running around in a Y.M.C.A. dormitory, or to trust with the fifteen-year-old soprano of the choir.

Before discussing this side of him, I shall have to digress for a moment. Of late years I have come to the conclusion that religion is one of the two main phases of the sublimated amative impulse. The other phase is the aesthetic, and I think the two are usually mutually exclusive. That is, the person who is predominantly religious is rarely aesthetic, and the person who is predominantly aesthetic is rarely religious. When you apparently have both together, as in the case, say, of a composer of church music, what you really have, I think, is an aesthete expressing himself resignedly in religious terms.

I am aware that studies in religious history support this view, but I didn't come by it that way. I got it directly: I became aware, either through my own feeling or through watching others, that there is almost an identical quality of exaltation in romantic love, in religious experience, and in aesthetic experience. I became aware of something else: that different religions gratify different kinds of sublimation. There is a lascivious quality in Christian Science, for example, that is different from the sensuous seductiveness of the Church of Rome, and these two are different from the anemic austerity of Episcopalianism. I became aware of something else: that all religions appeal to women vastly more than to men, and this, it seems to me, is because women are more often thwarted in their romantic desires than men are, or possibly because their more imaginative natures doom them to disappointment even when fulfillment is apparently theirs.

Scaling down from such astral forms as Christian Science, Catholicism, and Episcopalianism, it is obvious that the congregation of an evangelical church gets an enjoyment out of the proceedings that cometh not from the heart or spirit at all, but from a point slightly nearer the abode of Satan. Men and women jam tight in the vestibule; there is elevating intimacy, and a pleasant contact of manly thigh and fat female hip. Girls and boys, once the hymns are started, hold hands, and attain loftier communion than the back parlor induces. The pastor bellows about sin, and everybody knows what sin means: it is nice to be able to hear all about it here, and be doing the Lord a good turn as well. The pastor bellows about hell, and the same half-frightened, half-anticipatory shivers run all about as come upon stepping into a brothel. Excitement fills the air; a trance descends from above—a trance, it is true, slightly tinged with the bestial, but still, trance, and everybody is entitled to a trance.

These things being as they are, why do young men enter the ministry? I think the reason is easy to see. Having in them already a strain of sliminess, they hear the call to God—but not with their ears. They have an appetite for sneaking vicarious romance, and the holy office offers a way to gratify it. One or two of these young men whom I seduced into my confidence, told me plainly that all this was so. They have a pretty nice time when they are preachers—at least their idea of a nice time. I have spoken of the lady their kind usually lead to the altar. As I have said, she is usually no homely wallflower, but very toothsome. She is the kind who gets appointed handshaker to the departing congregation, who goes on tour as hymn leader with the travelling evangelist. There is a cold glitter in her eye and a soft moistness about her mouth that mirror perfectly those rosy dreams of her water-eyed husband. Never overlook the woman a man marries. Much is to be learned from her.

So there he is.

Pathology of Service
(November, 1925)

I propose herein to isolate the bacillus of Service, the itch to make the world better. Why it has never been isolated before I don't know. The disease rages, it has a myriad symptoms, from the Harrison Act, the Mann Act, and the Volstead Act, in its simpler phases to such fabulous derivatives as the law forbidding the teaching of Evolution in Tennessee and the law compelling the finger-printing of infants in Pennsylvania. Yet little has been done to discover its essential nature. Those whom it oppresses carry on a desultory traffic in epithets; they denounce it as "fanaticism" and sneer at it as "uplift," but they add nothing to what is known about it.

Always they make a fatal mistake. They discuss it in terms of the symptoms rather than in terms of the disease. That is, confronted by a new delusion, a new movement for this or that, they accord it all the honors of a lucid idea, and seek to combat it as though it had sense in it. They discuss it seriously, with its supposed import of good or evil to the commonwealth, and its relation to the Bill of Rights. This is like calling out a posse to rope the pink elephants seen by a man down with delirium tremens. I shall fall into no such error. I shall treat all these fine schemes as having no objective validity at all; I shall regard them as a social phantasmagoria, whirling clouds and specks in a national fever dream, and so doing, I shall try to discover what has brought them into being.

First, I should like to outline the problem. Service is peculiar to America. It is unknown in the Orient, in France, Germany, Italy, Russia, and Spain, in short, in most of the civilized world. It is known in England and the Scandinavian countries, but in a mild form, and in these places its presence is traceable almost in its entirety to feminist activities. As a dominant social philosophy it is the exclusive possession of ourselves. Moreover, even here, it is relatively recent. As I shall show presently, in the form we know it it is hardly more than twenty-five years old. The problem, then, is to account for something which is peculiar to America and which has come into being in this, the glorious Twentieth Century.

If I am wrong, then all current theories about it are wrong. This is especially true of the theories put forward by the Servists themselves. Ask the average adherent of Prohibition why he believes in it, and if he does not cite the Bible, he will cite something which he calls "modern enlightenment." Society, he will tell you, as a result of the increase in its collective knowledge, has developed a new conscience, a new realization of the duty it owes itself and its posterity. Prohibition, he will explain, has come as a result of this enlightenment. Inasmuch as human knowledge has actually increased of late, a specious plausibility goes with this argument. But it goes to pieces on inescapable rocks. Certain changes, it is true, may be ascribed to the new enlightenment. An example is the modern practice of sleeping with the windows up instead of down. Previously, night air was thought noxious; now it is thought necessary to healthful sleep. The point to be noted is that all persons not ignorant agree on it. But about Prohibition and other forms of Service there is no such agreement. One man is a dry; his neighbor is a wet. Both sleep with their windows open, but their enlightenment does not extend to Service. If Service were properly ascribable to enlightenment, it would enlist all informed persons in its ranks. But it does not, and its origin must be sought elsewhere.

If the Servist is thus unable to explain himself, his victims are in just as bad case. They have evolved various hypotheses. One of them is that Service results from the inferior man's envy of his superiors. The inferior man, it is held, by reason of his hoggish nature, cannot enjoy the principal pleasures of his superiors. Therefore, acting collectively, he prohibits all such pleasures. Another hypothesis, almost identical, is that Service results from the country dweller's envy of the city dweller. Still another is that Service, at least that part of it which is concerned with sex morality, results from the suppressed sex desires of the Servist. Still another is that Service is but a smoke screen to hide a mass scramble for government jobs. And finally, there are the hypotheses which ascribe Service to bigotry, malice, and intolerance, and let it go at that.

It needs but a glance at any of these, however, to show that they won't do. Service is not the exclusive business of the inferior man. Rather it is the other way around. It is notorious that Prohibition was foisted upon the working classes against their wishes. Service may not be the business of the very superior man, but it is the business of the comparatively superior man; the mediocrity, perhaps, but surely not the boob. Nor is it the exclusive business of the country dweller. The yokel has a few simple schemes to save the world, but all the rare and beautiful ones originate in the cities. Nor is it the exclusive business of those who hope to get jobs out of it. For one prospective jobholder in Service there are five hundred disciples who listen to the speeches, give the Chautauqua salute, and pledge $10 each as sustaining members. As for the sex theory, and the bigotry, malice, and intolerance theories, they collapse before space and time. Sex, bigotry, malice, and intolerance are as old as man. They exist in France, but Service is unknown in France. They existed in 143 B.C., but Service was unknown in 143 B.C. Our problem is located on the American continent, roughly between the year 1900 and 1925. Factors must be found which operate in this particular place and this particular time.

II

These factors, I think, like the factors which produce cancer, are two: there is a general agent and a specific one. Of the specific agent, or factor, more in a moment. The general agent, I think, has its roots simply in the appetite for drama. That is, the Servist yearns to shine before his fellows and himself, to play a role which is heroic; unconsciously, he seeks an escape from the meanness of his everyday existence. In a superficial way this is often noted. The lustful satisfaction which he gets out of his labors, a satisfaction out of all proportion to anything they bring forth, is a matter of common comment. The trouble is, that this satisfaction is thought to be purely hedonistic. The Servist is thought to go his queer way because he gets pleasure out of it, of the same sort that other men get out of wine and music; and it has even been suggested that he might be cured if he were provided with other simple pleasures, such as those offered by band concerts and bull fights. This is all wrong. There is hardly any pleasure, in that sense, in a Servist's day. Snooping down alleys and behind speakeasies must be far from pleasurable, and operating on amorous husbands must be downright nauseating: knights of such rococo grails are requited with a satisfaction that is far from pleasure, in any proper use of the word. It is my contention that this satisfaction is dramatic, that it has nothing to do with good and evil, pain or joy; that it is the satisfaction which a little girl gets when she dons her mother's hat and parades before company.

The chief buttresses of this theory, of course, are intangibles, not facts of record: you observe the Servist's grimaces, and you penetrate to his soul or you don't. But certain concrete facts bear on it. To begin with, there is the manner in which the Servist goes about his work. He is forever holding meetings, parades, and demonstrations, and for all these he provides badges, banners, and slogans. All this bears a suspicious resemblance to a college football game, which is also marked by badges, banners, and slogans, i.e., yells, and which is so transparently an effort on the part of the many to dramatize themselves by seeking identity with the heroic few that it needs no detailed discussion. There is nothing about improving the world which calls *per se* for such tactics. Business men, launching schemes which are demonstrably beneficial, often do so with a brief notice on the company bulletin-board. When the Servist invariably uses whoops and noise, he lays himself open to the suspicion that improving the world is not his only object. He appears, to use childhood's expression, to be "showing off," to be seeking an inflation of his ego by merging himself with a great and glorious procession, one in which all participants are knights in shining white armor, and the despair and envy of those who line the sidewalks.

Next, I point out the sharp contrast between the kind of people who are Servists and those who are not. In Service, one finds bankers, druggists, grocers, superintendents of schools, proprietors of gents' furnishing stores, teachers, professors in third-rate universities, butchers, owners of Ford garages, proprietors of shoe-stores, grain and feed dealers, vendors of stationery and school supplies, ice, coal, and wood dealers, dentists, proprietors of soft-drink emporiums, agents for hygienic corsets, boarding-house keepers, insurance agents, proprietors of lunch-rooms, advertising solicitors, station agents, secretaries to associations, promoters of cemeteries and daylight mausoleums, realtors, and postmasters. Not in service, one finds cowboys, actors, bootleggers, opera singers, prizefighters, lumbermen, head waiters, pool champions, baseball players, stick-up men, writers, newspaper men, gangsters, sculptors, soldiers, prostitutes, acrobats, and doctors. There is a middle ground on which stand people who may be Servists or may not, depending on temperamental peculiarities; I leave them out of consideration, and mention only those who, on the one hand, are almost always Servists, and those who, on the other hand, are almost always not.

Examining these two groups, one is struck by two circumstances. The first, the group which is in Service, is made up of people who lead insufferably dull lives. It is not that they are such dull people intrinsically, or that they lack brains of a sort, or that they lack money to seek pleasure, for most of them, in a petty way, are fairly well off. It is simply that as they survey their lives the tiny spark of imagination which flickers in all humankind must revolt at a drab, utterly pointless spectacle, and so it is not surprising to find them casting about for means to cast a bit of glamor over it. The second group, the group which is not in Service, is made up of people who according to their own notion lead a heroic existence. The people who are indifferent to Service, it is commonly thought, are infected by a liberal spirit which renders them immune. But looking over my samples, I find this hard to believe. That a liberal spirit infects an actor is surely not plausible. I think it is simply that an actor can admire himself hugely, and that in consequence he has no need of Service. Of course, *you* may not admire an actor, but be assured *he* does, and that is all that matters for the purposes of this inquiry.

If I am right so far, it would seem that a person consecrated to Service, if he were suddenly thrust into a heroic job, would become most shaky in respect to his vows, and that a person hitherto immune to Service, on quitting the original heroic job, would be extremely liable to contract the disease. And so in fact we find it. For an example of back-sliding Servists, we need go no further than Congress. It is full of up-standing Methodists, once ardent Servists, who on election to the heroic toga forsook the good, the true, and the beautiful, and became addicted to licentious practices. Representative the Rev. Mr. Upshaw, of Georgia, has made bitter complaint about the scandal, and as I write the outstanding facts about it are being entered on court records, as an incident to a congressman's divorce suit. As examples of heroic buckaroos who quit their original calling, and then went into Service, the names of John L. Sullivan, Al Jennings, the Rev. William A. Sunday, Robert Downing, and Benny Leonard come to mind at once. None of these gentlemen, so long as he followed the profession he first engaged in, was ever heard of in Service. Yet on retirement, each became a Servist in his own way, Sullivan as a temperance lecturer, Sunday and Downing as preachers, Al Jennings as a moral writer. Benny Leonard, after taking leave of the ring in an elegant valedictory, conceived the ambition of making the world healthy, and sent Heywood Broun an exerciser. There are hundreds of lesser lights who have gone the same way: a revival meeting is hardly complete without one of them. And as a wholesale example of the process, we have only to look at our soldiers. So long as they were heroes, they were fine scoffers at Service, especially in the form it took under the red triangle; but a soon as they doffed their uniforms, they went in for Service with the most fanatical zeal, and were a menace to public order until they were finally reshackled safely to the oars.

There is much more evidence that I could adduce bearing on the impulse of the Servist, but I leave it out for lack of space. It seems to me, however, that the considerations I have touched on make a strong presupposition in favor of the dramatic hypothesis.

III

The specific factor brings me to the saddest part of my discourse. For it is my solemn and awful conclusion that Service, which rallies to its banner Fundamentalists and all other right-thinking men, was sired by these three: Darwin, Nietzsche, and Spencer, and that the greatest of these was Spencer.

Service, in so far as it has a philosophic basis, involves the idea of Progress. That is, humanity is conceived to be moving toward a goal, in accordance with God's holy law, and this goal is the millennium which should be ushered in as quickly as possible. This is a new idea in the world. Before the Twentieth Century you will find no record of it: men had advocated reforms a-plenty, for the general convenience or on theological grounds; but they had never conceived of Progress, apart from the specific steps which marked it, as an end in itself. The notion, obviously, did not arise of its own accord, and it is necessary to find something to account for it.

This will be found, I believe, in the writings of Spencer. He announced the thesis that society is itself an organism, and that it is in process of evolution exactly like a biological organism. He showed that social groups in their lower forms are small and of simple structure; that as they develop they become larger and more complex, with a growing specialization of individual units and interdependence between them; that finally, in the big national groups, a structure is attained similar to the structure of the higher forms of animal life, with sustaining system, distributing system, and regulatory system all complete. Here is the beginning of the idea of Progress. It is only fair to Spencer, however, to absolve him from responsibility for the godly results his theory later led to. In his hands, it produced no godly results at all, but appeared to lead straight to atheism and despair. Pursuing his studies in the evolution of moral ideas, he was led to the conclusion that there can be no such thing as an absolute standard of human conduct. What is right in one society is wrong in another; what seems so conclusively in accordance with the will of God is usually quite illusory. To obey the dictates of biological instincts and appetites was about as far as he ever got in the way of a maxim for the young.[1]

All this, of course, was equivalent to giving the Summum Bonum a kiss on the head with a potato masher, and indeed it has never been the same Summum Bonum since. It is small wonder that Spencer's English colleagues were loath to concede much sense to his ideas. Leslie Stephen and S. Alexander are very polite to him,[2] and even manage to fit evolution into their argument, but it is quite plain they had no intention of subscribing to his heresies. Huxley joined issue with him, and on his own ground, contending that if society is evolving, it is the evolution of species, since the evolution of species acts to eliminate weak strains, whereas the evolution of society, with its tendency toward "humane" treatment of the unfit, acts to preserve and perpetuate these strains.[3] It goes without saying that American moralists conceded him nothing, for they had apparently never heard of him at all.[4] Down through the eighties and nineties and early nineteen hundreds they went their untroubled way, occasionally giving him space in a footnote, but preoccupied mainly with their categorical imperatives and four major virtues. Then all of a sudden, some time during the reign of the immortal Theodore, they had a great awakening. They embraced all that Spencer wrote thirty years before, they endowed it with evangelical overtones—and the philosophical basis for Service was complete. How did this come about?

As to that, I can only guess. But my guess is that it came about through the writings and speakings of Borden P. Bowne, who, during the closing years of the last century, was professor of philosophy at Boston University. Although forgotten now by the laity, Bowne enjoyed tremendous academic prestige in his day, and his influence must have been considerable. His specialty was examining the arguments as to whether there is or is not a God, and his bias was in favor of God. Writing at a time when evolution had rocked men's faith, he did much to hearten them for another try at the trail. Atheists confronted him, demanding proof of God, and he had back at them by demanding proof that there was no God. If a burden of proof lay on believers, he said, an equal burden of proof lay on non-believers: here were phenomena which could be explained two ways, and neither side could claim exemption from logic. Having thus cleared his decks for action, he opened up his guns, and he had pretty good guns. It is absurd, he said, to hold a mechanistic view of life and the universe. Matter could not spontaneously have sprung into life, and life could not mechanically have developed into Man. We must have another conception of causation and teleology. We must get away from that theory of causation which regards the cosmos as a series of pool balls in a row, with man as the No. 1 ball in the side pocket. Rather we should regard the cosmic process as a great musical composition, wherein each part has a separate existence taken by itself, and yet fits into a planned and logical whole, and wherein all the parts move toward a preconceived goal.

Thus he took the small orchestra of Spencer, the orchestra of the flora and fauna, and augmented it by adding an infinite number of pieces; he set planets and fixed stars to banging great instruments in the heavens, and earthquakes to rumbling down in hell. And above all, he said, it is unthinkable that all this fuss could have been set going as mere caprice; there must have been some reason for it, and this reason, this purpose, must include all of it, and all of it must be moving toward some goal worthy of it.[5]

It was a fine cacophony, and even the professors could catch a little of it. The orchestration was beyond them, but the main tune they could hear, and this they fashioned into a stave of their own.[6] They forgot about the planets and the fixed stars, and all of Bowne's cautions about abstractions, and seized on the idea of society moving toward a goal, a moral goal. At last, they said, we have something which hooks up with Darwin, and the descent of man; with Spencer, and the evolution of conduct: with Nietzsche, and the superman, and with Holy Writ. So sing a little lay about progress, and the job is done!

This nonsense in one form or another is now poured into thousands of our college students every year. Every year a new crop of clear eyed young men and women, fit in mind and body, all convinced that it boots not where we are going, so long as we are on our way! And the Liberal editors wonder what has come over the country!

IV

If I am right about the dramatic instinct, and right about Progress, it remains for me to show what the dramatic instinct did with itself before Evolution came along, and why other nations have remained immune to the disease which is a plague among us.

America, I take it, needs more artificial bolstering up of personal roles than any nation on earth. We are a complete democracy. Others nations have representative government, and to that extent are political democracies, but ours is both a political democracy and a philosophical democracy. Here, men not only have the right to vote, but they have the right to consider themselves equal to all other men. And for this last right they pay a terrific price. Since in America, all men are equal, all men must justify their existence, must get ahead. In other countries, where it is impossible to move from one caste to another, men do not try to. In England, if a man is born a valet, he may remain a valet for the rest of his life, and retain the respect of his master, his friends, and himself. But in America, if a man is born a valet, he must become a butler, a headwaiter, and finally a bootlegger, else he is a failure, despised of all men. Thus there is a frantic scramble to attain what is called success. But in the nature of things, all men cannot attain success. The vast majority must play lowly roles indeed, and the national imperative being as it is, this sets them to brooding and self-castigation. Naturally, even if they have not attained success, they seek a way to make it seem that they have, some means whereby they can induce other men to look at them with respect, envy, and maybe a little fear.

In the early days of the Republic, of course, this craving for drama was just as strong as it is now. The necessity for getting on was just as great, and the failures were just as numerous. But the despair of those days discharged itself in a great national adventure which has now come to an end. This was the adventure of winning the West. It was something which everybody could participate in, everybody could identify himself with, just as the howling freshman identifies himself with a fast half-back, just as a Servist identifies himself with a parade on Fifth Avenue.

Everybody was on the move or wished he was; everybody had relatives who were going or had gone; everybody read about it in the newspapers and heard it talked about at the village store. It was forever on the floor of Congress: whether to send a company of regulars to some corner of Colorado, whether to slaughter the Indians or geld them, whether to admit Missouri free or slave, what to do with Kansas and Nebraska, whether to insist on 54-40 or fight. That great region over the horizon came to be the symbol of romance and opportunity. If you have any doubts about the appeal that it carried, have a look at the names of the railroads which were built in the past century, and notice how many of them bear the expression "and Western." This was the magic shibboleth that evoked epic, mystery poetry, poetry which stirred the hearts of all the citizens of the land. But along about 1900, the adventure was over. The West was won, and the rest was faint perfume. Giving up that glamorous frontier was a wrench. Magazines continued to print "Western" stories long after the cowboy was extinct in every place except the rodeo, and after the magazines quit, the movies carried on. But bit by bit, people realized that the big day was gone.

Now it is easy to see that when the West no longer offered an easy way to heroism, people should have turned to something else. But why did they turn in the peculiar direction they took? Why did they embrace this philosophy of foreigners? Why didn't they go on with the philosophy of Emerson, or William James, or even Elbert Hubbard? I believe it is because this philosophy of progress was the only thing on the market which satisfied the craving to regard America as a land of destiny, a craving which had been acquired during the winning of the West. Previously, Westward Ho! had been the watchword, and since people rarely think more than one generation ahead, it never occurred to anybody that Westward Ho! would not be our destiny until the end of time. When we were brought up short by the Pacific Ocean, the spell of a destiny had become too strong to be cast off. We had to have a destiny, and the idea of progress, of doing God's will by hastening His divine plan, by bringing nearer His great millennium, and of beating all other nations in the race, held an appeal stronger than all other ideas. Thus we see why America embraced the doctrine while other nations let it alone. Other nations are not harassed by the scramble for success, the way we are, and their citizens have less need of bolstering up their roles; other nations have rarely held the notion of destiny, so they have no need to find one for themselves. We alone have need of this philosophy, and we alone have embraced it.

V

Well, can anything be done about a cure? It seems to me that much can be done. I need hardly point out that the specific factor, misapplied evolution itself, appears a bad place to begin. You may argue about this until the cows come home, and never prove anything; indeed, I doubt if you could even get the average Servist to admit the origin of the ideas. But the general agent, the craving for drama, is surely vulnerable. All that is necessary is to make it impossible for the Servist to derive a thrill from his work, and ridicule is the obvious way to do this.

I do not speak without clinical data. Ridicule has been tried, as a matter of fact, and with marked success. In Baltimore, the fair city by the Chesapeake, lives a publicist by the name of Hamilton Owens. He is editor of a newspaper which is opposed to Service in all its forms. But he never makes the mistake of taking Service seriously. He ridicules it, mocks it, tweeks its nose and pulls its whiskers. He produces grotesque maps and charters, showing how far the Servists would reach if placed end to end; he demands to know, if x Prohibition agents collect y bribes in z number of days, how many bottles of booze can be stored under the Brooklyn Bridge; he makes up terrible slogans, and offers them to the Servists. In short, he does the one thing Service cannot stand: he strips it of its glory. The result is that the Maryland Free State is probably the hardest State in the Union to perform Service in. Servists there have become timid and skittish. The Servist who would thrive and grow fat on ordinary abuse thinks long and hard before he braves the deadly ridicule of Mr. Owens.

The plan, I think, is practicable all over the country. Moreover, I do not see that it violates any of the Servist's rights, moral or civil. He, uninvited, holds a parade and asks the help of the police to compel us to get in line. If we not only refuse to get in line, but jeer at him and withhold the admiration he so plainly desires, I do not see that he has received anything but his deserts. His plea that he works for God and morality is all bosh. Actually he works for his own aggrandizement, and I see no reason why we should not suppress him as we would suppress any other nuisance. Progress be damned! I am a Fundamentalist.

Mr. Mencken and the Multitudes
(*New York Times Book Review*, April 16, 1950)

H.L. Mencken is superficially the easiest set-up awaiting the biographer. He offers no dearth of material, any more than does the aurora borealis. In his heyday, indeed, he was a sort of neon Northern Light, our leading literary luminary, the arbiter of books, idol of college students, editor of our leading intellectual magazine, scourge of frauds, hypocrites, and windbags—all this and a wit besides.

Mencken wrote more than most men of his time, was more written about than any of his contemporaries, unless it was Coolidge. Yet in some subtle way he is booby-trapped, so as hitherto to elude biography. His detractors hated him too much, his worshipers were too dazzled to achieve objectivity; as for Mencken himself, though he got out reams of memoirs, he missed profundity, because he always underrated his own stature, perhaps not being aware of it.

From the plethora of material Edgar Kemler has drawn a face that seems real, told a tale fresh on every page, and on some pages a tale packed with staggering surprises. One suspects that Kemler, a new product of Hopkins, Harvard, and Baltimore, has done a standing broad jump into the front rank of American biographers.

Probably wisely, he retires the familiar caste of Mencken's own writings. Gone the ice cream-eating pony, the dim-witted horse, the bartenders, livery keepers, painted ladies, brass band leaders, mourners at the multiple funeral of Joe Gans, heroes of the Baltimore Fire, and Democratic delgates to the convention of 1912, who almost, but not quite, nominated Mencken for Vice President. In their place are the editors, writers, politicians, and adversaries of various sorts who actually made his life, who pushed him to such acclaim and brought him such grief.

Combat is the steady theme, and we soon see Mencken's propensity for quarrels. Some of them were small, such as those with John Adams Thayer, over management of The Smart Set; Theodore Dreiser, over strategy toward the censors; George Jean Nathan, over policies of The American Mercury. But some of them were gigantic, such as those with the churches, over many moral matters; with the Babbitts, wowsers, and bigots over hypocrisy in general; with the United States Government, over his attitude toward World War I, which he opposed, over censorship, persecution, and prohibition, which he not only opposed, but almost single-handedly smashed, if a solo credit can be given for a movement that eventually, but not initially, involved millions of citizens.

Yet it is soon apparent that no man can face such odds and win. As Kemler puts it, Mencken became "over-extended." It was up to him to change his music, shorten his lines, or in some way bring his resources and the tactical actualities into proportion. He did nothing of the kind.

It is dismaying, yet at the same time inspiring, to discover that he had no capacity to trim, compromise, or switch. You took him that way or you didn't take him. But the fact that many did take him, that a "civilized minority," as he called it, provided him an audience no matter how violently majorities disapproved, led indirectly to his undoing. He began assuming he needed no majority approval, and thus contumacity got into it, perhaps catching the eye of the gods.

Death, which was one of their guys, suddenly appeared, when Mencken claimed, no doubt as an owlish jape, divine intervention in the demise of some of his persecutors. From there on in Death rode with him, claiming members of his family, his dearest friends, dealing him blows he never recovered from. To relax, he took a trip west, barnstorming all the way, smearing himself on the front pages, cutting capers in Hollywood, getting himself talked about.

To put some color of sobriety over these carryings-on, he gave out he was bound for San Francisco to honor George Sterling, America's greatest poet. Mr. Sterling, understandably touched, prepared a welcome. But as the guest's arrival was more and more delayed, he began drinking the welcome up. When Mencken knocked on his door he was forever unable to answer, having already downed the last of his bottles, the one that was full of prussic acid.

Then the gods switched music on Mencken. They began flinging things at him that defied combat in any form, such as the depression. He ran up all the old flags, but thier legends, in so far as they could be deciphered, seemed to read Let 'Em Eat Cake. This American Mercury readers couldn't stomach. They flung Hitler at him, but instead of fighting him, Mencken embraced him, or at any rate flirted with him noticeably. This Baltimore couldn't take. They flung Roosevelt at him, and fighting Roosevelt was like stabbing a rapier into the Mississippi River. And, ironically enough, the one time Mencken was a good boy, behaved himself, cracked jokes and hurt nobody's feelings, Roosevelt staked him out in one of the most fiendish jokes every perpetrated on an adversary.

This was at the Gridiron Club dinner of December, 1934, when Roosevelt, grinning at Mencken, read to the assembled journalists an attack on the press unparalleled for deadly virulence. But it soon turned out, as Mencken's face got redder and the chill got colder and colder, that this wasn't Roosevelt's indictment. It was Mencken's from "Prejudices," Series VI.

It was the beginning of the journalistic end, though after that Mencken produced the Days books, another edition of "The American Language," and "A New Dictionary of Quotations," one of the most delightful bedside companions in print. Then, there was last year's "Chrestomathy," a collection of many rare, prized Mencken pieces.

Now, at 69, Mencken lives happily with his brother August, and seeks his old friends, especially Nathan, who has never wavered in his devotion. Yet one hears his health precludes further work, and this is somehow frightening. For we live in troubled times, with the censor, the patrioteer, the bigot in full cry once more. And one wonders who the big bull elephant will be, to smash at them hard again, and whether there ever will be another one quite as big, quite as brave, quite as mad, as Mencken.

II. Lippmann and The World—*The Corporate Awfulness*

II. *Lippmann and* The World—*The Corporate Awfulness*

Introduction

As we have seen from his *Mercury* article, Cain did not have a very high opinion of the work produced by editorial writers when he was introduced to Walter Lippmann on that September day in 1924. At the *Sun*, they had called them "idiotorials" and "to a working stiff in the news departments," said Cain, "they are thinking pieces not respected at all, done by trained seals with green eye-shades, most of them very elderly. Their only qualification was that they be in favor of motherhood and against the man-eating shark." And when Lippmann, after reading some of Cain's magazine articles (which Cain had hastily asked his mother to send up from Baltimore) asked Cain to try his hand at writing a few sample editorials or "leaders," as he called them, Cain was not sure what to do. He had to face the simple fact that he did *not* know *how* to write an editorial.

Lippmann handed him a bundle that contained all the New York newspapers for that day and Cain took them upstairs to a little cubicle under the golden dome, overlooking the Brooklyn Bridge. He sat down at the roll top desk and opened the bundle to peep at the editorial pages which he hoped would give him some idea what to write about. They were all deep pieces—on the Ruhr, the tariff, the coming presidential election, Calvin Coolidge, and the Teapot Dome scandals. He scanned the rest of the news but found nothing to spark him. A kindly gentleman from the typesetting room said the Ruhr was a good subject to write about, and Cain said, sure, he could write about it "as soon as I find out where it is."

After an hour of trying to decide what to write about, Cain found himself coming back to the man-eating shark. He thought: Well, everyone's in favor of motherhood, but what about this fish? Why should one oppose it? "Leave us never forget," he said to himself, "the man-eating shark is viviparous—it brings forth its young alive. It's kind to its young and it'd been doing this over ten million years before the human race was ever heard of. The man-eating shark was the first mother, and in a very real sense the man-eating shark is motherhood." That, Cain decided, was his editorial, and he wrote it. Then he wrote another in somewhat the same vein, about a Congressman who purposely had himself indicted for making home beer.

But then he decided this was enough. He did not have a prayer in the world of becoming an editorial writer. He dropped his impish efforts on the desk of Lippmann's secretary and "slunk down the circular stairs and out of Lippmann's life"—and into a speakeasy on Grove Street, where he was supposed to meet a friend named Malcolm Ross. He was convinced that he had failed miserably in his first attempt to write editorials. Around 11:00 P.M., Ross arrived with two bulldog editions of the *World*. Cain did not open his paper but continued drinking his scotch. After Ross ordered his drink, he began reading the paper, and then he began to laugh. "Pretty funny! Did you write this?"

Cain looked at the page a minute and said, "Yeah, I wrote it." He could not believe his eyes, Lippmann had used one of his editorials, the one about the Congressman. It was headed "Maryland's Merry Andrew," appeared in the September 26, 1924 issue of *The World* and, for the record, is reprinted below:

In his patriotic efforts to find out what the Volstead law means, Representative John Philip Hill of the 3d District of Maryland has finally been indicted. May he speedily be brought to trial. Not that we want to see him jailed, but we confess a hankering to see the show.

When he began his manufacture of wine and cider in his Balitmore home, he gave notice by a series of fearful and wonderful proclamations in the newspapers. He tested his brew with devices bearing strange but apposite names, and as the bubbles rose he recorded the mounting alcoholic content upon great charts, looking like thermometers, in front of his home. He besieged the Prohibition Commissioner with pathetic pleas for information as to whether he was breaking the law or not. Finally, to add a subtle touch, he revealed that he was using formulas furnished regularly upon application by the Department of Agriculture.

In brief, without ever losing sight of his point, he staged fine comedy, conducting his fight always good-humoredly and like a gentleman. What is in store for him next is not apparent, but it seems safe to say that Hill will be equal to the emergency and that the show will be worth seeing.

Still skeptical, Cain went to the *World* office the next morning and found everybody friendly with "hellos," especially Lippmann, who asked if he had any leader ideas for today. Cain said no, "but I'll think of something." "Well, do it," said Lippmann. "Those are very funny pieces. I was very glad to get them. I didn't use that piece about the shark—a very funny piece, but I don't like pieces about the newspaper business itself." "Oh, inbreeding," Cain said. "That's the idea," Lippmann replied.

Cain now had a job—at a minimum of $20 a day. A few days later, he had two editorials in the paper, including one on baseball, which would soon become one of his favorite subjects. The Washington Senators, with their great fast-balling pitcher, Walter Johnson, and boy-wonder manager, Bucky

Harris, had just won the American League Pennant, and Cain wrote a nice, lighthearted piece hailing the conquering heroes. Ten days later, Washington won the World Series, the victory coming over the New York Giants in the bottom of the twelfth inning of the seventh game on a now-famous grounder hit down the left side of the infield. When the ball struck a pebble and bounced over third baseman Freddie Lindstrom's head, the Senators had their first (and only) World Series title. Cain joined the hysteria.

Within a few months, Cain was making $125-a-week. And, by rough estimate, from September of 1924 until *The World* folded in February of 1931, he wrote at least 1,300 editorials, varying in length from 15 to 1,000 words. Fortunately for the researcher, they are easy to identify because Lippmann instructed his secretary to write the name of the author of every editorial on his page during the years he edited it and these pages are on microfilm in the Lippmann papers at Yale University Library.

As a result of his six years on *The World*, Cain became something of an authority on editorial writing, which he expressed in a long, thoughtful piece for *The Saturday Evening Post* in 1927 . Reading it, it is obvious that his view of editorial writers and writing had changed substantially since his iconoclastic piece on the breed he had written for Mencken and *The Mercury* three years earlier.

Cain had been on *The World* less than six months when he had a minor confrontation with editorial page policy. In 1924, the *World* had led the attack against those critics who tried to suppress *What Price Glory?* But early in 1925, Lippmann decided "the line must be drawn somewhere," i.e., certain plays should not be performed. What prompted the turnabout was a play entitled *A Good Bad Woman*. The *World*, in an editorial written by Lippmann, said it pandered to a low public taste and that it was the producer's responsibility "to protect the stage against corruption from the inside, which can lead only to censorship from the outside."

Cain, who by now had become a dedicated foe of censorship in any form—a lifelong preoccupation—responded to Lippmann's proposal for what he called a "play jury" by counterattacking in *The Nation. The World* eventually backed away from its "play jury" and Lippmann never gave any indication of having been annoyed with Cain's independent stand on the issue.

By 1928, Cain was well established as one of the city's most respected editorial writers. Lippmann, perhaps more than anyone on the paper, appreciated his talent, and when contract time came around again Cain was given a $1,000 bonus and a three-year renewal at $125 a week. However, now that he had remarried and was paying $150 a month alimony, $125 a week did not go very far, especially in New York. So Lippmann arranged to have him contribute to the Sunday section (at $25 a week) and the *Evening World* editorial page (at $50 a week), bringing his weekly income to $200.

His contributions to the *Evening World* editorial page consisted of one editorial a day, in addition to what he called "five comic paragraphs." Cain's only editorial achievement of note on the *Evening World* was his unsuccessful campaign against the Third Avenue Elevated Railway.

The by-lined columns he wrote for the Sunday section were not much more successful, although they attracted quite a following. But Cain learned, somewhat to his surprise, that he could not write personalized casuals. "I have no capacity to be Cain. I can't be Cain. I can be anybody except Cain," he said. On the *World*, he learned to be "the corporate awfulness" of the paper, as he called it. "This newspaper job," he said, "as the whole of the paper talking through a solemn editorial 'we,' was, in its way, a portent, a sign of my latent strength ... and of my very real limitations."

In fact, his experience on the *World* taught him perhaps the most important single thing he ever learned about his writing: *He could not write unless he pretended to be someone else!* And that someone could apparently not be a New Yorker. He had to be down-home, country rube, a "low life" character, as his mother called them, whom he had known growing up on the Eastern Shore. Later, he found he could pretend to be the California roughneck, "the boy who is just as elemental inside as his eastern colleague, but who has been to high school, completes his sentences and uses reasonably good grammar," as he wrote in his "Preface" to *Three of a Kind*. Once he had "put that on wax," James M. Cain was ready to write the novels for which he eventually became famous.

By 1929, James M. Cain was writing stylistically perfect editorials, but they also seemed to have lost some of their originality; his creative energy apparently had shifted to his *Mercury* by-lined pieces. Nevertheless, he could write a brief essay on almost any subject under the sun, and the world, you might say, was his oyster—or lobster, or frog's leg, or huckleberry pie, or any food that would inspire letters to the editor. In 1929, he came out solidly in favor of the hot dog; and when a Massachusetts lobsterman caged a lobster measuring 34 inches from the tip of its claw to the end of its tail, he said that big lobsters were superior in every way to little lobsters—arousing a storm of letters. He also applauded and explained the need for the proposed bridge over the Chesapeake Bay several decades before its completion, and said that if radio did nothing else but rid the world of tenors (who sounded squeaky over the air) it had served its purpose. He continued to comment on new evidence in the Sacco-Vanzetti case; was intrigued by a new sport, the six-day bike race; applauded doctors' suggestion that we should all take winter vacations; was concerned about presidential handshakes (on one day, Hoover shook 1,757 hands; on another 1,095). He also worried about the country's not utilizing ex-presidents and ex-presidential candidates; came out against another Yankee pennant; deplored Floyd Gibbons' writing a story for *Liberty* about the Second World War, to be fought in 1933-36; supported the appointment of

Robert Hutchins, at the age of thirty, to be president of the University of Chicago, pointing out that Alexander, Shakespeare, Washington, Beethoven, Jefferson, and Jackson all had important jobs or achievements by the time they were thirty; came out against roadside signs and for Mother's Day; cited a study that showed 65 percent more arithmetic is taught in schools than is required by "life situations"; wasn't sure that "Miss Universe" was the proper title for the winner of a beauty contest in Texas, but conceded, after seeing her picture, that the Republic of Mars would be hard put to beat her; and when it was reported that Yale had been forced to sink its goalposts in concrete, he said if the school wanted to win games it should be putting the concrete in the heads of its players.

The future author of *The Postman Always Rings Twice* and "Double Indemnity" was also skeptical that talking pictures would ever be any good and deplored the amount of crime in the talkies. "If you've seen one crime movie," he said, "you've seen them all, and you haven't seen very much at that." Responding to a *Nation* article criticizing the black and white morality in the movies, Cain explained why it was inevitable. "Nice subtle colors are the product of single minds and they will be found only in those arts produced by single minds .... [Movies] are a broth condemned to the talents of too many cooks, and we all know what such a broth tastes like." It was a belief Cain never lost; in fact, his years in Hollywood would only confirm it.

When the *World* was finally sold by the Pulitzers to the Scripps-Howard chain, many ex-staffers wrote the paper's obituary. Cain wrote his for *The New Freeman* and *The New York Herald Tribune* said it was "the sharpest and most original" of all the articles about the end of the *World*. And for Cain, it was the end of his professional relationship (although not his friendship) with Walter Lippmann.

In 1975, after Lippmann had died and Cain was in his eighties, he wrote an article about Lippmann for *The Washington Post* magazine, *Potomac* which was not only a fine tribute to one of his early mentors, but played a significant role in his long career as a writer. Although Cain had written a couple of short nostalgic pieces for *The Post* the year before, the piece on Lippmann was a major article which attracted considerable attention around the country and helped spark his "resurrection," which he called the magazine articles he did for *The Washington Post* late in his life. Carey McWilliams, the editor of *Nation*, wrote expressing his admiration for the Lippmann piece, saying he hoped Cain could be persuaded to write for *The Nation*. Andy Logan, on the *New Yorker*, wrote him that it was the "only account I ever read that made [Lippmann] seem living and real rather than a disembodied and occasional wrong-headed philosopher," and expressing the hope that Cain would write more: "There's a pile of feckless nonsense being printed nowadays, and whatever you feel like putting out would be a wonderful change."

One of the things Cain liked about Lippmann was his gentle manner. "In my work," said Cain, "he was courtesy itself, and he never once raised the question of who was boss and who was employee. He seemed to understand instinctively that at this kind of work, writing editorials for a newspaper, opinions can't be commanded; that those can be aren't worth very much. He didn't want men around him who could be commanded to think in a certain way." But most important, Lippmann never disparaged Cain or looked down on him for his painstaking efforts to improve his style. His attitude toward writing, said Cain, "as compared with the attitude of the average city editor I was accustomed to, who thought it all right to assign some copy boy to yank pages out of your typewriter before you had even read them over, was so startling to me I could hardly believe it . . . . He didn't laugh at me, or sneer at me, or look down on me for rewriting my editorials. He knew, of course, he had to know, that some of them went through the chopper a dozen times— something the newspaper business scorns, in spite of its supposed dedication to 'good writing.' And he didn't mind that I polished and repolished and polished six times more, as though it was a Wilkinson Sword Blade."

Lippmann gave Cain something else indispensable to the development of a writer: freedom to write about the things that concerned him and to say what he wanted to say. "He never tried to dictate what I should write," Cain recalled. "Just once he suggested an editorial, and I said, 'Well, I don't know,' and he said: 'Forget it'."

This section on Lippmann and *The World* contains mostly Cain's writings about his boss, the paper, and the craft of editorial writing. Some of his editorials and by-lined columns are reprinted, including his editorial on a rather unusual boxer of the 1920s named "Battling Siki," which *The New Yorker* reprinted and which Cain said was rumored to have been considered for the Pulitzer Prize (which subsequent research proved not to be the case). Very few editorials by any writer, however, will withstand the test of time and his personalized by-lined pieces only tend to confirm why Cain himself did not especially like them. But I thought that for the record, some should be included—and they do reveal the roots of one of the finest writing styles to emerge in American journalism, as well as literature, between the two world wars.

R.H.

Walter Lippmann Had Style
(Washington Post/ Potomac, February 2, 1975)

Once, when Walter Lippmann was editor of the New York World, in charge, that is, of the editorial page, and I was an editorial writer under him, he went away for some days, and the morning he was due back, several of us were standing around waiting for him, and of course, having a pleasant chat: Miss Lashin, his tiny secretary; Nina Dumas, Arthur Krock's secretary; John I. Heaton, an elderly editorial writer; Rollin

Kirby, the cartoonist, and myself. Then suddenly he stepped out of the elevator, but instead of the suave, friendly, and elegant chief we were accustomed to, a stranger stood before us, savage with rage. When his eye fell on me he snarled: "You! It would be you!"

"... Well!" I said, utterly caught by surprise. "Obviously, I'm charged, and I plead guilty at once, without hearing any more about it. But just for laughs, I would like to know what I've done."

He had in his hand what I'd done, an editorial I'd written while he was away, on the subject of writing, the last sentence of which seemed to be what infuriated him: "Writing, apparently, is not as easy as it looks." I confess, as he kept pointing at it and rereading it out loud, that it left me baffled, but I'm not the only one. For 40 years, I've made a parlor game of this tale, and I have yet to have one guest detect what the shouting was for....

"Don't you know," he bellowed, "that after the negative the word is so?"

"Oh, so it is, so it is," I replied. "I forgot for the moment—I'm sorry."

So I wrote another editorial, giving an "Old Subscriber" credit for detecting my fault, and winding up, "Apparently, it isn't." This eased the situation, so, presently, he was back to normal, a considerate, gracious superior, and life could go on. I recall the incident to point up a side of his nature that those writing about him since he died seem unaware of: his obsessive interest in style, writing style. He wrote beautifully, as we all know, but this was more than a natural gift. It was also the result of an exhaustive study of rhetoric, down to a point as small as the one he held against me— which, incidentally, wasn't as clearcut as he said. *So*, after a negative, is mainly to the ear. *As* parses just as well, and it must be noted that one's man euphony is another man's pain in the neck. But what I'm trying to say is that when something throws a normally courteous, sensible man into a silly temper, it means a great deal to him, and should be taken into account, in any discussion of him.

But I wasn't the only one he got unreasonable with on this same subject. Once, in a column he wrote, he said we must revert "to the status quo." Or at least, that's what appeared in the paper. But the next day brought a letter from him to The Washington Post, saying he had written "to the statu quo," and demanding a correction. Owlishly the Post shirtailed his letter with an apology, explaining that "our specialist on the Fourth Declension of Latin nouns was having his day off at the time"—as accounting for the blooper. Now this was even sillier than the complaint he made against me. True, the dative case of status, in Latin, is statu, but who cuts it so thin? Status quo, or status quo ante actually, is so often used in English that it is almost a part of the language, and to be mixing it up with Latin case-endings is affectation verging on pedantry.

And yet, I have to confess, when I got back to my office that day, after my bawling-out in front of the girls and my friends, I wasn't upset, but rather pleased, actually, that I was working for one man in the newspaper business to whom such things mattered. For, leave us face it, the newspaper business admires good writing much more than it achieves it. It achieves terse writing, true enough, and libel-proof writing: "It is alleged" is the foundation of newspaper style. But for one Art Buchwald, Holmes Alexander, or Crosby Noyes, who can really write English, there are dozens who can say it, but in a way that leaves you wishing that they would bone up on rhetoric a bit, so their writing would have something describable as charm. Also, I couldn't forget that it was Lippmann's obsession with style and its basic principles that actually got me my job. But to explain how that came about, I must make a personal digression.

It was 1924, and I was 32 years old, just out of the lunghouse at Sabillasville, where I'd been chasing the cure, as they say, for a case of TB I'd come down with. And I needed a job—not desperately, as I was fairly well-heeled at the time, but when you need a job you need it. Also, I wanted to go to New York, as I'd gone about as far as I could on the Baltimore Sun, and craved a shot at the big time. However, it had to be a special job, for at the lunghouse the doctors had warned me that any attempt on my part to hold down the job I'd been holding, as a reporter on a newspaper staff, would surely lead to disaster. It had to be a job I could hold sitting down. So, on trips to New York I had read the World, and noted that the editorial page lacked articles. So I picked myself out to chase them up—to think up subjects, find people to write them, bull them through to completion, and in that way improve the page. I may say, I had a theory that in seeking a job, you shouldn't just ask for "a job." Pick out some particular, special job, and then go after that. Having got that far, I asked Henry Mencken to write me a letter of introduction, if he knew anyone on the World, and it turned out that he did. He wrote a letter to Arthur Krock, assistant to the president, and I tucked it into my pocket. I didn't tell Mencken, but my practice with a letter of introduction was not to spring it at the outset of my call. Get in on my own face was the system I had, speak my piece for what it was worth, and then if I got anywhere, to remember the letter and use it to warm things, and also to arouse respect, for not making a personal matter out of business. But Mencken had his system too, and without telling me, he supplemented the letter he gave me by writing Krock direct. So when I got there I was expected, and my carefully rehearsed speech, for getting Krock's ear; for selling him on myself, had the wind taken out of its sails. There I was. "You *are* in," as Fields told the boy in "Poppy," and I was left with my mouth hanging open with nothing coming out. And then Krock crossed me still further by saying: "I'm taking you in to see Walter Lippmann, who's in charge of the editorial page."

So in a few seconds, there I was, face to face with this man I'd heard of for years, a blocky, handsome guy not much older than I was, who sat staring at me with big, brown, uncomfortable searching eyes. I began my sales talk, sounding like a frog in a well, and not even talking naturally. For actually, I speak two tongues. One is the speech of my childhood, learned under a father obsessed with the way people should talk. I could hardly say ten words without hearing: "Not preventitive, preventive. Not sort of a, a sort of. No him and me went over, he and I went over. Not cyoupon, coupon." Then I met Ike Newton, who put in the brick walk on the campus of the college my father was president of, and learned with delight at last, how people actually do talk. He completely enchanted me, not only by what he said, but by the incomparable way he said it. I went home talking like him, to my father's great irritation. In spite of this, I continued to talk like him, and still do, with accretions from the streets of the cities I've lived in. But when upset, I revert to the speech of my childhood, the stiff, correct way of talking my father beat into my head. I did that day with Lippmann, but knew at once that on the articles I was getting nowhere. I also knew, that for some reason I couldn't fathom, he was paying attention to me. And what I didn't know was that Maxwell Anderson, who had been writing Lippmann's human interest editorials, had quit the week before, after "What Price Glory" smashed, to devote himself to the drama, and that Lippmann needed a writer. And, as he told me later, when we compared notes on that interview, "when my ear caught the participles that didn't dangle, the infinitives well buttoned in, the pronouns with all the antecedents, it occurred to me that you could take Anderson's place." So, he suddenly interrupted to ask if I had any samples of my writing, leaving me utterly crossed up. I thought: What has writing got to do with it? Nobody's mentioned writing, so far.

However, anything to please, and I got my mother in Baltimore to send some magazine articles by me, took them in, was given a tryout, and at once knew I had no more qualifications to write editorials than a Junebug has, and after writing three japes as gallows humor and slinking out of the place, I charged the whole thing off as a dreadful mistake, and tried to think what to do next. But my japes came out in the paper, and then more japes that I wrote, and more japes after them. And then I had a triumph: I wrote a jape called "THIS EVIL MUST CEASE," alleging that the Pie Trust was debasing the blueberry pies by adding cornstarch to them, to thicken the filling so they would stack. I called for an end of the practice, saying "Give us back our free-running juice"—and so forth and so on, for a passionate paragraph. Well, the whole country took up this burning issue. Every editorial writer from Maine to California got into the act; the Literary Digest gave two pages to it; the New York Rotary Club debated it, and Mr. Shattuck, president of Shrafft's, sent two of his pies over, to prove that Schrafft's wasn't guilty. And I was suddenly put under contract. I could go down to Baltimore and tell my mother: "You've been proclaiming for years that I don't have good sense, and events have proved you right—but in New York they pay you for it."

By that time, I was getting to know Lippmann a little, as he took me to lunch once or twice at the Hardware Club in the Woolworth Building, and when he found out that in addition to my father's tutelage, I had taught freshman English in two colleges, and had had to bone up on the rhetoric he made a religion of, it was the beginning of a beautiful friendship, as I don't think style, as such, was ever far from his mind. Once I had to be late with my copy, held up, perhaps, by the outcome of some World Series game, and when I took it down, everyone, including Miss Lashin, had gone. I found him in his office, working under his desk lamp, pitched my piece in my basket and started to go. He looked up, however, and said: "You get a lot more stuff in this paper than your God-given talents entitled you to. I suppose you know that?"

"Well I didn't," I replied. "If so, why?"

"Because I know, once I've read it for sense, that I can pitch it in that basket without having to spend the next hour translating flat-wheeled sentences into English."

In that era, the first electric car out in the morning always had a flat wheel, and went through the city waking everyone up, "Vloomp, vloomp, vloomp"—and his reaction to the copy certain of his writers turned in gives a clue to his reaction to writing of all kinds: It was aural; bad writing tortured his ear. And some of his writers, while encyclopedic at their specialties, had no ear at all. He had to iron out kinks, and I think this irked him from first to last. But nothing of this has come out in the pieces written about him; or about other things that were part of him too—for example, about his appearance. One piece called him "a smallish man, with a brisk manner of speech." Another said he was "tall and rather slender." A third gave him "a slight stoop." He seems to have been described circumstantially by those who never saw him. So perhaps it may not be amiss if I fill the lacuna now, and describe what he looked like. I would guess his height at five feet, eleven inches, as he was just a shade shorter than I am, and I'm 6 foot neat. His physique was rather blocky, his chest heavy, his waist small, his legs sturdy and straight. His face was round, his eyes brown, his features a bit stubby, the total effect quite handsome. But the main thing that came through was an impression of physical strength. His hands weren't large but they were thick and massively strong.

Once, as we were going to lunch and I was about to step off the curb in front of the Pulitzer Building, he said: "Jim, I think it's up to the few to keep civilization from being torn down by the many. Don't you?" I was so astonished my head snapped around, and at that moment this iron hand caught my arm, to pull me, almost lift me, back from the curb, as a taxi shot by within inches. If it hadn't been for that hand, I would have been killed. It yanked me back, make no mistake about that. It would. It was that kind of hand and he that kind of man. And yet his handwriting was so small it was microscopic: the printers, on the occasional times his copy went down without being typed by Miss Lashin, had to read it under a glass. It was one of his contradictions.

His voice, on the basis of his appearance, should have been dark, rich, and full—it was put together, of course, like a grand opera baritone. Actually, it was always a bit ghostly, with what the singers call "escapement." On TV, it didn't sound like that, and my little opera singer wife, Florence Macbeth, who was his devoted fan, insisted he must have had lessons, some sort of preparation, before going on. "There's also his breathing," she said. "When you go on TV, you sound like a porpoise blowing, but not he. You can't hear him breathe at all." But the last time I talked with him, when he called me from Maine about a letter I'd had in the paper that dealt with his stand on Vietnam, he said he hadn't had any lessons at all.

However, brilliant though he was on those interviews, he did have rehearsals for them, of a sort, and that may explain his willingness to try something that in some ways seemed as weird to his mind, "as though I'd taken up ballet dancing"—or "belly dancing"—nobody seemed quite sure what he said. And the rehearsals came in this way: After some dinner party at which he would be a guest, the host would lead into the drawing room, when the doorbell would start ringing, as the after-dinner guests would begin coming, and be presented to him. Presently, the host wuld say: "Sit over there, Walter," and all would know what was coming. The sweet young things with pretty legs would gather around on the floor, the men would pull up their chairs, and the host would begin being Mr. Interlocutor, as in the old-time minstrel show. And for the space of two hours, Lippmann would hold forth, answering questions, the host's, and also the guests', as an occasional hand would go up, exactly as he answered Cronkite's on TV. I think he enjoyed these sessions, giving out from on high with wisdom, but everyone else did too, as he was incomparable to listen to. I never heard a dull word from him. But many such sessions, of course, taught him to trust his improvisation. His TV appearances weren't wholly an untried venture.

In dress, he was what's called conservative, being given to dark pepper-and-salt suits, quiet overcoats, and dark gray Homburg hats. In the twenties he carried a stick, as we all did. He was always annoyed by Jimmy Walker, and the legend that he was "well-dressed." "I think he's horribly dressed," he said. "He's dressed like a vaudeville actor." But the last time I saw him, at the Metropolitan Club one day, where I was Arthur Krock's guest at lunch, he had on a suit gaudy Yale blue in hue, with fuzzy white stripes and plaids, so I confess I was startled—by comparison, Jimmy Walker would have looked like a monk. I took that to be Helen's influence, Helen Byrne Armstrong, his second wife, who probably tried to lighten him up, get some sparkle into his nature. One other thing startled me, shaking hands with him that day: his color. In the twenties, when I worked for him, his complexion was the pale color of health, but this day it was a bright pink—a pink that comes out of two pots, one alcoholic, one stethoscopic. As I knew he drank very little, it had to be from the other, from blood pressure, a somewhat ominous sign, well borne out later on, when strokes laid him low, and he had to retire to a home .... In manner, he was pleasant, courteous, and what colored people call "easy"—he waived rank, in favor of gracious informality, which made him of course quite likeable.

I come now to the final thing that has been skimped in the writings about him— what he wrote about, what he stood for, what he added up to. It is said that he "sought truth in a baffling world"; that he "told it as it was, always"; that he "never compromised, especially with his principles." But as to what his principles were, apart from his distrust of mobocracy, the commentators are vague, and I'm not sure I'll be much help—but I'll give it a try. So what *did* he add up to?"

It was said of him occasionally that when he was secretary to the Socialist mayor of Schenectady, he was a Socialist: that when he was on the board of *The New Republic*, he became a liberal; that when he was editor of *The New York World*, he was a Democrat, and that when he was handled by the New York Herald-Tribune syndicate, he was a Republican—and there is just enough truth in the charge to preclude its being dismissed out of hand. He was a realist, and adjusted to the realities of his situation, whatever it happened to be. But the adjustments, always, were on marginal matters, not involving his inner convictions. It is those inner convictions we are discussing, and it seems odd that no one seems able to state them. So, once more, what were they? I shall now astonish you. It became my belief, when I'd come to know him quite well, that he didn't have any.

I had begun to notice, early on, though with other writers of that era, with Westbrook Pegler, say, or David Lawrence, or Heywood Broun, that while I couldn't predict what they would say on any given subject, I could predict their bias, the general approach they would take. To give an example of his unpredictability, there was his stand on the Vietnam war. On the basis of that, you would suppose he would oppose the sending of troops into Santo Domingo. The island it seemed, was in our "sphere of influence," and as such, subject to troop assistance, or whatever the troops were supposed to be giving.

This is one instance of apparent inconsistency, but a researcher would turn up a hundred. And the reason, for this apparent lack of coordinates, of any general approach that would pull things together, was that he planned it that way. I think, in the morning, when he started to work, he tried to fashion his mind into what

Sholasticism called a *tabula rasa*, a wiped-clean slate, with no preconception, no party affiliation, no bias of any kind, so he could tackle each thing as it came up, strictly on its own merits, and not on any other. Or in other words, he wasn't like Marquis Childs, say, who tackles everything with the underlying color of a fairly regular Democrat. I don't think, far from being a Socialist, Liberal, Democrat, Republican, or whatever his employment seemed to call for, that he was ever *anything*. As a columnist, of course this gave him special point, enabled him to elucidate, as he syndicated it, with a beautiful absence of prejudice, and gained him a position in the newspaper world that was unique—but, as a columnist. Don't get the idea it made him a perfect editor. It was an approach which early on aroused deep misgivings on the World, that caused Broun to kick over the traces and lay down a barrage against his own paper, and on one occasion, caused me to do it too. Broun's defection came over Sacco and Vanzetti, two Massachusetts Communists who were not guilty of payroll robbery but were burned for it just the same. The case was a cause celebre, but Lippmann, unable, apparently, to get through his head that two human lives were at stake, began making an etude out of it, an intellectual exercise in logic-chopping, especially in regard to the Lowell report. The Lowell Commission was appointed by the Governor of Massachusetts, to review the trial evidence, and ascertain if these men were guilty. Lippmann bought the idea, and it was hard to escape the suspicion that the Old School Tie figured in his approach, for A. Lawrence Lowell, the chairman, was also president of Harvard, of which Lippmann was a graduate, and with which his ties were close. The commission reported that the men were indeed guilty, and Lippmann, without any question of any kind, accepted the report and put his paper back of it.

But by that time, things had gone very far: a man confessed that he, and not these Italians, had held up the payroll truck; the judge in the case had publicly betrayed a bias incompatible with justice, and public opinion was inflamed cherry red, with sparks coming off it. Broun broke over the traces, and all sorts of people indicted the World, which was torn apart by the issue. And it wasn't until Felix Frankfurter, not yet on the court, but on the faculty of Harvard, showed up with his exhibit that Lippmann realized the commission might be wrong. Mr. Frankfurter, I think, was the most offensive, disagreeable human being I ever had contact with, but he had with him one of the three copies of the Lowell Report, and it showed all too plainly that the commission hadn't even read the testimony at the trial, that its findings were perfunctory, and that any endorsement of it was silly. So we had to start all over, reopen the case with an editorial, a setpiece of which I wrote part, to plead with Massachusetts not to go through with this travesty on justice. But even then Lippmann didn't wake up. When I rang him, to tell him when my segment would be ready, he said there was no hurry now, that the piece would run in two parts, and that I could take my time. I thought that over, then went downstairs to see what the reason was, for the difference between one block-buster to run all in one piece, and a continued-in-our-next that only half said it, was very great indeed. He was a bit impatient with me, saying the editorial would be so long it couldn't possibly be set up in time, so hurrying had no point. I stood there staring at him in utter disbelief, then slowly realized that in his ignorance of newspaper mechanics, which was fairly thorough incidentally, he supposed that one printer started at the beginning of an editorial, and ran it out to the end, and didn't know that the composing room foreman cut it up into "takes," and could get it set in ten minutes if he had to. I said: "Walter, will you for Christ's sake wake up? Don't break this thing apart—run it all in one piece so it scores, if scoring is possible now. Give it to me when it's finished, and let me take charge downstairs. I'll get it set, don't worry."

So prodded, he reversed his decision, and we ran it all in one piece the next day. I had plenty of time, down in the composing room, to play with it, get some lead in the lead, have centered asterisks set, to drop in every few paragraphs, to give it some appearance.

However, the men were burned, but it wasn't the end of the story. Next morning, as usual, I went down to work on the subway, alongside of a woman who I saw was reading the editorial page of the World. I hadn't opened mine yet, and didn't pay too much attention. But suddenly, on one of the editorials, three gray spots appeared, that had to be caused by spit. When I opened the paper at breakfast, I found that what she had spit on was a piece Lippmann had written without telling the staff, saying in effect that those associated with the case were all honorable men, and had done what was right as it was given them to see the right, and the rest of us had best get on with our lives and forget the whole unfortunate incident. What I'm trying to say is that first to last, he was unable to see that some things can't be forgotten—I don't forget this case, even now. To him, first, last, and all the time, it was an intellectual exercise, nothing more.

Then there was the case of the "Play Jury," which he endorsed, saying "the line must be drawn somewhere." But where? And by whom, It was this that made me kick over, and come out with a magazine piece protesting. Which brings me to a conversation I had with him, that has been extensively quoted recently, as it came out in a magazine piece I wrote when the World was finally sold. He had been worked over savagely by Amos Pinchot in the Nation, and betrayed, at lunch, that it hurt. But I said: "I don't see why you should be upset, actually, you played in luck. Where you were vulnerable he didn't mention at all—perhaps missed it, boning up on his piece of back copies of the paper. I mean, the Scopes trial. You took seriously what was basically a clown show, with all the publicity hounds out in force, Bryan, Darrow, Malone, Mencken, the whole bunch. But you made a serious issue of it, even dredging up basic principles. You can't do that on a newspaper—in a book, but not on an editorial page." And then, reaching for an analogy, I said: "Look! a piano has eight octaves, a violin three. But a bugle has four notes, and if what you have to blow is a bugle, there's no use camping down with a piano score."

"You may be right," he told me, "but God damn it, I'm not going to spend my life writing bugle calls."

It turned out however that when the occasion arose, he could write bugle calls, and that his were better calls by far, than the calls most people wrote. The best writing of his life, as I personally think, was the series of columns he did against the Vietnam War, at the end of his career. They made the general point that it is not up to the United States to be the world's policeman, a big, profound observation, a real contribution, which, if remembered, could save millions of lives in the future. It was in connection with these columns that I heard myself say one night to some guests in my Hyattsville home, "He can't be frightened and can't be bought." I think it a very high tribute and the fact that it was true justifies everything else, and indeed puts a laurel wreath on it.

Are Editorials Worth Reading?
(The Saturday Evening Post, December 24, 1927)

The other day I was the recipient of fulsome compliments on a story that had appeared in the newspaper I work for. But as it happened, I had not written it; another writer bearing the same name was responsible. "But you write for that paper, don't you?" asked my eulogist, obviously anxious to retrieve his blunder by offering me some kind of compliment.

"Yes," I said, only too eager to be thus placated, "I write editorials."

"Oh," he remarked somewhat vaguely. "Oh, yeah." Then, apparently having decided that since the case was hopeless, he had just as well be frank, he added: "You know I never read the editorial page—in your paper or any other paper."

I reflected on this. He was an intelligent fellow, as I had discovered from previous acquaintance with him; he was well read, he knew what was going on in the world. In fact, he was precisely the type of enlightened, hard-boiled American citizen for whom I had supposed that my own erudite compositions would have an almost irresistible appeal.

"Why not?" I asked at length. "What's the matter with the editorial page?"

"Oh, I don't know," replied. "All that dry stuff—I just won't take the time to wade through it."

I have been thinking that fellow over ever since then, for I know there are a great many people like him. They are the kind of people, I take it, who have almost a pathological fear of being bored; the kind of people who make their livings in such a fashion that they do not come in close contact with the practical, prosaic aspects of life; the kind of people who do not join the clubs, attend the meetings or listen to the speeches that engage practical folk; the kind of people, in short, who have no direct concern with many of the things which a newspaper discusses, and who demand that their reading matter be interesting on its own account as well as in relation to some practical problem that stands at the moment in need of a solution. And it must be admitted that if the editorial page has nothing to offer them there is something radically wrong with it; it may be a force for the community good, but it is woefully lacking in intellectual punch.

Well, does it offer them anything? Taking one American newspaper with another, I should say that it does. Of course, it labors under a dreadful handicap at the outset in the matter of its appearance. It is solemn, austere, forbidding. Moreover, casual inspection of its lengthy paragraphs shows that they do not belie their looks. They deal with stuffy subjects, exactly the dry stuff that bored my friend, and they are filled with many a tedious whereas and windy wherefore.

Yet it would be a mistake to judge the page by these things alone. The undertaker clothes are to some extent obligatory. The corporate awfulness of the paper speaks here, remember, and any undue frivolity in attire would not be seemly. And the whereases and wherefores, together with all the dull discussions to which they relate, get into the paper by reason of circumstances whose existence the layman does not suspect at all, and which, if they are explained a little, may help to clear up a number of misunderstandings.

The truth is that the editor is just as bored by the dry stuff as anybody else. Yet he has to publish it, because to neglect it would mean a withdrawal from that contact with everyday life that is the heart of every newspaper. It may be classified roughly under the following heads:

1. Party editorials. During campaigns, and even between campaigns, newspapers must lend support to the parties with which they are affiliated, else they forgo all chance of being heard when legislation is enacted.

2. Civic editorials. Innumerable movements of a public nature must either be indorsed or opposed, else the paper loses a real opportunity for public service.

3. Policy editorials. Practically every newspaper has certain pet schemes which it thinks are for the public good, and on these, if it is to get anywhere with them, it must dingdong year in and year out.

4. Big-news editorials. Almost every day a tornado sweeps some state, somebody else flies the Atlantic Ocean or a local boy wins the welterweight championship, and comment is absolutely imperative.

Now if you will put yourself in the position of a writer who must turn out pieces that fall into any of these categories, you will see that he has a tough job on his hands, and that it is almost impossible for him to write anything that will be interesting in the absolute sense. Party editorials, as the man who writes them is usually aware, are hollow on the inside, for they assume something which is palpably not true—that a Democrat is better than a Republican, or vice versa. Civic editorials are sound, perhaps, but flat. It is hard to take a lofty intellectual flight on the question whether Main Street should have two traffic lights, red and green, or three traffic lights, red, green and orange.

Policy editorials are usually intolerably repetitious. After a newspaper has said for the thousandth time that there should be a seat for every child in the public schools it has said it.

But the big-news editorials are the worst of the lot. When the Coast Guard cutter Seminole makes a great rescue at sea, taking twenty-two Lascars from the sinking tanker by skillful use of the breeches buoy, you may think it is a simple matter to turn out two graceful paragraphs of tribute. Try it. You will be amazed to discover how many banal phrases your brain can hatch in the course of an hour; you will be surprised, too, to discover that there is nothing rational to say about a great rescue at sea.

This was illustrated in comic fashion when Lindbergh flew from New York to Paris. Now the only sensible thing to say about Lindbergh was "Hooray!" But this, unfortunately, was not dignified enough for an editorial page, and neither was it long enough for a leading editorial. So manfully the editorial writers of the country sat down to the job of stretching it out for a column. They made him the Spirit of Youth, the Spirit of the New World, the Spirit of the Twentieth Century; they called him Ace High, Lone Star and Young Eagle; they said he was borne on the Pinions of Destiny, the Wings of the Dawn and the Prayers of Humanity. But when they were done, although he had written the blobbiest prose that had been seen on these shores for a long time, and although they had embarrassed Lindy horribly, what they had said was "Hooray!"

What's What in Editorials

Thus, since such chores claim much of the editorial space, it can be seen that all the wit of G.B. Shaw, Georges Clemenceau and Bugs Baer taken together could not save much of the editorial page from being something of a bore. These pieces are of interest to those for whom they are of interest, but the most gifted pen in the world could hardly make them of interest on their own account. Well, then, what does the editorial page offer that is interesting on its own account?

That depends to some extent on the paper, the locality and the tastes of the editor. But there are some pieces that are likely to be of interest in any paper. At the head of the list I should place the discussion of national affairs when they assume larger importance than party wrangles; or, if they involve parties, when the division is along philosophic rather than partisan lines. Such a discussion is continually carried on in regard to the tariff, which has always bulked large in our national politics, and which lately has been an especially lively issue by reason of the relation it bears to war debts, and by reason, too, of the paradoxical twist that has been given it by France, which has started a game of freeze-out with us whose outcome is not predictable at this writing. Such questions as this are usually threshed out in a highly intelligent manner by our editors, and anybody who is even slightly interested in political economy will find their comment instructive.

Next, I will surprise you by nominating the obituary editorials that commonly follow the death of some prominent citizen. For here the editor addresses himself to the subject of subjects, which is man. And if the deceased is not merely a local bigwig who must have his wreath of lilies but a man in whom the editor is really interested, you are likely to see something well worth your reading indeed. I doubt it any finer writing ever appeared in American newspapers than that which followed the death of William Jennings Bryan. This was a man who offered rich material for appraisal, a man of baffling contradictions, of talent that amounted to genius in some directions and incredible limitations in others. And on the Monday morning after his death, the editors of the country rose to their opportunity magnificently. Some of them were dazed by the dramatic manner of his passing and gave themselves over to mushy platitudes. But most of them handled him realistically, and the best of what they wrote would make a brilliant volume on later-day American history.

Anthology of the Hog Call

Next, I nominate the comment on the fine arts which appears pretty regularly in every newspapers. It is not commonly realized that some of the best criticism of literature, drama, music and such things which is printed in American newspaprs appears in the editorial columns rather than in the columns regularly devoted to them. There are several reasons for this. In the first place, when a book, say, is important enough to command notice on the editorial page, it is likely to be a book that is really worth writing about, and not merely another book. In the second place, when your editorial writer turns critic he is able to couch his remarks in much better English than most other writers employ. His work lies regularly in the field of analysis, which is the very essence of criticism; so that when he begins to talk about a book he can say with perfect ease what he means. Also, since his page is addressed to the general public and not to a limited few, he must keep his feet on the ground, use plain words, argue his case with sense and reason. Thus he avoids the fault which is the curse of critical writing on American newspapers—the critic stuff, which is only too often gibbering nonsense.

Next, I nominate those editorials where the editor puts his tongue in his cheek and deliberately spoofs his readers. You may have read such pieces and thought them a little heavy. That is because you regarded them as efforts at pure humor. That is not the idea at all. In fact, the editor is careful not to provoke too loud a cackle, for that would defeat his real purpose. This is to start something that will lead to an amusing flurry in his letter column—a department that always needs a little artificial pepping up lest it become insufferably tedious with the effusions of Civitas, Veritas and Pro Bono Publico. And if you read such things with an understanding eye, and then watch from day to day to see what happens, you can have many a snicker with the editor at the queer fish that rise to his bait.

One of the most adroit exponents of this kind of spoofing is a man associated with the Baltimore Evening Sun, who will have to be nameless here. He does his deadly work not in the editorial columns but in the letter column itself. His trick is to take something hitherto regarded by all as perfectly innocent and then discover that it is immoral. For example, when the grand opera Tristan and Isolde was given in Baltimore, he took exception to it on the ground that it condoned free love. And always a deluge of letters follows, all of which take his nonsense with complete seriousness. Some applaud him, some denounce him, but few penetrate his hoax. If you read the Baltimore Evening Sun, you can spot him easily enough, as he invariably signs his letters "American Mother."

On the paper I work for we once started a queer tempest indeed. This was in regard to the hog call. Noticing that there was to be a hog-calling contest in Omaha, Nebraska, we feigned great ignorance of this branch of the vocal art and inquired whether one really called hogs on a farm, and if so, why and how. Our remarks had hardly been published before things began to happen. Letters poured in, all of them setting us straight on this important matter. Other newspapers, not deceived in the least, also undertook to set us straight, until within two weeks the thing had spread from coast to coast, the Literary Digest had devoted two whole pages to it, and the Omaha contest took on the proportions of a national event.

We were able, however, to confound our critics. For most of them rushed into print with detailed descriptions of the hog call, several of these having a musical score as well as words. But as it happened, no two of these descriptions were alike. One gave the hog call as Soo-e-e-e-e-e! So-e-e-e-e-e! So-e-e-e-e-e! Pig-pig-pig! Another gave it as Soo-pig! Soo-pig! Soo-pig! Still another gave it as Soo! Soo! Soo! Soo-e-e-e-e-e-e! And so on. As we pointed out, with crushing logic, that if the experts themselves could not agree what the hog call sounded like, it would be presumptuous for the layman even to have an opinion. To rout them completely, we published an anthology of all the various calls that had appeared. And this, I submit, was one of the strangest anthologies that ever saw the light of day, and a precious piece of Americana to boot.

Writing Their Hobbies

Finally, I nominate those editorials which are born of the editor's hobby. What this is for the editor of your paper you will have to find out for yourself, which will probably be a matter of five minutes' gumshoe work. But every editor has one—has some pet subject that he would rather write on than anything else, and as a result he usually turns out during the course of the year two or three dozen editorials that are out of the ordinary and very well worth reading.

For example, Claude G. Bowers, assistant editor of the New York Evening World is a historian of parts, having written among other books Jefferson and Hamilton which was a best seller for several months and is probably known to you. Bowen writes innumerable editorials in this field and there is nothing he likes better than to skin publicly a dead Federalist. John L. Heaton, on the New York Morning World, likes to write about swimming. He is sixty-seven years old, and during the warmer months it is his practice to swim a mile each day before coming to work, marking the distance in the ocean off Brighton Beach by bringing himself in line with the city blocks on shore. So when Gertrude Ederly swims the Channel or George Young swims from Catalina Island to the mainland, he usually has something out of the ordinary to say.

Frank M. O'Brien, of the New York Sun, winner of the Pulitzer Prize in 1921 for his editorial The Unknown Soldier, likes to write about pedigreed horses. Nicholas Roosevelt, of the New York Times, bears a grudge against the schedules of the Long Island Railroad, and some fearful and wonderful pieces appear in the Times on his subject as a result. Arthur Krock, of the same paper, takes special delight in fabricating bogus American folklore. Being a walking encyclopedia of true American folklore anyway, he can manufacture the spurious article so skillfully that you will have trouble to tell it from the genuine. Thus you are likely to see any kind of fabulous yarn in the editorial columns of the Times, from the lamentable behavior of the race horse which had been trained by a one-legged man to the equally lamentable behavior of the overly proud dog whose tail curled so tight that it lifted his hind legs right up in the air.

A Maxim to Follow

Arthur Brisbane, when he has nothing else to write about, loves to do a gloomy philosophic piece involving the gorilla, the prize fighter and the Nietzschean superman. Tiffany Blake, of the Chicago Tribune, likes to write about music, but likes still better to write hot pieces roasting the South. F. Lauriston Bullard, of the Boston Herald, winner of the Pulitzer Pize in 1926 for his editorial on the Sacco-Vanzetti case, likes to write about New England localities and customs; while Julian Harris, of the Columbus, Georgia, Enquirer-Sun, winner of the Pulitzer Prize in 1925 for his stand against the Ku Klux Klan, likes to polish off a piece on intolerance. John W. Owens, of the Baltimore Morning Sun, likes to utter learned words on labor questions; while Hamilton Owens, of the Baltimore Evening Sun, likes to write about Marylandism, which he is sufficiently deluded to believe is different from some other kind of ism. As for your humble servant, he likes to write about prize fighters, and the greatest moment of his life came when the New Yorker republished the piece he had written on Battling Siki on the question of that gladiator's sudden demise. This editorial, it is said, almost got the Pulitzer Prize for the year 1925.

The list could be extended indefinitely. The thing to note about it, however, is that it tells the story of pieces that come from the heart, and such pieces as these, it hardly needs saying, are always worth reading, even if they deal with the Einstein physics.

To sum up, I should say that if you read the editorial page with a little discrimination, passing up what is not even expected to interest you and taking what is, you will be amused as well as instructed. And always remember that the workmanship on this page is probably the best that goes into the paper. The men who write for it have time to write carefully, and as I have already pointed out, the nature of the practice they get trains them to write a little better than the average reporter. And if occasionally you find something that bores you to tears, remember the maxim that Wilde found in the Western dance hall: "Don't shoot the pianist—he's doing his best."

Editorials
Washington Wins the Series
(October 11, 1924)

It is given to some cities to be Carthage, and rule the seas; it is given to some to be Rome, and rule the world; it is given to others to win the World's Series. The greatest of these is Washington. For, think of it, Washington has actually won the series. They thought it was history when they won the pennant. But the pennant—what was that? Something soon forgotten, something for a few old-timers to tell stories about in the wintertime, when the park is covered with snow. But to be the world's champions— that is something to be remembered, something to chisel on marble.

And what a game! None of your dull, one-sided affairs, a foregone conclusion from the third inning. No, a real ringtail lalapaloosa, twelve gorgeous innings, when anything might happen and anything did happen, when not one of the players or coaches or thousands of screeching, jumping, praying fans knew which way the cat was going to jump.

Was there anything lacking? If so, nobody noticed it. Every hero gave more than anybody hoped he would give, showed heroic stuff from beginning to end. There was young Bucky Harris, who would be unanimously elected Senator if Washington had a vote. First he made the homer that brought Washington's first run. Then he clouted the hit that tied the score. What a boy, what a boy! And Ruel, who got on with one out in the twelfth. And McNeely, who drove in that run, that run of runs, the run that won the game. And finally—

Walter Johnson. Let us take off our hats. Walter Johnson, who we thought had been counted out. Walter Johnson, who went down to grim defeat in New York, who they said was too old. Walter Johnson, tried and true wheelhorse of a great team; who took the box in the ninth, faced those deadly youngsters from New York, and delivered what was asked of him. Three innings and he was the Walter Johnson of old. A brief space, but the greatest three innings of his life.

The Giants? The Giants are our own, and we sorrow when they lose. But they have already tasted such victory many times; had they won, they would merely have been champions once more. They can afford to skip a year. This time, we frankly rejoice with Washington. We know how they feel, and it is a feeling like which there is none in this vale of tears.

The Glorious Kid
(May 24, 1927)

We have had two days to get used to it now—this flight to Paris—and most of us cannot get used to it; still we gobble up all the papers have to tell us about it; still we chuckle delightedly over some new tidbit, such as the news that the hero sought letters of introduction to Paris; still we marvel and still we thrill. Why? The Evening World explains it by saying this is the "greatest" let us say "most glorious." For in all truth, this flight was not great in the sense that the voyage of Columbus was great; it added little to human knowledge, it will not affect by a hair's breadth the history of the world. The very charm of it is that it was not useful. Lindbergh did not do a service, he scored a touchdown; over the most hazardous field ever tried by man, he scooted away to the biggest touchdown of all time. And say what you will about those who do us a service, those who add to human knowledge, human comfort or human health, it is the boy who scores the big touchdown that sets the stands to cheering, the girls to throwing flowers and the old grads weeping tears of sheer joy on each other's necks.

And a large part of the glory of the feat arises from the charm of the performer. Was there ever such an irresistible fellow as Lindbergh? "Well, here we are!" he announced, as the crowd tore open his plane on his arrival. And that, to our American way of thinking, was the one perfect remark for the occasion. Again, there is his face. It is seldom that a man looks his part, and especially the American idea of his part, as does Lindbergh. He is a synthetic portrait of Ted Coy, Penrod Schofield, and Abraham Lincoln at the age of nineteen; that face suggests everything that we associate with this kind of achievement. He captured our imaginations the moment he appeared. Two hops from San Diego and no talk after he got here—there, we knew instinctively, was the stuff that Paris flights are made of. As he hung around waiting for the weather to clear up and gawkishly allowing the photographers to take his picture he grew upon us. And when he finally took off we had a sort of superstition about him: he was Casey, mighty Casey, and we could not conceive how he could possibly strike out. Well, he did not strike out.

August, How Could You?
(August 27, 1927)

August, in all sooth has not been one of those months of which the poets sing. Thumbing our copy of Bartlett's Familiar Quotations, we are unable to find a single reference to it, although May has twenty-three and even December has six. For this state of affairs, of course, there has been a sound reason. August was just one of those things that you couldn't write a poem about, even if you tried. And until this year it has seemed that August was content with its lowly lot and would stay that way until the end of time.

But now what do we find? We find August trying to horn into the quotation book just as though it were the social equal of other months. When it started off, one suspects that it had its eye on the fine showing of May. You could almost hear it saying to itself, "If May could attract all that notice by merely blowing fair weather, then watch what happens when I show what I can do." So it blew fair weather. And what happened was precisely nothing. Our poets penetrated the ruse and to a man refrained from writing a single line.

Enrage, it went into a sulk, and then obviously it turned an envious eye on the comparatively good showing made by December. "I see, I see," it no doubt said to itself; "when you try to be polite and still they won't have you; then you have to crash the gate." So it has been running a temperature-chart five degrees under the normal, and for the past four days it has been using strong-arm methods, and the result at this writing is still in doubt. We urge our poets to stand firm. And if they feel that they must write something, then we urge them to compose blasts that will wither the upstart, quatrains that make contemptuous references to dog days, and then inquire whether hot-dog days are not, after all, preferable to cold-dog days. By such means, perhaps, August will learn its place, so that when next year rolls around we can anoint ourselves with citronella in relative comfort.

The New Flivver
(December 4, 1927)

The unveiling of the new Ford car last Friday certainly took on the proportions of a public event. It had been heralded for months in advance, the prospect of it had whetted curiosity to a fine edge, and when it finally took place excitement could hardly have been greater had Pah-Wah, the sacred white elephant of Burma, elected to sit for seven days on the flagpole of the Woolworth Building. Moreover, in all this there was not the faintest suggestion of the ridiculous. Even the most godless scoffer must have realized that the magnum opus thus offered for sale was worth all the commotion it was causing.

It is this aspect of the ceremony which sets you to pondering in an effort to discover why this seems to be an authentic epic and not the usual trite story of commercial success which we all find so tedious. And the first thing you notice about it is that it represents a tremendous gamble. How many millions were spent in rebuilding the factories which are to make this car will perhaps never be divulged. But there were many millions, of that we may be sure. And they were spent without a jet of direct proof that they would ever be returned in the shape of profit from sales. This is a very unusual way to do business.

The ordinary procedure would have been to experiment on a small scale, to make a few of the proposed cars, put them on the market and see how the public liked them. Then, if they were a hit they could be offered in quantity. And if they were a flop they could be withdrawn without representing much loss.

But that, evidently, is not the way this company works. It closes down its shop, fits it up with an entirely new set of tools and then stakes it all on one great throw of the dice. Thus you got a quality of boldness into the story from the beginning of it. You felt as you feel at the beginning of another epic enterprise, the building of a tunnel. There were the boring starts on both sides of the river at once, with no assurance save that given by delicate instruments and intricate calculations that the two tubes will meet under the middle of the river.

But when the tunnel is done the two tubes meet, and so it proves with the new Ford. It is a success even before its buyers have seen it. And thus you get another quality: the quality of intellectuality, the triumph of mind over matter. "There is no guessing," said Mr. Ford, "as to whether it will be a successful model. It has to be. There is no way it can escape being so, for it represents the sum total of all we have learned about motor-car building in the making of 15,000,000 automobiles." The bland confidence of that is simply staggering. What would be guesswork on the part of other men is exact calculation with Mr. Ford; he has succeeded in making the automobile business as scientific as the engineer has succeeded in making the business of driving a tunnel.

Thus one begins to understand why this story differs from lesser stories, and why Mr. Ford, often so absurd when he tries to discuss philosophical matters, suddenly appears as a colossus when he steps into his proper role of automobile builder. Indeed, he appears almost as the genius of modern America. This thing which he makes is surely the symbol of the advance which the modern age has made over any other age. And the way he makes it, with efficiency calculated to the nth degree, with a vast organization by means of which, as he says, "we make our own steel—we make our own glass—we mine our own coal—we make virtually every part used in the Ford car"—that is what we like to think marks off America as superior in at least one respect to the rest of the world. Other people may make better music than we make, better rugs, better singers, better ships. But at the business of taking a great machine of steel and men and making it work we acknowledge no superior, and we believe that is our contribution to civilization. And Mr. Ford personifies it better than any man living.

The Beautiful Snow
(December 5, 1927)

Turning a sour eye out of the window yesterday, we fell to pondering on the extent to which a mechanical civilization has robbed us of one of the elemental facts of life, which is to say snow. There was a time when it meant as much to us as sunshine, or rain, or fire, or the forest or the sea. It produced a definite emotional effect, as witness the great number of poems that have been written about it. We yielded ourselves to it without question, making ourselves almost a part of it. In those days we travelled much by horse, and the ground was hardly white before bells could be heard and in a few hours we were all in sleighs, engaging in races that we could not win, laughing at nothing in particular, faking spills which for some mysterious reason did not hurt. At night we called a halt on ordinary pleasures and went out to the big hill, where we coasted for hours on the old bob-sled. If we were very young we pressed the snow into little balls and poked each other with it, or rolled it up into great balls and made snow men to whom we gave coal nuggets for eyes, nose and mouth and a corn cob pipe for a bit of artistic verisimilitude.

And in addition to all this we used to sit and look at it and reflected that it was beautiful.

Now that is all gone. One never sees a sleigh any more, and a taxicab rattling through the snow with chains on its tires is a rattling taxi-cab and nothing more. The big hill is a thing of the past, for a State road has been built on it and the grade has been reduced to 5 per cent, which is hardly enough to stir the old bob-sled out of its tracks. The snow, once a thing of beauty and primitive significance, is nothing but a wet, dirty nuisance. By its passing we have lost something. The glitter has gone out of the romance of winter.

Battling Siki
(December 16, 1928)

What a monstrous fellow was this Battling Siki, who has just been bumped off in so lamentable a fashion! Here was the brute primeval: musing on him, one could conceive him as the ancestor of the whole human race. But how different an ancestor from that hairy spectre which used to haunt the late Mr. Bryan! He was no hulking clod out of a scientist's note-book but a human figure out of the early epics of mankind. He had, it is true, the mentality of a backward toad: he could speak nine languages, and his total vocabulary in all, it is said, was 157 words, counting profane expletives.

But he had the soul of a god. He was the victim of moody fits, not comprehensible to us who have not lived in the paleolithic age; he was subject to berserk rages, when life was not safe within a mile of him. He also had strange humors and whimsies: he marched the streets of Paris clad in frock coat, silk hat, monocle, yellow gloves and tan shoes, carrying a monkey on his shoulder and dragging a yowling lion cub at the end of a chain: he liked to ride all night in a taxi and then, just for merry play, refuse to pay the driver, lashing out with his great fists if protest were entered. He had vast and engaging conceit: he appeared one time in Pennsylvania Station with a wine-bearer bringing up the rear; and while he argued with the small gray-haired clerk at the information desk he quaffed mighty quaffs from a two-gallon jug, until he became so drunk that the small, gray-haired clerk seized him by the seat of the breeches and threw him out in the street, where he sat down on the curb and apostrophized the stars on the ingratitude of man. He was perpetually in difficulty over women, but survived somehow. And in all this grotesque career, search of the records indicates that the greatest punishment he ever drew was a $5 fine. He faced the Magistrates, grinned that grin out of the primordial forest, the grin grinned by the first man when he discovered he was a man, and the Magistrates turned him loose as they would turn loose a lovable child.

What is all this but the sulks and tempers of Achilles, the prank of Siegfried and the boars, the strutting of Beowulf, the armours of Lemminkainen? We have had a walking image of our beginnings among us and did not know it. Let us pause and admire ourselves. If we had such an ancestor, we had something of which we can be proud.

The World Hits the Trail
(*The Nation*, March 4, 1925)

One of the greatest blows ever struck at the American theater came when the New York *World* turned its guns on current Broadway plays, on the ground that they are indecent. Coming from another source, the attack might have been negligible. Coming from the greatest libertarian newspaper in the country, it has played havoc. The public, accustomed to seeing the *World* fight all sorts of oppression and bigotry, assumed that when the *World* led the way the case must be clear indeed, and joyfully joined in the hue and cry; and the civilized minority, although aghast at the proceedings, was left without leadership or even means of expressing a protest. Already the campaign has borne a fine crop of fruit. The two plays originally proscribed by the *World* have swelled to thirteen, as the petty gentry contributed their mute. The pernicious "citizens' jury" plan has been put into effect. The District Attorney has bestirred himself and one of the first things he did was to send a little note to the producer of Eugene O'Neill's "Desire Under the Elms," telling him to close up.

The *World* enunciates two fallacious and intolerable principles:

1. That there is a general standard of decency that the theater must conform to; in its own language, "the line must be drawn somewhere"; and

2. That artistic excellence or intent is to be the measure of how much obscenity is permissible in a given instance.

It would be difficult to imagine two principles worse than these. In aesthetics, all that can be said is that one man's art is another man's poison. It has only been a few months since the *World* was hot against those who would suppress "What Price Glory?" This play, held the *World*, was art. Yet ask the average army officer whether he thinks it is art. It is quite as offensive to him as any play now running is to the *World*. Who is to be the judge? Why have any judge at all? The average burlesque show is pretty vulgar, but is that any reason for closing it? If it amuses sailors, soldiers, and taxicab drivers, then these citizens of the United States are entitled to their amusement. Why should they be bothered with art? In the theater, one cannot "draw the line somewhere." What takes place there is a matter between the manager and his patrons, and if the rest of us do not like the show, we can stay away. We don't have to look at it.

The particular show singled out by the *World* for attack was "A Good Bad Woman." I went to see this show. I found a third-rate play written around an amiable female guttersnipe. I found it dull but innocuous, with here and there a few lines undeniably amusing. When I came down to the *World* office the next day and innocently reported my findings, they were pooh-poohed by some of my colleagues on the ground that I was an immoral reprobate whom nothing could shock. I take exception, but let it pass. Now bear in mind that this is the play which moves the *World* to allege that a low public taste is being pandered to and that "the spokesmen for the theater know, know from the inside, whether the producer is playing the game honestly or whether he is cheating. It is for them to protect the stage against that corruption from the inside which can lead only to censorship from the outside."

Now I, an immoral reprobate, whom nothing can shock, open the *World* these mornings while the crusade is going on, and what do I find? I find a pictorial comic called Mutt and Jeff. I find one of the characters in this comic favorably depicted as swindling Florida real-estate dealers out of $500 on false pretenses, to wit, a fake telegram from one Joe Spivis: "Will you accept $1,000,000 for your Fifth Avenue property?—Morgan." Now, being an immoral reprobate, I am not shocked by this. I am amused, and I wish Jeff all luck with his confidence game. But a day or two later, I find Jeff paying court to an heiress, a bootlegger's daughter. To hide his baldness he has donned a wig, and to add verisimilitude to the deception he has imitated the symptoms of a certain disease of the scalp. Although a reprobate, I find this offensive. So, I may add, do a great many other persons find Mutt and Jeff uniformly coarse and occasionally indecent. This one time I am fortunate enough to be lined up with a large section of both clergy and laity.

Let us now examine the implications of this. Let us apply some of the *World's* own logic to it. Is it art? No. Does the *World* think it is art? I doubt it. Does it pander to a low public taste? Unquestionably it does; if a reprobate like me finds it low, then it must be low indeed. Why is it published? I am not privy to the reasons for its publication, but I suspect it is published because it sells papers. In other words, the motive is commercial, pure and simple. Papers have to be sold to make possible the lofty idealism which uniformly marks the editorial pages.

So, then, we have a most uncomfortably close analogy between the theatrical business and the newspaper business. Applying the standards which the *World* has set up, one would say that the *World* knows, "knows from the inside," that Mutt and Jeff is pretty shoddy stuff. One would say that it is up to the *World* to "protect the press against that corruption from the inside which can lead only to censorship from the outside." In fact, a great many people do say that very thing. Only a few weeks ago, the *Christain Century* was out with some such proposal to the newspaper owners of Chicago. But do I say that? Nay, I am a broad-minded reprobate. I have scrutinized my young morals and found them, so far as I can judge, absolutely uncorrupted by Mutt and Jeff. I have no impulse to sell real estate by means of fake telegrams. I have no impulse to be vulgar about diseases of the scalp. I have no impulse to deceive a bootlegger's daughter. In fact, as I say, I feel absolutely uncontaminated; and I am in favor of printing Mutt and Jeff as long as anyone wants to see them.

Why assume that I was contaminated by "A Good Bad Woman"? Is this a free country, or do we need to be protected by the *World* against our free, white, sovereign, independent, 100 per cent American selves?

Byline Columns
Close-Up
(November 2, 1930)

Lighting cigar after evening meal, our hero opens evening paper and prepares for quiet half hour. Sees editorial captioned "The Price of Apathy," discovers paper is urging readers to take interest in coming election, on ground that if we are ever going to have good government we shall not get it by public indifference. Thinks this is reasonable enough, puts paper down, and conscientiously gives himself over to meditation on issues of election.

Decides Tammany needs lesson, that much is clear. Tries to think over scandals Tammany has been involved in, remembers Maurice Connolly, wonders if Tammany extends as far as Queens, first decides it does, then decides it doesn't, thinks well, anyway, the principle is the same. Remembers Vitale, tries to remember some others, can't quite seem to place them, decides there must be a lot more if he could only place them. Name Tommaney pops into his mind, wonders who this guy was, thinks how much his name sounds like Tammany, tries to make jingle beginning Timmany, Tommaney, Tammany, tries to rhyme it with alimony, decides that doesn't sound so good, thinks a while, decides only other word he can think of is simony, tries to remember what simony means, can't quite place it.

Decides another thing that ought to be looked into is Union Square. Clenches fist, says "There's an outrage all right, square right in front of Tammany Hall and look how it's all full of mudpuddles." Decides Tammany is going to have plenty to answer for this election, thinks somebody ought to write a book about it for benefit of people like him that can't quite keep it all straight. Thinking of books, is reminded of Healy, tries to remember which Healy took the book money and which Healy had his sister-in-law knocked out, can't seem to remember how this goes, wonders if there's still another Healy, decides there probably is, decides the place is probably full of Healys. Thinks of good college yell:

> Healy, Healy, Healy,
> Siss Boom Ah!
> Hold 'Em Team!
> Hold 'Em Team!
> Hold 'Em Team!

Thinks of all dismal sounds in world "Hold 'em team" is probably worst, wonders whether to put some money on Yale against Harvard, thinks maybe it wouldn't be bad bet at that, recalls time he made touchdown from kick-off after other side got impression from locomotive whistle that umpire had blown horn to signalize off-side play.

Says "Well, well, well, this ain't getting us anywhere, how about that election." Knits brows, decides Tammany has lot to answer for, says "Well, damn it, you figured that out once, is that all you know about it?" Frowns, decides now he's really going to reason this thing out and know how to cast his vote. Wonders what district he lives in. Decides it is probably 17th but it seems to him he heard a guy say it was 21st. Decides he must look this up. Thinks of good wheeze:

"If they'd named him Volcano instead of Crater maybe he wouldn't have got lost so easy."

Decides this is pretty good wheeze and he'll pull it down to the office next day if he gets the chance. Decides Crater case is little old by now, maybe he'll have to work around to it carefully, decides maybe some lead like "You know, I'm still thinking about the Crater case" would go all right, somebody would be sure to have something to say to that, then he can work in his wheeze.

Says to self, "Come on, snap out of it. If this ain't apathy, what is?"

Wonders if "apathy" wouldn't fit in with his little rhyme, decides to give it a trial, fixes it up like this:

Timmany, Tommaney, Tammany,

The public was stricken with apathy.

The vote apathetic

Was extremely pathetic,

Simmony, Sommany, Simony.

Decides this might do if it had some sense to it, but as it stands it is not so hot. Goes over list of rhyme words again, thinks of "dommie" decides he's never going to get anywhere with this until he finds out what "simony" means takes down dictionary, looks it up, finds it has something to do with sale of church offices, gets excited, decides he's getting warm now, and his rhyme may turn out better than his wheeze.

Decides he's there with the funny stuff all right.

Decides, hell, if he had a mind to he could probably hold F.P.A.'s job. Thinks why doesn't he send some contributions to F.P.A. anyhow. Decides that's what he'll do with this thing after he gets it shined up, send it to F.P.A. and get it printed. Wonders why he never thought of doing that before.

Says to self, "Come on, get your mind on this."

Concentrates very hard. Reads rest of editorial, discovers it is state and national election, with Tammany only indirectly involved anyhow. Says to self, "Oh, hell. I wonder what's on at the Roxy."

Panhandling
(December 14, 1930)

Some weeks ago, in the belief that if panhandling is unavoidable it had as well be done in a competent way and inspired by a particularly fine exhibition of the art given at my own expense, I set down in this place a set of rules by which I thought the citizen could be relieved of his money with a minimum of pain to the beneficiary and, more importantly, to the citizen. They were as follows: That the person in need of funds learn to frequent show windows, excavations and other places where knots of people would be likely to collect; that he become adroit at little humorous remarks that would bring a smile to the face of some one of these spectators and that, with the ice thus broken, he proceed to make his touch, confident that whatever else a man might go back on he would not go back on a smile.

I am by no means prepared to admit that this is a poor scheme—on the contrary. I think it is a very good scheme, for, as I have said, it works when it is tried on me. Nevertheless it is now my duty to reveal that I have discovered a much better scheme. I say "discovered." This, of course, is a careless phrase: actually it discovered me, to the tune of 25 cents and not even a "thank you" at the end. But that is part of its surpassing beauty, so I think it would simplify things all around if I were to allow it came to my notice, and then proceed to the conclusions that are to be drawn from it.

It all happened very quickly, as I was leaving the house the other morning on my way to work. I was a little late as usual, and not really in the humor for the delays incidental to philanthropy. But, as I turned west on 19th Street I knew I was going to engage in philanthropy whether I was in the humor for it or not. For in front of me was a battered little man, a most preposterous little man, who seemed to be on his way to some destination of the geatest importance to him and at the same time to be going nowhere in particular. He was the kind of little man, if I make myself clear, who is able to go nowhere with all the bustling dignity that the rest of us exhibit going somewhere. When he saw me he stopped. A look of annoyance appeared on his face— he became aware of his surroundings with the bored start that a process server might give when at last he sighted his quarry.

I stopped too; it seemed the least I could do under the circumstances. Then without saying a word he stretched out his hand, at the same time turning his face away with the expression of disgust that one shows in the presence of some disagreeable rite, like the removal of a dead cat from the gutter. Then he stood there. When I had fished the 25 cents out of my pocket it was I who walked over to him, not he who walked over to me. The 25 cents received, he moved on without saying a word.

And I—what did I do? I moved on with a light, gladsome feeling in my heart, not because I had given a needy brother 25 cents but because the needy brother had vetoed all talk, before, during and after, on his part, and all mumbling don't mention it's on my part; it boiled down to handing over the money, really the easiest part of the whole transaction. I am convinced that many another citizen would prefer to be approached in exactly the same way. In the first place, the very curt manner of it acknowledged the hard realities of the situation. I have spoken before about the Judas Iscariot feeling that comes over one when a man asks for money on the street, that horrible feeling of guilt that reduces you to gulps and stutters and makes you claw feverishly for your coins with the single thought that you may hand one out and get away. It is the same feeling that you had when you were a little boy and papa caught you in a lie and asked you all sorts of stern questions, which you were utterly unable to answer for the reason that you were helpless to say anything at all.

Well, why should you feel guilty under these circumstances? In my opinion, you feel guilty because you are guilty. It is all very well, when Dec. 31 rolls around and you cast up what you have done in the year, to pat yourself on the back about the long hours you have worked and the admirable way in which you have performed your tasks. But God, up in heaven, knows this is all hooey. That you happen to have 25 cents in your pocket at this moment is nine-tenths luck. The man before you probably worked hard too and performed his tasks quite as admirably as you. Yet there he is and here you are.

There is no reason in the canon of eternal justice why he should not be here and you there; nor is there any assurance, for that matter, that in 1940, when we have the next cycle of Republican prosperity, those are not the identical places where the two of you will stand. So you feel guilty with good reason, and why a man who is for a moment behind the game should be so very polite about borrowing a few chips from the man who is ahead is a little hard to see. Indeed, it is something of a relief when he treats you like a felon, for at least the air is somehow cleared and you breathe freely.

In the second place, there are some situations so stark that they are utterly sublingual. When you win a new love, or leave an old one, when your belly is full, another man's empty—what is there to say? My battered little friend said nothing and for that I am profoundly grateful.

Good Resolutions
(December 28, 1930)

Placing feet on desk and lighting cigar, our citizen decides the time has come to have a showdown with himself on certain matter. Thinks to self, this stuff about New Year's resolutions may be all hooey, but one thing is certain, and that is he's not saving enough money. God knows he's making plenty. Not as much as last year, but still plenty. Fact of the matter, if anybody had told him ten years ago that he'd be making as much as he's making now, he'd have thought they were kidding him. And where is it? It isn't anywhere. It isn't anywhere. Well, cut out the fancy talk and say what you mean: It ain't nowhere. That's where it is, it ain't nowhere.

Here you've let a whole year slip by, and all you've put in the saving account is $117, and you can't count that because you've let the checking account drop so low you've had to pay the service charge three months running for not having a minimum balance of $500. A swell business man you are. Whoever said you were a business man anyhow? Say boy, you got to cut this out. You got to remember you got a family. Suppose you should die? Would you like Ethel and the kids to go out and sell apples? No? Yeah? Well, that's what they'll be doing if you don't get a shake on. Apples, nice red apples only a nickel apiece. A nickel, a nickel, a half a dime, the twentieth part of a dollar.

Frowns, thinks to self he could maybe cut down on his cigars and find cheaper place for lunch. Thinks to self, will you for God's sake get your mind on this and act like you were awake? Suppose you cut out all the cigars? Suppose you didn't eat any lunch? How much would that save? About $7 a week. Here you're up against a tough proposition and you're wasting time with foolish schemes for saving $7 a week. Come on, snap out of it. You've got to get at this thing comprehensively. Likes sound of this, mutters it over several times to self: Comprehensively, comprehensively, comprehensively.

That's the stuff. Comprehensively....

Feels he is getting somewhere now, knits brow, puffs at cigar. Tries to think how you go about a thing comprehensively. Wonders how the big shots go about it.

Puts feet back on desk, thinks, well then, how about Ford? Anyway, he won't turn into Hoover on you, soon as you look at his picture. Has hardly thought of Hoover before word pops out at him: Facts. Thinks to self, a fine guy you are, not to think of that sooner. Of course that's what you need, facts. Facts. Opens desk drawer, gets out old bank statements, begins to riffle through checks. Takes pen and piece of paper, begins to write down items beginning from first of year:

Snowdrifts Laundry	$13.62
J. Rossi (ice)	5.25
N.Y. Telephone Company	5.60
Consolidated Gas Company	2.48
N.Y. Edison Company	1.85
Elco Realty Corporation (rent)	160.00
Cash	1.02

Wonders what that cash item was for. All right, never mind, we're getting somewhere now. Turns over next check, finds it is to Robert P. Hill for $10. Thinks to self, what the hell. Robert P. Hill, hey? Robert P. Hill. Don't know any Robert P. Hill. Looks at signature, wonders if it is forgery. Looks O.K. but when them crooks start to forge your name they do it so good you couldn't even tell it yourself. Thinks to self, no wonder you couldn't save any money. Facts, hey. I'll say we're getting facts. Facts and then some. Wonders whether he ought to send wire to bank. Guesses as check is nearly a year old the bank couldn't do anything now. Better call the Detective Bureau, though. Picks up telephone, starts to call Spring 3100, feels pretty important that he can remember the number quick like that. Puts phone down quickly, thinks to self, now wait a minute. We'll just make sure about this thing. Gets out old check book, begins to riffle through stubs. Finds Snowdrift, Rossi, Telephone, Consolidated, Edison, Elco, Cash, begins to get pretty excited. Is sure next stub will not be marked Robert P. Hill. Turns leaf, finds next stub marked Robert P. Hill.

Well, what the hell?

Something wrong somewhere.

Picks up phone, calls wife, finds out Robert P. Hill is Dr. Hill, the dentist. Says all right, just wanted to know. Is unable to get mind on checks any more. Says, listen bimbo, to hell with facts. There's only one way to save money, and that's to save it. Hoover, hunh. Sure he's got plenty of facts, and look at him.

Vacuum
(February 22, 1931—Cain's last World column)

This piece, I am afraid, is going to be like Mr. Charles Winninger's scene in "Show Boat" when he told what the show would have been like if there had been one. For what I propose to do is explain why, at the end of an hour or more of fiddling the keys of my machine, I find myself with nothing to say, and then perhaps to draw certain conclusions thereupon.

It is not, I should say at the outset, because I lack ideas. I am fairly gabby, and during the week a number of things have occurred to me that I would like to write about, as follows:

1. Why I prefer Washington to Lincoln.

2. Where Washington, who had no country to yield allegiance to, was able to find the enthusiasm that carried him through five years of the Revolutionary War.

3. A sketch portraying the exultation of a business man who has been through a dismal year of firing and now has an opportunity to perform the ancient rite of hiring.

4. What makes a bad writer.

5. Why the reds, in spite of my undeniably anarchistic cast of mind, have never made any impression on me.

Nor is it that I lack the capacity to get my reflections on any of those things down on paper. I get plenty of practice at writing, alas, and once I know what I am going to say, saying it is an absurdly simple business. No, it is merely that at this particular time, on this particular day, I am unable to care enough about these subjects to set down in coherent sentences what I would ordinarily feel about them.

There are, it is true, extenuatory circumstances. I have had a bad spell of some mysterious liver complaint that I suffer from periodically, and it has left me somewhat weak in the legs. Also, I have been listening to a harangue from my doctor, one Vorhaus, who takes what strikes me as unseemly delight in telling me what is going to happen to me if I do not do what he tells me to do, and that hasn't exactly filled me with pep. Nevertheless, alibi or no alibi, the main point remains intact. What ails me, so far as doing any of these pieces is concerned, is not in my head. It is in my heart. What Washington brought to the Revolutionary War is what I am unable to bring to this typewriter.

Now what I am getting at is this: that what I am now afflicted with temporarily, the feeling that Washington, Lincoln, business men, waiters and reds will only put me to sleep if I try to write about them, is probably what afflicts permanently the average person who wants to write and, for some reason not known to himself, can't. Like all who work for newspapers, I run into quite a few such persons each year. They send me, show me or read me their manuscripts, or tell me the plot of some story they are "working" on, or the first act of some play. And unlike most who work for newspapers, I always lend them a very sympathetic ear. I cannot say this is because I have any belief that anything will come of it, for nothing ever has; perhaps it is out of curiosity as to what the trouble is. And the trouble, as I diagnose it is rarely cerebral. The ideas, as a rule, are good enough. Sometimes they are excellent. The writing is almost invariably better than that turned in by professionals. It is surprising how well the person who can't write writes. Somewhere inside of him, I think, is a secret feeling that the trick is to be learned out of grammars, rhetoric books and lexicons; you will usually find that he has conned these with diligence and is aware of nice distinctions in usage, delicate shades of meaning, that the average writer has never heard of. The typing is always perfect.

The pieces, however, are hopeless. Somewhere, perhaps on page 3, but more likely on page 1, immediately after the brave, fine opening, they go to pieces, wander off on trivial irrelevancies, end their paragraphs on four dots, head nowhere and get nowhere. I know the symptons for I show them every time I try to do a fiction story. The only way I can keep on the track at all is to pretend to be somebody else—to put it in dialect and thus get it told. If I try to do it in my own language I find that I have none—a style that seems to be personal enough for ordinary gassing refuses to get going for an imaginary narrative. So long as I merely report what people might have said under certain circumstances, I am all right; but the moment I have to step in myself, and try to create the impression that what happened to these people really matters, then I am sunk. I flounder about, not knowing whether I skip to the scene at the church or pile in a little more of the talk at the post office. The reason, I think, is the same as that which explains my mood today. I don't care what happened. It doesn't matter to me. Narratively, I do not exist. I have no impulse to show off, to hold an audience. I want to hide behind an assumed ego. I feel foolish. I am merely going through the motions.

And this, I think, is the real explanation of people who want to write and can't. They do not really want to write. They want to be known as writers, that is all. The brutal fact is exactly as Mr. Morris Markey once described it. "Those who can write," he said "do write."

The End of the World
(*The New Freeman*, February 11, 1931)

In the spring of 1926 I was spending an evening with Mr. Philip Goodman, the theatrical producer, and formerly an advertising man. We had been talking about various things, when abruptly he said:

"The *World* is for sale."

"Yes?" I replied. "Interesting if true."

"I know," he said. "The will prohibits it. Well, it's for sale. Listen: You and I are going down the street, and we pass a buildng. I say, 'Nice piece of property there.'- You say, 'Yes, it's a pity you can't buy it.' I look at it, and something tells me you *can* buy it. I don't know what it is, but I know it. So I go and buy it, and make a nice penny on it. Well, it's the same way with the *World*. Will or no will, it's for sale."

"All right," I said. "Go ahead and buy it."

Somewhat to my surprise, he tried to. He found a buyer, and within two weeks had entered into negotiations with Ralph Pulitzer, through Arthur Krock, at that time assistant to the president of the *World*. I was present at the talk between Goodman and Krock, which took place at Krock's home in Central Park South. A price was mentioned: it was $18,000,000.

"But," said Krock, "this is only a hypothetical figure, mentioned chiefly to give you an idea of the size of the project you have in mind. As a matter of fact, the *World* is not for sale. Mr. Pulitzer reminds you that disposition of the property is forbidden by his father's will. Lawyers, of course, might find a way to get around that. He directs me to inform you, however, that he has no desire to get around it. He is deeply interested in the *World*, has published it successfully for fifteen years, wants to continue publishing it, and sees no reason to abdicate now. In short, while he appreciates your interest, he wants you to understand that your whole idea is chimerical."

"Nevertheless," said Goodman after we had left, "it's for sale."

Shortly afterward, Goodman's buyer lost a lot of money through an adverse court decision, and shortly after that he died, so the deal fell through. I think, though, that the episode is illuminating at this time, for two reasons: first, because it shows that as recently as five years ago Ralph Pulitzer had no intention of selling the *World*, and probably did not realize that it was in difficulties, as it had made money the year before, and had paid a bonus to its employees; second, because Goodman's analysis of what was wrong with the *World*, made at a time when few suspected that anything was wrong with it, is naturally more impressive than the innumerable analyses that have been made in the last few months, when anybody could see that everything was wrong with it.

"What is it," I asked him, "That makes you think the *World* is losing ground? What ails it?"

"Well," he said, after thinking a few minutes, "remember what I said about the two men and the building. If you have any eye for that kind of thing at all, you know without knowing how you know. In general, I would say that nothing ever ails any newspaper but the man at the top. That may be a little like saying that the *World* is no good because it is no good. More specifically, I would say that one of the things that ails the *World* is want ads. They pay well, but no matter what they pay they cost more than they bring in.

Nobody knows how many people buy the *World* just to get a tip on a job, but my guess is that there are a lot of them. They don't do any advertiser any good, and don't kid yourself that the advertisers in this town don't know it.

"Next, the *World* is not read. It is bought, but it is not read. You have one crowd buying it for Broun, another for Adams, another for Igoe, another for Lippmann, another for Webster, and all of them add up to quite a few thousand. But I don't believe there is a single subscriber who buys the *World* to begin on Page 1 and read it through. The stuff is simply not there. The *World* hasn't got the news. People heave it into the nearest ash-can as soon as they have finished the feature they bought it for, and there again you have circulation that doesn't do advertisers any good.

"Next, nobody in the shop seems to have any idea what the composite reader of the *World* looks like. You've got an editorial page addressed to intellectuals, a sporting section addressed to the fancy, a Sunday magazine addressed to morons, and twenty other things that don't seem to be addressed to anybody. Who can strike a common denominator among all these? I can't. If nobody in the shop knows what the composite reader looks like, nobody outside of it knows what the composite editor looks like. The *World* is not a newspaper. It is an agglomeration of twenty different newspapers, one or two of them good, most of them bad. And it's for sale. You wait, and you "see.""

II

This, I think, was as sound on the last day of publication as it was at the time it was spoken. The most important part of it, of course, was the reference to "the man at the top," who was at that time Ralph Pulitzer, and who still is for the purposes of this discussion, for Herbert Pulitzer was in office only a year, and must be regarded as a quarterback sent in for the last five minutes after the game was hopelessly lost, with no idea but to stall for time and hold the score down. What kind of newspaper Ralph Pulitzer would have got out if he had been free to follow his own inclination I don't know, but my guess is that it would have been a newspaper of opinion, manned by as fine a staff of contributors as he could possibly get together. Indeed, for a time, that was about the kind of newspaper he did get out. When you recall that his editorial writers included such men as Walter Lippmann, Charles Merz, Maxwell Anderson, Laurence Stallings, John L. Heaton, L.R.E. Paulin, Claude G. Bowers, Harold L. Pollard, William O. Scroggs, and Allan Nevins; that his news staff included such reporters as Leonard Cline, Oliver Garrett, Louis Weitzenkorn, and Frank Sullivan; that his columnists included such men as Heywood Broun, F. P. Adams, Deems Taylor, Alexander Woollcott, St. John Ervine, and Harry Hansen; and that his regular contributors included such men as H.L. Mencken, Ring Lardner, and Will Rogers; you realize that he succeeded pretty well in getting his kind of newspaper, and you also realize that his kind of newspaper was pretty certain to fail. But it cannot be argued that his kind of newspaper was not worth getting out. It was, and I shall always believe that when his crew was hitting on all six, the *World* was probably the most interesting newspaper in the United States, and possibly anywhere.

But he was hamstrung by the will, and in a much worse way by the "ideals" of his father, to which I think he was sincerely devoted, and which he felt he had to carry on. Now these ideals are quite well known, for they were carried at the masthead for years; but they happen to be about as representative of Joseph Pulitzer's newspaper practice as the Gettysburg Address is representative of Abraham Lincoln's political practice. They had a lot to say about progress and reform, but they had nothing to say about bringing in the hottest news that a big staff could collect; and they had nothing to say about the most important part of Joseph Pulitzer's formula, which was to leave the rabbits to less ambitious competitors, and then go hunt elephants. Elephants he hunted, as for example Roosevelt, and when he got done he had the finest collection of tusks that was ever asssembled in this country: in his day the *World* was not only respected, but wholesomely feared.

I don't think Ralph Pulitzer enjoyed hunting elephants, not because he lacked courage for the business, but because it was usually attended by grubby details on the news side that offended his fastidiousness. In other words, one of his handicaps was that he was a gentleman. Moreover, when the old editors began to die and retire, he had a tendency to employ gentlemen in their places. By some accident, one of his most important appointments, Herbert Bayard Swope, was in the old tradition. Now Swope is a gentleman by any conceivable standard, but he is also a newspaper man; nobody can bulldoze a cop, a Governor, or a President any more ferociously than he can, and nobody knows better than he that the main product of a newspaper is smoke. Smoke was what he wanted, and smoke, as you can see by reading the Florida peonage stories and the Ku-Klux exposé, was what he got.

But others were in the new tradition, and especially Lippmann. Many curious things have been said about him lately, some in the vein of Broun and Villard, who hint at a certain faint-heartedness in him, and some in the vein of the local liberals, who regard him as a great editor. He is not faint-hearted and he is not an editor. Nobody who ever tried to buck him on any issue whatever could have any doubts about his spirit: he will not trim, he will not back down, and he will not compromise, whether his personal fortunes are involved or not. And nobody who watched his boredom with the job of getting out his page, his impulse to wish all chores off on Merz, his frequent betrayals that he had not even read the letters in his own forum, could have supposed that he was an editor. He had no interest in editing, and it is not surprising that his page often showed it.

Lippmann, I think, is a poet of ideas. He stews out theories, hypotheses, explanations as profusely as a scenarist stews out gags. If you will read his books, you will see that he seldom bothers to prove any of them; the pages are full of foot-notes, but most of them refer not to sources of facts, but to sources of suitable quotations, i.e., to other men's ideas, where they happen to have a bearing on his own. The adjective which reviewers use most frequently about these books is "stimulating," and I think this is a fair description of Lippmann's present function as a publicist, and certainly if he were only that he would be a great deal.

But to a poet, obviousness is utterly intolerable. And here, probably, is the clue to why Lippmann often seemed to be out of tune with the newspaper business. I think it could be argued that obviousness is almost indispensable to a newspaper. The moment it departs from the outstanding realities of what it is discussing it gets into the realm of shadow-boxing. But Lippmann recoils from the obvious as a cat recoils from water. He was always trying to get away from the plain banalities of polemic, and find the grain of ultimate truth, the aspect of the discussion which might conceivably be valid ten years from now. Possibly I am talking too generally to make myself quite clear. I can illustrate well enough if I tell of a talk I once had with him.

We were having lunch a few days after Villard published the article that caused so much talk. "I don't see that you need lose any sleep over it," I said. "It has the weakness of everything that isn't sound. For my part, I think you played in luck. For where you really had your chin hanging out, and showed all your real weaknesses, was in the Scopes trial. And he evidently forgot it."

"Maybe that wasn't good," he said. "I've often wondered about it."

"There," I said, "you rode a hobby without any regard to whether it was worth all you were writing about it and you were also guilty of trying to make an editorial more than it can be, and usually achieving something less than it ought to be."

"I don't quite know what you mean," he said.

"Well," I said, "if you ask me, the most that any newspaper should try to do is choose sides in a fight, and then fight as hard as it can, even when it secretly wishes the fight were going a little differently. But you are always trying to dredge up basic principles. In a newspaper, it won't work. For example, turn to music. A piano has eight octaves, a violin three, a cornet two, and a —searching idly for an instrument of still smaller compass—a bugle has only four notes. Now if what you've got to blow is a bugle, there isn't any sense in camping yourself down in front of piano music."

"You may be right," he said. *"But God Damn it, I'm not going to spend my life writing bugle-calls."*

There I think you have the explanation of Lippmann, his strength, his weakness, his pride, his general attitude toward his work. He never felt, I think, that while a bugle-call may be the most utter banality as absolute music, it may be the most glorious thing in the world when the battle is going hard. Partly as a matter of intellectual pride, partly because as I have said he is really a poet, and jarred by all banalities, he never let himself lose his perspective through the emotions of combat. Indeed, when he was aware of the combat, he was always trying to bring it to a gentlemanly level; he seemed to regard it as a sort of amateurs' tennis tournament, as indicated by his invariable desire to shake hands afterward. He published a piece praising the good intentions of the Lowell Committee after Sacco and Vanzetti were burned, he had a kind word for Mr. Hoover after the election of 1928, he "saluted" the new owners when they finally took possession of the *World*. What he never seemed able to see was that the handshake after a tennis match is public proclamation of the fact that it didn't really matter. But the sole excuse for a newspaper's activity is that it *does* matter. For my part, I esteem a certain churlishness in a newspaper. But Lippmann is, always has been, and always will be, a gentleman. You have to admire it, but at the same time you have to query it as a qualification for an editor.

For my part, in ending these somewhat disjointed remarks, I shall reserve my salute for Mr. James W. Barrett, who headed the employees' movement to acquire the *World*. When Barrett stood up in front of the meeting at the Astor and stuck out his jaw, it was the most inspiring sight I think I ever saw while I was on the *World*. I felt that what he was attempting could not be done, and yet he tried to do it, and stuck out his jaw. Is there anything in the world so fine as a stuck-out jaw? It is the prelude to a bugle-call, and the older I get the more respect I have for it.

III. Six Decades of Journalism—1917-1977

Introduction

In the Spring of 1917, when James M. Cain went into the building that housed *The Baltimore American* looking for a job, he had no idea what qualifications were needed to be hired on a newspaper. He ended up talking with William Kines, the city editor, and must have impressed him, because Kines offered him a job as a reporter at $10 a week. He was assigned the southern police district, and his first story was a drowning. He went back to the city room to type his story at around 10:00 P.M., and dropped it in the "in" basket. Back at his desk, he watched the night city editor, Raymond Hoblitzel, pick the story up and study it. Hoblitzel was a fine, experienced editor, who talked with a slight stammer. Cain noted that something seemed to be wrong as Hoblitzel fingered the story, until finally he came over to Cain's desk and stammered: "Mr. Cain, you've b-been in the newspaper business bef-f-fore? May I ask where?"

"No," said Cain, "I'm new at it." And then, as Hoblitzel stared, he added: "Matter of fact, that's the first story I ever wrote."

Still Hoblitzel stared, and then finally said: "I—compliment you on it. I would say—you're in—the right business. I predict—you'll go far."

Mr. Hoblitzel was, indeed, a man of foresight. Sitting in front of a typewritter was the right business for James M. Cain. He did it continually for the next 60 years—and three days after he died in 1977, his last newspaper piece appeared in *The Washington Post.*

Cain worked nearly a year on *The Baltimore American* as a reporter, then was offered a job at $3-a-week more on the rival *Sun.* But he was only on the *Sun* few months before deciding to enlist in the Army and he spent most of the war in France with the 79th Division. When the war was over, it was several months before the 79th received its orders to return to the States and during this period the division started a newspaper, *The Lorraine Cross,* of which Cain was eventually made editor. Alexander Woolcott, who was working for *The Stars and Stripes,* called the *Cross,* "a snappy young journal" and gave it credit for putting out the first "extra" ever printed in France. Cain also became the chief publicist for the Division and when the 79th returned to the States in 1919, he wrote the *New York Times* article which described the division's exploits during the war.

102

Cain returned to *The Sun* in 1920 and the following year asked to be assigned to what he considered one of the most important stories since the war—the treason trial of William Blizzard in West Virginia. It was a significant milestone in Cain's career and also marked the beginning of a life-long fascination with the subject of treason. Blizzard was president of UMW District No. 16 and leader of a group of coal miners who had staged an armed march against some mines in Logan and Mingo counties, where the "deputy sheriffs" were actually hired guns paid by the mine companies to keep the union out. An increasing number of people had been living in tents, unemployed and just waiting for some spark that would start trouble. "They're a-murderin' the women and children," was often heard, and although reporter Cain never saw any evidence that women and children were murdered, it was an effective rallying cry. In August 1921, open warfare between the mine operators and the union organizers erupted, and a state of martial law was proclaimed. Ten men were actually killed in a battle when the miners marched on the town of Matewan, and two union sympathizers were shot down in cold blood in the town of Welch. The miners, two thousand strong, then assembled on one side of a ridge at Blair Mountain. On the other side, the sheriff deputies, state police, and a few patriotic citizens dug in, and Governor John J. Cornwell ordered his forces to neither advance nor retreat. The state also brought in four airplanes, armed them with makeshift bombs, and sent them up to attack the miners. Both sides held their positions and fired machine guns and rifles at each other for three days—before federal troops finally arrived and sent everyone home. It would have been a comic war right out of a Marx Brothers movie except for the fact that three men were accidentally killed.

After the dust had settled, the Logan County grand jury met in a special session and, in addition to wholesale charges of murder, conspiracy, and unlawful assembly, indicated twenty-three union men—including William Blizzard and Walter Allen—for treason against the state of West Virginia. Although the *Sun* editors were more interested in the coal companies' fight with the unions, it was the charge of treason that intrigued Cain. "I simply don't believe," Cain later told his editor, "that a glorified riot that was somewhat provoked should be blown up to an act of war."

Most of the papers covering the trial were pro-coal company, but Cain's coverage was essentially pro-union. And because the subject was treason, the conflict between the coal operators and the miners became a national story. Cain's dispatches and features for *The Sun* attracted considerable attention and when he returned to Baltimore he queried *The Atlantic Monthly* editor, Ellery Sedgwick, who replied: "The attitude of the *Baltimore Sun* regarding the West Virginia mining situation long since attracted my attention, and I consider its treatment of a difficult and dangerous situation as a public service of a high order. I am therefore very warmly disposed to say Yes to your proposal of June 5th.... Of your own work, except so far as I have read the columns of the *Sun,* I know nothing, and so I cannot promise you to accept what you may write, but...any manuscript you send will be read by all of us here with close interest and attention."

Sedgwick wrote Mencken inquiring about Cain and Mencken replied: "I don't know Cain personally, but I am told by friends at the *Sun* office that he is a man of exceptional quality." Cain wrote the article and sent it to Boston, but nothing happened. Then he received a letter from Sedgwick saying he was buying the article, but that he was holding it for two or three months to give it "better display," which Cain took with a grain of salt. When the check for $125 arrived, his first sale began to seem real, but still the article did not appear. Then one day, Henry Hyde, a columnist for the *Sun* dropped by Cain's desk and said: "I see you lead the *Atlantic* next month."

Cain also wrote two pieces about West Virginia for *The Nation.* Then, with his writings in *The Sun* and two national magazines attracting not only attention but applause, he suddenly developed the confidence to think he might write a novel about the situation in the mines. He took a leave of absence from *The Sun,* went down to West Virginia to gather more material, returned to Baltimore and wrote three drafts of what he hoped would be the Great American Novel—then gave up in despair. Part of his problem was that he was still too much of a reporter: "I was so preoccupied with background, authenticity and verisimilitude, that I had time for little else," he said. Discouraged, he decided that he simply could not write a novel, a decision from which he did not waiver for 10 years. So, for the next decade, James M. Cain was essentially a journalist, writing, primarily, as we have seen, for two publications—H.L. Mencken's *American Mercury* and Walter Lippman's *New York World* editorial page. However, during the 1920s, Cain also wrote articles for other publications—most notably *The Bookman* and *The Saturday Evening Post*—selections from which are included here.

It should be noted that in assembling the articles for this section I have arranged them more or less chronologically in relation to the experiences in Cain's life, rather than the time in which they were written. Thus, the first article is a profile of John Garfield Moore, written in 1933 about a young man who was a hero of Cain's boyhood in Chestertown Maryland; and "Treason, By Any Other Name," although written late in his life for *The Washington Post,* was inspired by the treason trial of William Blizzard which Cain covered in 1922. All Cain's articles draw heavily on his own experiences and, read consecutively, the book, as a whole, adds up to a loosely organized autobiography.

When Cain reported for work at the *New Yorker* in February of 1931, its essential character and quality were well established due, it was generally agreed, to the genius and talent of six editors—Ross, Ralph Ingersoll, James Thurber, Katherine and E. B. White and Wolcott Gibbs. Thurber and White wrote "Comment" and "Talk of the Town" as well as bylined "casuals." They also performed a variety of chores, such as writing captions for cartoons and those little bright one liners commenting on some absurd, pretentious or asinine item culled from the world's press, or sent in by a contributor, and reprinted at the bottom of a page. Katherine White handled the literary talent and developed the short fiction which was gradually becoming a required element in the *New Yorker* format. Wolcott Gibbs could handle almost any editorial assignment and was probably the best parodist the country ever produced.

Cain, himself, wrote very little for the magazine while he was there. His two contributions consisted of an amusing little piece called "Sealing Wax," (about trying to mail a registered letter and learning that the Post Office no longer provided the sealing wax) and a poem, "Gridiron Soliloquies."

It did not take Cain long to find out that Ross was going to be a peculiar boss. "As he passed by my desk," Cain said of the first day, "I looked up to say hello, but he went by without seeming to see me, apparently preoccupied with whatever was on his mind. However, almost at once, within a minute or two, he was there by my desk again, a grin on his face, to tell me something funny Benchley or somebody had said the night before—but with no 'good morning,' 'hello,' 'hi 'ya,' or anything of that kind.... When this entrance of his was repeated day after day, with his invariable reappearance, affable but always without any greeting, I began to realize that in this otherwise courteous man, so easy in conversation, there lurked something peculiar, a streak of self-consciousness, or shyness, or social kinkiness, that was anything but easy, and was in fact downright wacky."

And Cain was also convinced that the way Ross ran the *New Yorker* was, at the very least, wacky. The main problem, he thought, was Ross's refusal to pay enough money to hire good secretaries, which meant *New Yorker* editors spent too much time doing the work of their incompetent secretaries. Another thing that annoyed Cain was the *New Yorker's* system of drawing accounts. He was opposed to it in general, and insisted that if he was to do his job properly, he had to be informed about each advance to a writer or artist and the exact amount. But Ross was devious about this. He would put through an advance without telling Cain and when Cain confronted him he would have some excuse like: "I didn't want to tell you 'til the money was actually paid," always adding: "I know your hostility to the whole idea of advances." Cain would explain that he was not against an advance, just the left-handed way the magazine had of getting them paid back—or not paid back, as the case may be.

They also haggled over the rates paid to "Talk of the Town" and "Comment" writers—especially Thurber and White. Cain recalled that, at the time, White was getting 19 cents a word for his contributions and Thurber 17 cents. The difference upset him because he felt that after *Is Sex Necessary?*

(written by Thurber and White) was published in 1929, they were equally well known. He also felt that if Thurber ever found out he was getting less than White, he might get angry and leave. But Ross insisted that in subtle little ways, White was better, which finally Cain admitted, but in a peevish way: "Could it be," he asked Ross, "that White's superiority is due to having a wife on this magazine, in charge of fiction pieces, who wouldn't like it at all if Thurber were held to be equal to the man of her dreams?"

Ross made no answer but it was obvious he didn't like the inference. Cain realized he was skating on thin ice, but he also was beginning to feel that he did not much care. He was slowly coming to accept the fact that the *New Yorker* was no place for him. Furthermore, his reputation as a writer of dialogue had now become a salable commodity in Hollywood, and his agent, Jim Geller, was tempting him with offers from the studios.

New Yorker alumni of the early 1930s remember Cain as a personable, likeable staffer. "He got along well with everyone at the *New Yorker* except Ross," said B. A. Bergman, "But who did?" Bergman said he especially enjoyed talking with Cain, who "was a rare conversationalist." Alexander Woolcott Cain described as "cold, androgynous, fat, gabby, brilliant, but not really likeable." On the other hand, he liked Dorothy Parker immensely, recalling that "she had the most beautiful manners, along with those luminous dark eyes...Sure she could destroy you, but you had probably put her in pain first by boring her."

E. B. White remembers Cain as "a compulsively neat man, an ash tray mustn't have any stale ashes in it." The Whites both felt friendly toward Cain—and they continued a correspondence over the years—but there was no close relationship. "I remember his entertaining us one Thanksgiving Day at his apartment with a turkey dinner.... The turkey was bigger than the platter, and Jim delivered a monologue as he carved, while the slices of meat slipped quietly to the floor." White was always impressed by Cain's ability to ignore the disappearing meat—"an exercise in imperturbability."

James Thurber said that some of the staffers at the *New Yorker* were baffled by Cain, who liked to work on the floor, where he put the "Talk" department together. They called him "Dizzy Jim" and they called Thurber "Daffy Jim." Cain found Daffy "damned hard to like" but said Thurber "cared not a hoot whether you liked him or not."

Ross was the most unusual person at *The New Yorker* and one aspect of his peculiarity was his continuing war with publisher Raul Fleischman and the business department. Cain remembered Ross having contempt verging on nausea for anything resembling a businessman. He thought they were fakes and once said to Cain: "If the magazine is right, anybody can sell advertising in it; if it's not, nobody can."

Every now and then Lois Lang, one of the "Avenue" writers, would mention in her column that she found it at Macy's and "all hell breaks loose,"

Cain recalled. "Russeks and Lord and Taylor and the Cutie-Pie Shoppey all call up and the smell of ozone is in the corridors and the copy boy is running memos and then at last there is a CONFERENCE. It is attended by Ross, Fleischmann, Jesus, the Front Office Contingent, and perhaps a secretary or two, to get it all in writing. Fleischmann, affably, opens it and we're off to a pleasant start. Then the front office boys explain what has to be done in words of one syllable, so Ross can get it through a head not born for the intricacies and subtleties of business. To all this, Ross listens with obvious pain, but with some sick imitation of a smile pasted on his face. Then one of them pats the arms of the chair, with a that's-that air, as though we could all now go home. It has been sensible, friendly, and constructive, and Fleischmann, a born optimist, looks quite hopeful. Then nothing happens for five minutes. It becomes obvious that back of the pasted smile, the conscientious efforts at courtesy, Ross hasn't been listening at all. Then slowly, haltingly, he begins to talk. He announces, not in the I-want-to-speak-on-the-motion way the others have done, but in a flat, definitive tone, like a rector beginning 'I'm the Resurrection and the Life.' Presently, he says: 'So this is the way we're going to do it.' He explains the way. He explains the reasons. They're solid, cogent reasons that take account of pesky business angles the business men don't appear to have thought of. It's wholly different from their way, but before he gets through all of them know it's the right way and the only way.

"As he talks he gesticulates with his hands. They droop off his wrists like dead things, all the fingers hanging separately, and seeming to have grown twice as long. He finishes, then gets up and goes out, with no farewell of any kind: too preoccupied. All sit looking at each other, then somebody looks at his watch. Fleischmann looks relieved, as though at last it's settled with less fuss than might have been expected, considering Ross."

As for his own virtues as a *New Yorker* editor, Cain felt he had few. He found it impossible to think up ideas in July suitable for November. His mind was geared to a newspaper deadline, not magazine publication. He also could not get used to the idea that the magazine was conceived as entertainment rather than news. Cain continually came up with ideas that would have been good on a newspaper—and Ross would respond: "Cain, let's let the other magazines be important. We're just a little package of entertainment that sells for 15 cents—We don't have our mind on big things."

Within a few months after becoming Ross's Jesus, Cain "was about as miserable a human being as I have ever encountered," said his successor, B. A. Bergman. And Cain confessed that "I was so little qualified for my job on the *New Yorker*, and detested it so, my mind began to play me tricks. I would talk to someone in the waiting room, then next morning have no recollection whatever that any such meeting took place."

This amused his secretary, Eileen Collins, at first, but then it began to worry her. Cain appeared to be a "nervous wreck" and he admitted to Andy

White that on "my last days on the *New Yorker* I was going somewhat mental," which made it even more irritating when Ross would do something like fire a boy Cain had promoted without telling him about it. But the incident that finally triggered Cain's break with Ross concerned John O'Hara, who was now writing regularly for the *New Yorker*. Ross promised O'Hara an advance of $1,000 without telling Cain about it and this was the last straw. He said: "I'll be goddamned if I'll sign for this thing since you didn't clear it with me." But when he went home that night, he was furious with himself and thought: "What in the hell are you making an issue of these things for? Here is a man, O'Hara, who's personally cold but who is a very gifted writer. He ought to be in this magazine; you're making an issue of the thing! What in the hell are you doing this goddamn job for anyway?"

So the next day, early in November of 1931, he had lunch with his agent, James Geller, and told him: "You've been making noises about sending me out to Hollywood. O.K. If you can get me an offer, I'll take it."

By three o'clock that afternoon Geller had the offer firm—$400 a week at Paramount. Cain accepted and by 5:30 he was through at the *New Yorker*. As a parting gesture, he framed in leather one of Ross's memos—preserving the misspelling,—that Ross had sent him with a rejected manuscript:

"WHAT IS THE SIGNIFIGANCE [SIC] OF IT ALL?"

He presented it to his successor, B. A. Bergman, who still had it when he died.

Years later, at the time of Ross's death, Fleischmann wrote Cain that he remembered him as "probably the only 'Jesus' who was smart enough to know that he couldn't live forever in the unbelievable atmosphere of topsy-turvy-dom in which the magazine was functioning in those days and departed under his own will without any pressure from behind."

Cain's feeling about the magazine, at least immediately after leaving it, can be seen in a note of advice he wrote Sally Benson in 1934: "For God's sake can those little *New Yorker* pieces and spread out. That magazine, excellent as it is, is dedicated to precociousness, which means it is got out by a lot of precious amateurs, who are not the less amateurs because they are very gifted."

After *The Postman Always Rings Twice* was published and Cain was a nationally celebrated author, Wolcott Gibbs wrote Cain asking him to consider writing something for the magazine. It is unlikely that any *New Yorker* editor ever received such an emphatic rejection: "On the whole, I would rather be dead," replied Cain. "You see, by the time I thought up a list of ideas and submitted them and found out the one I liked Ross didn't like, and then submitted them and found out the one I liked Ross didn't like, and then wrote one up and sent it on and then got it back again with 32 numbered objections from Mrs. White, and then rewrote it and sent it back, then considered the proposal to buy the facts from me for $50 and have Andy White rewrite it, and finally it came out as a Reporter piece by Markey,—I would probably be dead anyway."

Cain's first job in Hollywood—with Paramount Pictures—lasted six months. And suddenly he was at one of the low points in his life. It was 1932, the middle of the Depression, and he was broke, 40-years-old, out of a job and with his professional contacts and reputation 3,000 miles away. He wrote Mencken that he did not know exactly why, but "I am washed up in the newspaper business." He decided magazines were now his only outlet but when he started trying to conceive articles and short stories, he became depressed. Then he began to think: "Unconsciously," he said, "I had assumed that the East was the only good seat for the show that started in 1492, and the white man began his reduction of the continent, but actually, if the Atlantic was the starting line of the great trek, the Pacific was the goal, and just as valid a place to study it from as the other side of the country."

He began to study California, its people and the life they were developing out there: "I had supposed the West to be a bit naive, a bit wild, wooly and absurd. Actually the country is the heir to a prodigious, rich colorful civilization" that had begun even before the first gold strike of 1848.

Before he went West, Cain had written two successful short stories for Mencken and *The Mercury*, so now he decided to try another, using California as the setting. The result was "Baby in the Icebox." Then he started to work on a major article about California, which many students of Cain (and I concur) consider his finest essay. He called it "Paradise," sent it off to Mencken, who said it was "the first really good article on California that has ever been done." And Mencken was not the only one who admired "Paradise": Ralph Thompson, who by 1937 would be writing "Books of the Times" for *The New York Times*, recalled running across "Paradise" in a university library and thinking it was "a positively vicious masterpiece, who was this James M. Cain?"

"Paradise" (see page 165) is 10,000 words, the longest article Cain ever wrote. And it is not so much vicious as a ruthlessly honest evaluation of the pros and cons of living in California. The vicious piece came next—on Malibu Beach and the movie colony there ("The Widow's Mite") written for Clare Brokaw (later Luce) on *Vanity Fair*.

When "Baby in the Icebox" was published in January of 1933, it also brought Cain his second Hollywood opportunity—this one at Columbia Studios. He was, however, no more successful writing scripts for Harry Cohn than he had been trying to rewrite "The Ten Commandments" for Percy Heath at Paramount. In six weeks he was out of a job again, but now he had a little money in the bank and the success of "Baby" and encouragement from Mencken and Alfred A. Knopf gave him the confidence to try another novel— "a simple story," he wrote Knopf, "laid in California, about a youth who commits the perfect murder with a girl, then has fortune kiss him on the brow, then, gets so bored with her as she murders her former husband every night for the kick it injects into their carnal relations, that he is sunk. That is, he finds that the bond which put such a tingle in their doings in the beginning can also be a chain that he doesn't dare break. An accident saves him the trouble but he is hung for this one anyway. Sounds dull, I suppose, but I might pull it off."

With Vincent Lawrence, a very successful screen writer, helping him, not only pulling if off and also loaning him $1000, Cain wrote the novel eventually titled *The Postman Always Rings Twice*, sent it off to Knopf, then turned again to his magazine journalism, convinced that, at best, *Postman* would make him a little money. "More than 500 novels," he told his wife, "come out every year in this country, and not many of them attract attention. If I sell a couple of thousand copies, get my name in the papers and pick up a little money, we'll be all to the good and I'll try to think of another one."

With the novel behind him, Cain did an article about writing for the studios ("Camera Obscura"), then another about John Garfield Moore ("Tribute to a Hero"), an idol of his childhood in Chestertown—both written for *The Mercury* and his last pieces for Mencken. About that time, he was also approached by B. A. Bergman—who had succeeded him at *The New Yorker*, but was now working for the Hearst syndicate. Bergman asked him to write a two-times-a-week column for Hearst for $85-a-week. Cain would be traveling in good company: Also on Bergman's page were Aldous Huxley, Emil Ludwig, Frank Sullivan, G. K. Chesterton and other equally distinguished authors. Cain's column started well enough, with the first one, in which he discussed novels about the West, being perhaps the most significant (see page 183). Over the next few months, he had further thoughts on the plight of the modern novel, but he also let it be known that he was not writing a literary column, as he picked up on such subjects as formal parties for teenagers (invented by girls, just as sports were invented by boys); the next war (inevitable); catfish sandwiches (ate five and loved them); nostalgic recall of reflections in his World War I observation post; textbooks (they were terrible); homework (he was against it); telephone calls (far too many, especially by teen-age children; recommended installing pay phone in house); tipping (nonexistent in the West, which he applauded); and so on. Cain was a human-interest writer in his column, just as he had been on the *World* editorial page.

But soon he began to detect the same problem he had had writing signed columns for the Sunday *World*. When writing as "the corporate awfulness" of the paper, his editorials had had point, definite style, and they had moved. Writing under his own name he bogged down in awkward self-consciousness. But he did not hear any complaints from Bergman or Hearst—at least not for a while.

Meanwhile, Cain was seriously contemplating a book growing out of his researches about the West. He summed it up to Knopf as "a new history of the

United States," but written "not in terms of government, but in terms of, let us say, conquest. It would trace the movement (across the continent) in terms of great staples, tobacco, cotton, lumber, fur, gold, corn, cocoa, and wheat, and show what happens when these big lodes of export staples begin to run out." He hoped to write it in a year and though his Hearst job would support him. "As a publishing venture," he said, "it will be worth a dozen novels," and added that this project gave him "the first real feeling I have had, of being headed somewhere, since I came here." Knopf liked the idea and gave it his encouragement.

However, before he could start to write an *American History—James M. Cain style,* an event occurred that would change his life forever, the publication of *The Postman Always Rings Tiwce.* The story of this phenomenal little novel which was not only an immediate and controversial bestseller, but a widely acclaimed literary success, has been told many times. And its primary impact on Cain was to make him an overnight literary sensation, sought after not only by the publishers back East, but the movie studios in the West. But, at first, Cain's instincts were still as a journalist and he flabbergasted his agent in New York, Edith Haggard, with a proposal for a series of articles on one of his favorite subjects—food. "With the magazine's world at your feet," she wrote him desperately, "with their hands raised high over their heads pleading with you for short stories, you want to write food articles"—which he did, three of which were published in *Esquire* in 1934 and '35. Another favorite subject was home singing and he too took time out from his fiction efforts to write an article for *The Mercury* on that subject too, which he called "Close Harmony."

However, the pressure from his agent, publisher and the studios, following the success of *The Postman,* for Cain to write stories was too great and for the next three decades he devoted most of his time to either successfully writing novels, magazine serials and short stories, or unsuccessfully trying to write screenplays. In fact, James M. Cain's 17 year career in Hollywood was one of the most unusual in a town famous for unusual careers. While he was trying desperately (at salaries up to $2500-a-week) to turn other people's stories into screenplays (while never achieving a single major movie credit to his name), he was also writing a string of best-selling novels (which other writers were turning into successful screenplays). In all, 15 movies were made from Cain's stories—but he did not do the screenplay for any of them. He did, however, make $130,000 from the sale of his stories to the movies, in addition to the royalties from the books.

Despite the lure of big money from the movie studios and his books, Cain never completely lost his love of journalism. In fact, when he was in his 70s, Cain told someone that he regretted ever giving up editorial writing and wished he had returned to his trade, instead of hanging around the studios trying to make it big in Hollywood. And despite the prodigious amount of fiction he turned out in the three decades following the publication of *The Postman*, he never completely abandoned his non-fiction. Another favorite subject was animals and in 1937 he wrote an article on chinchillas for McCalls; and he continued his column for a couple of years until he proved to his satisfaction—and Hearst's, who ordered him fired—that he could not write a personalized column. He also wrote Prefaces for several of his novels, as well as for the 50th Anniversary Issue of *Who's Who in America* (see page 225) and continued to write about Hollywood and the movies, including a little essay on what was wrong with British films and a series of five articles for *The Screen Writer* and *The Saturday Review* defending his efforts to launch the controversial "America's Author's Authority." This is much too complex a story to tell in detail here, but Cain's essays on this subject reveal that, in addition to everything else, Cain was also an accomplished polemicist. As an illustration, I have included his most important article on this subject (see page 216).

In 1947, Cain quit writing for the studios—in part because his advocacy of the AAA had made him *persona non grata* in Hollywood and, in part, because he wanted to go East to research a trilogy of novels on the civil war he planned. He and his fourth wife, the former opera star Florence Macbeth, settled in Hyattsville, Maryland, and after he had completed his research at the Library of Congress, they made a decision Cain regretted the rest of his life: They decided not to return to Hollywood but settle, instead, in Maryland.

The last 30 years of his life, Cain spent in Hyattsville, Maryland, nursing an ailing wife and trying to regain the spark in his fiction that had been ignited in California. He wrote 11 novels during these years, only five of which were published and none of them achieved the success of the books he wrote in California. And, as his literary career sputtered out, he tried to revive his journalism. He began sending pieces on random subjects to Philip Geyelin, editorial page editor of *The Washington Post*. Ocassionally, Geyelin would use one as a signed column, but most were returned; then finally Cain confessed his reason for submitting the pieces: He wanted to work up a close relationship with Geyelin to make his real pitch, which was "to be taken on as an if-as-and-when-editorial writer for the *Post*, contributing pieces on non-political subjects, like holidays, sporting events, book hits and so on. My trouble as a columnist as a psychological block I've never surmounted, on paper I can't be myself, always having to put my novels in the mouth of some queer characters or else be stiff, self-conscious and queer. But pretending to be the corporate awfulness of the newspaper, I'm in my element." Geyelin declined to hire Cain as an if-as-and-when editorial writer, and it appeared as if James M. Cain, like an old soldier—would never die, but just fade away.

Then, in the early 1970s, Cain experienced what he called his "resurrection." David Madden started it with his James M. Cain study for the

Twayne literary series: Then Tom Wolfe mentioned, in one of his essays, that Norman Mailer should take a few writing lessons from the master of momentum and Knopf re-issued three of Cain's novels with an Introduction by Tom Wolfe (*Cain X 3*) which was widely reviewed and praised; and John Carmody, a *Washington Post* editor, wrote a moving piece for *Potomac* magazine—"James M. Cain At Twilight Time," which was given national syndication.

Cain himself also published a new novel, *Rainbow's End,* which was well received, with most reviewers agreeing with Richard Fuller in *The Philadelphia Inquirer* that Cain still "has the old momentum." Then he published another new book, *The Institute,* which was not as well reviewed, but by now Cain had established a friendship with an assistant *Potomac* editor named Marian Clark, the leader, perhaps, of the James M. Cain fan club at the *Post.* This led to occasional lunches at Trader Vic's in Washington attended by Cain and his chauffeur of the day (usually one of several ladies in Hyattsville who had volunteered to take care of the elderly gentleman) and the *Post* fan club, which included Carmody, Clark, *Potomac* editor Shelby Coffey and writer Kenneth Turan. Cain was in his element: *The Post* writers knew they were lunching with a legend and loved to hear his Hollywood and newspaper stories and ask him questions about writing and writers in the old days, which Cain answered candidly. Coffey also invited Cain to contribute short pieces to *Potomac,* which Cain did and as they grew longer and longer, it was obvious that the old master had lost none of the style he had developed writing for Mencken and Lippmann. Cain's twilight articles for *The Post* were a mixture of nostalgia and personal experiences and, if nothing else, demonstrated that he had finally learned how to write personal casuals, which were not too stiff, self-conscious and queer, as he had described his earlier efforts.

The best of Cain's *Post* articles was the tribute to Walter Lippmann which attracted widespread attention and delighted Cain. When Carey McWilliams, editor of *The Nation,* read the piece and wrote Cain asking him to contribute to his magazine, Cain replied that he would meditate on it (he eventually declined) and said he was pleased to find "the old worse war horse could still jump to the sound of the bell and send it out in two days, that being *Potomac's* deadline they slapped on me."

I also read Cain's Lippman piece when it appeared and was pleasantly surprised to learn not only that he was alive, well and living only a few minutes of Washington Beltway driving away from me, but that he had had a long life in journalism as well as his literary and Hollywood career—all of which seemed to make him a natural subject for a biography. I assumed, however, that someone must already be writing it—or that he was working on his memoirs. But I called him and found that neither was the case. "I don't believe any man should write his autobiography," he told me, "unless he can give it the same subtitle Booker T. Washington gave his: *Or, Up from Slavery*. Unless you can say that, you've got no story to tell." He eventually agreed to me writing his biography, which took me almost four years and was published by Holt Rinehart and Winston in 1982.

As Cain faded into his last years, he was obsessed by the urge to write: "I'm just a has-been," he wrote one friend, "a senior citizen waiting for the clock to strike. I don't mind the clock, but waiting for it and doing nothing else terrifies me."

To keep from just looking at the clock, he continued writing—a novel called *Cloud 9* (recently published), another one, *The Cocktail Waitress* (never published), his memoirs (never completed) and his articles for *The Washington Post*. And he wrote until the very end: "I always intend not to, then I do work," he told me in one of my first interviews with him. "I go upstairs about eleven, although sometimes I sit down here thinking about what I'm going to write.... I get about six pages-a-day now at the typewriter, and that poops me out. But six pages is about 2,000 words and that's what any writer regards as a day's work.... I finish writing about two o'clock. Then I come down and sit twiddling my thumbs for about twenty mintues, then I fix my lunch.... I seem to have a zest for writing. I can't say I enjoy it. Anyone who enjoys writing can't write. It's laborious and frustrating. But it excites me and possesses me, no less so today than it did 50 years ago."

I asked him if he had ever waivered from his decision to become a writer, made in 1914, sitting on a bench in Lafayette Park, across from the White House: A low laugh came up out of his throat and became louder. Shaking his head he said: "Hell, yes, a hundred times. Every now and then, I used to say: 'For Christ's sake, why don't you become a carpenter, or something?' But I'm still at it."

James M. Cain kept at it steadily from 1917 until 1977, finishing his last piece ("American My Foot") and sending it to *The Post* just before he died.

Tribute to a Hero
(The American Mercury, November 1970)

In the year 1903 my father was elevated to the presidency of Washington College, at Chestertown, Md., having previously been vice-president of St. John's College at Annapolis. So that Summer he put us on a steamboat, took us across Chesapeake Bay, and invited us to survey our new place of residence.

I think we all felt the same way about it. It had, to be sure, certain agreeable features. There were rose bushes in our yard, and pear trees, and a walnut tree, and a grape arbor; there were neighbors with horses, who came with grins on their faces and invited us to take a ride; there were farmers with peach orchards, who told us to help ourselves, and apparently meant it. But when all this had been duly inventoried and marked on the pleasant side of the ledger, there were other entries in red which gave us great uneasiness, and which struck at parts of our natures much deeper than could be reached by flowers, horses, or the freshest of fruit.

There was, for example, the matter of the lower campus. At St. John's, to say nothing of the Naval Academy, the grass was mown to the semblance of green velvet. But here it grew as high as your knees: daisies were mixed with it, as well as bumble bees, and altogether it presented a distressingly unkempt appearance. Two or three weeks after we got there a man showed up and announced that he had the contract to cut it for the hay. He cut it, and Brown, the college janitor, trimmed around the trees with a scythe. In the hay I caught a young rabbit. After feeding it lettuce and pondering its destiny, I turned it loose. A rabbit is a big event in the life of a boy of eleven, and yet I couldn't help reflecting that it was an odd sort of beast to be gamboling on a college campus.

Then there was the windmill, with an auxiliary engine in its basement. The college was perched high on a big hill, so high that it couldn't make use of the town water-supply. This explained the windmill, but it didn't dispose of the windmill's bucolic appearance. Nothing could dispose of the boardwalk that led down the campus to the town. Even the smallest of us children knew that a college walk should be of brick. There were the stoves in the students' rooms, which betrayed that this college didn't even have steam heat. Then there were queer things about the town itself. It had no saloons. My father seemed to understand, but the rest of us had never heard of local option, and it seemed strange to see the family liquor arrive by boat in a five-gallon demijohn.

My sister Virginia named this the Dominus Vobiscum. The neck of the demijohn, where it stuck out from the box, was protected by two pieces of wood, nailed at an angle to form a little tent. She said they looked like the hands of the priest, as he stood ready to dispense the blessing. This struck us all as a nifty, and even now any liquor *en gros* is referred to in the house as a Dominus Vobiscum.

There were no cabs. There was the Voshell House hack, which met the trains and the steamboat, but it was built like the Toonerville Trolley, and it had no magnificent fellow with crashing whip and high silk hat on the front seat. Simon, the colored gentleman who drove it, beat his single horse with a stumpy buggy whip, and wore a cap with a patent leather visor.

There was no boathouse. At Annapolis, I had done all my swimming at the Severn River Boat Club, where we dived off the springboard and climbed out on the float, disdaining anything but deep water. Odd as it sounds, in all these years for swimming I had touched bottom only once. It was at low tide, and I had swum around to the shoreward side of the float, where there was a sandbar. My foot scraped sand, and it almost scared me to death. I think it was the first time it had occurred to me that a river had a bottom.

But at Chestertown it was all bottom. You undressed in the bushes, with flies and gnats buzzing around; you waded in, limping over shells, stones, mud or grass; you started to swim with no crisp plunge to begin with; you came out and shook the ants out of your clothes before you dressed. The other boys didn't seem to mind, but I hated it. I was annoyed, too, at the way they swam. If, perchance, there did happen to be a boat that they could dive from, they went off holding their noses, came up swimming dog fashion, and in other ways showed that they had no idea how the thing should be done.

Then they had customs that didn't make sense to me. When they met you they said "H'y." "What in the world," we asked each other at home, "is this 'H'y' that they yell at you?" We said "Hello," and mulishly stuck to it. It was years later before I realized that "H'y" was supposed to be "How are you?" They went down every night to see the steamboat come in. I went down, too, but when the exciting business of landing was over, with the hawser in and the gangplank out, I was ready to go up for a chocolate soda. I couldn't understand why they stuck around to see the passengers come off. I didn't know then that it was news if Dr. Twilley came home with a steel fishing pole, or Mr. Bacchus with a new suit of clothes.

What I got out of it, in addition to the landing, was the lights of the boat as she came into view below the town. They were pretty, but they got me in trouble. Having grown up around Annapolis harbor, I innocently referred to them as the port and starboard lights, causing some mirth among my companions. They began to bandy the words around, but with an annoying confusion as to which was which. I suggested they could remember the port light by port wine. This drew a blank. They had never heard of port wine.

At parties they permitted themselves to be shoved out to tread in idiotic measure called the Virginia Reel. In Annapolis we had been dressed up now and then and sent to things called germans, where we marched around and got ice-cream if we kept in line. They were unpleasant, but not insulting to the intelligence. But this thing was a palpable phoney. My father, however, seemed to understand it, and out of his snickers I got the explanation. These people, although they held their noses when they dived, and said "H'y," and raced home from the steamboat to tell who had been to the city that day, and in other ways exhibited the familiar symptoms of yokelry, all prided themselves on their fine Southern blood. If there was one thing my father detested it was fine Southern blood. I do, myself. It gives me the pip.

Then there was the church, which brought us presently to the decision to pull out of it, as at heart we weren't Catholics at all, but merely *Feinschmecker* of Catholicism. In Annapolis we hadn't thought about it, for there the faith was professed in an impressive way, with a convent on one side of the church and a monastery on the other, and all services mounted in a manner worthy of Ziegfeld. But here High Mass was a farce painful to behold. The priest was tone deaf, and did nothing but harangue the congregation about money. The choir couldn't sing, and was always muffing its cues. Once, when the organ started the introduction to the offertory, the lady who was to sing it whispered in panic to my mother that it wasn't the one she had learned. My mother picked up the music, adjusted her glasses, and sang it at sight.

It was the first time it dawned on me that she must be good. I knew she had a voice, an enormous thing that could trill and do acrobatics that other ladies apparently couldn't do, and I knew that for years she had been a professional singer. These, though, were facts I had grown up with and never thought much about. But when she stood up there that time, and put on a show that to me was black magic, I knew she must have something. What got me wasn't that she could do it, but that she knew she could do it. If that got me, the other side of it got me too, in reverse. For that woman, her face chalky and her voice quacking from fright, I had nothing but contempt. She was like all the rest of these people. She couldn't do anything right. She couldn't even learn the right offertory.

This place, then, made us uncomfortable. It violated all our ideas of how things ought to be done, and in obscure ways was at odds with our scheme of life. It was a hick place, while we were incorrigibly of the city, with all of the city dweller's love of agreeable superficialities: smartness, competence, and class. Alas, I fear it still is a hick place. My father got it policed up after a while, with the grass cut and the windmill removed and steam heat installed and brick walks all around, and a couple of new buildings to fatten its leanness, and Henry Powell Hopkins, an architect of real attainments, invested it with a great deal of charm.

But these changes, apparently, were all on the surface. After my father left, it reverted to type at an appalling rate of speed. Co-education, which he despised as the first earmark of the Methodist ethic, and managed almost to extinguish, has got the upper hand again, and the place is over-run with a lot of twittering girls. The climax of the year, I judge from the literature that reaches me, comes when the college is host to a convention of preachers. Mark one up for my father on that. He never wanted anybody around that wouldn't take a drink.

II

After the pears had been eaten, the swimming sampled, and the steamboat given the once-over, all business was suspended, so far as I was concerned, until one paramount point had been settled. Did this college have a football team or didn't it? And boy, I was hard to fool there! I came from a place where footballs grew on every tree, and I knew the stuff when I saw it. So when I went down to the field, the afternoon they held the first practice, I knew what to look for.

What I saw was a dreadful shock. Only two or three of the candidates were what I considered the proper size, and even these didn't have the right look on their faces. The suits were appalling. Several canvas jackets were on view, although canvas jackets had been obsolete since the Battle of Manila. Some of the stockings were black with maroon rings, some were maroon with black rings, some were plain maroon, and some were plain black. This was truly alarming. Football is a peculiar sport. Cost what may, it must have class. For this, there is good reason. As the mettle of a regiment can be estimated by the condition of its equipment and the way it salutes, so the mettle of a football team can be estimated by the condition of its gear and the snap with which it goes about its work. This outfit had no gear, and God knows it had no snap.

It practiced with a lot of noisy gabbling. It tackled around the neck. It hit the line with its belly. It took big slugs of water between scrimmages. And the cheering section, when it was assembled for a work-out some days later, was even worse. Girls were admitted to the rite, and ruined it with their shrill yipping. The place didn't even have a song. St. John's had a song. Adolph Torovsky, leader of the Marine Band, had seen to that, and composed a beauty. But not this place. Only some miserable version of "A Hot Time in the Old Town," with allusions to the Maroon and Black.

Presently my father went down to have a look at the practice. And if I was hard to fool, he was impossible to fool. He had learned his football at Yale, in the days when Camp really had his mind on it, and he had vastly increased his knowledge at

Annapolis. For years, as a sort of sideline to his teaching, he had coached the St. John's team, and St. John's was pretty good then, as any old-timer will tell you. I take exception to many of my father's notions, for example his notion that he can make a speech. But one thing that I have to hand him is that he knows football. Even now, at the age of seventy-three, he could take charge of a squad of gorillas in September and bring home a winner. So when he spoke, God was talking.

"They're a sad lot," he said, as he twisted a lemon peel over his drink before dinner. "St. John's will murder them."

"Why do they talk so much?" I asked.

"That's something you'll learn when you stay on the Eastern Shore a while. All these towns have some kind of bush-league baseball team, and most of these boys play ball in Summer. In bush-league baseball, you're supposed to talk it up, as they call it."

"What for?"

"God knows."

"Haven't they any suits?"

"The suits are bad, but maybe we can fix that."

"Why do they tackle around the neck?"

"Ah, why do they? But all that, that's not the worst of it. They don't play hard. That's the toughest thing to teach a football team. Plays are easy. One play is as good as another, so far as that goes, if you can execute it. But to get them to jump into every play with every ounce they've got, that's something else. I've nagged teams till they cried, but you can't win football games taking it easy. That's what this gang hasn't found out yet. They'll find out."

He sipped his drink, shook his head, and sighed. In justice to him, I must say he always tried to regard football as nothing more than a game, but down deep inside, he loved it.

"Still," he said after a while, "there's one boy out there that might be a football player."

"Which one is that?"

"His name is Moore. I like the way he goes about it."

That was the first I heard of Mr. James Garfield Moore. I was out there next day and spotted him. He had none of the big, raw-boned look that I associated with football. He was compactly made, with the neat, precise movements of a tightrope walker. His head was smallish, and round, and covered with silky sorrel hair. Even in his football clothes there was a touch of fastidiousness about his get-up. His manner was one of bored fretfulness, and altogether he seemed as unpromising a candidate for fullback as I had ever seen. I so reported before dinner that night.

"That," said my father, "is because you do nothing but watch the man with the ball. There are eleven men out there, and you must learn to see them all. Didn't you notice how he helped Hitch through the line that time he went down for a touchdown?"

"Were you out there?"

"I dropped by for a minute."

"Hitch is fast."

"Hitch is fast, but that won't help him if he doesn't shake loose. He made the touchdown, but Moore put him through the hole."

This, I have to explain, was before guiding the runner through a hole was prohibited under the rules. At that time, it was an important part of the play.

"But he's a little guy."

"He's not as little as you think. That skimpy suit makes him look small, but there's a good stocky boy inside of it. Always notice a man with those sloping shoulders. They come from big ropes of muscle leading down from the neck. He's got good powerful legs too. And he plays hard. He's got that quick, nervous energy that a football player has to have. There never was a good one without it. And God in Heaven, he keeps his mouth shut."

All that season, both before and after the predicted St. John's fiasco, I watched him, and I couldn't see anything. Occasionally, I would note a quick plunge through the line, but beyond that nothing. It wasn't until the next season, indeed, in a game with Western Maryland, that I saw what my father saw. I was within a few feet of the sidelines, and a Western Maryland runner started around, toward where I was standing, on a wide end run. Moore, from his fullback position, came up and forced him out and back. The runner cut in, or as the modern newspaper jargon has it, reversed his field. Moore left his feet. I think it was the hardest tackle I ever saw. They landed with a terrific thud at my feet, and both men were out cold. As they jerked Moore's headgear off and sponged his head, my first feeling was of paralyzed, frightened wonder. It seemed amazing that such a sleek little pate could command an act of such electric ferocity.

Then, after play was resumed and my wits returned, this was succeeded by a surge of gratitude, of exultation, of downright worship. Here was a guy who could do it the way they did it at Annapolis. Here was a guy who could do it so it lifted you, gave you that incomparable ecstasy, made you feel that man after all was a god. Here was a guy, *one* guy in this whole God-forsaken, lousy hick country, that could do it right.

III

That was the year he was captain. He wasn't a senior, you understand. As I recall, he was a special, which meant he was so twisted up on his studies that the faculty couldn't classify him. But this college was so benighted it had never heard of electing a senior as captain of the team. It did that the way it did everything else. It elected anybody at all, and then wondered why it didn't win any games.

So the next year he was back, but then the most dreadful rumors began to circulate about him. It seemed there were dark matters the year before, which had been kept secret by the team, for the sake of appearances. It seemed that he had been something less than an inspiration to his men. It seemed he had been all right on the field, but that before the games he was so "nervous" he was a demoralizing influence. And it seemed, most horrible of all, that "nervous" wasn't exactly what was meant. I fought this off. I wouldn't believe it. I got into acrimonious wrangles, and quoted my father, who ought to know, to the effect that this was one of the really great football players, and how could such a one be "nervous"? Alas, it was only too true. I heard it from the great man himself. He sat on the steps of West Hall one day, and explained to all within earshot why he wasn't going to play that year.

"What the hell?" he demanded to know. "I don't like the game. I hate it. It gets me so bad I can't even sleep nights. Why should I go out there? I had to do it last year, because I was captain. But I'm not captain any more. All I do is set the rest of them crazy, and it's better if I quit. I'm not going out any more. I wouldn't go out for a million dollars."

He encountered a stony silence. But my father, that night, seemed strangely unmoved by his perfidy. "The trouble with Moore," he said, "is that he doesn't like football. I suppose that's what comes of being a voluptuary."

"What's a voluptuary?"

"A voluptuary is one to whom the Fall of the year means Indian Summer instead of football. He'd rather sit in the sun with some girl than go out there and take it on the shins."

"They say he's yellow."

"Who says so?"

"Everybody."

"I bet you the team didn't say so. Well, you tell them to find me ten more men as yellow as he is, and I'll beat Yale. Yellow, for God's sake! That guy—yellow!"

That didn't help any, and there was to be worse, and more of it. Our big game that year, the one we were to wind up our season with, was with Maryland Agricultural College, what is now the University of Maryland, at College Park. St. John's, for some reason, wasn't scheduled. And two weeks before the game, an ominous piece of news appeared in the papers. Maryland had not only cleaned up the other teams it had met, but had actually beaten St. John's. St. John's, the invincible, had been drubbed by the incredible score of 27-5. And some days later there appeared an item to the effect that while Maryland regarded the Washington game as more or less of a foregone conclusion, it was going to bring the whole squad over as a reward for faithful practice. These would not be required to put on suits. They would function merely as rooters. There would be thirty of them, count them, thirty. And when I read that, I could hear their teeth grinding, and their ugly snouts chanting fee-fie-fo-fum.

They came. They came on a special boat, tumbled over the side, fell smartly into line, and marched up through the town. They wore gray uniforms and blue overcoats. It was the first I knew that Maryland was a military college, and it was a disturbing discovery. For St. John's, gallant St. John's that had been lately licked by this outfit, was a military college too, and so was the Navy. The brass buttons, somehow, knew how to handle leather. Behind the rooters, at a more leisurely pace, came the team. They looked like giants, and some of them I had heard about. There was Church, the center, and Bowland, one of the guards, and Barney Cooper, a halfback. Barney lived at Worston, near Chestertown, yet he had treasonably gone to Maryland instead of Washington. Years later, talking with him, I learned with complete astonishment that he had gone there to study agriculture.

And there was Curley Byrd, now coach at Maryland, and a terrifying apparition. He was tall, and as the saying goes, built like a whip. He had a startlingly handsome face, with big, flashing eyes, a splotch of florid red on each cheek, and a mane of black curly hair, from which he derives his nickname. His real name is Clifton Byrd, but he has long since bowed to the inevitable and become Curley. He looked like Rupert of Hentzau, and had all of that worthy's cold, sinister resolution about everything that he did.

After the team came Professor Richardson and Professor Spence, and them I escorted up to the house for the football lunch. It was a gay occasion, with the air full of the aroma of Turkish cigarettes and spiced cocktails, to me still the football smell. My mother, with fine bravado, bet Professor Richardson a box of candy on the outcome of the game, and he, after a show of hating to take such easy loot, accepted the wager. We children were awe-stricken at my mother's audacity. Even Professor Spence seemed a little impressed.

But after all, why not? For James Garfield Moore had consented to play. He didn't consent with any great grace, to be sure, but on the Thursday before the game he had come out, and stood around sourly while Henry Wilson tried to explain to him the signals and infuriated Halbert, the coach. Halbert had been imported from St. John's that year, and he wasn't used to any such goings on. But Halbert had never seen Moore play, so it made no difference what he thought. The main point was that he was to be in the game, so I left the house in a happy frame of mind, even with a slight tingle over the box of candy.

When I got out on the upper terrace, the team was there, dressed and ready to take the field. Halbert was there, his face white with rage. And Moore was there, all dressed up in the new suit that had been ordered by wire from Spalding's. But what a shocking spectacle! His face was green, and it twitched as though some invisible battery were shooting charges into it. He was slumped against a tree, as though unable to stand up. His mouth was half open, and around it foamed white, cottony spit. And he kept saying, in a dull, whining monotone:

"I can't do it. I can't play, I tell you. Oh, for God's sake, let me alone. I can't play. I can't do it. Why can't you leave me alone?..."

I walked on. It wasn't his face. It wasn't the way he leaned. It wasn't what he said. It was the spit. That awful foam around his lips told its own story. It made me sick.

IV

Washington—17		Maryland—0
Raisin	L.E.	Byrd
White	L.T.	Russnar
Maddox	L.G.	Hatten
McMaster	C.	Church
Voss	R.G.	Bowland
Gibson	R.T.	Iglehart
Long (capt.)	R.E.	Bosley
Wilson	Q.B.	Galt
McGinnes	R.H.B.	McNutt
Hitch	L.H.B.	Cooper
Moore	F.B.	Firor

Referee: Neilson. Umpire: Massey. Linesmen: Maryland, Parker; Washington, Porter. Touchdowns: Moore, McGinnes (2). Goals after touchdown: White (2).

I went down to the field, and stood around miserably during the preliminaries, which seemed to take intolerably long. Our team trotted through signals, and no sign of Moore. The Maryland team trotted through signals, and still no sign of him. Maryland lined up to kick off, Washington to receive. And then, all of a sudden, there he was, down under the goal-posts, spacing them out, getting them ready, with all his old fretful impatience, just as he used to be before this miserable business started.

Something had happened up on the terrace. I wasn't there, but I found out later what it was. The team had gone down. Long, the captain, and McGinnes lingered, hoping still that they might be able to get him out there. And then my father, late as usual, came bustling along on his way to the game. Moore looked at him, as though here at last was one who would understand, who would touch him on the shoulder and say, Go thou to the showers, who would give him the pity that he so deeply craved. And this is what he got:

"Well God damn it, Moore, make up your mind. Don't stand there slobbering like a baby."

He wheeled around, stared after my father, wiped his mouth. Long and McGinnes seized him, to rush him down on the field by main force. He shook them off. He buttoned his headgear and charged down on the field under his own steam. And as he went he snarled, "I'll show the long-legged——if I'm a baby or not."

The few seconds before that kick-off are high tide in all my recollections of football. I can't convey to you the effect of those hands, as he spaced the men out where he wanted them, nor the obedience they commanded. Mind you, he didn't know a signal, for Wilson's efforts to explain them to him had been a complete flop. He was barely familiar with the plays, and he was quite out of condition. That made no difference. All authority on that field, Halbert's authority, Long's authority, had dissolved into his authority. Stories of the Little Corporal and his hold on his troops have been credible to me since then. Such leadership is not based on inspiration, or on any of the gaudy things that the layman always imagines. It is based on trust, that simple, childlike faith which knows it is not going to be let down.

The kick was a little to one side. McGinnes took it, and ran it out to about the twenty-yard line. Washington's ball, first down, five yards to go. Then there was a hitch. From the sidelines, we couldn't tell what it was, but afterward we learned this was it:

Wilson: Eighty-five, ninety-seven, forty-one, sixty-two.
Moore: Signal!
Wilson: Eighty-five, ninety-seven, forty-one—
Moore: Quit yelling them goddam numbers and gimme the ball! I'm going through right guard.

Through right guard it was. If the Maryland line had been made of paper he couldn't have smashed it quicker. He wasn't a hurdler, or a twister, or a dodger. He was a true line plunger, a very rare breed. He came up to it, there was the impact, he was through, he was driving straight ahead, a string of tumbling tacklers behind him, he was down. He did it, my father said, by his unerring instinct for the hole, that place between two struggling players which could be struck, and if properly struck, would yield.

Ten yards that time, and once more the hands were spacing them out. This time McGinnes took it, the hands on his hips, shooting him off tackle for five yards. McGinnes once more, and another five yards. First down, five to go, the ball about on the Washington forty-yard line. The hands took command again, and Moore plunged the line. There was the same impact, the split second of suspense, the catch of the breath as he went through, the line of tumbling tacklers behind. But this time he didn't go down. He shook clear, and was off down the field. The Maryland quarterback dived, and tackled empty air. Moore was down under the goal-posts, hugging the ball for the first touchdown of the day. George White kicked goal. Score: Washington 6, Maryland 0, and the game not yet five minutes under way.

Maryland kicked off again, and once more their line was crumpled. But this time Moore let McGinnes, Hitch, and Wilson do most of it. McGinnes and Hitch, brother of the first Hitch we had had, would go slicing off tackle, and always the hands would be at their hips, guiding them, helping them, shooting them through the hole. Under those ancient rules, Wilson, as quarterback, had to go out five yards when he carried the ball, and Moore would be ahead of him taking him around. He was a beautiful blocker. He could take a man out with neat precision, then go on, still in the play himself. Once he took Byrd out, and that was the last of Byrd. Byrd, one of the greatest athletes that ever put on a suit, had to be replaced with a player named Wilson.

McGinnes made a second touchdown, and George White again kicked goal. He made a third, but this time George missed. The score at the end of the first half was: Washington 17, Maryland 0. Then, however, a bad thing happened. Moore, being all out of condition, folded up. He couldn't play any more, and was replaced by Bob Gill. Maryland sensed that the change meant weakness, and started a desperate battle to score. Three times they drove for a touchdown, but they had as well have tried to make it through a cage of wildcats. The power, the cunning, the skill for offensive play might be gone, but the spirit was still there. After what Moore had done for them, that team wasn't going to wash out on him. They didn't. It was almost dark when the game was over, but at the end the score was still 17-0.

V

So ended the first chapter of my life at Chestertown. Washington College at last had done it. It had been the brass buttons. Nay, it had beaten the brass buttons. But more importantly, a great man had come through, had proved he was really great. Did you ever have that happen to you? It is like nothing else in this world. It can happen only when you are young, for when you get older there are no more great men. Yet if it does happen to you, it stays with you through life, and warms you when you think of it. To me now, football is of as little consequence as anything I can imagine, and a football player rather less than a superman. Just the same, I lay this wreath at his feet unashamed, as he still seems great to me.

P.S. Charley Richardson, when you read this, you had better come across with that box of candy. It will be twenty-eight years late, but even so it will greatly improve your standing in certain quarters. The address is 201 Hawthorne Road, Baltimore, Md., and the acceptable brand is Whitman's Sampler Package.

Silent Night—1918
(*The Washington Post, December, 1974*)

Christmas, 1918, in France, is the one I best remember, but it really started September 30 of that year, when my division, the 79th, was being hauled back from the front, after four days in the Meuse-Argonne Offensive, for a little R and R, as it came to be called later—actually, for a little reorganization, so our parts could find each other, grow together again, and return for more fighting. My outfit was the Headquarters Troop, and we were slogging along on foot, our packs on a truck, when a small plane flew over. Dropping newspapers, L'Echo de Paris, all over the road. Several soldiers, knowing I could read French, came running with them to me, to find out what they said. The big headlines were all about the Bulgarian request for an armistice. It was, I thought, a tremendous piece of news, and after translating I popped off excitedly: "Hey, hey, hey! This thing's almost over! We're in sight of the end!"

"Us and who else?" demanded a soldier, known to us as Bryan, as he'd been born in 1896, and named for the great Commoner—he could recite the Cross of Gold speech by heart, and often, unfortunately did. But his last name I never knew. "Read what it says," he went on, "—and leave out all them damn yelps."

"But it's a crack in their wall!"

"Crack, crack, crack! Three more krauts bit the mud."

One thing led to another, but to his great surprise, the other soldiers were on my side, and wanted to hear more about when the war would end. At last, fed up by his gibes, one of them said: "Why don't you shut his mouth for him, Cain? Tell him say it with money? Tell him why don't he bet?" So taunted, Bryan did offer to bet, daring me, since I knew so much, to name a date and the amount I would lay to back it. I chose December 1, in the amount of ten francs, and, quite derisively, he accepted. But word of the bet got around, and I became more and more popular, spreading the word as I did, of the light at the end of our tunnel, and the possibility, at least, that we might soon see a rosier sky.

We reformed, went back in the lines, and fought on, and I would see Bryan daily, and listen to his gibes. And then one day he was gone. At Vachereauville, he was led out from the dugout, along with twenty others, including Captain Madeira, blind, after a mustard gas attack. I would have been led out too, except I had found for myself an extra-big gas mask for my extra-big face, so I could keep it on for the whole two hours the shells kept dropping around. And then, a week or so later, there was General Kuhn, out on the road with his aides, looking at his watch, nodding, and striding back to his dugout: The war was over. Now a great deal has been written as to what went on that night, the whooping, the hollering, the singing, the drinking, and the amounts of liquor consumed, but what actually happened was: nothing. In the first place, nobody believed it. By eleven o'clock, no guns had been firing, and after eleven they still weren't. So what? It was dismissed as one more mess-line rumor, G.H.Q. rumor, or latrine rumor, of which there had been a thousand, each one sillier than the last. In the second place, it rained. But the next night was something else again, something to remember till the day you die. We were suddenly detailed, a dozen of us under Corporal Riebel, to go up and clean out a German P.C. (post-of-Command as we called it then, later changed to Command Post by some genius in the Defense Department—for such inspirations we pay out our money).

But sweeping, to Cain, was never a pleasurable exercise, and slick conniving was. So, knowing Riebel's weakness for eating, I offered to go out, to the various infantry P.C.s then being set up nearby, collect the making for flapjacks, along with the syrup and butter, in return for exemption from work. At first Riebel said no, but then sorely tempted, he put it to a vote. Unanimously the soldiers said "Go!" and I took a gunny sack, got a sad look on my face, and faced the mess-sergeants that by now were encamped all over a great bottom land, with a river running through it, that the German P.C. looked down on. We didn't know it then, but we were actually in Germany, and the river was the Moselle, a world-renowned stream, celebrated for Wein, Weiber, und Gesang. My quest was completely successful, my gunny sack being so big as to make my loot look small and thin and pitiful, so each sergeant would throw in a little bit extra, to help out this out-of-luck. Headquarters detail, caught out by itself with no rations—at least I said it was. They kicked in with the flapjacks, and makings; also with bacon, a whole flitch, potatoes, beef, sugar, condensed milk, and a can of instant coffee, so the spit ran out of Riebel's mouth when I returned in late afternoon. Oddly, it was the coffee that interested the soldiers most—after months of tired mess-kitchen stuff, the prospect of one decent cup was highly exciting to all, and Riebel was besought to "make it strong enough, will you, so it don't taste no more like dishwater?" So Riebel, who took charge of the cooking himself, made it strong, a little too strong, it turned out.

For the instant coffee of that era knew not the decaffeinization process that later prevailed and was almost pure caffiene. Or in other words, it was a heart stimulant of frightening strenth. We ate our flapjacks as cooked by Riebel, our beef stew with potatoes, and then had our reaction. We staggered out on the boardwalk the P. C. fronted on, and went capering up and down, yelling, laughing, singing, and comparing ourselves like idiots. But down below, an even madder scene went on. For the ration trucks weren't the only ones that caught up with the infantry regiments, now on their way to Germany. Also, from the rear echelons, had come the trucks with band instruments on them. And also, raised up on high by God, came the brightest moon I ever saw. And then, for one night, I knew what joy felt like, the purest, most innocent joy I had ever imagined—thousands of doughboys, as we called them then, out under the moon, listening to their bands play music, and watching while their signal details shoe off their ammunition—starshells, all sorts of shells, in all sorts of beautiful colors. The mere recollection of it still makes me shiver.

No, I haven't forgotten Bryan.

As I said, he was led out as Vachereauville, and then vanished completely, to reappear in front of me, on the wall of a bridge at Dugny, where I was eating dinner. It was Christmas dinner, for our orders, how did you guess it, had been countermanded, so we didn't go up into Germany after all, but stuck around Northern France, the Headquarters Troop in a village we'd been in before, for a few dreary days in mid-summer—to spend nights without stars, and days without sun, so it always seemed to be ten o'clock in the morning or four in the afternoon. And now it was Christmas, with scum being served for dinner, and there I was eating it on the stone wall of a bridge, when I looked up and there was Bryan. "Hello, Cain," he said glumly. "I was wondering if you'd be here. I've made you goddam famous."

"Yeah?" I answered. "If so, how?"

"You know how. Spreading it, what you said—the bet we made that day. I been telling them guys in hospital. They all know who you are."

"What hospital they have you in?"

Would I know? Does it make any difference which one? Some goddam place— Souilly I guess it was. For six weeks I couldn't see. Today they sent me back. I think they're shipping me out."

"Some people are born lucky."

"Listen, Cain: Is it true?--

"Is the war over or not?"

"Well, don't tell me you didn't hear?"

"If I did would I be asking? In hospital, with your eyes bandaged up, you don't see nothing, and they got no time to tell you. They put your plate on your belly and run, and sometimes they empty your pot. And that's all. I asked you—"

"Yes, of course it's over."

"Then say how it was, why don't you? It all looks the same to me. Here's where we were before, and here's where we are now. I don't hear no guns, but I didn't used to, before. Not here in this place—further up it was different. But—"

"O.K., then, I'll tell you."

I told him, about as I've told it here, with attention to the moon, the Roman candle effect of the star-shells, and the music. "What songs they play?" he wanted to know.

"Oh, you know: "Over There," "K-K-K Katy." "Last Long Mile," "I'm All Bound Round"—same old ones, no change. On the "Long Long Trail," the guys all joined in."

"I would have. I love that song, Cain—you know, "Land of my Dreams," I know the words by heart...So, they played stuff. What then?"

"They blew Taps."

"...Yeah, they would."

He closed his messkit, got up, and said: "I got to see him before he goes back." And then, as I must have looked blank, a bit impatiently: "That drive—so he can tell them, when he goes back, them other guys in hospital, what you just told me—they'll know if you said it's so. I told you you're famous down there. I'll give you your ten francs if my pay ever catches up—it's been chasing me around. And thanks, Cain—you've made Christmas for me."

He left, and I never saw him again, or heard from him, or got my ten francs. I don't know if he's living or dead, though with mustard gas in your lungs, you didn't live long, as a rule. But I like to remember that once I made somebody's Christmas.

The Battle Ground of Coal
(*The Atlantic Monthly*, October, 1922)

I

As you leave the Ohio River at Kenova and wind down the Norfolk and Western Railroad beside the Big Saridy and Tug rivers, you come into a section where there is being fought the fiercest and most unrelenting war in modern industrial history. The country furnishes a suitable setting. Rocky hills, small mountains, rise on each side. They are gashed by 'creeks'; looking at these, you see that the wild region stands for miles back from the railroad. There is no soft, mellow outline about these hills. They are sharp and jagged; about their tops grows a stunted scraggly forest. Their color is raw: glaring reds and yellows, hard, watersoaked grays. Here and there you see the blue-black ribbon of coal.

In this untamed section of West Virginia two tremendous forces have staked out a battle ground. These are the United Mine Workers of America and the most powerful group of non-union coal-operators in the country. It is a battle to the bitter end; neither side asks quarter, neither side gives it. It is a battle for enormous stakes, on which money is lavished; it is fought through the courts, through the press, with matching of sharp wits to secure public approval. But more than this, it is actually fought with deadly weapons on both sides; many lives have already been lost; many may yet be forfeited.

As the train carries you southeastward, you see some signs of it. You pass many coal mines, and some of these are closed down. At the stations, pairs of men in military uniform scrutinize all who alight. These are the West Virginia State Police; a strong force of them is on duty here, for bloodshed became so frequent that one of these counties, Mingo, was placed under martial law. You pass occasional clusters of tents— squalid, wretched places, where swarms of men, women, and children are quartered. Everywhere you are sensible of an atmosphere of tension, covert alertness, sinister suspicion. It is not by accident that these State policemen appear always in pairs.

If you get off the train at Williamson, county seat of Mingo, you will be at the fighting front. People there will tell you that this struggle has been going on for three years. They will tell you of the bloody day at Matewan, May 19, 1920, when ten men, including the mayor of the town, fell in a pistol battle that lasted less than a minute. They will tell you of guerrilla warfare that went on for months; how Federal troops had to be called in twice. They will tell you of the 'three days' battle, which resulted, in May, 1921, in the declaration of martial law. Union partisans will tell you of the exercises on May 30 last, when the graves of a score of union fallen were decorated with all the ceremony accorded soldiers who have died for the flag. The operators will tell you of attacks from ambush: how their men have been shot down from behind; how witnesses for trials were mysteriously killed before they could testify. The atrocity list and quantity of propaganda give this war quite an orthodox flavor. It is very hard to sift out the truth.

II

Back in 1898, when the coal industry was quite as unsettled as it is now, the union and the big operators evolved a working plan to stablize conditions and equalize opportunity. This was the conference in the Central Competitive Field, whereby a wage scale was arrived at for this region, and scales in all other union districts were computed by using this scale as a basis and making allowances for different operating conditions, freight rates, and so forth. This was in order to give all districts an equal chance at the market. Coal is probably the most fluid commodity sold: coal from one section competes with coal from another section remote from the first. It is not analogous to a trade-marked article, for which an arbitrary price can be obtained by advertising campaign and kindred methods. No amount of advertising can make coal of a given grade from one section outsell the same grade from another section at a higher price. This peculiarity of the coal market was the reason for the basic wage-scale arrangement which gave all districts as nearly equal chances as possible, and precluded the possibility that a miscalculated rate might put whole mining fields out of business altogether.

The plan worked fairly well for a time. Within a few years, however, it was discovered that large new areas of coal lands had been developed, and that most of these were being worked with nonunion labor. They had been left out of the original calculation largely because the existence of such large virgin fields was not known until after the opening of the present century. Some of them were in Pennsylvania, but most, and by far the largest, were in southern West Virginia. Employing nonunion labor, they worked at a lower wage-scale than the union areas, and had become a formidable factor in the industry, for they were underselling union coal constantly. In the years just preceding the war, their effect on the market—and particularly the greater number of days their labor worked during the year—had become definitely noticeable. During the war, there was demand for everybody's coal, and there was no pinch then. The pinch came, however, in the year following the peace.

In 1919, there was a big strike, and the country saw that the nonunion mines had become a big factor in the industry. During the six weeks of that strike, the nonunion mines averaged about 4,000,000 tons of coal a week and *the bulk of this came from southern West Virginia*. There was a demand for much more than 4,000,000 tons; but it was clear, too, that these fields were capable of much greater production had transportation been available. The chaos incidental to government control of the railroads precluded an adequate car-supply, and so production was retarded; but the potential strength, the strategic position of these fields, had been demonstrated.

In 1919, even before the strike, the union had realized the necessity of getting into southern West Virginia. Early in that year, it began to send organizers into Logan County, one of the most important in the whole area. It encountered a stone wall. For when these fields were opened (which was only about twenty years ago), the operators there had determined that they were not going to be hampered by the union. In this determination they were doubtless reinforced by big subsidiaries of the United States Steel Corporation,—the great antiunion capitalist group in this country,—which had acquired large holdings in several of these counties. To keep out the union, they had developed a system of 'mine guards,' or 'private detectives.' The duty of these guards was, ostensibly, to protect property, but, in fact, to maintain an armed barrier to the union. The operators discharged all employees suspected of union leanings, and compelled all others to take oath that they would never join a labor organization. It was a rule of iron, backed by pistols and rifles, and it worked. The union had never obtained even a foothold in the big southern West Virginia field, including Logan, Mingo, McDowell, Wyoming, Raleigh, and Mercer counties.

It was this system the union met when it tried to organize Logan. In this county there was a slight variation. Back in 1912, Don Chafin, the legendary sheriff of Logan, had done away with the private-mine-guards system, but had substituted one of his own that was in all essential respects the same. The guards were sworn in as deputy sheriffs, but they were still paid out of an operators' pool, and their duties included ejection of union sympathizers. When the union entered Logan, its organizers were beaten, its members were discharged, evicted from their homes, and made to leave the county. Its meetings were broken up.

Finally, word came over the hills that women and children friendly to the union were being murdered. The report was not true, but a thousand or more union miners gathered at Lens Creek, about fifteen miles from Charleston, the state capital, and marched on Logan. They were halted by Governor John J. Cornwell and C. Frank Keeney, president of District 17, United Mine Workers. Governor Cornwell promised the men an investigation, and kept his word. A volume of startling testimony was compiled, and there was a wide demand that something be done. Governor Cornwell asked the legislature to act; so did the next governor, E. F. Morgan; but the legislature has done nothing, and the mine-guard system is still in effect.

And the union had failed to organize Logan. Next, in 1920, it struck at Mingo. It encountered the same obstacles here; but the resistance was not so effective, for Mingo is on the Kentucky border, and is easier of access than Logan. This union quickly got a foothold. Some of the county officers saw that its meetings were not disturbed, and locals were organized. The union demanded a wage conference with the operators, and, when they were refused, called their men out on strike.

Then the operators acted. They began to evict union miners from their homes (for in a coal camp the company owns homes, stores, churches, Y.M.C.A., and everything else). A party of Baldwin Felts detectives went to Matewan, to evict miners, and the big shooting ensued. Evictions went on however, and as fast as the miners' families were 'set out,' the union lodged them in tents. Within a short time there were some five thousand persons under canvas. They have been there ever since. The union feeds them, clothes them, and buries their dead. They sit by the Tug River, watching the coal trains pass on the railroad, flotsam cast up by the backwash of a mighty struggle, pathetically loyal to a cause of which they understand nothing.

'It's kinda slow-like,' they will tell you, 'and sometimes a fellow don't hardly know what to do to pass the time. Some of the boys fishes a little, and some of the women raises a few chickens and gardens around, on'y you cain't raise much on them mountains, like-a-that. But most of the time we jest set around and talk about when they're a-goin' to sign up.'

Then came the guerrilla warfare. Recall that these people, who were being evicted by thousands, were the same who had become such picturesque characters in popular fiction. For two centuries they had been frontiersmen; they had interbred and lived to themselves so much that there had come into being an atrophied race, a weaker strain of American stock. It was inevitable that they should furnish the labor for the mines. Nevertheless, although to the eye they seemed a singularly shiftless type of poor whites, they had high spirit of a sort. They were capable of cherishing life-long feuds. In the prosecution of these they had a most peculiar code, and resorted quickly to the rifle, whether the enemy was a family inheritance or a federal revenue officer looking for moonshine stills. The evictions aroused their bitterest resentment, and in these circumstances activism was predominant. Shootings and reprisals became the regular order of the day and night, whether union officials or coal-operators sanctioned them or not.

Federal troops came and went, and came and went a second time. The departure both times was the signal for renewed violence until in May 1, 1982, Morgan proclaimed martial law.

The state martial-law commander forthwith promulgated a set of regulations.

The union was given so many days a week in which to visit its ten colonies. There were to be no meetings and it was decreed that three or more union men gathered together would constitute a meeting. For violation of this last fantastic order, scores of union men were jailed. The union fields in the north, as in 1919, were thrown into a state of seething indignation. Then Sid Hatfield and Ed Chambers, two union sympathizers, were shot dead by Baldwin Felt's detectives at Welch in McDowell County (August 1, 1921). The volcano went into full eruption. The march of 1919 was reenacted, on a scale three times as large and with the additional object of going through Logan to Mingo and liberating the prisoners in the jail there. The marchers were turned back once by Keeney. Two days later, however, two union miners were killed and three others wounded by Logan deputies and State Police.

The miners reassembled, and whereas at first, they had numbered hundreds they now numbered thousands. At Blair Mountain, in Logan County, the mob was met by a force gathered to defend Logan, and a three-day battle was fought. The operators hired four airplanes, and bombed the miners. Both sides used machine guns; both sides had a number of men killed. Our war had broken out afresh. It did not stop until two thousand Federal troops were sent in on September 3.

This aroused the public again, but the thing was quickly forgotten, and except for a Senatorial investigation nothing was done. The union membership now had Mingo on its hands. It was hampered by a set of regulations more effective than all the mine guards it had ever encountered. For, however, they were intended, the martial-law rules worked to preserve the status quo, and the status quo was precisely what the operators wanted. The tent colonies became a heavy drain on the treasury. The union has spent on them in the two years of their existence not less than $1,500,000 (the figure is probably over $2,000,000). The money is the smallest part of the tent-colony story; however, these staggering figures suggest the iron determination of the union to get into these fields; suggest, too, the magnitude of the issues it thinks are at stake. At present, it is absolutely stalled in Mingo; yet it is hanging on desperately, pouring out money there at the rate of $11,000 a week. At first it was $25,000.

III

What happened during the 1922 strike makes it clear that it is a life-and-death matter for the union to get to these fields. There was probably never a strike when the union shutdown in its areas was so complete; union miners to the number of more than 600,000 who walked out and stayed out. Yet at the first week of the strike, with consumption averaging 8,000,000 tons a week, there were mined 3,784,000 tons. In the next few weeks the price began to climb; it soon became profitable for every little mine in the nonunion area to start up. Mile-long trains of coal gondolas began to groan and creak around the bends in the Tug River, through the idle staring tent colonies; it began to come out of the Winding mine in the great Pocahontas field. The weekly production rose. It passed the 4,000,000 mark, the 4,250,000 the 4,500,000 mark.

Finally, by the end of June, it has passed the 5,000,000 mark and the great mine-strike was hardly 40 per cent effective. It was fortunate for the miners, but quite fortuitous, that the strike of the railroad shopmen came on July 1. Again, transportation was a factor; the physical equipment of the carriers deteriorated so quickly that they could not supply coal cars, and production slumped sharply. It fell away below the 4,000,000 mark weekly, and, with reserve stocks already depleted, there was a crisis which brought the situation to a head and gave the miners an advantage they could not have secured otherwise. But the lesson was as plain as in 1919: the nonunion fields could practically break any strike henceforth, and the Gibraltar of the nonunion fields was southern West Virginia. These West Virginia fields mine more than a third of the tonnage for the whole country; and, leaving out of consideration the locally consumed output of small fields in the South and West, they produced much more than half the coal available for general distribution.

It would be a mistake, however, to consider the union's position only with reference to its effectiveness in time of strike. These fields are a menace to it in time of work as well. For the nonunion mines always have work, boom times or slack. If times are good, demand brisk, then all operators can sell their coal, the nonunion along with the rest. If times are bad and prices slump, then the union operator closes down, for there is a price below which he cannot afford to run his mine. The nonunion operator then gets the orders that might have gone to the union mine, for his costs are lower, and he can sell cheaper. The price that closes his mine is much lower than that which closes the union mine.

This is not theorizing. It is precisely what happens—what happened during the past year. In the union field of Allegany County, Maryland, for example, operators could not afford to run their mines. They offered the union miners work if they would take less pay. In view of the principle of 1898, the union held that this would be in violation of other contacts, and would not permit it. There was no strike, but there was no work; privation and suffering were widespread. Yet the operators who could not run their own mines, having contracts to fill, *bought coal in the nonunion fields of Connellsville and Somerset, Pennsylvania, and filled their contracts more cheaply than they could have done by mining the coal themselves.*

Most often, the way it works out is not so easy to trace as this. The union mine, unable to sell at the price offered, closes down and its men lose a day. The nonunion mine, able to sell at a lower price, can accept its orders. Its men do not lose a day.

All this can be checked up by a glance at government tabulations of the average number of working days to the year in union and nonunion fields. In 1916, the year just before the war, the average number of working days in three wholly-union states was: Ohio, 197, Indiana 187, Illinois, 198. The average for three nonunion states was: Georgia, 280, New Mexico, 292, Alabama, 262. The partly union state of Pennsylvania averaged 259; the partly union state of West Virginia, 237. In 1920, which was another fairly typical year, the averages were as follows: (union) Ohio, 188, Indiana, 192, Illinois, 213; (nonunion) Georgia, 294, New Mexico, 302; Alabama, 247; (partly union) Pennsylvania, 244, West Virginia, 198.

Statistics for 1921, one of the worst years the industry ever knew, have not been completed. The tendency, however, may be traced by the current weekly bulletins issued by the Geological Survey for that year. These bulletins include and estimate the percentage of full-time production attained by mines in various districts. The reports are divided by fields, hence it is not necessary to examine partly-union figures, as is the case when returns are made only by states.

For the week ending June 4, 1921, when the market had entered the second slump of the year, the percentage of full-time output was as follows: (union) Ohio, 25.5,

Indiana 34.2, Illinois, 37.1, (nonunion, in West Virginia) Winding Gulf field, 68.9 Pocohontas, 52.9, Logan, 55.6, Kenova-Thacker, 53, Tug River, 74.2 This relative activity continued, with the union fields gradually gaining ground, until October, when the peak for the year was reached. Percentages of full-time output for the week ending October 22 stood: (union) Ohio, 47.8, Indiana, 55.9, Illinois, 62.4; (nonunion, in West Virginia) Winding Gulf, 65.5, Pocahontas, 63.7, Logan, 62.9, Kenova-Thacker, 44.3, Tug River, 55.1 From then to the end of the year, production in the union fields fell off sharply, as the market went into another slump, with the nonunion fields holding their own, now and then gaining a little. Nonunion mines supplied a large proportion of the coal used last year, for the reason that they were the only ones which could afford to run. The union miner has come to such a pass that, even though paid at a reasonable rate, he is starving to death because he cannot get work. And the net result is that not only the union itself, but unionism as an idea, an economic scheme, is getting the blame for this condition. The union faces the most persistent fight against it that it has ever known—a fight no less in earnest because it usually appeared under the guise of agitation for the open shop. The union is literally on the defensive for its very existence.

IV

From the foregoing, it would seem, indeed, that the nonunion fields are more soundly organized than the union, and that the solution of the problem lies in putting the whole country on a nonunion basis. This is past what the operators are trying to prove. Not only the nonunion operators, but the union operators as well, distribute this sort of propaganda; newspaper offices are flooded with it. Yet it is clear that the argument of the operators is valid only in a superficial sense, even though present conditions lend it considerable plausibility. For obviously the prosperity of the non-union fields prevails, not through any variety of nonunionism per se, but from the artificial advantage they have on account of their lower wage-expense. One third of the industry, the non-union, works at one level of costs; the other two thirds, the union, work at a higher level; and all slumps and reverses are born by the less fortunate two thirds. At the first sign of hard times, they are stranded high and dry, while the nonunion fields still feel the pulse of business—a bit slow, perhaps, but enough to sustain life.

It would be a step back to the Dark Ages to put the whole country on a nonunion basis. No sooner would this be done than there would begin a cut-throat hammering of wages on the part of every operators' association in the country. It would be forced on them. If coal mined in Pennsylvania, with 70 cents a ton, say, as a wage-basis, began seriously underselling coal from Indiana, which might have 75 cents as a basis, Indiana operators should have to cut wages to survive. Pennsylvania, to retain its advantage, would cut wages in return; and so the thing would go on.

When you recall that coal from every big section competes with coal from every other big section, you can get an idea where this sort of thing would lead. The miner would be reduced almost to peonage, and the troubles of the industry would be multiplied a hundredfold.

Nor is the regional wage-agreement plan, recently advocated by the operators, much better. Indeed, this looks suspiciously like a move to divide the union against itself and thus pave the way for the end.

The trouble with this plan is that it allows independent agreements to be arrived at between operators and union representatives in a given section, whereby that section may enjoy a temporary prosperity comparable to that of the nonunion fields at present. Then the operators and union heads in another section will agree on an underselling scale, and this section will be prosperous while the first section will be stranded.

There is a point below which district presidents of the union would hardly dare go with this sort of thing; so the plan might work better than no union at all; but it is apparent that it holds unlimited possibilities for sharp dealing, and for disorganization of the business more serious than that which obtains at present. It should be borne in mind that subordinate union leaders, under pressure in their communities, are often willing to make clever bargains with the operators, and have to be restrained by international headquarters. But the trouble is that this kind of dealing, if carried on long, would inevitably bring the miner to a more degraded living than he has reached at present.

With these palpable defects in the nonunion and the regional agreement schemes, there is one plan left,—short of a big government corporation to run all coal mines,— which promises some sort of solution. This is to put the whole country on a union basis, and give all operators an equal chance at the market, and all miners an equal chance at regular work.

There is probably no Federal agency that could compel this; it is unquestionable, indeed, whether it would be wise to try to accomplish it by government agencies. Yet it could be accomplished if there were sufficiently insistent public demand that the armed-guard system, by which the union is forcibly kept out of the nonunion fields, be abolished. With the public more and more inclined to think of coal as a national problem, a sort of public utility, it is less and less inclined to put up with the amazing mediaeval methods whereby the nonunion operators maintain their advantage. It is their declaration that they are opposed to unionism as a principle; that their labor does not want it; that they are splendidly isolated and intend to remain so. Their reason, in fact, is that under the nonunion system their coal mines have become gold mines; their object in keeping out the union is money, and nothing else. Their labor joins the union whenever it gets a chance. When it becomes more generally known that this sort of industrial feudalism is what is wrong with the coal business, more than any other single defect, then the public may voice a persistent demand that be abolished.

V

In West Virginia, the union, all of a sudden, has a chance to profit by the greatest blow that has been dealt unionism in years, that is—the Coronado decision. This makes unions liable to suit, but it also gives them the right to sue. There is a law in West Virginia which prohibits private payment of deputy sheriffs. It carries no penalty, and has always been considered a dead letter. But it now becomes possible for the union to go into court as a plaintiff, and invoke the old bete noir of labor, the injunction proceeding, to prohibit such a system as is maintained in Logan County, and, on a lesser scale, in several other West Virginia counties. That is, it might ask the court to enjoin payment of deputies by the Logan sheriff, out of the operators pool. It might also ask the court to enjoin mine guards from interference with union meetings and union organizers. Its attorneys, indeed, are considering such a step now. If it should succeed, and the union could get its organizers into southern West Virginia, then the unionizing of these fields would be virtually accomplished. And if this end could be attained peaceably the long war in West Virginia might be ended, to the great advantage of the coal business all over the country.

The Coal Baron
(Written in 1945—Unpublished)

"As one of the seven men who have actually read *Das Kapital*," I began, for the edification of the lawyers, reporters, and fixers who were in Charleston, W. Va., in connection with some crisis in the mines; but I never finished my apothegm, whatever it was. For a large, grave man in his fifties looked up from the paper he was reading in the lobby of my hotel, held out his hand, and said: "I'm one of the other six." It was the beginning of a beautiful friendship, and a still more beautiful war. For at that time I was opposing, in various journals, the practices of certain coal operators, to say nothing of their press, courts, and gunmen, and he was doing the same for the union. We were thus at the diagonals in a large, grievous conflict, and soon came to feel we were paired. And so began a wrangle that lasted for years, in the strangest places, over the widest assortment of food, cigars, and drinks, all over the east.

His name was Wiley, and I think he was the most impressive-looking man I ever saw. I am six feet, and weigh over 200, but I felt like a squatty little Princeton quarterback in that overshadowing presence. Locally he was known as Colonel, but when I asked him why he said: "It is a brevet, and implies no military service. When I first came to this state, your colleagues of the newspapers felt that for a thing of such beauty Mister was grossly inadequate. Chief they held to be inelegant, Governor misleading, and General somewhat too elderly. Considering my Charleston, S. C., origin, Colonel was indicated, and as I couldn't but admit a certain cogency in their idea, I submitted with little protest but a great deal of grace."

Naturally he was outstanding in operators' activities, both as whip in caucus and spokesman in public affairs. He didn't, however, seek these offices, and they didn't, with any enthusiasm, seek him. Fastidious, groomed, learned, and intimate with the smallest details of fine speech, he was fully aware of the ursine aspect of most coal operators, and the tedious nature of their deliberations. But the point is, so were they. Having a reasonably realistic picture of themselves, they knew his value, to preside at banquets, deal with the press, and have his picture taken with the picture stars of the era.

But at the same time they didn't want anybody getting the idea they really liked him. For if he took their side, and represented them or it might be more accurate to say misrepresented them, in a wholly satisfactory way, he did so for all the wrong reasons. When it came to what he really thought, he held opinions that made their blood run cold. He didn't believe miners were low, lazy rats, who stubbornly refused to learn how to live without food, and then when they did do it, died. He thought they were human, and entitled to human things, like baths, music, jokes, fishing in the creek, and hot roasted peanuts on Saturday night. And his quarrel with unionism was not that it did too much for its followers, but that it didn't do enough.

He had curious observations on unions, for example their resemblance to other concentrations of power, which he said invariably produced a favored hierarchy and an exploited rank and file. He constantly pointed out the discrepancy between their words and their acts: they call themselves bargaining agents, he said, but actually they are instruments of coercion; they say negotiation, and mean direct action; they pretend to picket, and intend to riot. But these were incidental points, the by-product of much thought, rather than the main issue he took with them. This, he wanted it clear, was their hopeless, inevitable, and eternal alliance with inefficiency. To begin with, he would point out, they are opposed to the greatest means of human progress, which is invention. They resist any later-saving device, because it throws men out of work. But, he would emphasize, *all* invention is labor-saving, and if their stand had been taken soon enough, and had in any way been successful, we would still lack the wheel, as the Aztecs did. They condone bad work and tolerate, almost venerate, the bad workman. They slow down production. And they set up the intolerable situation in which one partner of an enterprise claims the right to hold a gun to the other partner's head. "While you," I would usually say at this point, "claim the right to cheat him out of what is rightfully his."

"Which is?"

"A share, in the profits."

"That he's not entitled to."

"He is if he assumes risk, which he steadfastly refuses to do. I agree, if he shared in the profits, he would no longer resist the machine. But a share in the profits is a share in the business, and I think you'd find the courts would so hold. But no man who risks nothing can make wise decisions in management, any more than a man can play winning poker while using another man's chips. It's simply trifling with the quest for you to suggest that the solution is to seat the shop committee at the same table with my directors. In a year we'd be out of business, that's all."

This was the state of the argument when I arrived at his mines in the fall of 1922. I had accepted the invitation, or perhaps it was a challenge, issued me by the operators to come down, visit the mines, and see what a sap I had been making of myself; I took a job, went underground, joined the union, and saw that I had indeed been making a sap of myself, but only for not saying it in times stronger. But after such labors, a visit to Wiley seemed enticing, so after an exchange of wires I set out for the empire of the Boone County Coal Corporation, which for some reason wasn't in Boone county at all, but at Sharples, in Logan County. He met me at the train in a yachting cap, set me up at the directors' lodge, then conducted me on a tour of inspection. I sensed something different in this camp. Even the shacks seemed better cared for than in other camps, and the flower gardens were positively startling. "Rather odd for a coal camp, Colonel Wiley."

"We have an annual contest."

"Your idea, I presume?"

"I'm on the committee."

But at the Community Hall, with recreation center, bowling alleys, pool tables and a library I had actually to be fanned. The company store he insisted that I investigate without him, so I could make sure the prices were fair and the management decent, a very rare state of affairs, indeed. "It couldn't be, darling, that you're really a romantic?"

"These things promote efficiency."

"And that's your only interest in them?"

"They represent an appropriation of profits to uses that should promote more profits. People work better when contented, and it's possible in this way to make a communal matter out of things that as individual luxuries would be prohibitive. Our school, church, and various community activities provide our people with things they couldn't afford separately, but I never heard of a union that thought of that, or appropriated any share of its profits to it, or to anything."

"Your mines organized?"

"No, they're not?"*

"You resist organization?"

"Not with force, but I oppose it."

"Your people want it?"

"Some of them, I suppose."

"I never heard of a camp that had a fair chance at a union local that didn't want it and didn't take it. If that's the case here, what you've got is pretty but it's paternalism."

"Maybe so, but it's right."

"No, it's not."

"Why?"

"It will only work if some crazy idealist like you sets out to work it. The beauty of democracy is that it assumes quite a few men in public office will be dirty sons of bitches, and intends to work in spite of them. What you've got here is Russian Communism upside down. It assumes the dictator is perfect, and generally he's not. You don't think those operators up the line are perfect,

*Since 1933 they have been.

do you? They toe the line when Lewis, Murray, Keeney, Mooney, and Bittner kick them in the shins and make them do it."

"I'm a benevolent despot?"

"That's it."

"You ought to see my production sheets."

That night Mrs. Wiley, a pleasant, well-bred woman, invited me to dinner, and after gay anecdotes of the Bohemian Club in San Francisco, of which he seemed to be a member, he asked me: "Do you know what you're eating?"

"Beef, isn't it?"

"That's chuck."

"Very good."

"That's another thing I work on, or Mrs. Wiley works on: to teach these people how to cook the cheaper cuts of meat. I wouldn't ask them to do anything I wouldn't do myself, so now nothing comes on this table but chuck, brisket, round, and plate."

"Also, of course, you could pay them more."

"That is not the point. I pay them more than a union mine does, you may be surprised to learn. The rate is lower, but they work twice as much. But if I paid them a million dollars a day, it would still remain true that if they will buy nothing but a steak, I can't buy whole carcasses for the company store. I have to have special cuts sent down from Charleston, and they're insanely expensive."

"It may interest you," I cut in, "how they cook those steaks. I found out, in the course of my researches, living in a miner's boarding house until yesterday. First, they beat on the steak with a hammer till it spreads out like a German pancake. Then they cut it into pieces. Then they fry it in cottonseed grease until it curls up at the edges. Then they put flower, water, and stuff into the pan and make a gravy. Then they pour that in a round yellow bowl, put the steak in it, and when it's floating around nicely and the potatoes have been taken up from the pot—".

"I know. Mrs. Wiley knows."

"They serve it on tin plates—"

"Please. My stomach isn't what it used to be."

"How's the campaign going, by the way?"

"It's precisely nowhere."

"Maybe they *like* fried steak."

"My contumacious young friend, *you can't have steak until you eat chuck.* You talk about food, and you've evidently eaten food, but what you know about it is exactly nothing. You spoke of a 'steak house' just now, but failed to mention the first thing to look for in a steak house, because it will tell you more about the steaks than you can find out by eating them. I mean the way it gets rid of ground meat. If it features enchiladas, hamburgers, stuffed peppers, or meat sauce for spaghetti, it has the ground meat problem under control and can buy carcasses. In that way it can afford prime meat. But if it only sells steaks, its meat has to be second-rate, because no place in the world could get the prices it would have to charge for prime meat bought by the special cut. My problem is identical. But I can't solve it unless my miners' wives help me solve it. So far, I'm sorry to say, they won't. And I don't have to tell you, it seems, that they eat very badly."

After a liqueur, we went through his library, pausing briefly to examine the great collection of books there, then into a music room which was rather dimly lit and didn't disclose its real nature to me at once. He offered to play me, on the phonograph, "anything you want," and as we had been talking of Pasquale Amato at dinner, I called for his record of the Pagliacci Prologue. But putting it on the machine seemed to involve various preparations, such as peering at cards, adjusting the revolution govern or, etc. Talking with Mrs. Wiley, I didn't pay much attention, even to his dissertation on synchronization of pitch, the great difficulty in getting player piano rolls made, etc. When I next noticed him closely, he was seated at the console of an organ in one corner of the room, with the player piano roll running in front of his eye, and the phonograph nowhere to be seen. Then he snapped a switch, and there assailed my ears the worst cacaphony I ever heard in my life, and I've quite an appetite for vocal punishment.

The phonograph, you see, was synchronized with the electric organ, and he had had special roles made, so he could accompany the phonograph with player rolls on the organ, while he conscientiously pulled out stops, and fondly supposed he was giving a bang-up exhibition of something hardly to be told from the synchronized original. Technically, as the movie cutters say, the two instruments were "in sync," but religiously, angrilly, painfully. It was as though riddles, brasses, woodwin, tympani, organ, and Pasquale had all been dropped in a cistern, and were in some mad, screaming stampede to get out. I peeped at Mrs. Wiley, and she was looking at him with a little smile that seemed to betoken affection mixed with pity. I knew, then, I was in the presence of the loneliest man on earth, one who was trying not to lose his soul on this desolate mountain top in West Virginia, a sojourner on a desert isle, reciting Shakespeare so as not to forget how to talk. At last, when it was mercifully over, I said: "Nice, but they do it better in New York."

"Or Philadelphia, for that matter."

"Oh yes. Once a week. I'd forgotten."

"Our home office is there. I can go, if I want."

"And?"

"...I've a job to do, and it's here."

Years later, having occasion to drive through West Virginia in connection with a book, I came upon Sharples unexpectedly, being a little confused as to my roads. Of course I stopped, saw the familiar Community

Hall as I had left it, with library, bowling alleys, and pool tables all doing business. But in the office, the gentleman behind the desk hesitated before he told me: "I'm sorry to tell you, but Colonel Wiley died some years ago."

"Oh...Where is Mrs. Wiley living, or do you know?"

"Mrs. Wiley died two days before he did. In fact, he was dressing for Mrs. Wiley's funeral when he was stricken. The whole camp was at her services. They all thought it strange he didn't appear, and naturally it seemed an inappropriate moment to make the announcement."

After a long time I said: "You'll have to excuse me if I'm terribly upset. We stopped corresponding some time ago, but we were very close friends, and it simply overwhelms me to learn he has gone out like a candle, with nothing I can do about it."

He walked out with me as I left, and stopped, in the hallway, in front of something I hadn't noticed as I came in. It was a large bronze plaque, bearing Wiley's portrait in relief, and the following inscription:

IN MEMORY OF
WILLIAM MELIN WILEY
Vice President and General Manager
BOONE COUNTY COAL CORPORATION
August 1918 — June 1931
This tablet is affectionately dedicated by his fellow officers, employees, and associates in grateful recognition of his outstanding qualities of integrity, friendliness, and leadership.
"Not quite like a candle; Mr. Cain."
"No, not quite."

Treason by Any Other Name Would Make a Hell of a Lot More Sense
(*The Washington Post*, January 30, 1977)

In mid-August of 1921, just after midnight, deputy sheriffs of Logan County, West Virginia, rode into a Logan County village to serve warrants sued out by anti-union coal operators on pro-union miners, thereby touching off a chain of events that went on and on and on, including a march on Logan by 15,000 miners, indictments for treason, and a trial, which I covered for the Baltimore Sun. The march was quite a thing, with a password, "I Come Creeping," and a song, "Hang Don Chapin to the Sour Apple Tree." Don Chapin was the sheriff of Logan County and the deputies' boss, of course—a stocky, handsome man in his early forties, who never went anywhere without four bodyguards, two in front, two at rear, their hands in their coat pockets, their eyes shooting around. The operators hired four planes to drop bombs on the miners, which did give the proceedings a warlike look, until federal troops, requested by the governor, came in and one H.H. Bandholtz, Maj. Gen., U.S.A., bade the tumult cease and it ceased.

No one got killed, nothing got damaged, and no great harm was done, and that might have been the end, except that one Logan coal operator, William M. Wiley, general manager of the Boone County Coal Corporation, located at Sharples, now Clothier, in Logan County, could read. He not only could read, but was a vastly cultured man, a personal friend I ought to say, who treated his own miners beautifully, so much so that they put up a plaque in his honor when he died in the 1930s—but was implacably against the union, and now saw the chance the march had created: To indict union officials for treason, try them, convict them, and thereby attainder the United Mineworkers of America so they could never erase the stigma.

So William Blizzard, among others, was indicted by the Logan County grand jury for treason to the state of West Virginia, whose constitution included the same definition and safeguards to the accused as our federal Constitution does: "Treason, to West Virginia, shall consist in levying war against her, or adhering to her enemies, giving them aid and comfort; but no person shall be convicted of treason except on confession in open court, or on the testimony of two witnesses to the same overt act."

Blizzard was president of District No. 16, United Mineworkers of America, a boyish-looking man still in his twenties, with a little boy and a very good-looking wife, whom I still claim as a personal friend. And where I got in it was in 1921, when the march began, when I pleaded with the late Spencer Davidson, acting news editor of the Sun, to let me go down and cover it, but as an interim officer he hesitated about the expense, and I didn't get to go. But when the trial opened, Stanley Reynolds, the regular editor, sent me down—I by that time, as financial editor of the Sun, having got into labor relations as a sort of related sideline.

So the trial, which had been transferred, on a motion for change of venue, from Logan County to Charles Town, the very courthouse where John Brown had been convicted sixty-three years before, got under way, with me sending a daily dispatch.

Then at the end of three or four days, John W. Owens, our big political reporter, showed up, for reasons he didn't explain to me, and then suddenly was gone. But over the weekend, when I slipped back to Baltimore, I found out what he was doing there. Stanley called me into his office and told me: "Jim, coal operators have been in here, trying to get you fired, on the ground that your stories are biased."

"Well," I told him, "I'm not surprised that they think so. I simply don't believe that a glorified riot, that was somewhat provoked don't forget, should be blown up to an act of war. To pretend that those miners meant it as such is to strain the fact beyond credence. However, if you feel I'm getting too fundamental—?"

"I don't feel that way at all. I sent Johnny Owens up there, he checked on the way things are going, and whether you're giving a fair report, and he okays your stuff completely. The story is not panning out, but we can't have coal operators telling the Sun who we fire and who we don't fire, and taking you off the assignment would be playing their game for them just as they want us to. So to let them know where they get off, I'm afraid you're stuck with it for the duration. So, look around for whatever amusements Charles Town has to offer—and God bless. So, I'm sorry, but that's how it has to be."

So for six weeks, morning, noon, and toward the end, night, I listened while treason was argued, frontwards, backwards, crosswise, and on the bias. And little by little I began changing my ideas about it. I started out with a conviction that three days of whooping and hollering, even with some shooting mixed in, fell light years short of war. But then I found myself going further, so I soured on treason itself. The first jolt came with the discovery, mentioned casually by counsel for the defense, that John Brown had been hung for a crime he couldn't have committed—treason to the Commonwealth of Virginia, which of course included Harpers Ferry at the time he took it over. And the reason he couldn't have committed treason to the Commonwealth of Virginia was that treason hangs on allegiance—and he owed none to Virginia. He wasn't a Virginia citizen, and in fact had never set foot in the commonwealth before he arrived, just before his raid on the arsenal. It came out, in more incidental comments by lawyers, that Benedict Arnold's guilt was somewhat equivocal too, for the reason that at the time of his deal with Clinton, no country existed for him to owe loyalty to. Well, did it? There was a Confederation, but were they in fact a country? The only solid allegiance he had, it was said in court, was to England, and to that allegiance he returned.

Cited almost daily were the John Marshall rulings on Burr, from which it was easy to see that our most celebrated Chief Justice took a very bilious view of treason and meant to make a conviction tough. So Burr, of course, was acquitted. And I suddenly realized after a while, that I disbelieved in treason too. It bothered me that to qualify as treason, an act, no matter how heinous or how overt, had to be committed by a citizen. If somebody else did it, it might qualify as sedition, but as treason, no.

This, I confess, bothered me, and still does. It seemed to me that a crime is a crime is a crime, and that the law against it should be the law for all, regardless of where he was born or if he was naturalized. It began to nag at me there was something familiar about treason that wholly aroused my distrust. And pretty soon I had it: It much resembled heresy, which also depended on allegiance, on faith, which is allegiance to a creed. When I got that far with it, I really didn't like treason. So, to wind it up about Blizzard, he was acquitted.

But it wasn't the end of the affair, for me. I confess treason lay heavy on my stomach, and as time went on and we got into another war, the way treason figured bothered me no end. For example, William Joyce, known as Lord Haw-Haw, was hanged for it by the British, with Miss Rebecca West keeping watch in the rain as an act of patriotism—but he couldn't have been guilty of it, as he wasn't a British subject. Born an American, he did, it is true, take out British papers, but on falsified information. He was guilty, then, of making untrue affidavits, but still had taken no lawful step to become a British subject. It didn't stop the British from hanging him—it seemed they couldn't forgive him his inept imitation of a thick British accent. But really, should the penalty be death for saying *haw* every ten seconds?

Then there was La Gillars, Axis Sally known as, whom we convicted and sent to prison. But she did her stuff in Berlin, where an American grand jury does not, under regular law, have jurisdiction. Then, of course, there was Mrs. d'Aquino, who became Tokyo Rose—or, more accurately, was one of six Tokyo Roses, all of whom went free except her, she being tried, convicted, and sentenced for treason—on the basis of her American citizenship. Finally, there was Ezra Pound, who did pro-Nazi broadcasts from Italy, was arrested, indicted, and brought to trial in the U.S. for treason—and then committed to St. Elizabeth's as being somewhat mental, where he stayed for ten years or so, before being finally released, as a result of the persistent pressure of many eminent persons, of which I'm sorry to say I was not one.

Then came Korea, but with a hitch in the script that somewhat inhibited treason:

Americans did the fighting, but the United Nations flew the flag. So what allegiance did we owe, anyhow? It was a question that underlay the whole war, and that lurked in the soldiers' minds, as many confessed, especially when they came into your home and no one was there to repeat what they said. No treason cases arose, by a funny coincidence. And then at last came Vietnam, the oddest war of all, in its legal implications. It all started when a wake was seen by a seaman, of white water behind a destroyer, not far from the Vietnamese coast, which could have been caused by a shark, but could have been caused too, by a torpedo, fired from a North Vietnamese torpedo boat. No torpedo boat was seen, but it was nighttime and no voices were heard, nor anything else observed to reinforce the torpedo possibility. Nevertheless, the United States Congress passed resolutions authorizing Mr. Johnson to take reprisals—not on the shark, which was the most likely possibility, but on the discharges of the torpedo assumed to be North Vietnamese. This, this one scattershot resolution, was the only legal basis the war ever had. War as such was never declared, which made treason impossible, under the constitutional provision, and so we fought a big war, losing 46,397 men in combat, that was at the same time not a war. This fact had some odd results, not all of them bad.

Since, without a declaration of war by Congress, wartime rules shouldn't be put into effect by the Army, the correspondents were comparatively free to tell us the truth, and so we got the truth, for the first time in our modern wars, with all sorts of odd details, about body counts, search and destroy missions and North Vietnamese successes, that we wouldn't have got otherwise. And no prosecutions for treason.

So what am I getting at? A pardon for Mrs. D'Aquino, of course, to start with. She doesn't have the gift of public relations, of getting liked very much if at all, but this is not a popularity contest, and I would say she was over-punished. Next, that we revised our conceptions of treason, so we toss it into the discard, for all intent and purpose. An overt act in wartime, if committed on American soil, can be adequately prosecuted under the laws which forbid sedition, and sedition is a crime which all may commit, regardless of citizenship. Or in other words, I would say let's get rid of a crime which is a crime if one man commits it, but not a crime if some other man does. I would say, let's make all of us equal under the law. And an overt act committed on enemy soil by an American citizen, I would accept as that person's right to commit in the place where he committed it. "But," I would say, "though you chose a new allegiance and we of course respect it, don't try to play it two ways. You have a new love, so keep it—or in other words, don't come back—don't try to come back, we won't have you."

Such a policy, I suspect, if announced at the outset of war, would do more to the passion of some anti-patriot than a lot of tall talk about treason, which is the hardest crime to prove and also to punish of any crime in our calendar. My system would save the expense of a trial, and the whoop-de-do that goes with it. It would be quietly announced, and put into effect by executive order. Or in other words, it would be cheap, simple, and quick, and get rid at long last of a crime that is an anachronism, as well as an utter anomaly.

So who am I, some long-haired pacifist, waving a bed sheet around? No, I'm as patriotic as anyone, and wear my hair in a butch-cut. I fought in the First World War, volunteering, and getting, overseas service within three weeks of my induction then doing duty at the front, under fire. Later, I was editor-in-chief of the Lorraine Cross, my division's paper, and got a letter of commendation from the commanding general, and close personal friend. I was a buck private in the rear rank, but he and I shared a night neither one of us ever forgot, and after the war we became quite close. In the Second World War, I worked for motion pictures, which were declared an essential industry, and while I wouldn't claim that work at pictures salaries entailed much sacrifice, I did pay some $150,000 in war taxes, which changes the picture a bit. Or in other words, I'm patriotic, but *don't* believe in treason.

I occurs to me that it might amuse you to learn what happened to Blizzard, and the idiotic part I played in the trial. So, for a month the prosecution presented its case, and then the defense started—mainly, with a procession of miners, who swore they had no warlike intentions, and in fact weren't even carrying guns. But one of the prosecution lawyers was a man named Osenton, who had a strange effect on these men. He didn't bark three questions at them before they turned to jelly, unable to say a word. He seemed to hypnotize them. He would fire question after question at them, and they would just sit and stare. It was, I knew, playing havoc with Blizzard's case, for I kept watching the jury and their annoyance with these miners, was obvious—though until that time, as well as I could see, they had been as little impressed with treason as I was. Which was the way things stood when Dave Fowler came to town. Fowler, like Lewis and Murray, was a Welshman, a big wheel at Indianapolis, and due to testify in the afternoon about some union headquarters angle—his efforts by phone, as I recall, to head the big march off. But I knew him quite well and we went to lunch. "Well how does it look?" he asked me, and I answered, "Bad." Then I told him about Osenton, and the affect he was having on the miners, "who are really telling the truth, at least as I think—but when he gets done with them, they all look like hang-dog crooks, and the jury is getting annoyed. What this wants is a comedian, someone who can talk back to Osenton—or if not that, at least talk, instead of just sitting there, not able to say *anything*."

"I see. I see," said Fowler.

He went on the stand, and on direct examination gave his testimony briefly quietly and simply, taking no more than a few minutes. Then Osenton started in. Fowler answered him, with easy, pleasant courtesy, but asking Osenton's name, as a friendly matter. Osenton gave it, but Fowler didn't quite get it, and had to have him repeat it. But being made to do something, instead of running things himself, was a new departure for Osenton, and he betrayed his annoyance. But when Fowler pleasantly thanked him, it got a big laugh. Even the judge, caught by surprise, had to smile. Then Osenton began working Fowler over, but at each question getting a mild, slightly off-center, answer. I wish I could remember what these answers were, but I was watching the jury and didn't do any memorizing. Anyway, Fowler was now running the show, that much Osenton knew, but instead of cutting it off, saying "No further questions," and grumpily sitting down, he had no more sense than to get sore, to lose his temper completely. So Fowler just sat there, owlishly studying the ceiling, and answering him with perfect good humor and perfect respect—almost. And the jury ate it up. All the previous harm was repaired, that I knew, for Osenton at last was cut down to size. It went on for twenty minutes, and when Fowler stepped down I knew Blizzard was going to be acquitted. He was.

So, Mr. President, and Mr. President-elect, if you want to pardon Mrs. D'Aquino, you may cite this piece by me, but put in, please, about haircuts, and how brave I am, and that I don't drink or smoke any more. I used to, but quit—showing my great willpower. And put in that I almost saw General Pershing once when he visited our division. I missed him but the stars on his shoulders, they told me, really reflected the sunlight.

The Man Merriwell
(*Saturday Evening Post*, June 11, 1927)

Through the streets of a little town in the state of **Maine**, on a winter night in the early 80s, a woman was running madly. Behind her, in **half-hearted** fashion, lumbered a man. As he puffed for breath he besought her to ease the **pace**. "There's no hurry," he kept repeating, and in between times he tried to reason with her.

Of course, he admitted, he was glad Willie had come home. Any man would be glad if his only son had run away and then come back again. But shucks, if the boy had kept body and soul together for six months, all on his own, it stood to reason he wouldn't up and die in the time it would take them to walk home. And another thing—just because a fellow had poked his head in the door and said Willie was back, why had they left the meeting and lit out this way hell-bent for election? They ought to have stayed until the meeting was over. It wouldn't hurt Willie to wait a little while. It would teach him a lesson. Maybe then he would get it through his head that when he ran away from home he might have to whittle his chips awhile before he saw his folks.

And as he argued thus the voice of Patten Pere sounded the least bit wistful; for as it happened, Brother Nickerson was to expound the Book of Revelation at the meeting tonight, with the aid of a great chart whereon would be depicted all the queer creatures of the Apocalypse. And when Brother Nickerson expounded the Book of Revelation, a man didn't stay away if he could help it.

His wife paid him no heed whatever. Leaving him far behind, she ran on, plunging through snowdrifts and scrambling over icy pavements. In a few minutes she was flinging open a door, racing down a hall and bursting into a kitchen, there to fly into the arms of a tall, lank youth who had been thawing himself out by the parental stove. Her joy was brief. For this boy of sixteen, who had ideas so strange that he must needs run away from a home where he had always been cock of the walk, had come home with ideas stranger still. No penitent prodigal he, ready to atone for his transgression by settling down into the first useful occupation that might present iself. Not at all. He pleaded guilty to nothing; he had money in his pocket and clothes on his back; and these, he seemed to think, proved that he had not wasted his time. As for a useful occupation—poof! He had loftier aspirations. His lordly dreams, it appeared, were filled with the screech of bullets, the snorting of buffaloes and the whooping of Comanches. In brief, he would an author be, and sign his name to books.

Far, far into the night his father and mother talked over the blow that had befallen them. "How'd he get that fool idea in his head?" fretted the father. "Seems like to me after he spent six months out in the world he would of learnt some sense."

"I was hoping he would be a preacher," said the mother sadly.

"I was hoping he would be a carpenter, and maybe earn enough to pay for his keep," replied the father. "I know where I can get him a job at a dollar and a half a day right now, and he can make two and a half as soon as he learns the trade." His voice grew warm as the full enormity of the situation began to dawn on him. "Dog-gon it!" he exclaimed. "I got a notion to take him over to that job tomorrow anyhow. I got a notion to put him to work and see if that don't beat some sense in his head." And as he stood six feet three, and was so huge in proportion that Abraham Lincoln had once singled him out of a crowd and challenged him to a rail-splitting contest, it seemed that he was able to make good on his notion.

"No, you can't do that," said the mother quickly.

"What's going to stop me?"

"He might run away again."

"Yeah, he sure is bull-headed." The father was silent a few minutes. "Well," he reflected after a time, "you got to admit he's got the pluck." Dark though the future might appear, he could not resist a sneaking pride that his son had gone over to Biddeford, the mill town, and held his own there without asking help from anybody. "He sure ain't afraid of nothing," he mused.

The mother sighed. The pluck in question seemed a long way from the ministry and the Book of Revelation.

"Guess we better leave him alone," said the father. "I don't know much about this writing business; it ain't in my line. But it's a cinch he ain't like no other boy that we ever seen, so maybe he knows what he's doing."

"Yes, I guess we better leave him be," said the mother sadly.

And the decision, no doubt, was a momentous one for the boy who was snoring away in another part of the house. For this William Gilbert Patten was presently to rewrite his eminent name as Burt L. Standish, and in no great length of time to give a waiting world that noblest Roman of them all, the Hon. Frank Merriwell, A.B., Yale.

He did not, of course, call for an ax and have the prodigious Frank cloven full-grown from his brow at one fell swipe. He had not, in fact, even thought of Frank at this time; other matters were more pressing. For one thing, although his parents were committed for the moment to an attitude of watchful waiting, they were practical folk; and if the usufructs of literature were not visible pretty soon, they might deliver an ultimatum that would mean the ministry, the carpentry, or another trip into the cold, cold world. For another thing, there was a little affair of honor with Mr. Gooch, boss of the mill at Biddeford.

Mr. Gooch, in firing him, had not only refused to give him the raise he demanded but had bidden him go get some hair on his face, else be thankful to work for the ninety cents a day he was getting. And it had become his ambition first to get some hair on his face, and second to make enough money to go over to Biddeford and snap haughty fingers at Mr. Gooch and Mr. Gooch's $1800 a year. So heigh-ho for the inkpot.

After three weeks, however, things looked black indeed. His first story, A Bad Man, had hardly been dry on the paper before he shipped it off to the Banner Weekly, a publication of the Messrs. Beadle & Adams, in New York, and it was rejected by return mail. What was almost as distressing, it had not come back with the note of rejection. With heavy heart young Patten went to work on another, The Pride of Sandy Flat. To his father, who made inquiries a little more pointed than mere courtesy demanded, he made evasive replies, neglecting to mention the note of rejection.

"It always takes a little time," he explained. "A whole lot of editors have got to read the stuff before they take it."

By the time The Pride of Sandy Flat was done he was blue indeed, and when he sent the story off he enclosed a very humble letter to the editor of the Banner Weekly, Mr. Orville J. Victor, in which he respectfully asked whether he revealed any talent as a writer. And P.S.—where was his other story?

He trembled when he opened the reply. Yes, said Mr. Victor, literary talent was plainly visible. The Pride of Sandy Flat was accepted. Through some oversight A Bad Man had not been returned, but now that it had had a second reading it, too, was accepted. Check was enclosed to pay for both stories—for six dollars.

He drew a long breath. Perhaps out of that moment he got something which enabled him to describe so feelingly, in later years, how Merriwell felt when the plotters had been foiled and our friends would breathe freely at last.

"Heard from those stories today," he said nonchalantly, tossing the check to his father as he sat down to the supper table that night.

Long and hard did the elder Patten stare at it. "How long did it take you to do them stories?" he asked.

"Oh, couple of days apiece, I guess."

"H'm!" said the elder Patten, in the manner of a man who makes mental calculations.

The third story, which was really a short novel, sold for seventy-five dollars. The check he showed not only to his father but to Henry Clark, a friend. And that night a boy pedaled frantically up the village store on his high-wheeled bicycle and burst into the room where men were buying cut plug, twist and loose chewing.

"Willie Patten got seventy-five dollars for one of them stories he's writing!" exclaimed the boy.

Up spoke Hosea Rackliff, the school-teacher. "Henry Clark," he said sternly, "you shut up with that foolishness. Willie Patten ain't got sense enough to make seventy-five dollars even if he worked for it, let alone making it by something he wrote."

But Henry Clark insisted that he had seen the check; and later on Bill Patten came in and confirmed the great news about his son, and excitement was intense in Corinna that night. The fourth story, a full-length novel, sold for $150, and by that time Willie Patten felt himself seasoned for a venture he had had in mind for some time. He would try his hand at dime novels.

A singular ambition? Not at that time. It is now quite forgotten that the dime novel has an ancient and thoroughly honorable history. In the beginning it was not the biographer of detectives, horse thieves and train robbers at all, but the historian of an epic achievement—the conquest of a continent. Its originator was Erastus F. Beadle, a native of Otsego, New York.

In 1857, when he was in his thirties, Beadle made a trip from Buffalo, where he had set up shop as a printer, to Nebraska, where he had taken up land and expected to settle. For various reasons his enterprise did not turn out very well, and he was forced to come back. But he had seen things that opened his eyes. He had found out first hand what was happening on the plains; he had had his own provisions stolen by Indians and had come into uncomfortably close contact with a scalping expedition.

What he saw convinced him that there was something radically wrong with the literature that his country was producing. The imaginative tales turned out by the disciples of Irving, Hawthorne, Longfellow, Whittier and Poe might be all very fine in a literary way, he reasoned, but they were woefully out of touch with the times. Such stuff, it seemed to him, gaped at the clouds while the elephants were marching by; the real romance of America, the great field for her literature, lay in the West. That was the land that was on everybody's tongue; that was the land that was forever on the floor of Congress, with great debates on whether Missouri should be admitted slave or free, and whether we should insist on fifty-four forty or fight; that was the land where supermen were rolling back a frontier on Indians and buffaloes; that was the land where the excitement was, where life had color, flavor and zip; that was the land that people wanted to read about.

Accordingly, as soon as he could get his affairs in order, he moved to New York and prepared to sing its saga. His plan, first, was to publish novels based on life as it was lived on the plains. His plan, second, was to sell them for ten cents.

When they heard the price at which the books were to be sold, his friends threw up their hands and threatened to have him put in the booby hatch. Other publishers, when rumors reached them, smiled. It was a pretty dream, they said, but the thing couldn't be done. Beadle went ahead with his preparations. It took him a year or two, selling joke books, song books and such things, to get together the necessary money, but presently he was ready. He would need a printer, he realized, so he engaged Robert Adams, who had set type for him in Buffalo. He would need an editor, so he engaged a shrewd young man named Orville J. Victor, the same Victor who many years later was to write a letter of encouragement to a very discouraged young man living in Corinna, Maine.

Victor soon made connections with a staff of writers; and on June 15, 1860. Beadle published his first dime novel. It was called Malaeska, or the Indian Wife of the White Hunter, and it was written by Ann S. W. Stephens, who was to follow it with a number of others. It set the pattern for Beadle publications for a long time to come. In format it was a little booklet of 128 pages, about the size of a baseball guide. The printing was on white rag paper and compares favorably with good printing today. The cover was of heavy salmon-colored paper, bearing on the front a steel engraving of the heroine. The story itself was most dignified. Several of the chapters start off with quotations from poetry; the style is rather literary; there is no suggestion of cheapness anywhere in it. It had a sale, in its first year, of 300,000 copies, and within a few years it had been translated into five languages.

Malaeska was followed by others in rapid succession. Some of them, in their day, were celebrated. Seth Jones, or the Captives of the Frontier, by Edward S. Ellis, published also in 1860, had a sale of 750,000 copies, and was translated into seven languages. Maum Guinea, or Christmas Among the Slaves, by Mrs. Metta Victor, wife of the editor, caused almost as much talk during the war as Uncle Tom's Cabin. When Henry Ward Beecher came back from England, where he had gone as Lincoln's representative, he wrote that this little book had done much to influence British public opinion. Lincoln himself, after Beadle had sent him a little package of samples, became a dime-novel fan. The soldiers in camp, finding that dime novels helped to while away many a tedious day, gobbled them up by the million, boosting sales beyond Beadle's wildest dreams. By the time the war came to an end the experiment was an assured success. In 1866 Robert Adams died, and Beadle took his two brothers, David Adams and William Adams, into partnership, the firm becoming Beadle & Adams, under which name it was to do business for thirty years. Beadle was made. It was his turn to ask, "Who's loony now?"

To this flourishing concern Willie Patten submitted his first dime novels. They were, at the most charitable estimate, pretty bad: Clear-Grit Cal, the Never-Say-Die Detective; Fire-Eye, the Thugs' Terror; Wild Vulcan, the Lone Ranger Rider, and so on. But they were published. Money began to pour in—or at least so it seemed in Corinna. Bill Patten's eyes bulged many a time at the $250 checks which his queer fish of a son received for one of these tales; down at the village store they shook their heads and muttered, for all this smacked of black magic.

So, after four years of it, when he was just turned twenty-one, Willie Patten decided it was time for him to go to New York. He had a little money now; he had served his apprenticeship as a writer; he had even, on the money received from the sale of The Corinna Owl, a weekly newspaper that he had started, taken a trip West and viewed at first hand the scene of the epic tales he had been writing. Within a short time he had wound up all his affairs and was ready to start.

All his affairs? Not quite. There was a little affair of honor, one that involved the light but genuine hair that now grew on his face, and the $2500 he had made in the past year as compared with a certain $1800.

When he got off the train at Biddeford he headed straight for the mill. "Where's Gooch?" he demanded of the first millhand he met.

"Hey, Willie!" exclaimed his former buddy. "Boy, I didn't hardly know you at first. You're a sight huskier than you was.... Gooch? Ain't you heard? Gooch is dead."

Col. Prentiss Ingraham limped fretfully around his small room on Fifty-eighth Street and glared belligerently at Patten, who had buckled up his long legs on a trunk.

"No, suh!" he roared, while his small frame quivered with indignation. "The West'n story nev' will be dead. So long as the American people have one drop of red blood left in their veins, I tell you they're goin' to read West'n stories!"

"Custer's been dead pretty near twenty years," said Patten.

"Buffalo Bill ain't dead!" the colonel shot back with heat that was pardonable, since, through the medium of the dime novel, he was Buffalo Bill's official biographer. "If you think he is," he went on, "go down to Philadelphia, where he's shownin' now, and watch him shoot. He can hold up his end of it, even with that little Oakley gal."

"They say she's pretty," said Patten, who had an eye to such things.

"Pretty as a picture," said the colonel, who also had an eye to such things, and stroked his flowing silky mustache. But in a moment he resumed fiercely: "And while you're down there, just count the people that come to see that Wild West show and see if Buffalo Bill is dead yet. And if you'll pa'don a little pride of auth'-ship, I'd just like to call to you' 'tention that my last stories about Buffalo Bill are sellin' bigger than ever. No, suh, Buffalo Bill's not dead, and neither is the West'n story."

Patten listened with half an ear. He was an older Patten now, with ten years in the literary trenches behind him, several of them devoted almost exclusively to this same kind of Western story that he was now beginning to have his doubts about. They had been glorious years in all truth. He had come down to a New York that was probably gaudier than any New York before or since. It was a New York as yet innocent of Subways, wherein you traveled uptown and downtown on elevated roads that still used steam engines, and cross town on cars still drawn by horses. Brooklyn Bridge was then one of the wonders of the modern world, and Steve Brodie had just settled the big argument by jumping off it and living to tell the story. The theatrical district still lay between Fourteenth and Twenty-third Streets; grand opera was given in the Academy of Music on Fourteenth, hard by Tony Pastor's Theater and Huber's Museum; Maggie Cline was just then singing Throw Him Down, McCluskey! John L. Sullivan still reigned supreme, holding court nightly at one or the other of his three saloons. Irish gangs still ravaged the Bowery, where beer gardens, open of front so you could see the drinkers and the dancing girls within, lined most of the way. The Pulitzer Building was still the tallest building in the United States, and visitors to New York ascended in its dome of "solid gold" to refresh themselves with a bird's-eye view of the city. The Hoffman House still attracted many customers with its celebrated oil paintings of the female nude. It was a wide-open town, with everybody having a roaring good time.

Patten loved it. Especially he loved the humbuggery of it. This crowd loved to be fooled and it good naturedly didn't give a hoot how often it was fooled, so it was fooled by a good glow. He loved the humbugs who provided the literary show, who hashed up preposterous tales about Indians chasing pioneers over the plains and being in turn routed by a thundering herd of buffaloes. They were a picturesque crew, who loved the West because it was the big show, and who were as much a part of it as the advance press agent is part of a circus—fellows like Joseph E. Badger, whose master creation was Mustang Sam. . . . "You ax who I be? I'm Mustang Sam, the high muck-a-muck of E Pluribus Unum. . . . I kin yell louder, run furder, ride faster, shoot straighter, jump higher, tell bigger lies, eat more poor bull, and jump outside o'more chain lightnin' than any two-legged critter as was ever puffed." Oil Coomes, who lived in Iowa, and was one of the few dime-novel writers canny enough to invest his money profitably; Edward L. Wheeler, who called everybody pard and was suspected of never having been farther West than West Philadelphia; Harlan P. Halsey, who wrote the delectable detective stories signed Old Sleuth; John R. Coryell, who originated the Nick Carter stories; Buckskin Sam, properly known as Sam S. Hall, who occasionally showed his virile Western manhood by going on a shooting rampage at his home in Wilmington, Delaware.

And Patten laughed as loud as any at the monkeyshine staged daily by Buffalo Bill and Ned Buntline, his first official biographer, known in private life as Col. F. Z. C. Judson. That was when they were first trying to put over Buffalo Bill as a character in dime-novel fiction. Six of eight times a day, both Cody and Judson, in full Western regimentals, would come galloping down Broadway and dismount at the office of the publisher in Rose Street. Ostensibly they were occupied with business of the very first importance; actually they were occupied with nothing more important that to provide a show for the crowd that always awaited them and incidentally to make a little extra publicity for the Buffalo Bill stories.

Most of all, Patten loved this same Colonel Ingraham who was now pacing the floor in such wild excitement at the very suggestion that the Western story might be on its last legs. The colonel had lived such a life that when he recounted his most prosaic experiences he was thought to be making up chapters for his next story. He had fought in the Civil War on the side of the Confederacy; he had soldiered in Austria, in Crete, in Africa, in Cuba, and with Juarez in Mexico. He had shot buffaloes with Buffalo Bill, to help fulfill the celebrated contract with the Kansas Pacific Railroad, under the terms of which Cody delivered the carcasses of more than 5000 buffaloes to be served as meat in the construction camps and thereby earned his highly valuable moniker. When Cody and Buntline had a disagreement, the colonel became Cody's biographer. And so well did he do his job that Buffalo Bill became such a character as not even Cody had dreamed was possible: There is many schoolboy, even now, who is astonished to learn, in sixth-grade history, that this magnifico of the colonel's creation actually lived and breathed. Add to all this the fact that the colonel was a gentleman of the old South, and could cuss in rhymed hexameter-verse, and he stands out as a most colorful writing man.

Now, however, Patten was beginning to be worried about the western story. This was not entirely a matter of art. It was more a question of bread and butter. Since the night when he had come back home from the Biddeford mill, he had written stories for his living, and it was something to be concerned about that the stories he had been writing were beginning to look bleary and frayed around the edges. Wherefore he lent a very dubious ear to the colonel's eulogy of Buffalo Bill.

"It's just like what they're saying about that contraption that this fool Haynes monkeying around with," the colonel was saying. "Some of them say it's going to put the horse out of business. Well, if Hayne was to hook a whistle on his machine, maybe it might do for a peanut roaster. Or if he was to put some bars around it maybe it might do for a cage for that talking dog they've got over at Worth's Museum. But put the horse out of business. Come over here, Gil—just look at the going out to the pa'k. Don't you just love to see 'em step? Gil, there's some thin; that won't never be put out of business. One of them is the horse and the other is more a question of bread and butter. Since the night when he had come back home from the Biddeford mill, he had written stories for his living, and it was something to be concerned about that the stories he had been writing were beginning to look bleary and frayed around the edges. Wherefore he lent a very dubious ear to the colonel's eulogy of Buffalo Bill.

"It's just like what they're saying about the contraption that this fool Haynes monkeying around with," the colonel was saying. "Some of them say it's going to put the horse out of business. Well, if Haynes was to hook a whistle on his machine, maybe it might do for a peanut roster. Or if he was to put some bars around it maybe it might do for a cage for that talking dog they've got over at Worth's Museum. But put the horse out of business. Come over here, Gil—just look at them going out to the pa'k. Don't you just love to see 'em step? Gil, there's some things that won't never be put out of business. One of them is the horse and the other is the West'n story—that gave the horse his proper place in literature, if I do say so myself."

Shortly afterward Patten joined his family at Camden, Maine, where they had moved from Corinna, more than ever convinced that he had to find a new field if he was to continue to make his living by his facile pen. He had hardly landed there when he received a letter from O.G. Smith, president of Street & Smith, in regard to a new series of stories. By the time—1895 Street & Smith had long since taken the leadership of the dime novel herd away from Beadle & Adams. The firm had been started in 1855, several years before Beadle went into business, but had not published dime novels

until after Beadle had demonstrated that the thing could be done. Then gradually it
had pulled ahead, until by now it was the leading publisher in the field. No doubt the
death of Beadle, in 1984 had much to do with the dwindling prosperity of the firm.

Mr. Smith wanted to know if Patten would be interested in doing a new series of
stories for boys. Patten wrote for more details and Mr. Smith replied as follows:

December 16, 1895

Gilbert Patten, Esq.
Camden, Maine.
Dear Sir: Replying to your favor of December 13, at hand today, we beg to state that the material of
which we wrote you in our last letter is intended for a library which we purpose issuing every
week; something in the line of the Jack Harkaway stories, Gay Dashleigh series which we are
running in Good News and the Island School Series, all of which are expressed to you under
separate cover, the idea being to issue a library containing a series of stories covering the class of
incident, in all of which will appear one prominent character surrounded by suitable satellites. It
would be an advantage to the series to have introduced the Dutchman, the Negro, the Irishman,
and any other dialect that you are familiar with. From what we know of your work, we believe
you can give us what we require, and would be pleased to have you write us one of these stories at
once. Upon receipt of it, if satisfactory, we will be prepared to make a contract with you to cover
twenty thousand words weekly for this library and a sufficient number of Good News stories to
keep them running in the columns of Good News, if you believe you can turn out this amount of
work.

It is important that the main character in the series should have a catchy name, such as Dick
Lightheart, Jack Harkaway, Gay Dashleigh, Don Kirk [a character in two previous stories by
Patten] as upon this name will depend the title for the library.

The essential idea of this series is to interest young readers in the career of a young man at a
boarding school, preferably a military or a naval academy. The stories should differ from the Jack
Harkaways in being American and thoroughly up to date. Our idea is to issue, say, twelve stories,
each complete in itself, but like the links in a chain, all dealing with life at the academy. By this
time the readers will have become sufficiently well acquainted with the hero, and the author will
also no doubt have exhausted most of the pranks and escapades that might naturally occur.

After the first twelve numbers, the hero is obliged to leave the academy, or takes it upon
himself to leave. It is essential that he should come into a considerable amount of money at this
period. When he leaves the academy he takes with him one of the professor's servants, a chum. In
fact any of the characters you have introduced and made prominent in the story. A little love
element would also not be amiss, though this is not particularly important.

When the hero is once projected on his travels there is an infinite variety of incident to choose
from. In the Island School Series, published by one of our London connections, you will find
scenes of foreign travel, with color. This material you are at liberty to use freely, with our hero as
the central character, of course, and up-to-date dialogue.

After we run through twenty or thirty numbers of this, we would bring the hero back and
have him go to college, say, Yale University; thence we could take him on his travels again to the
South Seas or anywhere.

If you can do the opening stories of school life, you will be able to do them all, as we shall
assist you in the matter of local color for the stories of travel.

This letter will, of course, be held as confidential. After you have fully examined the Island
School material, kindly return to us.

Yours truly,

Patten hadn't got half through this before he knew that this was what he had been
looking for. He would get away from the absurdities of Western fiction and give the
boys something they could believe in. Also, he would give them a hero they could
really admire. An he would try to build the stories on character rather than on incident,

and in that way make them live.

Preparedness in a Name

Frank Merriwell was agreed upon as the name of the hero, this name suggesting the kind of boy Patten had in mind. And lest the import of the name be lost on the youthful readers, Patten was careful to describe Frank on Page 1 of the first story, thus; "His face was frank, open and winning, but the merry light that usually dwelt in his eyes was now banished by a look of scorn," and so on.

In order that the series could be continued by others if Patten fell ill or got tired of the job, or something of the sort, it was necessary that he have a nom de plume. But L. Standish was agreed upon for this, as being a good, substantial American alias. The pay was to be the pricely sum of fifty dollars a week.

Finally Patten was ready to write the first story, to be called Frank Merriwell; or, First Days at Fardale. As he hitched up to his typewriter he snickered to himself, for there popped into his head a story that was going the rounds about the colonel. It seems that somebody had asked the colonel how he managed to think of plots in such amazing profusion.

"First," the colonel said, "I take a situation, and then I work forward from that."

"Yes, colonel, but what do you mean by a situation?"

"Crack! Crack! Crack! Three more redskins bit the dust," elucidated the colonel. "There you have it. Now go on with your story."

"Better start it off in style," thought Patten, and this is what he wrote:

Chapter I
Frank Makes A Foe

"Get out!"
Thump! A shrill howl of pain.
"Stop it! That's my dog!"
"Oh, it is? Then you ought to be kicked too! Take that for your impudence!"
Cuff! A blow from an open hand sent the boyish owner of a whimpering poodle staggering to the ground, while paper bags of pop corn flew from his basket and scattered their snowy contents around.
"That was a cowardly blow!"

And so on. As may be imagined, the clarion defy at the end came from Frank; and fitting it was that the first words he ever uttered should quiver with magnificent contempt at the spectacle of a cowardly blow.

"It was an awful job, and don't you forget it," says Patten, looking back at the beginning of the Merriwell experiment. "Twenty thousand words a week! That means more than a million words a year—at the rate of one full-length novel a month. And when you turn out stuff that fast for seventeen years, you're grinding copy. All the Merriwell stories have been written and gathered into books. Two hundred and four of them—count them up and see how many they make. But when I was writing them there were times when I felt like a horse in an old country treadmill. I ground and I ground and I ground, and it seemed as though there never would be an end to it."

For the new series was a success from the start. The first number, published April

18, 1896, sold out completely; within three months the circulation of the Tip-Top Library, with Frank Merriwell as its leading character, had reached 75,000, with new readers, their nickels clutched in their dirty little fists, marching up to the news stands every week. And to satisfy them, Patten settled down to the laborious business of grinding out 20,000 words a week every week in the year.

"Over a period of years," he goes on, "I imagine that comes pretty close to setting a record. But don't get the idea that I was a remarkably fast writer. There were plenty of them who could turn it out a lot faster than I could. One time Beadle & Adams needed a serial in a hurry, and Victor locked Edward L. Wheeler in a room with a pile of paper. After two days there was a 30,000-word novel. I don't say it was a good novel, but anyhow it was a novel.

"But the colonel beat that. There was some misunderstanding about a story. Victor expected it, but the colonel hadn't written it, and when Victor wired him, in Washington, it was within two days of publication time. The colonel sat right down and began to write. It almost killed him, but at the end of twenty-four hours he had a 33,000-word story in the mail.

"But over a long pull I probably turned out as much as any of the rest, and maybe a little bit more. The first year was the worst, because I hadn't got any system into it. On those first stories I tramped the floor many a night, and there were weeks when I didn't think I could possibly get a story ready. I used to write a lot of them up in Maine, and if I didn't make a certain express with my copy, there wouldn't be any story that week. And more than once I finished the story so late I had to run down to the station and hand the envelope to the man on the mail car; the train would be already in and ready to pull out.

"After a while it came easier. I blocked the stories out thirteen at a time. Why thirteen? Well, there are fifty-two weeks in the year, and when you divide fifty-two by four you get thirteen, not twelve. Then I saved myself a lot of work by learning to dictate to a stenographer. My fingers got sore banging out that much copy on a machine. The dictation scheme accounts for one thing that many people laugh about in the Merriwell stories—a stilted effect in the style and a touch of artificiality in the dialogue. I guess the charge is true. But you shoot 4,000 words a day at a stenographer, and when she transcribes her notes, see how flexible and natural it sounds. Easy style and nice, homely dialogue are possible only when you have a chance to shine up your work. No chance for that doing the Merriwells. That was rough-and-ready writing, and if you couldn't do it that way, you couldn't do it at all.

"Plots? I never had much trouble with plots. No, I wasn't like the colonel; I didn't start with a situation and work forward from that. I built all these stories around a character. If you will read the first Merriwell story you will see what I mean. That is a story about a number of boys, one of them Merriwell, who were candidates for admission to Fardale Academy. One of them, as a result of the brawl at the railroad station which opens the story, takes a dislike to Merriwell and plots to keep him out of the academy. In the course of the feud, Merriwell rescues the beautiful Inza from a mad dog after the other boy had fled; he emerges triumphant from a fist fight and two or three other scrapes that he stumbles into. Superficially, that is a story made up of highly improbable incident. Look a little closer and you will see that Frank succeeds because he has certain outstanding traits of character. Even in the end, when he is freed from a cemetery vault into which his enemies had locked him, his rescuer is the same little shaver whom he had befriended a few days before at the railroad station in the scuffle over the dog."

"All the Merriwell stories were built on the same formula—to test Frank in some crucial way so that certain sides of his nature were thrown into high relief. Yes, one of his qualities, of course, was courage. But they laugh about Frank's bravery too much. As a matter of fact, he wasn't so brave; he was scared often, and badly scared at that. Much more important was his loyalty—something that boys esteem more than anything else. No matter how hard pressed Frank might be, he never played anybody a dirty trick. Of course, it was my business to see that he was hard pressed in every story. He was always getting into jams, so that if he would only turn against his friends he could make a million dollars. Of course he never did it. Another quality was a sense of humor. Another was a sense of justice, a capacity to see the other fellow's side. And another was a little vague; I can best describe it as decency.

"But he had a lot of very human weaknesses too. One of them was a love for gambling. Frank's battle to overcome this furnished many a chapter in the series, and the boys, I judge, found it just as absorbing as a lot of so-called action."

The popular story based on character was a novelty then; the publishers, although they had themselves suggested the idea, were a little appalled at the lengths to which Patten carried it. One day while he was at luncheon with O.G. Smith and his brother G.C. Smith, also of the Street & Smith firm, O.G. Smith wanted to know if the stories could not be sped up a little.

"It seems to me," he said, "that these stories ought to have more action—incident, you know, excitement, something going on."

Patten, a little surprised, asked where the stories seemed to lag.

"Well," said Smith, "last week you had a story that shows what I mean. For two pages Merriwell does nothing but take care of his horse—feeds him, waters him, rests him, and so on. I don't believe that appeals to boys."

"I think you're wrong," said Patten. "In the first place, Merriwell has been repeatedly identified as a humane character. He is kind to animals; it is part of his nature. In the second place, nine-tenths of the boys who read these stories are of the age when they are crazy over horses. They know all about horses. And when they read how Merriwell was considerate of his horse, that brings the story close home to them. Those two pages are just as interesting to them as though I had had Frank ride the horse in front of the express train and grab the girl off the cowcatcher. Get your mind off action. Action is what killed the old dime novel. It is all right for a few pages, but it gets pretty tedious unless there is some character mixed up with it that you can get interested in." Smith was still dubious. "I'll ask you one thing," said Patten: "Do the stories sell?"

Smith laughed. Turning to his brother he said: "I guess Patten's got us there. The stories sell all right. If they haven't got excitement, they've got something, so we might as well let him alone and let him do his stories his own fool way."

"Characters," Patten explains, "were perhaps the hardest. When you're writing regular fiction, you draw your characters from life. But when you're writing for boys, you draw your characters from the imaginary world that boys live in. When I conceived Frank, I think I hit on approximately the boy that every kid would like to be. Not, mind you, the boy that every kid ought to be. That was the Horatio Alger idea—a moral in every story. But my boy pointed no moral; he was just every boy's ideal picture of himself. And I never did anything cleverer than when I made Frank, right in the first story, an expert ventriloquist.

"The kids had all heard of this trick, and they had all gone out back of the barn to practice, in a secret effort to acquire it. So when Frank appeared as a master of this mysterious art they fell in love with him at once.

"But Frank wasn't the only character. There had to be others, especially villains. For a long time Bart Hodge was the chief villain of the series. He was the boy who cuffed the little pop-corn vender at the railroad station. Bart, however, eventually renounced his evil ways and became Frank's closest friend. Then there was Porfias del Norte, who appeared when I took Frank out West for a time.

"Friends have told me that Porfias del Norte was the greatest villain of all literature. He had every human depravity, and a few depravities that had not heretofore been regarded as human. He stopped at nothing—not even mayhem. His word was not worth the breath it took to utter it. He had not the slightest chivalry toward women and children. He associated with low characters. He was prolific of plots, schemes and intrigues. His lightest word was a curse.

"Then there had to be comic characters. It is a curious thing, but you cannot give boys a real humor. They do not understand it. Slapstick is what they get fun out of. That is the reason for such characters as Harry Rattleton, who always said things like "I feel filly—I mean, I feel silly." Boys think that very funny. And Hans Dunnerwurst, the Dutch boy; and Ephraim Gallup, the lank Yankee boy, who, every time things began to get hot, would moan, 'I wisht I was to hum on the farm.'

"Only twice did I draw characters from life. Once was when I used a friend of mine, Capt. Walter Wiley, and put him into the stories, name and all. He had been a seafaring man and was a picturesque fellow, and he went over great with the boys. In the stories he was always referred to as the Windjammer."

"The other time was a little different." Here Patten pauses to laugh. "One time I met a lady I knew, up in Maine—a Mrs. Gardner, and she said to me, 'Mr. Patten, my boy reads about Frank Merriwell every week, and he wants to know if you couldn't put him into a story'. "

"So I said that would be easy enough, and I asked her one or two questions about what kind of looking boy he was, since I had never seen him, and one or two other things about him, and then I put him into a story. He only appeared for a sentence or two, did Earl Gardner, as a freshman at Yale who wanted to meet the great Frank Merriwell, but never had the chance, and I thought that would be the end of it. But within two weeks I had a hundred letters from boys all over the country, demanding that I give them more about Earl Gardner. So Earl Gardner became one of the most popular characters in the stories."

"A trust," said O. Henry, "is its own weakest point"; and the same principle held true for Merriwell. It was his very popularity that led to his downfall. For in spite of all that Patten did to stunt his growth, he grew bigger and bigger and older and older, until no boy in the world could be expected to take an interest in him. His story, indeed for the last ten eventful years of his life, is the story of Patten's desperate efforts to keep alive the spark of youth within him. Other characters might stay the same age for years. Mutt and Jeff look the same now as they did seventeen years ago; the

Katzenjammer Kids never grow up, and neither does Chester Gump.

But Merriwell had no such luck. He was the idol of thousands of boys who kept book on him as closely as thousands of other boys now keep book on Babe Ruth. When Frank had finished the first year at Fardale he had to go on to second year; there was no more chance that he could be sent to repeat the course than that he could be sent out to rob a bank. And after four years at Fardale he was through at Fardale; the big question was what to do with him next.

In accordance with the original plan, he went to Yale. He was a great boy at Yale; he made the football team every year, and won all the Harvard games single-handed in the last minute of play. He was elected to all the best fraternities; he led his class with honors. In fact he was easily the most remarkable student that Old Eli ever had.

But at the end of his junior year, the same old question came up; in another year he would graduate, and be a man, out of the ken of boys forever. The situation was rather serious. The circulation was now 108,000; much depended on Merriwell, so far as Patten was concerned. His original $50 a week, after a number of raises, had become $150; and in the early 1900s this was not to be sneezed at.

To gain time to think, Patten took Frank out of Yale. He contrived a dastardly plot whereby Frank lost all his money and had to go to work on a railroad. Here, at least, it would be harder for the boys to keep tab on the hero, since there were no college semesters marking the time so easily. And while Frank worked on the locomotives, Patten racked his brain as to what to do. And finally he decided he would retire Frank and invent a long-lost brother, much younger than Frank, who would reawaken juvenile interest.

So Frank settled the great strike on the railroad, recovered his fortune, went back to college, graduated at the end of a year, and the stage was all set for Dick. The advent of Dick presented some difficulties, as Frank was an only child, as all the readers knew. Nevertheless, Merriwell pere had once taken a mysterious trip, and Patten let it be known that on this trip he had got married, and Dick Merriwell was the result of that union. So Dick Merriwell finally appeared on the scene, much to the surprise of Frank, as may be imagined.

But Dick was a dreadful flop. The readers still numbered thousands, of course, for the name Merriwell was potent. But the boys never took to Dick as they had taken to Frank.

"The reason," says Patten, "was that Dick was not the character that Frank was. I couldn't make him a replica of Frank, you know; he had to be different. But it was Frank who really stood for every boy's dream. Dick was all right, but not many boys wanted to be like him. And then I suppose I had got careless. Frank's ventriloquism was a big hit. But Dick's capacity to talk with wild animals never went over. It just didn't click. I guess I had written Merriwells too long."

And so, after a few years of Dick, the Merriwell series came to an end. After Patten gave it up, two or three others tried to carry on, but without success.

Shortly after the Merriwell stories started, Beadle & Adams closed their doors. After the debacle, Patten and Arthur Grissom, first editor of Smart Set, persuaded Street & Smith to give the colonel a berth. And there he continued to recount the glories of Buffalo Bill, but to an ever-dwindling clientele.

In 1904, just before he died, the colonel went up to visit Patten in Maine.

"How's Little Lord Merriweather?" he asked.

"Paying a hundred and fifty a week," said Patten. "How's Buffalo Bill?"

"Dead," said the colonel. "Cody's not, but Buffalo Bill is." He sighed. "Gil," he confided, "something's happened to this country. Things aren't what they used to be."

In addition to the Merriwell stories, Patten has written seventy novels of standard length, besides innumerable serials and short stories that were never gathered into book form. The Merriwells, in reissued form, are still on sale on the newsstands. He estimates that in his life he has written 40,000,000 words of fiction, or enough to fill eight five-foot shelves. He is now plain Gilbert Patten, having dropped the William because it reminded him of the days when he was called Willie. Oddly enough, although he is easily the country's most prolific *literatus,* you will not find him in Who's Who.

"Did I love Merriwell?" he says. "Not at first. Those early stories were more of a joke to me than anything else. But when it got so that a half million kids were reading him every week—and I think there were that many, when you stop to think how the stories were lent from hand to hand—I began to realize that I had about the biggest chance to influence the youth of this country that any man ever had. And when you get the messiah complex you are lost. Yes, I loved him. And I loved him most because no boy, if he followed in his tracks, ever did anything that he need be ashamed of."

The Solid South
(*The Bookman,* November 1933)

It is my purpose in this article to discuss certain twists in the Southern mind, especially the twist which leads it to vote dry and drink wet, and perhaps to hazard a few forecasts as to what the future may hold. But at the very outset I find myself stuck. As a result of the nonsense that has been published in recent years, it has become impossible to talk about the South with a person who has not been there, for he thinks of it in terms of all sorts of fantastic goings on, and appraises its mentality at such a discount that he is quite unable to understand what you are trying to tell him. If you will bear with me, then, for a few moments, I shall try to clear up any misconceptions that may have arisen in your mind, and then get on with the discourse.

The South, taking one community with another, is not lawless. Of course, there are parts of it where dreadful things happen. But there are parts of every section where dreadful things happen. Surely no part of the South can surpass in lawlessness the Egypt section of Illinois, whose capital is Herrin, or the coal mine section of Pennsylvania, or the oil-well section of Oklahoma. A certain amount of violence is an inevitable part of the human scene; it can be expected wherever hoodlums are in the majority, whether they be American hoodlums or Italian hoodlums, or Northern hoodlums or Southern hoodlums. If you ascribe any undue portion of it to the South, you merely befuddle all your thinking about the South. There are towns in the South where nobody has been flogged since the Civil War, where there has not been a lynching in the memory of the oldest inhabitant, and where the Ku Klux Klan is regarded as humorously as it is regarded in New York City. With regard to lynching, the truth is that it is all but extinct, in the South as well as everywhere else, as you can see for yourself if you will consult the figures on it as given in the *World Almanac*. The number of victims per annum, which ran into the hundreds in the nineties, is now down in the 'teens, and it steadily diminishes. In another few years lynching will take its place with the persecution of witches in colonial times as a historical curiosity.

The South is not insanely anti-Catholic. Of course, there are people everywhere who believe there is a gigantic Catholic conspiracy to put the Pope in the White House. But there are probably no more of them in the South than anywhere else. As it happens, I was a Catholic in my youth, and I lived in a typical Southern community on the Eastern Shore of Maryland, a section predominantly Methodist. If there was any discrimination against me because I was a Catholic, I did not hear of it, and I think a boy knocking around with other boys would have heard of it. And while my personal charm is undeniable, I don't think any exception was made in my case on account of it. Relations between my church and the other churches in town were very cordial. When we held our annual supper in October, all the money was made off hungry Methodists who had packed the hall to get a good meal for fifty cents, and when the other churches held their suppers in the spring, there were always a number of Catholics in the throng, Catholics who looked a little guilty, but who put down their fried chicken and deviled eggs nevertheless. In a political way, they had nothing to complain of. They got a fair allotment of county jobs from time to time, and I never heard a no-popery howl in any campaign. Mr. Dixon, who took up the collection, was Clerk of the Court for at least ten years. He was always unanimously elected, both parties agreeing that he was the man for the job.

The South is not backward in cultural development. There is a general impression that it is, I know, and it has made little effort to correct that impression. Nevertheless, the impression is false. It is true that the South has few resident practitioners of the bozart, and that it supports no symphony orchestras. But this state of affairs is due, not to any hostility to the bozart on the part of the South, for no such hostility exists, but simply to the fact that there are no large cities in the South. When you consider that Baltimore, which is three times the size of any other Southern city in the matter of white population that might be interested in the bozart, can boast a bare half-dozen men who have made any reputation as writers, musicians, and sculptors, you can see why no city lying south of it is likely to be able to boast of a great many. What happens when a Southerner decides to go in for the bozart in a professional way is that he moves north, as did Olga Samaroff, Thomas Dixon, Riccardo Martin, Joseph Wood Krutch, Laurence Stallings, Stark Young, Irvin S. Cobb, and dozens of others, not to forget Edgar Allan Poe. He has to, to make a living. So that a peremptory challenge to a place like Atlanta to produce a list of artists, or to support a big-time symphony orchestra, is just plain nonsense. You had as well demand that it support a big-league baseball team.

As for the bozart in a general way, the South does not differ much from the rest of the country. It has its circulating libraries, which carry books good, bad, and indifferent; it has its small choruses and orchestras; it has its professional concerts, when it can afford them; of late, it has its little theatres, which have sprung up everywhere to take the place of the late-lamented road companies. In addition, it has several excellent universities, notably the University of North Carolina, the University of Virginia, and Vanderbilt University. Vanderbilt, it should be noted, is in the heart of the Bible Belt in Tennessee, and yet it made not the slightest compromise with the dolts who staged the farce at Dayton, and a few years before, it made not the slightest compromise with the dolts who tried to purge its faculty of Huns. Independence is by no means uncommon in the South—although it doesn't seem to get much publicity.

In short, the kind of Southerner who runs the South is an intelligent, reflective, and informed man. It will help you a great deal, when you try to understand him, if you remember that. When you think of him as a simian farmhand, acting from pathological impulses and almost incapable of rational thought, you only make things a great deal harder for yourself.

II

One time I was talking with a candidate for Congress in one of the districts of Maryland. He was in a little difficulty. Although he had the backing of the Democratic organization, and although he was very well thought of, he wasn't attracting much attention. He lacked what is called an issue, something to make a fight about. I suggested that Prohibition was a lively issue, and that he might cause quite a stir if he ran as a wet. He thought this over for a moment and then he shook his head.

"No," he said, "that won't do. I believe you're right about a wet having a good chance in my district. A whole lot of those people don't think much of Prohibition. But I can't come out as a wet. It's a matter of principle with me. I'm a dry, I always have been a dry, and I always expect to be a dry. And I can't see my way clear to coming out as a wet just to get a few votes."

Then he poured himself a drink and asked me what I thought of the League of Nations as a campaign issue.

Now this, which is quite typical of a Southern politician, is at first glance comic. You feel that a man who could solemnly come out with such a statement, and then top it off with a glass of whisky, must be a lineal descendant of the late Petroleum V. Nasby. But when you trace back the reasons for it, the comic touches begin to vanish, and you see that it is consistent with a perfectly sane political philosophy, and, most paradoxical of all, quite sincere.

The truth is that the principles of democracy, as they are supposed to be accepted by other citizens of the Republica, are merely so much bombast to the Southerner. He has heard of them, of course, for they are in his school books. But he regards them as the graceful trimmings of the government, as pleasant rhetoric to be spouted on the Fourth of July. It has never occurred to him that they are actually to be put into practice. So far as he is concerned, all men are not created equal. Thus he sees nothing strange, and certainly nothing unjust, in laws that bear differrently on different kinds of men. To him there is no hypocrisy in denying a drink to one man, and in granting it to another.

His point of view in this respect is partly reasoned from the premises that confront him everywhere he turns, and partly inherited. It was many, many years ago that his ancestors noted that with regard to the principles of government there is a great difference between theory and practice. Specifically, they noted certain differences between the Declaration of Independence, which furnishes the theoretical basis for our government and the Constitution of the United States, which puts the theories into practice. The one said that all men are created free and equal. The other said that some men are slaves. It did not say that they were in so many words, it is true; it delicately referred to them as "such persons as any of the states now existing shall think proper to admit". But it made its meaning perfectly clear to all who cared to read.

Now there is a hopeless discrepancy between these two propositions. If one is true the other must necessarily be false. It was a discrepancy that caused quite a little trouble in the last century. In the end the North went to war to establish the truth of the first; the South went to war to establish the truth of the second. And the North won the war, but the South won the argument.

For we may as well be honest about this thing, regardless of the feelings of the sad young men on the liberal magazines. The Negro in the South today, no matter what he may make of himself tomorrow, offers conclusive evidence that the Declaration of Independence was a little previous with the things that it held to be self-evident. He is not the equal of the white man. In Harlem he is. That is to say, he has attained the white man's high estate and ½ percent in habitants who are civilized. 49½ percent who are dull middle class, and 50 percent who are muscular morons. But in the South he has made no such brilliant record for himself. There he runs 0 percent of inhabitants who are civilized, ½ percent who are dull middle class, and 99½ percent who are muscular morons. There are, it is true, occasional Negroes in the South who are civilized in every sense of the word. But when you add them up, and then divide by 8,064.377, which is the total number of Negroes in the South, the quotient is so small that it does not affect the percentages I have given above.

Now these are facts which face the Southerner as soon as he gets out of bed in the morning. And they are at the bottom of his conviction that laws must apply differently to different kinds of men; that government is a job for the few who are fit to govern and not for these millions of irresponsible children who are not fit to govern at all, or even to exercise the "rights" that are said to belong to them inalienably.

I wonder if you have ever stopped to think how alienable these rights really are. You are under the impression, I suppose, that you have the right to use the streets of the city where you live. So you have. But if you abuse this right it will be taken from you so fast that you will hardly know what happened to you. That is to say, if you are hauled up three times for driving your automobile while under the influence of liquor, you will have your license revoked and find that your right was alienable to a considerable extent.

Well, that is what has happened in the South. The Negro there has shown in pitiful fashion that there are certain rights that he cannot be entrusted with. So these rights, and only these rights, have been taken away from him. They are as follows:

(a) The right to demand admittance to the hotels, theatres, restaurants, and schools where white people are admitted, and to ride in the compartments where white people ride on public conveyances.

(b) The right to vote.

These are all. No other rights have been taken from him, and this is a very important point to note when people begin shooting their mouths off about "race prejudice". The Negro in the South usually gets a fair deal in the courts, and sometimes more than a fair deal, for often his employer shows up and intercedes on his behalf. He is free to engage in business, and often does so, with extensive white patronage. In the town where I used to live, the most prosperous barber was Jim Jones, a Negro and his customers were all white. Across the street from him Jim Robinson had a restaurant, also patronized by white people. In Harper's Ferry, W. Va., which really ought to be considered as in the Shenandoah Valley section of Virginia, the swank hotel is owned and run by Negroes, and its customers are also white. Scores of instances of this sort could be mentioned in all parts of the South. The only rights which have been abridged are those which I have listed; and there are solid, substantial reasons in both cases.

For the abridgment of the first right the reason is that the Negro, when you admit him to polite surroundings, is an entirely unknown quantity. He may be decently dressed and conduct himself in a decent manner. But on the other hand he may be dressed in filthy overalls, smeared with plaster, grease, canning-factory refuse, or whatever he has been working in, and smelling to high heaven; and he may conduct himself so boisterously that he is a nuisance to everybody within earshot. That is the story of the Jim Crow laws, and it is a hard story to dispose of. When the Negro in the South is as orderly, as well-dressed, and as well-bathed as the Negro in New York. I imagine the Jim Crow laws will go into the discard. But until then they are a public necessity.

With regard to the pother that is continually kicked up over the "nullification" of the Fifteenth Amendment, the abridgment, that is, of the Negro's right to vote, it is a little hard to speak patiently. Of course, if you conceive of the right to vote as the right to drop a vague sort of ballot in a vague sort of box in favor of a vague sort of candidate; and if you conceive of government in terms of vague legislatures passing vague laws about this and that. I can see that the disfranchisement of Negroes in the South will strike you as a monstrously unjust thing. But if you conceive of the right to vote in a realistic way, as the right to drop a specific ballot in a specific box in favor of specific candidate, and carrying with it per se the right to govern; and if you conceive of government in terms of the things which it is predominantly concerned with, then you must know that this disfranchisement had to come. Legislatures and laws are only a small part of the activities of government. When you get to political units smaller than states, they are almost a negligible part of government. The average county does not enact a new regulation once in six months. But it has plenty of other things on its hands. It must build roads, bridges, and schoolhouses. It must keep vital statistics, records of deeds, titles, and judgments; and it cannot make mistakes about them either. It must collect taxes and account for them accurately. It must apprehend, prosecute, and convict criminals, and keep a system of courts running. And it must operate an educational system whose cost, even in a poor county, runs to thousands of dollars a month.

Now if it were just a matter of sitting around passing laws all the time, I grant you the Negro might do just as well as the white man. He could hardly do worse. But if you can picture him as doing any of the things I have mentioned above, you can picture the impossible. Give him a year in any county, and everything, from roads to schools, would be in a state of chaos. And that is the reason he has been disfranchized. It would be more accurate to say that is the reason he has been allowed to disfranchize himself. For there has been pulled no rough stuff; Senator Glass is quite right when he says there is no "nullification" of the Fifteenth Amendment. The thing is done quite simply by means of a poll tax, a literacy test, or a property test. Election officials no doubt give a little assistance now and then, but not much. They don't have to. For the sad truth is that if the Southern Negro does not flunk out on one of these tests he flunks out on another: if he has $2 to pay his poll tax, then he flunks the literacy tests; and if he can pay the poll tax and pass the literacy test, he flunks the property test. Negroes who pass all three, as a rule, are allowed to vote. The Southerner likes to feel broad-minded like anybody else.

Thus the hue and cry about race prejudice in the South is a little out of joint with the facts as they exist. Race prejudice exists in the South, of course. But there is race prejudice and race prejudice. There is the race prejudice of the professional Southerner who "wouldn't eat with a nigger, no sir, if I was starving to death". And there is the race prejudice of the average Southerner who has no general convictions on the subject, but who will not associate with the rough, uncouth and unwashed Negroes he sees around him any more than he would associate with rough, uncouth and unwashed white men. What I am trying to say is that race prejudice, as it exists in the South, is not a philosophic, abstract thing, a credo that all white people are sworn to uphold, but a spontaneous physical thing, a state of mind that would be forced on the most open-minded person as soon as he spent a week in the South. As the Negro becomes more presentable, race prejudice tends to disappear. What the Negro race in the South needs is fewer organs of indignant opinion and more bathtubs.

III

I dilate on these things, not to hold a brief for the Southerner's way of dealing with the Negro problem, but to make it clear that he is distinctly class-minded, and has every reason to be. He would not call himself so, of course, for this expression has a rather sinister sound to it. If he were asked to give his point of view a name, he would probably say he was "element-minded". Elements play a great part in his thinking. "I tell you how it is," he will often say to you; "the reason I stick with the Democratic party is that it represents the best element in the community." And again: "There's an element in this county that we got to do something about pretty soon. I say live and let live, but when you've got an element that don't know how to behave, and all the time raising hell and making a lot of trouble, why then something's got to be done."

But whether you call him class minded or element minded, it amounts to the same thing. And, while this state of mind had its origin in the effort to devise a plan that would work with Negroes, it did not take long to branch out and take in other citizens as well. The Southerner, as I have said, is not stupid. And he saw that the yokels who swarmed the street on Saturday night were just as much of a problem, particularly with regard to public order, as the Negroes. They were noisy, they caroused until all hours of the night, they were a menace to the safety of law abiding people. And as he turned this over in his mind, he decided that something had to be done about this "element" as well as about the Negro element. The result was Prohibition. And the result, also, was this peculiar attitude that was revealed by my friend the candidate for Congress. The Southerner was no more concerned about alcohol as a moral question than you and I are concerned about it. Since he could hold his liquor or, if he could not, since he removed himself from public view when he was drunk he had no intention of becoming a teetotaler himself. But he had every intention of placing liquor beyond the reach of the farmhands and Negroes who were dangerous when they got hold of it.

But calculations go awry. This class consciousness, this element-mindedness, cannot be kept a secret for very long. It seeps down, and after many years, the whole population gets permeated with it. At least that is what happened in the South. Even the yokels heard of it, and grew accustomed to it, and made it a part of their thinking. The result was the Ku Klux Klan. It was, of course, a ghastly travesty on the original idea. Where the upper-class Southern had been class-conscious only to the extent that he had to be, and had kept a fairly clear motion of the implications of what he was doing, the Ku Kluxer was class-conscious for the pure thrill that his class-consciousness gave him. "If this is a government for the benefit of the restricted few, and no others have any rights whatever." Then he proceeded to proscribe everybody that he bore a grudge against, and especially everybody that he feared. Catholics, Jews, Negroes—all these looked alike to him, and it gave him a fine feeling of superiority, probably the first he had ever had in his life, to make speeches against them and send them anonymous notes.

In most parts of the South, as I have said, this did not amount to much in a practical way. The people who actually run the average Southern community would not for a minute stand for any such goings on as the Ku Klux is supposed to have indulged in, and did indulge in often enough to get a great many dispatches into the newspapers. But it was irritating nevertheless in an intangible way. It was a vulgar mockery of something that had had a real meaning; moreover, it held the South up to ridicule, gave it a bad name. And the upper-class Southerner, as I know from talking with him, has done some hard thinking about this Ku Klux business. He has it well under control now, as he always has such things under control. Ku Kluxers, lately, have been going to jail, and the Klan is losing its poor witless members everywhere. But it has been disturbing, nevertheless, because it has come perilously close to reducing a philosophy of government to absurdity.

Then Prohibition has worked out in a way exactly opposite to what was intended. In the beginning, as I have said, the idea back of it was that a gentleman could get his liquor, but that others must go dry. Until National Prohibition came along, only two Southern States, Georgia and Florida, were "bone-dry," all the others affording some means for a citizen to have liquor in his home if he had a home to have it in. But under National Prohibiton it has turned out that a gentleman cannot get any liquor, but that others can get all they want. Of course a gentleman can get liquor, too, but he cannot get liquor that he can drink. A yokel can get corn whiskey in any quantity, and at prices so low as to be ridiculous, and he is perfectly satisfied to drink corn whiskey. But a gentleman cannot drink corn whiskey. It peels the lining of his stomach.

Thus the South, from what I hear of it, is in a reflective mood, and it is not to be wondered at that it turns a kindly eye on the candidacy of Al Smith, the champion of equal rights for all. As to what is going to happen down there I don't know, for the factors are complex and they operate slowly. But I would not be suprised at some radical changes. The Southerner, I remind you once more, is an intelligent man; he knows what is good for him as well as anybody, and he is very little-swayed by moral zeal. The things which lined him up in favor of Prohibition have to a large extent disappeared in the last twenty years. The dreadful dirt roads, the isolation of whole sections of a community, the dimly lighted towns, all those things which made a cross-roads saloon a source of all sorts of disorders, are a thing of the past. More miles of good roads go down every year, the towns are well lighted, sheriffs have fast cars, there are motorcops on every highway. Thus the police problem that Prohibition was originally devised to deal with is to a large extent gone. Time is required for all things, of course. New slogans have to be invented, people have to think and change their minds. The religious ardor which is the outer seeming of Prohibition has to have a chance to cool. But it would not be unlikely that when a sensible plan to deal with the liquor question is devised the South will be as hospitable to it as any other section.

Paradise
(The American Mercury, March 1933)

I shall attempt, in this piece, an appraisal of the civilization of Southern California, but it occurs to me that before I begin I had better give you some idea what the place looks like. If you are like myself before I came here, you have formed, from Sunkist ads, newsreels, movie magazines, railroad folders, and so on, a somewhat false picture of it, and you will have to get rid of this before you can understand what I am trying to say.

Wash out, then, the "land of sunshine, fruit, and flowers": all these are here, but not with the lush, verdant fragrance that you have probably imagined. A celebrated movie comedian is credited with the remark that "the flowers don't smell and the women do," but in my observation nothing smells. Wash out the girl with the red cheeks peeping coyly from behind a spray of orange leaves. The girl is here, but the dry air has taken the red out of her cheeks; the orange trees are here, but they don't look that way: the whole picture has too much pep, life, and moisture in it.

Wash out the palm trees, half visible beyond the tap dancing platform. Palm trees are here, but they are all phonies, planted by people bemused with the notion of a sub-tropical climate, and they are so out of harmony with their surroundings that they hardly arrest your notice. Wash out the movie palazzos, so impressive in the photographs. They are here too, at any rate in a place called Beverly Hills, not far from Hollywood; but they are like the palm trees, so implausible in their surroundings that they take on the lifelessness of movie sets. Above all, wash out the cool green that seems to be the main feature of all illustrations got out by railroads. Wash that out and keep it out.

When you have got this far, you can begin quite starkly with a desert. As to what this desert looked like before it was touched by man you can get an idea by following it across the Mexican border into Lower California, where man is feeble and touches no more than he has to. On one side you can put an ocean, a placid oily-looking ocean that laps the sand with no sign of life on it except an occasional seal squirming through the swells, and almost no color. On the other side, some hundreds of miles inland, put some mountains. Between ocean and mountains put some high hills that look as if they were spilled out carelessly with a gigantic sugar scoop, and between the hills, wide flat valleys. Have both hills and valleys a grey sunbaked tan; put a few tufts of dry grass on the hills and occasional clumps of stunted trees in the valleys, but see that the naked earth shows through everything that grows on it.

You are now ready for the handiwork of man. I suggest that you put it in with water-color, for if it blurs here and there and lacks a very clear outline, that will be so much the better. The hills you can leave just as they were. In the valleys in addition to the stunted clumps you already have, put in some trees: a few palms, eucalyptus, orange, fig, pomegranate, and other varieties that require little water. You might smear in some patches of green lawn, with hose sprinkling them: it will remind you that bringing water in by pipeline is still the outstanding accomplishment of man in this region.

Now then, put in some houses. Most of them should be plain white stucco with red tile roofs, for the prevalent architecture is Spanish, although a mongrel Spanish that is corrupted by every style known on earth, and a few styles not hitherto known. But you can also let your fancy run at this point, and put in some structures *ad lib*, just to exhibit your technique. If a filling station occurs to you, a replica of the Taj Mahal, faithfully executed in lath and plaster, put that in. If you hit on a hot-dog stand in the shape of a hot dog prone, with portholes for windows and a sign reading "Alligator Farm," put that in. Never mind why a hot-dog stand should have portholes for windows and a new line of alligators: we are concerned here with appearances, and will get to that part later.

If you think a blacksmith shop in the shape of a gilded tea-kettle would be an agreeable nifty, put that in; by the time you get it there it will be an Automobile laundry, Cars Washed, 50c, but leave it in anyhow. You might throw in a few structures in the shape of lemons, oranges, pagodas, igloos, windmills, mosques, and kangaroo heads, without bothering to inquire what they are doing there; if you must have signs on them, mark them "For Sale Cheap." For the rest, long rows of wire poles, some advertising statuary done in papier mache, and the usual bungalows and tract offices. It doesn't matter much, so paint everything up gaudily and have it different from the place next door.

Now take your opus out in the noonday sun, tack it down on a board, and look at it. You will find that something has happened to it. In that dreadful glare, all the color you smeared on so lavishly has disappeared; your trees do not look like trees at all, but are inconsequential things reaching not .000001% of the distance to the heaven they aspire to; your green lawns are hardly visible, and the water that sprinkles them is but a misty mockery of water; your gay structures, for all their artistic incongruity, fail to apprise God of the joke: all that is left is the gray, sunbaked tan that you started with. Well, that is Southern California.

The main thing to remember is the sunlight, and the immense expanse of sky and earth that it illuminates: it sucks the color out of everything that it touches, takes the green out of leaves and the sap out of twigs, makes human beings seem small and of no importance. Here there is no oppressive heat, you understand. The climate is approximately as represented: temperate in Summer, with cool evenings when you often light a fire; almost as temperate in Winter, except for the occasional night that makes you long for the steam heat of the East. It is simply that the sunlight gives everything the unmoving quality of things seen in a desert. And of course this is greatly aggravated by the similarity of the seasons, in itself. Nothing changes. Summer follows Winter without a Spring, Winter follows Summer without a Fall. The citrus trees flower and bear all at the same time: you never get a riot of blossoms as you do in Western Maryland when the apple trees are in bloom, or a catharsis of stinking, primitive accomplishment, as you do in Delaware when the tomatoes go to the cannery. Here the oil wells flow right along, so do the orange trees, so does everything. It is terrifying.

You may suppose that here an addict of dark days is voicing an aversion to sunlight, and that I exaggerate the effect which the sun has on things, particularly on the appearance of the countryside. I don't think so, and I adduce one curious scrap of evidence to bolster my position. About halfway between Los Angeles and San Diego is a small beach colony, called Balboa. It lies on a lagoon that makes in from the ocean, an inlet perhaps half a mile wide and two or three miles long. This must be fairly deep, as it is a deep, indigo blue. Now this patch of blue is the only thing for miles, nay for hundreds of miles, that can compete with the sunlight and nullify it, so that you see things as they really are. As a result, Balboa seems a riot of color, although it is nothing but a collection of ordinary beach cottages when you get into it. You stop your car when you come to it, feast your eyes on it, as an Arab might feast his eyes on an oasis; think foolishly of paintings depicting Italy and other romantic places.

I think that this circumstance, the fact that one patch of blue water can make such a difference in the appearance of the landscape, shows what really ails the look of this part of the country; gives a clue, too, to why the inhabitants are so indifferent to the really appalling atrocities that they have committed. Balboa, although not pretentious, is built in some sort of harmony, for with its setting the residents had an incentive to build something to go with it; but elsewhere, it makes no difference what people do, the result is the same. If they erect a beautiful house, as many of them have, the sun robs it of all force and life; if they erect a monstrosity, it passes unnoticed, is merely one more thing along the road.

There is no reward for aesthetic virtue here, no punishment for aesthetic crime; nothing but a vast cosmic indifference, and that is the one thing the human imagination cannot stand. It withers, or else, frantic to make itself felt, goes off into feverish and idiotic excursions that have neither reason, rhyme, nor point, and that even fail in their one purpose, which is to attract notice.

II

Now, in spite of the foregoing, when you come to consider the life that is encountered here, you have to admit that there is a great deal to be said for it.

First, I would list the unfailing friendliness and courtesy of the people. It is a friendliness somewhat different from what you find elsewhere, for it does not as a rule include hospitality. The man who will take all sorts of trouble to direct you to some place you are trying to find does not ordinarily invite you into his house; it is not that he has any reason for keeping you out, it is merely that it does not occur to him to do it.

Hospitality, I think, comes when people have set down roots; it goes with pride in a home, pride in ancestors that built the home, conscious identification with a particular soil. These people, in one way or another, are all exiles. They have come here recently, and their hearts are really in the places that they left. Thus, if they do not do as much visiting with each other as you see in other parts of the country, or the gossiping that goes with visiting, they do have the quick friendliness that exiles commonly show, and I must say it is most agreeable. You may encounter many things you do not like in California, but you will go a long way before you meet a churl.

With the friendliness and courtesy I would bracket the excellent English that is spoken here. The Easterner, when he first hears it, is likely to mistake it for the glib chatter of habitual salesmanship. I think that is because the language you hear here, even from the most casual garage mechanic, is too articulate to seem plausible. For one accustomed to the bray of Eastern Virginia, or the gargle of Second Avenue, New York, or the grunts of the West Virginia foothills, or the wim, wigor, and witality of Southern Pennsylvania, it is hard to believe that the common man can express himself coherently, unless he has learned the trick somehow by rote. So that when the common man out here addresses you in easy grammar, completes his sentences, shows familiarity with good manners, and in addition gives you a pleasant smile, you are like to resent it, and assume that he is parroting the radio, or the talkies, or else that he has been under the tutelage of a high-pressure salesman somewhere, and supplied with a suitable line of gab. In other words, even when you hear it you don't believe it; instead, you keep your ears open for the "authentic" talk of the region, uncorrupted by influences tending to neutralize its flavor.

Well, I have listened to it for more than a year now, and I believe it, and I think I am middling hard to fool about such things. The authentic talk of the region is simply good English, and you will hear it wherever you go. The intonation is not what you may have supposed from listening to Aimee over the radio. Aimee comes from Canada, and her dreadful twang bears no relation to what is spoken here. The actual accent, to my ear, has a somewhat pansy cast to it; it produces on me the same effect as an Englishman's accent. It is clipped, not as clipped as the New England accent, but a little clipped; in addition there is a faint musical undertone in it: they "sing" it, which is probably why it affects me as an Englishman's English, since he also sings his stuff, although in a different key. Pronunciation is excellent. The populace seem to be on familiar terms with most of the words in the language, and you rarely hear that butchery of sonorous terms that is so common elsewhere.

With the good English goes an uncommonly high level of education. These people read, they know what is going on in the world, even if they hold some strange ideas about it, of which more later. And I might mention at this point a cleanliness hardly to be matched elsewhere. Except for the few Mexican hovels in every town, there is no squalor here, or dirt. The houses are very badly planned, but two rooms in them are built with the best of skill, and polished with the utmost care: the kitchen and the bathroom. There is no litter. As in some European cities, where even on the most crowded Sunday there is no scattering of lunch-wrappings in the parks, a homogeneous population takes pretty good care of its nest. And the sunshine, a blight in so many ways, may be due for credit here. It is a sort of general disinfectant.

Next, I would list the things that require an effective communal effort: schools, roads, gigantic water projects, recreation facilities, and so on. The schools, in my opinion, are the best in the country. I find three States ranked ahead of California, Nevada, New York, and Wyoming,—in the amount of money expended per unit of attendance, or population, or whatever it is that they measure by; but I say that money is not the only thing that counts in education. My brief for the California schools rests on the simple fact that our two children did terribly in the East, whereas here they do fine. They like school, learn their lessons, take an interest in what the school does; and so they get a great deal more out of their time than I got when I was their age. Also, they are treated with the utmost consideration, not only by their teachers, but by their colleagues in bondage.

This last is a great point with me, for they are foreigners (I am their stepfather, not their father), and I had been afraid they would run into the Ku Klux aspect of the American temperament when they got into American schools. They did run into it in New York: trust a foreigner who got here in 1930 to haze a foreigner who got here in 1931. But here they don't run into it, which gets me back to the friendliness of the people, probably one reason the schools do so well. For it makes no difference how much you spend on schools, if half your juice is wasted assimilating immigrants, as it is in New York, or fighting irregular attendance, as it is in rural sections of the East, or mopping up the swamps of illiteracy, as it is in the South, you are not going to have much of a school system. Here, the effort goes into the studies, the school paper, the sports and the other things that children ought to be doing; there is a minimum of waste, particularly on "discipline," that infallible symptom of rasping gears. There seems to be hardly any disciplinary problem in California schools. When children enjoy being there, like their teachers, and do their work, why start the bastinado?

As to higher education, I can tell you nothing, as I have had no chance to study it. I would like it better if these various institutions weren't quite so wild about football; but it is only one man's opinion, so let it pass. I shall have to pass up the water projects too, as they have a Metropolitan Water District here whose workings I can't quite get the hang of, so that it would probably be better if I just flunked out. The main point, though, is that the water is here: it is piped into houses, lawns, fields, and orchards; it is the staff of life. I doubt if any other section of the country uses as much water as this one does, and these States, as you may have heard, are quick on the spigot.

The roads are superb. They run for miles in every direction, eight tracks wide where traffic is heavy, with illumination at night, beautiful curves and easy grades, no mean feat of construction when you consider that they never get very far without having to cross a range of mountainous hills. Of course, they are not primarily ornamental: this section, to a greater extent than any other, is dependent on the automobile, as forty years ago it was dependent on the horse. The distances are so vast, the waste of time so cruel if you go by bus or street car, that you must have your own transportation, and whether she needs greasing is literally a matter of greater moment than whether the roof leaks. Everybody has some kind of second-or-third-or ninth-hand flivver; even the cook comes to work in her car. Of course, she can't cook when she gets there, but anyhow she arrives in style.

As you might expect, there is a great skill in everything that pertains to the automobile, that extends much further than the roads it runs on. No motor disease has been heard of that the local specialist can't cure, and at a reasonable price. Snagged top? A place that does nothing but fix tops. Crumpled fender? Another place that attends to fenders. Starter acting funny? Places everywhere that "Reweld starter teeth without removing flywheels." The markets, most of them, have smooth flat parking areas in front of them, so you can drive right up and have the potatoes lifted into the back seat; there are lunch places that hook a tray on the side of your car, so that you can eat without so much as getting out. Of course, this gives me the colic, but it gives you an idea how far the thing goes.

Traffic control is perfect, with no endless tinkering with it as in the East; I think it moves through Los Angeles faster than through any other city on earth. This is the one section I ever heard of that did something about a place to park. Driving in New York is one long nightmare of finding a place to leave the car, as it is in most other American cities; here, there are parking places everywhere, run by brisk fellows in white smocks who whisk your car out of the way, hand you a ticket, and charge you from a nickel to twenty-five cents, depending on the location. What a load off your mind that is!

The recreation facilities are endless. Every town has its country club, or several of them, which will take in almost any presentable person who will pay the very moderate dues. But there are plenty of public places, either privately operated, or run by municipalities, where anybody can play for a small admission charge: golf courses, riding ranches, tennis courts, and so on, many of the last being free, as they are maintained by the towns chiefly for children. Plenty of them, you understand: no calling up two days in advance to reserve a court for one hour in the afternoon.

For my part, what I take most delight in is the swimming pools. Anywhere you go you can have a swim: a clean swim, a pleasant swim, a swim run by people who really know their stuff. Think what this means. In all of New York City, except for three or four hotels that have pools, and one or two small places uptown, there is not one place where the six million can get wet without going to Coney, Brighton, or some other dreadful beach. The city maintains "bath-houses," where worthy widows of dead policemen dispense towel and soap for three cents; but they are intended primarily to provide bums with a bath, and only one of them has a pool, a small, horrible affair that I should certainly hate to fall into.

But here all you have to do is drive up, plunk down a coin, get towel, soap, and suit, if you haven't brought one, and dive off. You can be sure the suit has been steamed and properly dried before you got it. No dirt, no noise, no slopping around a filthy dressing-room where uncouth voices yell "Hey locker!" I swam all last Summer in a high-school pool. It was the best I was ever in: the charge was fifteen cents. One curious thing about it may interest you. As it was a public pool, it took in just an ordinary run of people, about half children, half grown-ups; all clean, well-behaved, and dressed in gay suits, but just average people. Yet out of all the thousands I saw there, not five appeared during the whole Summer who could really swim. Down at the Ambassador, in Los Angeles and at Agua Caliente, in Mexico, the idle sons of the rich dive, float, and crawl with the finest grace; but even so simple a trick, apparently, is beyond the idle sons of the poor.

III

Now I come to the tough part of my piece. If the foregoing is true, as it certainly is, and much more of the same that I could put in if I had space, why is it, you may well ask, that I don't break out into a decent hymn of praise at once, instead of making my bass a sour note under the twittering treble?

I wish I could, but I can't. The thing simply won't add up. When I take off the first shoe at night, and wonder what I have to show for the day, I usually know that I have nothing to show for it. I can't take a schoolhouse to bed with me, or a State road, or a swimming pool; some can, and if you can you had better come here at once, as this is the place you were born for. But not I. To me, life takes on a dreadful vacuity here, and I am going to have a hard time indicating it. Frankly, I don't know exactly what it is that I miss. But if you will bear with me while I grope a little, I shall try to get it down on paper.

Let us take a fresh start, a long way off, in a place that everybody can agree on: Paris. It may seem unfair to choose a city that had its beginnings in Roman times, and compare it with a section which in its present phase is hardly fifteen years old, but let it pass: an unfair comparison is precisely what I want. What is it, now, that charms me about Paris, that gives me what I don't find here? The so-called "culture"? The yodeling of the current Violetta at the Opera, or the pirouetting of her agile assistants, as they sway and whirl to thunderous applause and then sink lightly back into their wheelchairs? The actresses along the boulevards? The paintings in the art store windows? The symphony concerts?

Nay, none of these. If I want a Violetta, I should have heard the last one in Los Angeles, probably the best in the business; when I want hoofing, I can see better hoofers in Hollywood than in Paris, and the same goes for actresses; when I want paintings, I can see the best in the world in Pasadena; when I want symphonies, I can hear excellent performances in the Hollywood Bowl, and under pleasanter circumstances than in a stinking hall in Paris.

No, what I like is a jumble of the tangible and the intangible, of beauty and ugliness, that somehow sets me a-tingle: the sinister proximity of big things, and the smokestacks on hinges, pulled down as the boats go under the bridges; the glimpse of a medieval street, the way a boy charms *"Matin, le Temps, Echo de Paris!"*, the glow of lights behind the awnings as the gathering dark brings out the lettering, the captain in the Cafe de la Paix who looks like Otto Kahn; the patina on the arch at the Etoile, the salesman who says he has *les Camel, les Chesterfield, et les Lucky Streak;* the bronze statues in the park behind the Louvre, the fake artist painting the wrong bridge down by the river; the great facade of Notre Dame, the shiny faced nuns hawking souvenirs beneath the fish market, and the discovery that they tie a lobster's claw here, instead of pegging them, as we do, and an ancient peasant, bending beneath a rack that fits him with the terrible precision of a polished yoke on the neck of oxen; the meal I had in the Avenue Victor Hugo, the meal I had in the Rue de la Pepiniere, the meal I had in the Rue Royale, the meal I had—wherever it was. In other words, a perpetual invitation to explore, to linger, to enjoy,

I think this beckoning jumble, in great or small degree, is the essence of the appeal which any place has for you, and that if it isn't there, you are going to be most unhappy about it, even if at first you don't quite know what ails you. Well, it is what this place lacks. You can drive for miles and the one thing you can be sure of is that you are not going to be rewarded for so much as one little scrap, one little unexpected bit, one hint of charm, that you can sit down with for a moment, and as I have said, take to bed with you at night. Of course, the place does have a history, and there are many fine relics of the Spanish occupation, all preserved with an admirable regard for what is due them.

But they, after all, are a closed chapter. The one now being written somehow never manages to be delightful, produces nothing but an endless succession of Rabbit Fryers, 50¢; Eggs, Guaranteed Fresh, 23 Doz.; Canary Birds, 50¢, Also Baby Chix Just Hatched; Car Mart, All Makes Used Cars, Lowest Prices; Orange Drink, 5¢ Eat; Drink Goat Milk for Health, Drive Right; Finest English Walnuts, 15 Lb.; $100 Down Buys This Lot, Improvements Installed, No Assessments; Eat's Scotty Kennels, 100 Yds.; Pure Muscat Grapejuice, 35¢ Gal., We Deliver; Eat; I have got so that if I go out for an afternoon's drive, I usually wind up at Goebel's Lion Farm, smoking a cigarette with Bert Parks, the chief attendant. God in Heaven, a cat is something to look at! I have followed all the doings out there faithfully, from the birth of the leopard cubs to the unfortunate fate of Jiggs when he strayed into a cage with two she-lions who got frightfully chewed up. I learned with great interest what happened when Paramount sent a star out there to have his picture taken feeding Caesar, as a bit of publicity for a forthcoming picture. Instead of biting the meat Caesar bit the actor. First time I knew a lion liked ham.

Eat. That is the measure, alas, of the cookery of the region. You can go from Santa Barbara to the border, and you will not strike one place where you can get a really distinguished meal. There are, to be sure, the various Biltmores, and in Los Angeles the Ambassador, a restaurant called the Victor Hugo, a hotel called the Town House, and Bernstein's sea-food place. All of them have their points, and the Town House, I must say, really knows how to put a meal together. But they suffer from two circumstances. The first is that they can't sell liquor. If you want food *and* drink at the same meal, you have to go to a speak, and a California speak is so bad that there is nothing to say about it. The other is that they really have nothing to make a distinguished meal with. Meats are obtainable here, and vegetables, the best you can get anywhere; but when it comes to fish, and particularly shellfish, those indispensable embellishments that transform eating into dining, they are simply not to be had. Brother, God hath laid a curse on this Pacific Ocean, and decreed that nothing that comes out of it shall be fit to eat; and anybody who tells you different has simply never fished in another ocean.

The oysters are frightful. They serve what they call Eastern oysters, which means oysters that have been transplanted from the East to Puget Sound or some such place, and taken after they are grown. They are pale, watery, and fishy. Then they serve the native oyster, known as the Olympia, or Olympic—there seems to be some difference of opinion on the point. These are small, dark, and mussel-like in appearance. The taste is quite beyond the power of words to convey: I had to exercise all of my 90 hp. will to get down enough to call it a test. If you can imagine a blend of fish, seaweed, copper, and pot-washings, all smelling like low tide on a mud-flat, you will have some faint notion of what an Olympia oyster is like.

The crab is an ocean crab, smooth, without spines, and singularly coarse and tasteless. As a rule they serve it as cracked crab, which means that they steam it, chill it, and cut it up quite nicely, with the shell cracked so you can pick out the meat with an oyster fork. I think it would be better if they didn't let the ice come in contact with the crab, and thereby suck out the salt, but I hope they don't begin taking pains with it, just to please me. Any way they served it, I wouldn't like it. The only good crab I ever had out here was the other night, at a little party in Beverly Hills. It was in a salad, and I at once sought out my hostess.

"I've got to know more about this," I said. "I'm just writing a piece saying the crabs out here are lousy."

"I don't think so," she said. "I've had good crab in the Brown Derby, lots of times."

"Never mind the Brown Derby," I said. "I've got to be reliable and accurate about this thing, and what I want to know is: Where did you *get* this crab?"

"Well if you've got to know," she said, "that's canned crab, but I don't know why you had to be so inquisitive."

In other words, it was good old Crisfield blue-claw, and maybe it didn't taste good!

The lobster is that crustacean known in the East as a crayfish and in France as a *langouste*, and it's not much, any way you take it. It has eight big legs, but no giant claws, so that there is no claw meat. The fat and coral are incredible, and there is hardly any shoulder meat. The gigantic tail, when steamed and served cold, is white and of even texture, but tasteless. Broiling doesn't help any. The tail muscle of a *langouste*, when broiled, splits off into pieces, like a rope that has been unravelled, so that it is disagreeable to eat, and has no more taste than it had before.

But the prize monster of these parts is called an abalone. The abalone, if pulled out of the North Sea, would be a *coquille*, and if pulled out of Long Island Sound would be a scallop; but as it is, it is pulled out of the Pacific, which makes it different. The shell is large, some six or eight inches across, and fluted like a scallop shell, very pretty. The thing itself is a lump of muscle about the size of a small lemon, and so tough that if yo tried to cut it, it would jump off the plate and hit the lady at the next table on the eye. So they operate on it with a hammer to soften it up a bit. How many outfielders they have to post, to field it home when it jumps off the block, I don't know; but when they get through with it, it is a sort of Childs pancake, and this they dip in batter and fry. You can have it. I got half of one down once: what an experience that was!

There are barracuda, salmon, halibut, swordfish, and tarpon, but I personally don't regard them very highly. Swordfish, I suppose, is as good as it is said to be; but for my part, when they begin serving fish in steaks, it doesn't seem like fish any more. The medium-size fish, like shad and bass, which go so well after the soup, don't seem to taste right: perhaps the trouble is in the cookery. The only fish I can say much for out here are the sand-dab, which looks like a small English sole and tastes like perch; the grunion, a near-smelt that is against the law for some treason, and that you have to get bootleg, and the trout. The trout all seem to come from Noah Beery's trout farm, on the road to the Mohave Desert. They are pretty good anyhow at the Town House, where they know how to make a *meuniere* sauce.

IV

Now then, if there are no smells to caress my nose, and no sights to delight my eye, and no food to tickle my mouth, this gets us down pretty much to what we laughingly call my intellect. God knows I am not particular here, not anything like as particular as I am about oysters. I don't ask for talk about Proust, or familiarities with the cosmic ray theory, or acute critical appraisal of the latest Japanese painter; I can take stuff or leave it alone, and I actually feel better when I am off it. But I do ask—what shall I say? Something that peaks my imagination a little, gives me some sort of that, makes me feel that that day I heard something. And I am the sort that is as likely to get this from the comman man as his more erudite cousin, the high-brow.

But what do I get? Nothing. For when a gentleman appears at my door, orange peeler in hand, bows gracefully at my halting invitation to come in, removes his hat with the utmost aplomb, enters, sits down easily, and explains in accents that would do credit to a Harvard man that this particular article is manufactured by the O'Peelo Company, and bears the signed guarantee of that firm, handsomely engraved with one extra blade all for ten cents—when that happens, it is hard for me to escape the reflection that what this Wright has his mind on is an orange peeler.

Now, right here, I think, I finally get into words my main squawk against this section: the piddling occupations to which the people dedicate their lives. Bear in mind my disclaimer of high-brow leanings which is honest, and the earthy nature of the intellectual fodder that I ask. I am greatly stimulated by a trapper boy in a West Virginia coal-mine, or a puddler in a Pennsylvania steel-mill, or a hand on a Nebraska corn-farm. These people, although they usually talk a dreadful jargon, are frequently morons, and sometimes anything but admirable personally, all take part in vast human dramas, and I find it impossible to disregard the stature which their occupations confer on them. If they are prosperous, it is big news; if they are hungry, it is tragic; and no matter what their condition is, they share some of the electric importance of the stages they tread.

But what electric importance can be felt in a peddler of orange peelers? Or of a dozen ripe avocados, just plucked that morning? Or a confector of Bar-B-Q? Or the proprietor of a goldfish farm? Or a breeder of rabbit fryers? They give me no kick at all. They give themselves no kick. The whole place is overrun with nutty religions, which are merely the effort of these people to inject some sort of point into their lives; if not on earth, then in the stars, in numbers, in vibrations, or whatever their fancy hits on. They are not, as I have hinted, and as I shall show more clearly in a moment, inferior people. Rather the other way around. But they suffer from the cruel feebleness of the play which the economy of the region compels them to take part in.

If it were only possible to create for them a suitable play artificially, as it is possible to fashion a play for childhood, where libraries, schoolhouses, athletic fields, and a few leagues and debating clubs are all that is needed to set things humming—the thing would have been done long ago. But with grown-ups it is not as simple as that. The yarn has to be there. There can be no build-up, as they say in the movies, for the main situation; it cannot be evoked at will, and it cannot be faked. If the voltage cannot be felt, the whole piece falls flat, and it will throw off no jumble of delightful sparks of the kind we were talking about in connection with Paris.

They not only give themselves no kick, but they have developed out of the things they do, a curious slant on life, particularly on Labor, which you have no doubt read about and probably misunderstood. For these occupations are not only piddling, but also fly-by-night; none of them seem to pay, and it is unusual to find a man who is doing the same thing now as he did last year. If he has a poultry farm, a few months ago he fixed flats and a few months before that had a newsstand.

This makes for the most incredible incompetence at those routine things that you have always taken for granted. The paperhanger takes five days to do a job that a good man would finish in one; the restaurant has its lights so placed that your head casts a shadow on your plate, making it impossible to see your food; a house, well-designed otherwise, has one corner of the living-room gouged out to let in a trick stairway, the result being that you cannot lay a rug; the salesman has a persuasive line of talk about the merits of the article, and then has to look on the icebox door to find out the price; the telephone clerk reports that somebody called, but hasn't taken his number so you can call back; the waiter clamps a fork over the spoon when he serves peas, in the elegant manner of an Italian serving asparagus, not noticing that when it is peas he is serving, and not asparagus, this makes them bounce all over the table like shot; the bookstore is sorry, sir, but would have to know the publisher before it could order that book for you, apparently not knowing that the United States Index, which is lying open on the counter, was invented specifically to solve this problem; the apartment-house has its drawers built exactly three inches too short to hold a shirt; the movie impresario wires frantically to New York for a certain writer, only to discover that for a year he has had the varlet on his own lot.

You may think I overstate the case, in a strained effort to be comical. I assure you I do not. It is not only my observation. It is the observation of every Easterner who comes out here: I have talked with dozens of them on the subject, and all of them make the same report, most of them with much fancier illustrations than those I have given.

Now, this kind of thing, together with the state of affairs that lies back of it, has bred a fear of good, honest, well paid craftsmanship that is at the bottom of the very genuine anti-union sentiment that you find here. This sentiment, no doubt, had its origin in the disturbances that led to the dynamiting of the Los Angeles *Times* office some years ago, and Big Business certainly had a hand in that fight. But Big Business, so far as I have had a chance to observe it, is pretty sensible now. The core of the anti-union feeling here these days is not so much Big Business as Little Labor; and how this works out I can best show by quoting a man I talked with shortly after I came here.

"This is how it is," he said. "Your dirt farmer from Iowa, or wherever it is, gets here with a little pile, just about enough to keep him, and at first, after freezing his face in those blizzards for forty years, it's great. He has a swell time, sees the Mr. Wilson's Observatory, the Pacific Ocean, the millionaires' houses in Pasadena, the Huntington Museum, and Hollywood he's never seen anything like that before and he loves it. But then what? There ain't no more. After six months he's so sick of doing nothing that he'll take fifteen dollars a week, or ten dollars a week or three dollars a week; or he'll start any kind of cock-eyed business, he'll do *anything*, just to keep busy. And boy, maybe you think that baby can't hate union labor! Because union labor, anyhow the way he figures it, means that pretty soon he's out of a job, and there's *nothing* for him to do but water the grass."

That sums it up very simply, and it certainly takes the wind out of your indigestion, makes all your fine theories about collective bargaining seem as silly as your theories about civil rights seem in Mexico. For indignation, particularly in this controversy, rests on some sort of sporting sympathy for the under-dog; but when you find out that the under-dog has a couple of mice under *him* yet, in great danger of being mashed flat, what are you going to do? Begin feeling sorry for the mice, I suppose. There they are, and they certainly confuse the issue quite thoroughly. Just the same, I greatly prefer a dog fight to a mouse-fight; and the fact that these are worthy mice, down there through no fault of their own, doesn't relieve their doings of a certain what-of-it quality that I find very hard to get excited about.

What I would like to see here, to make an end of my carping, would be a vast increase in what might be called economic vitality. The whole place would be pepped up, I think, by big, slashing industries, industries that bind men together, make them feel their competence as workmen, fill them with the vanity that demands adequate recompense; industries that afford an afflatus of the ego that is requited only by fine food and drink; industries that produce pep, bustle, enjoyment of life. They are really what throw off the jumble of sparks, cover a country with things that appeal to the imagination. But so far there are not anything like enough of them.

Some, you understand, oil production is enormous: I must say that a trip through the well-forests, for all their dreadful reek, hands you something. Movie production is also important: I believe oil and movies account for nearly 25% of the revenues of the place from the outside. Furniture, Hollywood garments and various other manufactures are growing. But still, not enough of these to go around. The typical Southern Californian is still the middle Westerner who was a crack sidewalk contractor in Sioux City, and a punk rabbit breeder here. Nobody told him that many Southern California streets don't have sidewalks: no walking done, you know. So he is out of luck. So his talents are wasted. So it is not his fault. But he is terribly dull company.

A word about the nutty religions. They don't cut anything like as much ice as you might think from reading about them. They are here, and practically everybody polishes his discourse with "pass on," instead of "die:" he can't be quite sure what cult you may belong to. Even so, they are more like pastimes than the religions you are probably accustomed to. People find in them a relief from boredom, give them the zealous attention that a fad might command elsewhere; but they change off pretty easily from one to the other, and apparently don't care about them very deeply.

Aimee doesn't seem to cut any ice at all. The newspapers treat her with the amiable levity that New York reserves for the Metropolitan Opera House, and I personally have never met a Californian who has even seen her. I am an object of curiosity, in fact, when I let it be known that I have seen her, and a great disappointment when I have to admit that this was before she reduced and changed the color of her hair.

V

I wish now to do a little speculating about the future of this place. From what I have said, you may think it is pretty dark, but I wouldn't bet on it; there are a number of favorable factors, and I should like to check them over briefly.

First, let me emphasize again the distinctly superior human material that is on hand. Circumstances, particularly the fact that at the moment there are not very stimulating things for them to do, may have condemned these people to the kind of activity I was describing a moment ago, but they are capable of bucking stiffer winds, and when stiffer winds begin to blow they will acquit themselves impressively. I remind you that a selective process has affected the settlement here that has not gone on in many other American localities. In general, I think it can be said that most sections of the United States were first populated by failures. They are usually referred to as "pioneers," but that euphemism doesn't dispose of the fact that they were doing very badly where they were, and pulled up stakes to see if they couldn't do better somewhere else.

But that hasn't been the case here. Making all allowance for the automobile tramp and others of his kind who have come here, the person who has unpacked and stayed usually has had a pile. Sometimes it has been a big pile, for a great deal of wealth is visible: I hope I haven't given you the idea that everybody here is just one jump ahead of the sheriff. Oftener it has been a little pile, but anyhow it has been some kind of pile. The typical settler here has made what some walk of life regards as a success, and is here to enjoy the climate; that means that he is a person of some substance. Whatever he does after he gets here, the original ability is there; it is transmitted to his children, and it is something to be recombined with.

Next, I shall surprise you by citing as a favorable factor the Los Angeles Chamber of Commerce, which with various affiliated organizatons pretty much controls the commerical development of the region. It seems to me that the economic situation out here has forced it, perhaps unconsciously, to acquire a profounder notion of its responsibilities than you will find in most organizations of its kind. The average American chamber of commerce, in my experience with it, is a noisy, tiresome, and exceedingly childish booster affair, with no maturer idea of its function than to bring as many factories to town as possible, in order that merchants will have more customers, realtors more prospects for their lots, and property more benefit from the unearned increment. That, and a running wrangle with the Interstate Commerce Commission, carried on by the traffic department, over some freight differential enjoyed by a nearby city, is about the extent of its activity. As to whether the factories are desirable, as to whether abolishment of the differential would throw several railroads into bankruptcy, they seldom give a thought; and sometimes, as when one Eastern city proudly announced the advent of a soap factory that had stunk so badly it was run out of another city, you wonder whether they are quite bright.

But here the basic situation is different, and you can see what it is from the phrase you hear so often around the Los Angeles chamber: "We know we can't go on selling climate forever. People have got to have something to do after they get here." In other words, the boom is over. People fell for the climate all right, and bought lots, and settled **down.** But piles, whether big or little, have a distressing tendency to melt, so that the section faces the necessity of becoming an economic unit that can run under its own steam, piles or no piles. To that exceedingly difficult problem which is after all the problem I have been stating in a roundabout way, the Los Angeles Chamber of Commerce is addressing itself with a sobriety which I must confess impresses me.

It is not content to get a new factory although it has got plenty of these in the last few years. It has been forced to do what most Chambers of Commerce do not do: undertake an exhaustive study of the possibilities of the region, that takes into account the needs of the population as a whole, and that is much broader in its scope than the leather-bound "presentation" got up for some particular manufacturer.

Now, if this profounder attitude is real, and not something that I thought I detected and didn't, you would expect it to give some tangible evidence of its presence, something you could put your finger on and say, "There, that's what I mean." And so, in fact, you find it. The offices are quiet and run with swift efficiency. There are no signs telling you to "Smile, Damn You, Smile." There is an atmosphere not unlike what you associate with the research departments of a big university, with the difference that this research has a purpose, a smell of dealing with live, important things, that most university research plainly lacks.

And there is something that I pay a great deal of attention to when I try to estimate a man's integrity, which is a healthy respect for a fact. It amounts almost to a religion in this place. You hear frequently the rueful admission that "we've got a reputation to live down, all right";, they seem terrified lest old mistakes will be repeated and come home to roost. So that you are no sooner handed a table of figures than you get the footnote: "Now listen: This is not any of our hooey. This comes right out of the United States Census Reports, and you can bank on it to the last decimal point." Well, I buy that I am a sucker for the man who is worried about the last decimal point.

In other words, out of the Gethesemane of its woe these last few years, this Los Angeles Chamber of Commerce bids fair to emerge as what a chamber of commerce ought to be, and so seldom is. It is very powerful, much more so than the chambers of commerce you are probably accustomed to. It is a sort of government outside the government, bearing about the same relation to the body politic as the Communist party does in Russia (I suppose I put that in out of pure malice.) And, like the Communist party in Russia, it is most intolerant of all schemes for monkeying with the gears. Radicalism of any kind is anathema to it. I suspect that the big fellows enrolled in it are not anything like so hot on this subject as they are thought to be; but big fellows are not the only ones it must satisfy: the very fact that it has a large membership, has to study the problems of even the littlest fellows, and is the repository of a highly concentrated leadership, has forced it in this matter to go along with the crowd.

This, I must say, I find deplorable. I never feel that a city is really in the Big Time unless it has soap boxers damning the government in the parks, and parades that occasionally result in cracked heads. Why I regard such things as cosmopolitan I don't know, but I do. Yet it would be foolish to maintain that I miss them out here as much as I would if they were absent, say, in New York. Again like Russia, this section is not ready for that kind of thing yet. You have to get the gears turning before you can throw left-handed monkey wrenches into them. And, of course, the basic realities take some of the sting out, too.

The one basic reality that can dignify Red goings-on is hunger, and there is very little of it here. Ten cents will buy an incredible amount of food, and hardly anybody lacks ten cents; if somebody does lack it, the genuinely humane treatment he gets here alters somewhat the circumstance that he can't put up a general squawk. What I am trying to say is that the air, the sun, the lay of the land, the feel of what is going on here, make the inalienable right of man to talk, wrangle, and fight himself out of his daily bread seem somewhat beside the point; that maybe what other sections have their mind on, but not this one. It has its mind on something else, and it is only sensible to judge it by what it is trying to do, and not by what you think it ought to be trying to do.

Which brings me to my final point, which is the idea held by everybody here that some sort of destiny awaits the place. Of recent years, the implications of a destiny have bemused me greatly; and I believe that one of the troubles of the United States as a whole is that it no longer has one. In the beginning, its destiny was to reduce a continent, and that destiny, as long as it lasted, made everything hum; transformed the most shiftless bacon-and-beaner into a pioneer, placed an epic frame around our wars, gave the most trivial episode the stature of history. But the continent has been reduced, alas, so that destiny has blown up.

Now what? If you know, you are a wiser man than I am. We have a great deal of running around about it, visionaries providing us with a lot of past destinies: one set trying to make us the most cultured nation on earth, and demanding that we pile novel on top of symphony on top of skyscraper until we claim our place in the aesthetic sun; another set trying to make us the most moral nation on earth, piling Prohibition laws on top of cigarette laws on top of anti-Evolution laws on top of blue laws; another set trying to make us the most prosperous nation on earth piling tariffs on top of R.F.C.'s on top of apostrophes to the Forgotten Man. But all these stars, unfortunately, begin to make a great deal like fish-scales, and where we are actually headed, if anywhere it is pretty hard, for me at least, to see.

So that when you come to a place that not only thinks it has a destiny, but knows it has a destiny, you cannot but be arrested. Where this place is headed to be the leader in commerce, art, citrus production, music, rabbit breeding, oil production, furniture manufacture, walnut growing, literature, olive bottling, short and long-distance hauling, clay modelling, aesthetic criticism, fish export, canary-bird culture, playwrighting, shipping, cinematic creativeness, and drawing-room manners. In short, it is going to be a paradise on earth. And, with such vaulting ambitions it might pull off something; you can't tell. It is keenly aware of the Orient, and also of Mexico; streams are meeting here that ought to churn up some exciting whirlpools. I, personally, even if the act hasn't been so hot, am not going to walk out on the show. One thing it is going to be, within the twelve-months, is the wine center of the new World. I guess you think I'm going to walk out on that, do you? That will make a lot of things different.

No, I stay. The climate suits me fine.

The Widow's Mite, or Queen of the Rancho
(*Vanity Fair*, August 1933)

Whatever else may be said of Malibu, the place where the movie queens grow their sunburn, there is one thing that you have to hand it: it is probably the finest beach ever created by God. About a half hour's drive up the coast from Santa Monica, and not more than an hour from the studios of Hollywood, Westwood and Culver City, it lies between two snubby points of land, and swings in for about a mile, a perfect area of crisp yellow sand. This is free from shells, stones, and weed. It is also free from mud, that invisible deposit of fine silt which on most beaches causes the water to turn to coffee at the very point where you enter it. Here the water remains clear, even in its last scurrying rush at your feet. The bottom drops off evenly, so that the surf comes in with beautiful precision. Far out, a swell appears, and breaks into a curling lip. This spreads, until there is a wall of water a quarter of a mile long, which comes in slowly, and gets higher as it comes. Then it smashes down, and sends a smother of foam sliding up the sands. This recedes, and for a minute or more there is quiet, with the ocean still as a pond. Then the sea stirs again, there is another swell, and the performance is repeated. Each swell gives a strictly solo number, with entrance, build-up, punch-line, and tag all complete. While it is on, no other swells appear to crab its act.

They roll in, curiously enough, from the south, not the west: when you sit in the sand you don't stare at China cross the Bay, but at Rockefeller Ridge, or whatever it was that Byrd discovered on his Antarctic trip. That is because the west coast of the United States does not run north and south, but northwest and southwest, and at this point goes off on a slant which runs almost exactly east and west. Thus there are never any lengthening shadows on this beach, any hour of deep purple relaxation, with gulls white against the sea, and distant liners showing all their colors like models under glass. The sun is out there, over the ocean, until it goes down suddenly and abrupt night sets in. While it is there, it is always high noon and even the water has the restless glare that goes with that hour. As the sun is beyond it, it has a vivid green translucence, and when a big comber breaks, a rainbow hangs all a-shimmer, giving you a momentary feeling of snow blindness. The gulls and the ships having their shady side toward you, are a sombre and startling black and appear greatly exaggerated in size. It is dazzling, a little wearisome and more than a little unreal: it has that quality, whatever it is, that marks off the Pacific Ocean from all other oceans.

Yet you can't say that it is not beautiful, any more than you can say that certain other creations of God, here visible pretty much as God made them, are not beautiful. Isn't Sylvia Sidney beautiful? And Janet Gaynor? And Joan Bennett? And Betty Williams? And all the others of the same gilded profession? Are they the less beautiful that they wear skimpy bathing suits consisting chiefly of thin ribbons crossing areas of orange sunburn? All I can say is, they look beautiful to me, and the less they have on the more beautiful they look. They blend in with the seascape, being in much the same key; they too are dazzling, a little wearisome, and more than a little unreal; they too have that quality, that suggestion of having stepped out of somebody's fever dream, that goes with the Pacific Ocean and no other ocean. I suppose the same could be said of Ronald Colman, John Gilbert, Clive Brook, Warner Baxter, and other males who here hold leases. I hear they are beautiful, and God knows they are strange. But here I must call a halt, and ring down the curtain on this exercise in rhapsodical prose. Regardless of what you see, when you gaze on these gentlemen clad in even less than the ladies wear, all I see is hair; and this brings me with a bump to the hard, every-day realities, which are, to wit:

(a) Granted that this is a witching spot, is it yet so witching that it is worth $400 a foot? And,
(b) If not, did somebody take these pulchritudinous suckers for a ride? And,
(c) If so, what do they get out of it, now that they have been took?

The answer to the first question, of course, lies in the realm of opinion, so I shall merely note that at $400 a foot, a 30-foot lot costs $12,000; that $12,000 is almost exactly the amount required to cover such a lot with $1 bills; that this is a windy spot to make jigsaw puzzles out of United States currency: the bills might blow away, or the sand might blow away, or both might blow away—I note these points, and leave the reader to form any opinion that he likes. The answer to the second question takes us back many, many years, as far back, indeed, as the year 1926. It was at this time that Mrs. May K. Rindge reached a crisis in her affairs.

Mrs. Rindge is a widow, whose husband had left her with great beauty, a thorough knowledge of school teaching acquired at Marblehead, Mass., and the Rancho Topango Malibu Sequit, more or less paid for. Now a rancho, even a small rancho, and all paid for, is something of a problem for a woman. The cooks get sick, the hands get sick, the bulls get sick, and then they all get well and start to fight. But when it is a Rancho Topango Malibu Sequit, and runs for twenty-four miles along the coast, and in addition to the cooks, the hands, and the bulls, there are ships getting wrecked every month or so, and wet sailors tracking sand all over the place shouting that they are a cook and a captain bold and the mate of the Nancy Brig, and notes coming due at the bank, and the lighthouse keeper wigwagging that his daughter Nellie has the measles, and bugs getting into the fruit trees; and when, in addition to all this, the State of California gets absurd notions of where to put the road, and you have to go to war with it—then a rancho ceases to be a problem, and becomes a downright bore. I said war, and I mean war. The State of California sent its road builders out, and Mrs. Rindge sent her guard-out and there was in-fighting and out-fighting with shots. In the end, the State of California won the war, and built the road, and Mrs. Rindge didn't like it much, as she is a woman rather inclined to have her own way.

Still, it wasn't these things that brought on the crisis, for after all, cooks, hands, bulls, sailors, measles, bugs, and wars all come to an end some time: you win or you lose, and it is over. What produced the crisis was the bonds. After the road was built, people leased land, and then the varlets demanded water, and water runs in pipes, and pipes cost money. So Mrs. Rindge sold bonds and once you have bonds there is no end to them. Every six months they demand interest, and if the interest isn't paid, it is bad all around. So Mrs. Rindge faced a crisis, and it was at this time that she met one Harold G. Ferguson, a real estate man of Los Angeles, who had an idea. Why not develop that stretch of very charming beach, that lay about midway on the rancho, into a beach colony? Mrs. Rindge was willing, but on one condition: the land must be leased, not sold. Bond or no bonds, she would not break up the rancho.

So Mr. Ferguson chopped the place into lots, and sent Mr. A. A. Jones out to peddle the leases. Mr. Jones is the real genius of Malibu Beach. He is a tall young man, sharp of face, and still sharper of eye, who looks a little like Col. Charles A. Lindbergh. He takes it going, coming crosswise, and on the bias. You may get an idea how talented he is when he was able to dispose of the leases at all. For in all truth, it is coming pretty thick to ask a man to leave stand at $30 a month. Build a house on it, and then at the end of ten years have nothing but the privilege of loading his house on a truck and hauling it away. Yet Mrs Jones persevered, and at the end of a few months had a dozen or more lessors signed up.

And then, in 1927, history was made in one fell swoop. Miss Anna Q. Nilsson rented a lot. This may not sound like history, yet in fact it is. For Miss Anna Q. Nilsson was a moving picture actress, and it is a peculiarity of moving picture actresses that as soon as one of them does something, all the rest do exactly the same thing, not stopping to reason why. You might think this would keep them hopping around at a lively rate, but it doesn't, for it is not often that one of them thinks up something, or even thinks. Miss Anna Q. Nilsson rented a lot, and then Miss Marie Prevost rented a lot, and then a dozen more of them rented lots and then some actors rented lots, and some supervisors. So Malibu Beach was going over with a bang and the question of the bond issue, at any rate, eased up quite a bit.

Still, Mr. Jones was not happy. What depressed him was not that the thing had gone over, but that it had gone over too well. These people, he saw, were able to pay much more than $30 a month for lots, and it was the apparent impossibility of getting more than $30 out of them, *now* that the project had been launched on that basis, that made him melancholy. But then Mrs. O'Leary's cow got into it. The fire started from defective wiring at No. 83, what is now John Gilbert's house, on October 26, 1929. It spread. Actors and actresses rushed from their homes in night clothes, frantic to know what to do about it. One rushed in to rescue his private stock. All rushed in to rescue their private stock. This was all they did about it. Twenty-nine houses went up in flames that night, but when, came the dawn, Mr. Jones assembled the lessors together, he had a proposal to make to them. They would all, he pointed out, want to rebuild. They would all want to rebuild on a much more impressive scale than the $2,500 cottages they had had before the fire. But they would certainly not want to rebuild thus impressively on the basis of leases which would expire in 1936. In view of this, the company would take back the old leases, and issue new ones, running until 1941, and do this at only a slightly higher rental, say $75 a month.

This took them by surprise, but a supervisor took out a pencil and did some figuring. A supervisor, in case you don't know, is one who takes complete charge of a moving picture and commands its destiny from script to cutting room. He is always employed for his shrewd business judgment. And on a thing of this sort, a supervisor figures this way: If a lease costs $75 a month, it must be a lot better lease than one which costs only $30 a month. The supervisor signed. All signed, and then rushed off to Hollywood to tell what a marvelous new bargain they had made.

Thus Malibu rose phoenix-like from the ashes, and within a few months was a thing of beauty and joy. Mr. Jack Warner spent $100,000 on his cottage, and very pretty it is too. Mr. Robert Z. Leonard spent $60,000. Others spent paltry $50,000's and $40,000's, and $25,000's, and very few, as Mr. Jones points out, spent less than $8,000. It was at this point that Mr. James laid down a rule: all exterior plans must be approved by him. This was to keep the architecture within tasteful limits, and prevent such objectionable things as flat roofs. I must say that Malibu, with its peaked roofs, well chosen paint, and general air of good taste, appeals to the eye more than most places in this section of the country: its houses look like houses, and not like stables, shops, or hot-dog stands, as do many of the dwellings, nearby. Yet it would be idle to deny that Mr. Jones' rule makes it advisable to employ a builder of Mr. Jones' designation. Whether Mr. Jones takes a commission from the builder he designates, I must confess I don't know.

Things were very rosy, then, and all the more rosy since news of the new leases had brought a second big wave of lessors, so that the cottages now numbered more than a hundred. Still, Mr. Jones was not satisfied. He organized one or two little things, such as the Malibu Beach patrol. This affords water man service, fireman service, and garbage removal service, and the rate is $10 a month. He organized a lifeguard service, charging $20 a year for it. Also, he founded the Malibu Inn, which is a combination shoe-shine, magazine, newspaper, postcard, soda water, and hot dog service, and the social center of Malibu.

Still, he brooded, and he brooded pretty much alone, for Mr. Ferguson had had the bad taste to get sent to jail, and Mrs. Rindge was off attending to oil wells. Oil wells are a lot of trouble, too. And then, once more, Mrs. O'Leary's cow booted the lantern, and Mr. Jones was ready for his final stroke. While the ashes were still hot, he decided that in 1941 the lessors would be privileged to buy the land at $100 a foot, or $12,000 a lot; and he decreed, in addition, that if any leases should be sold, he would have to approve the new lessors. This had the effect of keeping out the riff-raff, and it also made it advisable to employ Mr. Jones as agent when selling a lease.

Well, it was a supervisor, as usual, who saw the force of this logic, and he reasoned this way: if they gave you the sand, it couldn't be any good; but when they charge $12,000 for it, it must have production value. It is the shrewd business sense of the supervisors which has put the movies where they are today. So the supervisor signed, and most of the others signed, and Mrs. Rindge, when it was pointed out to her that 147 times $12,000 equals $1,354,000 conquered her distaste for parting with land, and approved the new leases.

Thus the history of this Elysian spot, but we still have to ascertain what the residents get out of it, now that they are there. To get at this, let us spy on one of these lovely ladies, to see what she does with her time. She wakes up, I hear, about 7:30, summons the maid, and has breakfast. She gets up, bathes, dresses, and drives off to the studio. At the studio, she works all day, save for one hour in which she has lunch at the studio lunchroom without removing her make-up. At six o'clock, she drives back to Malibu, and on arrival there, dresses for dinner in a fetching suit of blue pajamas.

Dinner over, she has a cigarette, and starts for the party. There will be several parties going on, but she attends only one. If she is a Paramount lady, she goes where Paramount is going and so on. Next year, when her contract is sold, she will go to an entirely different set of parties. Arrived at the party, she has a brace of cocktails, here served at any hour, and surveys the evening. This is what she sees:

> 3 Extra girls in evening dress, grateful for having been invited down.
> 4 Actresses in blue pajamas.
> 1 Actress in bathing suit.
> 1 Actress in ceremonial Chinese robe, weighing ten pounds: cost, $2,300.
> 1 Man from New York, in dinner coat.
> 4 Men in sweaters and knickers.
> 4 Supervisors in middle of floor, shooting dice.

This is the party, except for the host and hostess, who haven't shown up yet, having forgotten about it. It is not only the party as is, but it is all the party there is going to be. There will be no dancing. There will be no necking. There will be no light, infectious gayety, with merry madcaps deciding to jump in the ocean at 1 A.M. There will be nothing but dice, drinks, and conversation. Yet our lady is not fazed. She examines it with a fishy eye for a few minutes, then decides that she likes it. She kneels down, puts her arm around a supervisor, and announces she has come to bring him luck. He replies that Christ, he needs it, baby. She joins the game, wins $200, cannily quits when the quitting is good, and joins the conversation. It goes like this:

"Well, he's got a hit."

"And who wouldn't? They buy him *Dinner at Eight*, paid a hunnerd and ten thousand dollars for it, Louis B. Mayer told me so himself and showed me the check, paid a hunnerd and ten grand for it, and then they give him Dressler, Beery, Harlow, Tracy, Evans, Hersholt, Morley, Tone, Cukor, and both Barrymores."

"And Robson."

"He was to get Robson, and then he didn't get her."

"He's got Robson."

"She was going to be in it but they yanked her. He told me so himself and Christ he ought to know oughtn't he?"

"Robson's in it."

"All right, then, he's got Robson. Well, who wouldn't have a hit?"

"He can have it."

"That picture was sunk before it started."

"All right maybe it don't make money but it makes him don't it?"

So it goes for upwards of three hours, in the tone of voice of a quarterback in the last five minutes of a desperate football game. But our lady hardly notices it, and by 11:30 she has had a fine time, and takes her departure to go to bed. As to where she goes to bed, it would perhaps be indelicate to inquire. The main point is that she leaves by the back door, and goes to bed somewhere, and that she hasn't been out on the beach yet. And so with the next day and the next, and on until Sunday, when of course she must run in to Hollywood for a change of air and some news.

Well, if she spends her days at the studio, and her evenings at the party, and her nights in bed, and her Sundays in Hollywood, when is it that she enjoys this ravishing beach? That is the whole point. She doesn't. I have been by this beach a number of times, and I have been on it a number of times, and I swear I have never yet seen or heard of more than three people on it at one time. It is the most deserted beach this side of Paradise. The only living creature that seems really to enjoy it is a chow dog. He stands there and barks at the waves to go back. Mr. Jones motions to them to roll in. And they roll.

Hearst Columns
(From *The New York American*)

Wanted: A Western Story
(First column for Hearst November 11, 1933)

What interests me of late is not literature by the piece but literature in the mass: books less for their own sake than for the sake of some great vein in the imagination of a people of which they are the outcropping. So far as I know only one such lode has ever appeared in this country. That was the adventure of the West. For four hundred years the reduction of a continent was our destiny: it was felt by every citizen, underlay all our wars, lent importance to the great debates in Congress, begot all the great writing we have ever done. The first man to tell this saga was James Fenimore Cooper, but he was a little before his time, and I think the real pioneer was a man you seldom hear of: Erasmus Beadle, who founded the Beadle & Adams dime library in 1860.

It was Beadle who first published the story of the West on a great scale, and he had scores of imitators, some of whom put out tales so lurid they came into disrepute; just the same, it was this mountain of cheap books which marked the departure from Hawthorne, Poe, Longfellow, Irving and the other polite writers of the first half of the Nineteenth Century. It was a literature of the people, and it knew what the people held to be romantic. And from it, almost directly out of it grew a literature of the nation. Mark Twain who wrote for Beadle, Bret Harte, Ambrose Bierce, Jack London, Frank Norris, O. Henry, Willa Cather and a host of others. The great works of these writers were all on one theme: the West.

Furthermore, these works have that quality so sorely missed today, when the Western adventure is pretty well finished; they are about something; they tell a story which the author feels is worth telling, instead of one, as his sour attitude toward it shows, which he feels is *not* worth telling. In other words, when you begin to consider books by the ton in this way you discover a curious thing: that what writers have to say is not the main point at all. Before they can have anything to say, the destiny, the national purpose of the deal must be there; there must be a story to tell, one that fires writers and sets readers a-tingle, one that transcends plot, characters, and writing as writing, however fine these may be.

These reflections are provoked by seeing in a book store the other day, side by side these titles: *A Farewell to Arms, Sanctuary, Miss Lonelyhearts, Ann Vickers,* and *Anthony Adverse.* I can't read these books. I have tried for I greatly admire some of their writers, but I can't get through them. The reason I think is that they bear no relation, except in a purely journalistic sense, to the times in which I live. I yearn, in these directionless days, for another Western story. I want something that knows what we are headed for. Can writers fill that order? I don't know. Before they can I guess it is essential that we be headed somewhere.

Romance Under the NRA
(December 5, 1933)

The story tellers and myself, alas, seem to be at a sort of deadlock. Tabulating their output, as it is reviewed in the periodicals reaching me this week, I find it foots up as follows:

9 books about far places;
5 books about distant times;
7 books about far places *and* distant times;
11 books about animals;
1 book, called "*Solid Citizen,*" by McCready Huston, which is about a present-day business man, and apparently tries to deal with these times in which we live.

In other words, after the vigor of the 1920s, after *Main Street, Babbitt, Arrowsmith,* and *Elmer Gantry;* after *The Great Gatsby* and *All the Sad Young Men;* after *Eric Dorn, Capitol Hill, Brawnyman, An American Tragedy, How to Write Short Stories, with Samples,* and all the other books that painted that era so accurately—after, in spite of, and notwithstanding that great renaissance, our novelists have gone Thornton Wilder.

And that is exactly where they and I part company. I understand, of course, the reason for these fairy tales, these stories about love among the ancient Peruvians, love in the Napoleonic era, love among the worthy Cajuns, love among the privateers in 1812 and so on. It has become quite hard to write about the present. For if you imply by happy ending, that everything is swell, then people wonder if you are quite bright, and if you imply, by your finish, or otherwise, that everything is terrible, then they wonder where you got the idea that *that* was news.

It is a tough assignment, and yet it seems to me that in passing it up in a body, as they seem to be doing, the modern novelists are missing a great opportunity. Terrible or not, these times are going to bulk larger in history than most other times, and it is important, for historical reasons if for no other, that they be recorded, vividly and imaginatively, as only the novelist can do it, before their flavor is lost forever.

Romance, no doubt, is all right in its place. But its place, I suspect, is in the works of second-rate writers, the Richard Harding Davises of literature, the F. Marion Crawfords, Anthony Hopes, Harold MacGraths, George Barr McCutcheons, and John Luther Longs who are never going to write anything very hot anyway, and might as well be doing this so long as people want to read it. But when a whole generation of writers begins to send the wind whistling through the rigging, whet the sacrificial knife for the beautiful princess, hoist the chest aboard the lugger, and rein in the horses to let them catch their breath—then it is time to call a halt.

These are important times, and it is up to the literary boys to quit fooling around, and go to work.

Dictators
(October 24, 1934)

It is surprising, and in a way gratifying, this loud razz that has greeted Mr. Hoover's book, *The Challenge to Liberty*. It is surprising, because this country has a habit of being too polite to its public figures, and it is gratifying because the razzers have laid their fingers squarely on the main point, which is that Mr. Hoover never showed any passion for liberty in the days when he could do something about it, and thus, in his present dither over it, seems a bit late, to say the least of it.

But a book, after all, is not merely a thesis. It is also the presentation of a thesis, a job of literary carpentry in its own right, and I wish somebody would go into this question of how badly Mr. Hoover writes. A half hour of his style, I confess, completely exhausts me. He has a genius for what Walter Lippmann used to call flat-wheel sentences, dreadful strings of words that torture your eye, rasp your ear, and leave your mind groping for their meaning, if any.

In addition, he is the kind of writer who never quite says it. He selects the word "work," decides that doesn't quite do it, and puts "and struggle for" on top of it. "Those principles of" comes glibly enough, but it has a plural in it, so that "Americanism" doesn't quite seem to match up right, and gets "an individual accomplishment" to keep it company.

But by this time the thing is in a dreadful snarl, and it takes three lines about the forefathers, involving a whole flock of do's, with "ands" in between, to unwind it and nail it down so he can go on to another one of exactly the same kind.

Of course such men never write, in any accurate meaning of the word. They dictate. And the mouth is such a spendthrift, so accustomed to send its words flying down the wind with no thought that they will never come home to roost, that it is incapable of the economy, the careful calculation of effect, that real writing demands and must have.

If stenography were abolished, and big shots compelled to hitch up to their typewriters as lesser hacks do, the quality of their prose might be distinctly improved or, more likely, they would decide not to write the book at all, which is probably what the situation really calls for.

Bagdad's People
(June 1, 1934)

When I revisited New York recently after an absence of three years it had the same effect on me that it always had. I respect it, and yet somehow I can't like it. I walked home one night, from lower Second Avenue to my hotel in the Forties, and I saw the heart of the city, the central essence which, after the brokers, the bankers, the actors, the writers, and other such super-cargo are stripped away, remains the substance of New York.

I mean the East Side mob. It was about the hour when the theatres were closing down, and here they came, spilling by the thousands out on the sidewalk—bowlegged girls and boys with hats on the sides of their heads, sallow girls and boys with handkerchiefs hanging out of their breast pockets, girls chewing gum and boys wearing undershirts. Girls wearing winter coats on a sticky spring night and boys talking in nosey, New York accents.

And yet, as I say, I respected them. For I knew that behind those shoebutton eyes, those jaws furiously chewing gum, a yeast was working, a determination to get more out of life than their fathers and mothers had got, an ambition to be more than slicers of salami in a corner delicatessen.

I knew that all this simian band were going to the City College by day, conning their books by night, attending meetings in between the grinding of what they take to be an education; I knew that all of them were slaving, straining, putting every ounce of effort into some fantastic dream, even if it was only to be fourth assistant instructor in mathematics at Columbia.

Well, I buy that. I buy it, for its intensity. I buy anything that is entered into with that desperate drive that seems to me the finest thing in life, and perhaps the only thing in life. In the jargon of the stage, these people have got a play. They know where they are going, and even if they don't get there they tried to get there. That is why I say I respect New York. I respect it more than I respect most cities, for in them I find only pettiness, an acceptance of the humdrum as absence of contagious eagerness.

I respect it, and yet I can't like it. It grates on me harshly, makes me want to run away from it. I never could like it. I tried to, God knows. While I lived there I made part of my living writing dialogues for a newspaper, and sound journalism demanded that the locale of these be New York. I couldn't write New York speech. The fault wasn't in my ear, for I have an excellent ear. It lay somewhere inside of me. I couldn't like these people. Their talk didn't delight me, as it delights, say, Arthur Kober. When I wrote it I was a phoney and knew it.

Take me as far as Manhattan Transfer and I can make characters come to life. But leave me in New York and I guarantee you they will be so many waxworks. This makes no sense, and I don't know why I bore you with it. But I spent seven years in the town, and it has just come to me that they were seven years that added up to nothing whatever.

Western Virus
(June 29, 1934)

One of the curious things in connection with my recent trip East was the discovery that I had gone Western in precisely the way that every Iowa farmer goes Western as soon as he treks over the Rockies, buys a ranch and settles down to raise oranges. The first symptom of it was a dissatisfaction with everything I saw back where I came from. Nothing was right. The traffic was handled wrong, the filling stations didn't give service, the hills were too small, the air was too hot, the rain came too often, but only half rained when it did rain.

Even the food tasted bad, which was odd, for I had once written an article saying Western food was terrible, and that I should now think it good showed how far the thing had gone with me. Then I did a lot of tiresome gabbling, boring everybody with my tall stories about the wide open spaces. And then I felt a constant pull to get away, to go back and see a desert once more, and eat an abalone, probably the worst-tasting beast ever taken on land or sea.

So far you would say I was the usual emigrant, back to the old country after three years and full of the wonderful things I had seen since I went away. But really it was much more than that. I was full of this Western thing, which goes a lot deeper than comparison of traffic systems, the lay of the hills, or the way the cooks fix salad. It involves, somehow, a belief that the West affords a better, richer way of life, that it offers something to the soul as well as to the body, that it is esoteric as well as material.

Well, if so, then how? That is what, after three years of trying, I have been unable to find out. The truth about the West is that there is something mystical in it; its appeal is elusive, as prone to vanish as soon as you come close and try to look at it, as the colors on its own mountains. You feel it, and yet you can't lay your finger on it. You tell yourself, say, that it is a matter of space but that isn't true, for if you were like me you had plenty of space in New York, and very nicely decorated it was, too. So with your other efforts to explain it. You can't do it. But this much you know: once it gets you, you are no good for anything else.

The Bosky Dells
(June 11, 1934)

Some time ago, by an accident of travel schedules, I observed the progress of Spring as it spread northward over the United States. I started from the West Coast, and struck it first in Texas. I had always supposed Texas was a state composed entirely of bleak tundras, baking hot in Summer and freezing cold in Winter, but that turned out to be a mistake. I saw miles and miles of meadows, and thousands and thousands of trees; small trees, to be sure, but all leafed out in gay green.

I then followed it up through Louisiana, Alabama and Tennessee, and then I lost it. It was a little cool for greenery in Kentucky, Northern Virginia and Maryland. But then, getting on the train again a couple of weeks later, I picked it up and followed it all the way up to the Great Lakes, where it was in full bloom.

Well, it would be idle to deny that Spring in these States is something to see. Every forest, every clump of trees is covered with the cleanest, brightest green that you can imagine. Under them, on the banks and hillsides, are flowers of every conceivable color and every conceivable size. And scattered through them, everywhere, was dogwood; sprays of waxy white flowers that somehow painted up the whole spectacle, made it look like a set for *Mid-Summer Night's Dream*. It is something for poets to write about, all right, and no wonder it makes them a little bit goofy.

It is something for poets to write about, and yet it left me cold. It had the same effect on me it had always had. It is too fragrant, too pretty, too contented. It makes me feel as church-bells do, when they ring on Sunday evening; that peaceful, pastoral ding-dong to me is the most dismal sound in the world.

In fact, it wasn't until I got far away from this highly poetical Spring that I felt what the average person seems to feel when he gazes on nature. We had just crossed the sink that holds the Salton Sea, and entered the last of the big deserts before you get to the Coast. It was so hot you didn't dare move; the club car was gray with a dust that not even the tightest doors and windows can keep out; all you could see was sand that drifted like snow, and bleak brown hills in the distance.

It would be hard to imagine a more horrible place, and yet as I looked out on those stunted desert bushes, all warped and twisted by a wind that never stops blowing, I got something. There was nothing sweet, contented, and pretty-pretty here. It was a grim, desperate and terrible struggle for existence, and all of a sudden I was stirred by it, excited by its drama, lifted by its stark, lethal beauty.

They say the desert gets you, after a while; that once you begin to feel it no other place seems like home. I suppose so. I have been in the Southwest now for three years, and like all the rest have begun chasing mirages

Literary Osmosis
(June 20, 1934)

One of the wisest writing men in the world, I suspect, is Sinclair Lewis. I don't refer to the wisdom that shines out of his pages, although no doubt there is some of that, else people wouldn't read his books. I refer to his manner of writing them. He traipses all over the world, and particularly all over this country, camping down in the locale of his stories, getting all soaked up with his people before he puts a word down on paper, and then he stays there until he gets finished with it.

This is sharply at variance with the usual practice among writers. They do not, of course, try to write about places they have never seen, or, at any rate, most of them do not; but they are always trying to do it from memory.

Now this much is true about writing: a man can write what is in front of his nose, and that is about all he can write. Once you get a hundred miles away from a place it doesn't seem real any more. Furthermore there are great gaps in your information about it. You can't remember whether the filling station attendants in that part of the world wear smocks or overalls, or whether the restaurants serve enchiladas for breakfast, or flapjacks. Thus your account of it is colorless, and shy on details. It is only when you can get up from the typewriter and look at it that you are confident and make no mistakes.

These reflections are provoked by what happened to me after a trip of mine recently. It was an extended trip, that took me across the country and back, and up and down it, and around it in circles, both by train and by automobile. And it was interesting. There were many things I wanted to write about it, and some of them I did write. But most of them I postponed until I could get home, to my own machine, where I could pound them out without a lot of engagements, sleeper jumps, and dashes for trains.

Well, here I am back, and here is my own machine, and it has vanished into the shadows, that trip. I wanted to write about the food in New Orleans. I wanted to write about the gigantic, black, and dignified Negroes in San Antonio. I wanted to write about the architecture of Annapolis. I wanted to write about these, and many other things besides, but they will never get written. Here in the sunshine of Southern California they seem blurred, queer, and faint. The next time I travel I am going to do as Lewis does. I am going to take my typewriter with me, and write it while it is hot. That is the only way it ever goes down on paper.

The Other Guy's Play
(July 20, 1934)

My life throws me with a good many playwrights, movie writers and novelists, and this much they all have in common: it is almost impossible to get them into a show, and even if you do get them there, still more nearly impossible to keep them there, for they can grab their hats quicker, and go sneaking out on a bad one faster, than any breed of man I know.

I used to speculate on this, and concluded that it was either boredom with a trade they knew too well, or else some sort of unconscious jealousy, that made for impatience with another man's work, even when you would suppose that they ought to study it, if for no reason but to learn something from it.

The other night, though, I got another slant on it, from a playwright. We had just walked out on a play of which the less said the better, and were drinking beer in a sour frame of mind. "A bad play is an awful thing, isn't it?" he said abruptly.

"Yeah," I said. "It is."

"You know," he went on, "it doesn't only bore me. I could stand that. If that was all. I would even sit there and look at it. But it *terrifies* me. I tell you what I mean. A good play, it makes it look easy. A good play is always simple. It makes you feel, why I could have written that, if I'd only thought of it. And it makes you feel that writing a play is hot stuff, something worth doing.

"But a bad play? It just makes you sick. It's always complicated and dull, and felt. The guy made all the mistakes you ever made, and all of a sudden, instead of it being him up there they're coughing on, it's you. And then it makes you feel it's a lousy trade anyway. It makes you feel like you ought to have stayed in the advertising business.

"That's what I mean. That's why it terrifies me. That's why I can't sit there and look at it."

It's a curious point of view, but I believe one that most professional story-tellers share. It is no part of the purpose of a play, or a book, of course, to inspire other men to write, but it is a pleasant reflection, I think, that a good one can have that effect.

Camera Obscura
(*The American Mercury*, October 1933)

Of the 300 or so writers actually employed in Hollywood, I suppose I know fifty, and I don't know one who doesn't dislike movie work, and wish he could afford to quit it. This is a singular state of affairs, for among the actors, directors, executives, and the other people engaged in the business the feeling is the other way around. They find it, to be sure, very trying. They rarely make a picture without getting into some sort of nasty mess; they find the studio is doing them dirt, they see their pet scene on the cutting-room floor, they quarrel among themselves, they live in a state of constant turmoil. But all this is temporal, accidental, and local. The cinema itself to them is Heaven, and however badly it may be run in spots, it is fundamentally so perfect that it would be impossible to imagine an improvement.

For writers, however, it is Hell, and it is Hell no less if their corner of it, as often happens, is very well run. For some, of course, it is worse than for others. The ones who find it least irksome, oddly enough, are those who were professional novelists, playwrights, or story writers before they came to it. This is not because they are better at it, or are more politely treated, or have thicker skins. It is because, for them, it is not the only egg in the basket. If they fail at it, or get into a row with some supervisor, or for one reason or another have to leave, they still have their trade to fall back on. To them, the movies are only a sideline, and an unimportant one except for the money that is in it; their real work, the thing that seems worth while to them, is something else. Thus they shed studio grief easily, and even manage to regard it a bit humorously.

But the man who used to get out notices for Ziegfeld is never going to write a play, and knows it, and neither is the man who used to cover fires for the New York *Daily News*, nor the man who used to write light articles for *Time*, nor the man who used to bust bronks for Hoot Gibson. If they don't get a whiff of stardust here, there is no place else they will get it, and so they are the bitterest about the business.

It sounds somewhat odd to hear one of them denounce it with passion, for to look at him you wouldn't think he was capable of passion, and to look at his record you wouldn't think he cared about anything much, so long as he got paid. But that is the curious thing about a writer. No matter what queer things he used to do, no matter what queer things he does now, such as advertising himself in the movie annuals, no matter how smugly he tells himself that 1,000 bucks a week pays for everything, no matter what kind of cheap hack he may be, to all signs and appearances, there comes a time in his day when he has to be a writer. Within his limits, he has to come to grips with his job, to do his best. Yet his best, if you are to believe him, is the one thing the movies won't let him do.

None of them, then, gets any satisfaction out of it. They get money, but nothing more. Some take the disappointment lightly, others tragically, but for all of them it is there, and it is what I want to probe into here. I have to warn you that I am a disappointed movie writer myself, so you can take my remarks at a proper discount. I have had two flops. I think they were due to bad judgment, i.e., to the acceptance of assignments I had no fitness for, rather than to any special ineptitude for the work, but I would mislead you if I let you think I only half tried, or that they weren't real flops. I worked as hard as I knew how, and yet both times I flopped flat.

But I would mislead you, too, if I let you think my failure at this task mattered as much to me as my failure at other tasks. When I am going through the back files of some magazine, and come across an article of mine that I feel was bad, I can't look at it. I have to flip the pages fast, and if it was an especially bad article, I am upset for the whole day, and have to pound the typewriter furiously to shake it out of my mind. The movies had no such power to punish me. I disliked the fact that two companies had paid me money, and had got nothing for it, for that was a new sensation to me, and a disagreeable one. I was in a scramble of personal emotions, for on both lots there were men who had treated me very decently, whom I had got to like, and whom I had let down. Moreover, I was sad in the pocketbook, for I like money as well as anybody else, and movie money will buy as much as any other kind of money.

But all that involved what you might call my social conscience. My artistic conscience barely stirred. And if I had turned in a fine story, I don't think it would have turned any handsprings either. That is what I want to get at here: Why is it that the movies seem unable to afford the writer the requital that he finds so quickly elsewhere; burning shame for work badly done, glowing pride in work that hits the mark? If I do get at it, I ought to be able to shed light on a somewhat broader issue, which is the cinema's claim to a place in the sun. Is this really destined to be one of the major arts, worthy of serious critical attention: Or is it only a rich relative of the Muses, dressed in all her fine raiment, but condemned to go forever without a lover unless she pays him a fat sum to get in bed with her?

II

The woe of the movie writer, of course, is no special discovery of my own: it is discussed all the time, together with various theories to explain it, and I think it would be well to clear the deck of some of these before going on.

You have heard, no doubt, that moving picture studios are dreadful places, run by barbarians with no idea of manners, and callous to all the finer ideals that are supposed to animate a writer. This doesn't happen to be true. I have worked in a number of places in my time, and I have never worked any place where courtesy was more in evidence than on a movie lot, or where the daily contacts were more pleasant. The capacity of a studio to make life agreeable for you, indeed, savors almost of the magical. If you are bothered by street noises, they will whisk you to a place where you can hear nothing but birds; if you dislike to talk over the telephone, the girl at the board will tell your lies for you; if you like tea at four-thirty, it will arrive at four-thirty sharp.

You can have no complaint about the arrangements for your comfort, and you can have no complaint about the treatment you get from your colleagues. If you are stuck, ten of them will sit around and try to pull you out; if you need a gag, somebody will think of one, and shoot it to you quick. Wash out all stories about the ghastliness of life on a movie lot. They are like stories about the illiterate Broadway producers: funny when told, but lamentably far from the truth. A movie lot, making all allowance for feuds, quarrels, and turmoil, is more like a big club than a place of employment.

Movie executives are anything but barbarians. The business is full of nepotism: the incompetent brother-in-law is a great trial to everybody, including his wife. But that is true of every business. And there is the occasional irritating roughneck. But taking one man with another, you can be sure that he didn't get to be supervisor, or associate producer, or production manager, without knowing a great deal about moving pictures. And you can't know much about moving pictures unless you know something of the world. These fellows have been around, they have good manners, they talk well, they have some presence. They are not, as a rule, very well educated, if by education you mean the possession of college degrees. Yet they will often surprise you by their exact information on some recondite subject: like most self-made men, they have to work hard for knowledge, and when they get it they have it.

They have one bad fault. They are prone to condone bad work if the picture makes money, and overlook good work if the picture flops. But here again, something must be said for them. The pressure on them to produce profits is simply enormous, and if it ever got around that they had their minds on anything else they would be very badly off indeed. Too, they have found out by rule of thumb that good work is usually profitable and bad work not, so that they don't lose much sleep over occasional exceptions.

This brings me to the most important legend of all, so far as this discussion is concerned, which is that the studios don't want good work from a writer, but only the cheapest stuff he can think up, and the more stereotyped, mawkish, and salacious, the better. This is an idea that is held, not only by the outside world, but by the writers themselves, to a very large extent. It is their most frequent out, what they blame their troubles on. Well, I don't believe it. I have sat in a good many moving picture conferences, and I have yet to hear an executive say, "Boys, it ain't sexy enough." What they usually say is: "Boys, it's no goddam good. Maybe you need more time. Take it. But it's got to be a whole lot better if we're going to schedule it."

When the boys get back to their office, no doubt they feel hurt. No doubt they feel that this is a story about a sensitive young something or other, and as such must be pretty good. No doubt they feel that they are sensitive young somethings or other themselves, and couldn't possibly have thought up anything but a masterpiece. No doubt they feel that the movies are run by a lot of ex-button hole makers who wouldn't know something good if it was handed to them on a silver platter. No doubt they pity themselves handsomely, but I'll tell you why their effort was turned down. It was no goddam good, and that was the beginning of it and the end of it.

They want good stories, and they will hire any writer, from G.B. Shaw to Mike Romanoff, who shows a glim of a shadow of a wisp of a promise of giving them good stories. By good they mean just what you mean by good. That is, they mean what you mean when you have paid your money and want something to show for it. They don't mean what you mean when you sit around as a kibitzer and think up bigger and better ideas for the movies. Sad experience has taught them that whimsical political satire in the Gilbert and Sullivan manner, hot appeals to reason in the Heywood Broun manner, screwy pictures of sheep in the Swedish manner, screwy pictures of feet in the German manner, and screwy pictures of flywheels in the Russian manner, produce only snores, even in the most cultivated noses. And sad experience has taught them that many of their own screwy tricks, effective enough once, nowadays produce only snores, too.

They have learned that good means good. It means what you paid for: that kick, that excitement, that emotion, which takes you out of the seat you are sitting in, transports you to where things are going on, and holds you there in hot suspense to see how it all comes out. They'll give you all those. If you want Gilbert and Sullivan, they'll get you Danforth; if you want Broun, they'll get him; they've got all the sheep, feet, flywheels, shipwrecks, ostriches, palaces, legs, wapitis, conveyor belts, and elephants there are. But one thing they demand: it's got to be good. And if sometimes it isn't good, be assured that they know it as well as you do.

They have to get out 550 pictures a year in this place, exclusively of shorts, newsreels, and novelties, and there just aren't that many good stories. Just the same, good is what they want. Nothing is too high-brow for them, or too fine, or too delicate; there is no technical problem they won't solve for you, provided it has that thing.

III

The first thing that catches your ear, when you go on a movie lot, is that these people don't say "movies," or "talkies." They say "pictures." And it is not long before you realize that this is no chance word. It states the essence of the business.

That thing up there isn't primarily the record of a novel, a play, or a story. It is a series of photographed pictures. All its main problems are identical with those of the old postcard series, where a cat stalked a bird in six views, or a dog rescued a boy from the water, or a hobo stole a pie from a pantry shelf. The basis of the cinema is a photographed picture, and that it moves, or that it talks, is incidental. This moving and talking may lend verisimilitude, or variety, or divertissement for the ear, but the main thing remains: a photographed picture.

Now, when you use a photographed picture as a means of expression, there are certain things about it that do not occur to the average person, and they bear directly on what I am getting at here. I can illustrate by quoting a conversation I once had with a cartoonist, at the time when a prominent lady tennis player was exhibiting her drawings and attracting some attention with them. I asked him what he thought of them.

"Oh," he said, "they're all right, I guess. They're not drawings, though. Anyway, not what an artist means by drawings. They're nothing but sketches from photographs."

"How do you know?" I asked.

"I don't know how I know. Don't *you* know? Can't you feel that lifelessness about them? All those figures are in poses no artist would ever think of. Look at that one. Only the camera could get a woman in a stoop like that. You see, to get the feeling of life in a figure, you have to pose the model, or imagine the model, in a position that makes the stresses of the anatomy effective. If you don't, you get something like the snapshot of a runner as he breaks the tape. Usually, he doesn't look to be running at all. He looks to be falling down, or walking, or standing still. It's the same way with these things. I don't know what to say about them. There's nothing to say. *They don't say anything.*"

Bearing in mind that last remark, which I put in italics as the key to this discussion, consider now photography in comparison with that branch of graphic art to which it would seem to bear the closest relation: portraiture. Consider the pictures of Sargent, who specialized in portraiture, and who always got a likeness as good as the camera gets. When you look at his portrait of Joseph Pulitzer, do you say, "What a man!"? You do not. You say, "What a picture!". But when you look at a photograph of Pulitzer, it is the other way around. You examine his face with interest, take in all details of costume, from the flapping black hat to the great cape, and never give a thought to the photographer at all. Why? Because the portrait *says* something. What you see is Joseph Pulitzer, but what you *feel* is John Singer Sargent. In some curious fashion, with paint as a medium and Pulitzer as a model, Sargent's imagination speaks to your imagination, says something that transcends all models, however eminent. It would be the same with any model, a peasant girl, say, or Lord Ribblesdale, a dull man, but the subject of a very fine portrait.

But the photographer imagines nothing, communicates nothing. He poses the model, adjusts the lights, uses a soft focus or a sharp focus, retouches afterward, goes through an elaborate routine, and in view of this, it is common to hear eminent custodians of the little birdie discussed as "artists." Yet obviously there is no art here, no message from one imagination to another imagination. No matter what lofty thoughts the photographer may be capable of, or the beholder may be capable of, what goes on the plate is the model, and that is all that goes on the plate. It is all the photographer can give, all the beholder can get. To the extent that the model is interesting the picture will be interesting, but only to that extent: even the best photographer couldn't make the Brain Trust look like anything.

But, you say, the writer is not a photographer. He makes up stories, and these are what the models narrate. Furthermore, he doesn't deal in still pictures, where a comparison can be made with drawing. His figures move and talk, and are so lifelike that the proper comparison is with the actors in a play. Well, I doubt that. The moving photograph, I think, is much closer to the face on the plate, in all its profounder aspects, than it is to the living actor. There is, for example, the matter of the period of interest. You get sick of the moving photograph with the same appalling swiftness that you get sick of the still photograph: all movie shots have to be brief, and intercut with close-ups and angle shots, else you would go insane from the monotony. Again, when drawing and photography do meet on the screen, drawing wins by so many miles that it is not even a race. I think it is agreed, both in the industry and out of it, that Mickey Mouse is the one outstanding accomplishment of the talking picture to date. Yet it is not photographic. It is made with a camera, but it is a drawing; that is, it is one imagination speaking to another imagination.

But let us waive these points, which may seem a little thin, and consider the proposition that the photographed model is to all intent and purpose like the actor in a play. Superficially he is, of course, but with this difference: the actor is not part of the play. He is part of the performance, but he acts only as surrogate for a character. The character has an imaginative existence apart from his performance of it, and the play has an imaginative existence apart from all performances of it. This is something that even the most naive realize, for you hear them as they go out! "Good show all right, but that kid was lousy"; or: "Nothing to it, but Cornell was good." The actor may hurt the play, or he may help it, but always the play is one thing, the actor another.

That is not true of a movie. The story has no existence apart from this version of it: the two are frozen together on that film for all time, and they cannot be separated. There is a script, and you can consult it, but you will not find a script in the sense that a play has a script or a symphony a score. It is a set of notes for a director, set down in jargon that only he can understand. Furthermore, it often gives no clue to what comes out on the screen. "Camera," it says, "pans to get section of crowd." But "section of crowd," as the director shoots it, may be the big scene of the picture. There is nothing in the script to show it. If you want this story, you have to get it from that film: for the first time in the history of such things, imagination and performance go together, and there is no way to get them apart.

Now, it doesn't help the writer any to realize that a studio, with its great resources, can give him a production such as no stage producer can give him. It can, and it does. But this is the spot he is in: since the whole enterprise is in one lump, it follows that things must be arranged so that this particular cast can do its best. If he has written for the stage, he has heard a producer say, "Don't write an actor. Write a character. When you get a live character on paper, we'll find the actor to play it." But the very nature of this movie business compels him to write for an actor. Chevalier, for example, likes to play in a straw hat. It makes him feel like Chevalier. And in his pictures you will usually find some comic bit that involves a straw hat.

Well, suppose the writer, assigned to a Chevalier picture, remembered his stage tradition and said: "To hell with Chevalier. I am not writing Chevalier. I'm writing a character, and my character doesn't wear a straw hat. Anyhow, I've got more things to worry about than spotting a hat gag so that Frog can get a laugh." The supervisor, I think, would look at him in some astonishment. What character? There will never be any character except as Chevalier plays it. It is sink or swim with Chevalier, and anything that helps him belongs in, as they say.

But suppose the supervisor were such a supervisor as never existed, and said: "Maybe you're right. Do it your way, and we'll see." And suppose, after it is finished, the studio sees that it isn't a Chevalier picture at all, but a Bing Crosby picture. Next day the supervisor will be back. "This guy, you've heard him, likes a spot where he can go la-de-da, m'm-m'm-m'm, you know, on the chorus? See if you can fix up a couple of those lyrics so it works in right, will you?"

First draft, second draft, final draft, or whatever draft it is, that is the way it works out. The words are the supervisor's, the voice is the camera's. It is the same with Blondell's legs, Cagney's sock, McHugh's laugh, West's bosom, Merkle's accent, Brown's mouth, Fields's juggling, Durante's nose: there is hardly an actor without an asset to be taken into account, so we are right back where we started. They move, they talk, they look exactly like actors in a play, and yet we have the same old model, the face on the plate: regardless of what the writer, the director, or anybody else is trying to say, that is what comes out on the screen.

It is this, I think, that makes a writer get sick at the stomach when he walks on a movie lot, causes him to feel that in some vague way he is a prostitute of the arts. It is not that he is jealous of the actor. It is not that he has highfalutin notions about the sanctity of writing as compared with other branches of the business. He gets off some nonsense to that effect, of course, and half believes it. But the trouble is not that. It is inherent in the business. Imagination is free or it is not free, and here it is not free. It serves the medium, instead of the medium serving it, and once that is felt, that is the end of pride, of joy in getting things down on paper, of having them appear in front of your eyes. And for my part, no matter what technical improvements are made, I can't see that it can be changed even a little bit. So long as this is photography, it is there to stay.

But even this is not the end of it, so far as the writer is concerned. If the camera has a defective capacity for conveying what somebody imagined, it has a positive genius for conveying what nobody imagined. Once I saw Charles Bickford in a picture called "East of Borneo," liked some things he did in it, and called him up to tell him so. He wasn't home, but Mrs. Bickford was, and we got to talking about the picture.

"Tell me," I said, "did Charlie really have to work with those alligators, or was his end of it all done in the studio?"

"He certainly *did* have to work with the alligators," she said. "And oh my, did you notice that place where the alligator was in the boat? That alligator wasn't supposed to be there. When Hobart screamed that time it was a real scream, and Charlie didn't know what to do. It was an awfully expensive set-up, and they had three cameras on it, and he hated to make them shoot it over. So he picked up the oar and beat the alligator over the back with it, and it got out of the boat, but he was scared all right."

It was the wow shot of the picture. It was very valuable, for it made possible fine lobby stills showing Bickford slashing at a snapping alligator, and it pulled them in by the thousands. But who imagined it? Not the authors. Not the director. Not Bickford, for he wasn't imagining about that time. He was trying to get out of a spot, and if you ever saw a half ton of alligators go into action against a man, **you can know** how hot that spot was. Nobody imagined it. It was an accident. But if he had collided with the story the story would have been scuttled so fast you couldn't see it go down. When a beauty like that is caught on a negative, story, and all such things must make way for it.

In the picture "Tarzan," a lioness went up a tree after a man. The authors didn't imagine that. How could they? Lions don't climb trees. It was in there because Goebel happens to have a cat that flouts zoology and goes aloft. So they baited her with meat and got her up there. "It looked funny," said Goebel, "but they went for it, so I guess it was all right."

In hardly any animal picture does the negative show exactly what the authors wrote. In "King of the Jungle," the script called for a lion to kill a bull. The bull pitched nine lions out of the stockade, and when he was withdrawn, being too clawed up by that time to look pretty in a picture, a second bull pitched out five more. The human race, apparently, had been under some slight misapprehension as to who the king of the jungle really was, and the lion never did kill the bull. So they cut in some footage of the fight, and let it go at that.

Then there is the kind of shot that depends on mechanical effect, and achieves, in verisimilitude, much more than could be achieved by any imagination has ever beheld such a thing. The gigantic ape in "King Kong," the rubber octopus in "Below the Sea," the sinking submarine in "The Devil and the Deep,"—all these go far beyond imagination, in the sense that no imagination could possibly pretend that it knew what such things look like. In other words, the writer not only works with a medium which grossly fails him at times, but one that runs hog wild on him at other times, and makes him say things which no man in his sober senses could mean or believe.

Were he an artist in paints, words, or musical notes, he would be working with a medium absolutely under his control. But this medium is always climbing down from its tripod and telling him what to do. "We can't do that, old man," it says to him. "No way to photograph a thought, you know. Of course, they put it on the sound track in

'Strange Interlude,' but for a thing like this, it's too screwy. I tell you what we can do, though. We'll sink this guy in a shipwreck. We've still got the tank we used in 'Hell Under the Waves,' and that ship model from 'Express Liner,' and we'll put the fast camera on it, so those bubbles come out slow and big; we'll do a real, first-class, up-to-date under-water job on it, that'll look like a million dollars, and we can do it for seven fifty, anyway a grand, what do you say?"

He obeys the medium, the medium doesn't obey him. And then, when his work has had its brief flurry, it is dead. Old movies can't be reissued. As we have noted, the story is shackled to a single set of costumes, sets, and technical devices, and when these are out of date, they sink it. If, as sometimes happens, a movie is made over, there is an entirely new version: not a scrap of the first author's work remains. It is the final garland of the movie writer.

IV

I think it is clear now why the serious critic so persistently holds aloof from moving pictures, and why he will probably continue to do so. Inevitably, he is Posterity's bookmaker, and Posterity is not going to be fooled by straw hats, legs, noses, alligators, process shots, or anything so ephemeral, however ingenious it may be. It pays off on wings, on that imaginative vitality which can fly down the cruelly long distance through the years.

Thus the critic is concerned with what, in telegraphy, is known as the phantom circuit, that electrical area which exists apart from all wires, all models, all costumes, all effects: the imagination we have been talking about. But when he looks for it on the screen, where is he to find it? Did the writer put it in, or the director, or the actor, or was it just an accident, like Bickford and the alligators? And suppose he does spot it, and thinks he knows whom to credit it to, how can he mark odds on it when it is glued to celluloid, is not free, and can never fly?

It is as though, in music, he were invited to pass on a composition, and then discovered that the only way he could ever hear it was on a particular phonograph record. It is imprisoned there, and he can't be concerned with things in a prison, any more than a scientist can be concerned with formulas reserved to a commercial trademark. Something snide gets into the business, and repels him. And he can never be quite sure that a crash of cymbals which he especially admires is not, in reality, the sound of the conductor falling off the podium.

I think it is clear, too, that the writer, if he has his mind on Bigger and Better Things, will forever be disappointed here, and that he will always yield place to the man in front of the camera, who is the model, and the man behind the camera, who is the director. Yet it might help him a bit to have a clear idea what his function is, and discharge that function, instead of aspiring to functions which simply are not there. I think an industry usually has an instinct for what is good for it, and from this industry you hear nothing about Bigger and Better Things. All that kind of talk goes on outside. This industry believes that its future lies in entertainment. "Give us down-to-earth stories," say the exhibitors, in the trade periodicals. "Give us something the customers like. Cut out the highbrow fol-de-rol, and learn *Showmanship*. Good human *Stories*. Stories with *Real Situations*. Stories with *Excitement*."

Well, there are worse trades than confecting entertainment, and if you realize clearly that you *are* at work on entertainment, something that lives tonight and tomorrow is forgotten, then the suspicions that you are a prostitute of the arts loses much of its sting. If entertainment is all that it comes to, then we are all workmen together, aren't we, putting up a little show? The question of who is most important hasn't much point if it is realized that nobody is important. With that always kept in mind, I think writers could have a lot more fun than they have now and do better work. There is good entertainment and bad, and a chance for plenty of honest resourcefulness.

For my part, when I go to a movie, I am entertained best if it is unabashedly a movie, and not a piece of dull hoke posing as something else. I fell for Jo Swerling's "Below the Sea," rubber octopus and all, but I detested "Cavalcade." I liked Frances Marion's "The Champ," but "Cynara" gave me a pain in the neck. I think that is the way most of the customers feel, and I think it shows the way to the proper sphere for moving pictures. In other words, it is better to shoot at a balloon and hit a balloon than to shoot at a star and hit a cornfield.

Fame and Hot Hollywood
(*The Washington Post*, June 16, 1974)

In Hollywood, it used to be that the test of your fame was the degree of your involvement in a war we had going on—except that nobody called it fame. You were hot or you weren't hot, and I never heard it called anything else.

The war was for the social supremacy of Beverly Hills, and it was fought by various ladies, always unsuccessfully, against Mrs. Edward G. Robinson. So, in due course, she called me and invited me to dinner, this being my first intimation that for various reasons, I had reached a certain degree of hotness, a delicious realization. In due course I went over there, and in addition to meeting her, met her husband, the eminent Eddie himself, and saw her house, a fantastic thing to look at.

It had in it all those pictures you had seen in Time magazine, except these were the originals, beautifully hung in the right places, in suitable frames, with lights at their bottoms, so you could see them without straining your eyes. Gladys was very good-looking, and Eddie most interesting, especially on the subject of acting, which I always nudged him into. He took it seriously, and was vastly informed about it, having resources at it not often suspected, much though he was praised. Gladys never had a caterer, and once, at a gigantic garden party she gave, took me into the kitchen to show me the gear involved in baking up steak and kidney pie for several hundred people.

But others took you up too, and as they came to your house too and there had to be a payback, you got invited to the big bash at which the slate was wiped clean and could start over again.

Of course, I lived in a Hollywood that had almost nothing to do with the Hollywood of the fan magazines, made up of perfectly sensible people, who lived sensible, well-bred lives and paid almost as little attention to the whoop-de-do of hotness as I did. To most of them, as to me, pictures were a sideline, except during the war, when they were proclaimed an essential industry; and to be patriotic, we all had to sacrifice ourselves at salaries, at least in my case, larger than the one then paid the

President of the United States.

It could bring odd consequences, as for example when I got home from Europe one time, to encounter bewilderment verging in reverence. The reason was a series of interviews with me, published in Amsterdam, Stockholm, London, and various places, which stood Hollywood on its ear. I was, and am, translated into Swedish, Danish, and various other European languages, and so was an item of news when I got to town. But to Hollywood, where foreign bureaus sent the news on, and most of whose geniuses are unknown east of Pasadena, this was a bewildering thing. And it may have had something to do with an odd conversation I had with a girl I was quite fond of, whom I don't name because I can't. She got married again, after Hollywood, and I'm ashamed to confess I don't remember her second name especially as she died, and I feel guilty about it. Anyway, though she didn't eat at the same table at Metro as the one I usually sat at, she would wait for me out on the grass and walk with me over to the Thalberg Building, or Iron Lung as it was called, where we both had our offices. One day she seemed a bit down, and presently I asked: "Well, wellamalla? I pour gravy on your ice cream, or what?"

"Oh, the usual," she answered. "My option. It's coming up tomorrow and though I guess it'll be O.K. I haven't heard yet, and I'm worried."

"Option?" I yelped. "Look who's bragging. I haven't seen an option in years. I work on a day-to-day basis. We could say hour-to-hour. We could even say minute to minute without fear of successful contradiction. Any time, any moment, the foreman could open my door, turn the light out over my typewriter, and that would be that."

"Aw for Christsake!"

The venom in the voice of this well-bred girl was unmistakable, and utterly startling.

. . . "What did I say?" I asked, somewhat stunned.

"Knock it off, will you?" she snapped, "with the comical stuff about the foreman, and let somebody talk that has trouble, and is not in the humor for jokes. A fat chance you would be fired."

"Well I have been, I assure you."

"Not any more. You're Arthur Hornblow's kept intellectual and everyone knows it and if you're not going to be fired don't gag at someone who could be."

I stood there, no doubt blinking at her, trying to catch up with what she had said, being utterly caught by surprise. At last I asked her. "What did you say—will you repeat it, please? What in the hell did you say?

"Aw," she snarled, "it's the new status symbol—they all have one now. Hunt Stromberg has Aldous Huxley, Arthur Freed has Bob Nathan, and Arthur Hornblow has you. So I'm not much amused by your foreman and the way he can snap off your light."

I should have been humiliated by such a charge, but when I got back to my office discovered I wasn't—just the opposite, I was a bit pleased. I knew, of course, that Arthur Hornblow wasn't keeping me on a tribute to anything except my possible ability to do him a script, but to discover that I was an intellectual, this was quite a sensation. I really enjoyed it, and still do. In fact, I recall the soft impeachment with some pride, even now.

But the only time I really savored it, this status of being hot, would come on this same Metro lot, on the occasions when I would be sold to Metro to work on a one-picture deal.

There was a man on the lot with a face not even a mother could be sure of, who, when I'd appear without hotness, would pass me on the walk to the commissary, with a frigid, distant bow, and say: "Mr. Cain!?" But if perchance I was hot, this same faceless object would stop on seeing me, gurgle ecstatically, and exclaim: "Jim! Jim! Long time no see! Aw gee, it's great having you back—just great having you back!" I would pass him, say "Kid, I love you," and continue to my office. He would still be on my mind, and then I would ask myself. Was he there? Did he exist? Or was he something the Special Effects Department ran up, as a pleasant little feature for my first day back on the lot? Probably, or at the very least possibly, he was done with mirrors, but I cannot deny he was pleasant.

Charles Laughton: A Reminiscence of a Revelation
(*The Washington Post*, August 22, 1976)

The new book on Charles Laughton, by Charles Higham, stresses his homosexuality, and gives adequate space to his origin, as the son of a Yorkshire hotel owner, yet almost ignores the effect that this had on him, and how he felt about it. Which leads me to wonder how well Higham knew Laughton, or if he knew him at all.

I first met him at a party the Samson Raphaelsons gave in their Beverly Hills home. He took no notice of me, though of course I took notice of him, as everyone did. He had just finished a picture, due shortly for release, "The Sign of the Cross," about which there was some talk, and within a few days, when it began showing in the theaters, I went to have a look. It was about ancient Rome, and he played Nero—but a thoroughly effeminate Nero with curled hair, a leer and all the other trimmings. It was the first I knew that Nero had such a bias, but of pictures, you don't ask too much historical accuracy, and the portrait was certainly effective, vivid, damning and unforgettable.

And yet, something about it didn't match up, at least to my naive mind, and I went to see it a second time. Then suddenly I knew what the trouble was, and the next time I ran into Laughton, at the Raphaelsons' again, I was able to tell him: "I checked on that picture of yours, that portrait you gave of Nero as a practicing homo, and there's nothing in the script that accounts for the way you played that part. You never heard of me, but I'm a writer, specializing in dialogue, and I know what I'm talking about; there's not one word in your lines that warrants the picture you painted. Nero, in the script, was a straight Cecil De Mille heavy, who corresponds to Gibbons's account in "The Decline and Fall." Where did that fag come from?"

His face lit up, in a moment he was at my side, and in two moments he was my pal. It delighted him that someone, at last, had detected the truth, that this character was his own invention, something he had hesitated to brag about, openly. He admitted his utter horror, when he read the De Mille script, at the slug that he had to play and began casting around for something he could do to make him interesting. He told how the opening shot was one he thought up himself, of having his toes pedicured, and how Freddie March, as he called him, had warned him it wouldn't work, that "you'll never get away with it, you'll see." But when he looked up De Mille was there, staring as the scene was shot, and when it was done, turned away without saying anything. "He has yet to say anything," Laughton assured me. "That's the reward I got, for doing, if I say so myself, a pretty good job."

From there on in, we had a real friendship. He came to a dinner at my house, Elsa Lanchester coming with him, on one of her nights off from the theater she appeared in regularly, and turning out to be a most amusing lady. Just once, at the table, there was a throwback to his origins. He was most critical, even derisive, of the way I carved the turkey, but it didn't upset me unduly, as at least my system worked, and had made me a bit of money, as I had written it up now and then, and been paid for telling about it. But the real basis of our religion was this game we constantly played, of my seeing things in his portrayals that everyone else missed, especially the newspaper critics.

For example, there was his Javert in "Les Miserables," which I never saw on the screen but which he did for me often enough, and which I pronounced "the perfect bureaucrat—that Jean Val-Jean is human he hasn't yet thought of. To this man, he's simply a fugitive, something to be caught and put back into prison." It seemed to clarify for him his conception of the part, and he seemed to be memorizing what I said. And about that time he was meditating Cyrano de Bergerac—if he ever played him I don't know. I calmly accused him of wanting the part "so you can have, for once in your life, a nice long aquiline nose."

And so we coasted along. And then one day I was at work writing, when the front doorbell rang. I was annoyed, as it was the maid's afternoon off and I was alone in the house. To answer I had to go from my workroom to the front door, quite a trip. When I opened, there was Charles—but you never saw such a sight. The man I had known, a sedate English actor, had become the Hollywood boy, in white flannel trousers, white open-throat shirt, white shoes and a grin. I was caught by surprise, but came up with a grin too and asked him in. It turned out that at last he had put over a coup at MGM, by getting rid of a part he felt he was wrong for, of Micawber in David Copperfield, and wishing it off on W.C. Fields, who he thought could do it. The studio thought so too, and when Fields checked in for work, Laughton, to celebrate, came up to tell me about it.

So I congratulated him, and we talked. He seemed startled at how well I knew Fields, but was pleased that my appraisal of his talents, especially at straight acting, coincided with his own. Then he got up to go, and suddenly asked if I'd like to go with him that night to see "Ruggles of Red Gap," his latest release. I was, and still am, a rabid fan of Harry Leon Wilson, on whose novel the picture was based, and had hung on every word when it came out in The Saturday Evening Post, so of course I accepted, and he left. He didn't drive himself, going about by charter car, which of course had been waiting outside the whole time of his visit.

We didn't have dinner for some reason, and I picked him up at the Garden of Allah, an apartment house over near Beverly, where he lived. He had phoned the theater, which was the Warner Bros. Western, at Wilshire and Western Boulevards, and they had saved us seats on the aisle, about half-way down to the stage. We slipped into them, he giving me the one on the outside and the picture began to run.

It was an eye-opener, as to how big Charles Laughton was, and also how childish he was. For the whole time we were there a parade went on in the aisle, of people, mostly young, who pretended to want the little boys' room or the little girls' room, but who actually wanted to walk by Laughton, glance down and actually see him, and then for the rest of their lives tell about it. Pure ecstasy showed on their faces, but no more than the ecstasy that showed on his. He paid no attention to them, seeming not to know they were there. What he did pay attention to was himself, up there on the screen. According to Higham, he hated watching himself on the screen, but all I can say is he gave no evidence of it that night. He giggled and laughed in utter spellbound enchantment. I didn't then, and don't now, think he was very funny, and it seemed to me the audience was laughing more at Roland Young, Wesley Ruggles, and Reginald Owen than it was at him. But whom he laughed at was he. (Work on it, it parses).

And to clear up what happened later, just after we left the theater, I'll refresh your memory as to what "Ruggles of Red Gap" was about. Laughton was an English gentleman's gentleman, a valet who was lost in a London poker game to the owner of a ranch out in Wyoming, or some such God-awful place, and so had to journey out there to Red Gap, and go to work. There Red Gap happened to him, and of course, the U.S.A., the Wild West, and Zasu Pitts, who just happened to be the maid. So one night, when a bar party got going, a loud bum argument started about what Lincoln said at Gettysburg, and, how did you guess it, the one who knew was this English valet, now doubling as butler, waiter, cook, bottle washer and sweetie to Zasu. He began to speak, in a scene beautifully done, a bit diffidently at first, but as the bedlam shushed down his words become more distinct, more confident. He had played this speech for me before we came down, on his phonograph at the Garden of Allah, having made countless records of it to get it the way he wanted it, and it climaxed the picture in a beautifully eloquent way—so eloquent the audience broke into applause, not only in tribute to his performance on the screen, but to himself, as of course the whole place knew he was there.

Going out, and still continuing our game, by finding things in his performance he hadn't quite known were there, I began: ". . . Government of the people," and went on with it, beating four-four time as I went, telling him: "It's not commonly known that it beats in measures, like blank verse," and he very eagerly cut in: "Yes, yes, yes! I could feel it—it's why I made those records, so its pulse would be in my voice." By that time, we had reached the parking lot back of the theater, and were standing beside my car. Suddenly, still continuing our game, I said: "I know why that picture delights you. It's an autobiography, isn't it?"

"Oh! You caught that, didn't you!"

And then suddenly this man of the greatest eminence, of such eminence that a theater full of people had been agog just to glimpse his face, perhaps of an eminence greater than any actor had ever enjoyed, was turned into a nothing, a snivelling, stammering thing, who grasped the lapels of my coat and started to talk, to gasp, to whimper, to whine, in a way I could scarcely believe. He said I could never know what it meant to him, "to say goodbye to all that—to come to this country—to make a fresh start—to hold my head up at last—to—" It went on for five minutes or more, and I felt horribly uncomfortable. Then he let go and stepped away, standing for some moments rubbing his fingers together, in a curious, fidgety way.

We got in the car, and I drove to the Garden of Allah, where he had paintings he wanted to show me—Mexican paintings he had bought. We went in, and there they were, not framed at all, but stacked, on their edges, against the living room wall, perhaps two dozen in all. When I began tilting them back with one hand against my other hand, I was startled, knowing a bit about Mexico, to see what these things were: beautiful works by Rivera, Orozco and Sequeiros. Tilting paintings, on their edges, from one hand to the other, and twisting your head to peer at them, isn't the best way to look at art, but it's one way, and I certainly looked as well as I could. As I flipped an edge, so a new one came into view, he would say: "Shattering!"—or "Shettering," actually. But then it seemed to me, allowing for all vagaries of pronunciation, that he sounded slightly different and when I looked up he was staring at me with a cold little smile that wasn't a smile—and I knew I'd never see him again.

I had committed, unwittingly, unintentionally, without knowing I would, the one offense friendship can't stand: I had let him pour out to me things he now wished he hadn't said. He never called me again, and certainly I never called him. I can only say, that while he lasted he was something.

The Gentle Side of W.C. Fields
(*The Washington Post*, September 26, 1976)

Comedians, as a class, are a notoriously churlish bunch, who smile when paid to smile. Maurice Chevalier pops into my mind. He was in California at Paramount when I was, and for six months I ate lunch within 20 feet of him. He always ate alone, in a blue coat with brass buttons, and surrounded with five stooges I took to be his dresser, his secretary, the agent's representative, the studio's representative and a messenger. I grew fascinated after awhile just watching him. And the reason for my interest is that never once in that time did I see him smile, or say one agreeable word to those faceless men who surrounded him, or one word to anyone else.

It was quite a sociable place, with big stars moving around, tablehopping, telling jokes: Talloo, Marlene, Bebe Daniels, Lupe Velez, all sorts of good-looking girls visiting with one another, but not one stopped by him. He was sour, scowling and ill-humored, as well as a notorious tightwad. The account of the studio bootblack, of how he tried to get an extra 10-cent tip out of Chevalier, the day before Christmas, 1931, became a classic, one that he was asked to repeat for weeks. P.S., he did not get the 10 cents.

But if Chevalier's behavior clashed with his public image, and confirmed the notion of comedians as a grumpy breed, I found that the outstanding exception to this rule in those days was the very man whose public image was the most churlish, W.C. Fields.

I met him in 1930, through Philip Goodman, who had more to do with Fields's success than anyone else—a close personal friend, of mine as well as of Fields. Goodman, father of Ruth Goodman Goetz, the playwright, also my close friend, started out in the advertising business, grew bored with it, and turned to publishing. He put out one book, Mencken's "In Defense of Women," and then switched again, to theatrical producing. He became convinced that Don Marquis could write a play, and though Marquis wasn't, finally got things started with "The Old Soak," which he produced with Arthur Hopkins, and which made theatrical history. Then, looking for more worlds to conquer, he became convinced that Fields could talk. Fields, like Marquis, was highly dubious, and Goodman had a battle on his hands. The difficulty was the principle that Tilden later plugged so indefatigably: Don't change a winning game. Field's game, until then, was winning and winning big. He was a headliner in vaudeville, in nightclubs, in the Follies, but always in pantomime: as a comedy juggler, magician and actor, he never said a word. So when Goodman began arguing with him, Fields listened, but had no intention of giving up something sure for something that might be a fiasco. However, Goodman could dangle one piece of bait like no other: Talking, Fields could star, not merely be featured. He could star on Broadway, something they all dream about. Then, little by little Fields began to listen, and by a funny coincidence, Goodman had a script called "Poppy," which would do very well for a vehicle.

Then, one night, Fields said yes, and together he and Goodman cooked up Eustace McGargle, the con man on a carnival lot that Fields played, in countless variations, the rest of his life. And in that 1922 production it turned out that Goodman was right. Fields *could* talk, once this seldom, sententious, cyncial character was clarified in his mind—a character like no other, who was quoted by everyone, and whose big laughs were stolen by everyone, the greatest compliment of all. For example, toward the end of "Poppy's" last act, the rich boy in white-tie who is due to marry Poppy, McGargle's daughter, bounced onto the set, asking Fields, "May I come in?" But one night, halfway through the run of the show, Goodman was in the theater watching the scene, and it suddenly occurred to him the qustion was somewhat silly, as the boy was already there. So he went back and told Fields. "Next time he asks that, tell him "You *are* in—it could get a laugh, who knows." Fields didn't think much of it, but the producer is the producer, so next night, when the boy came out with his line, Fields told him, with pompous annoyance, "You *are* in"—and got one of the most memorable laughs in the theater. Paul Palmer, Sunday editor of The New York World, told me about it first, before I ever knew Fields, and with tears streaming down his face at the mere recollection of it. He said, "Jim, what it was about it I don't know, but that was the funniest thing I ever heard in a theater." And for years other comedians were stealing the laugh—"You *are* in" was dragged into every sketch for the next five years, and still can be heard, occasionally.

Then there was McGargle's advice to Poppy, on the day of her wedding. With a soft, sentimental manner, he caught her arm, to give her one word of affectionate wisdom, before she would take her vows: The word: "Poppy, never give a sucker an even break." This also was passed along by endless comedians. It didn't quite do as well as "You *are* in," but was widely quoted nevertheless. There were other bits from "Poppy," and for a year, Fields was big. It was his last starring hit, on Broadway. He was starred, solo, one more time in "Ballyhoo," a thing about union derbies, a feature of the era, but it wasn't a hit, and he was starred in the Vanities, Follies and vaudeville, but not solo.

So, he was ripe for a new idea, and Goodman came up with one. He would star Fields in a picture—and Fields went for it big, perhaps realizing that the time had come for a change. And right away, he knew what the picture should be about, an Uncle Tom show of the '90s, with himself as the proprietor. Goodman picked me to do the script—by that time, I was getting known for dialogues, in the World, The American Mercury and various magazines. My contribution was to recall that Little Eva, a tot in the stage shows who goes to heaven in Act III, was not in the book a lot, but a comely teenager, who rode with her boyfriend in Audubon Park, New Orleans, buckety bucket. When Mrs. Stowe couldn't think of anything else for her to do she decided to let her die, and did of "author's disease," as Sinclair Lewis used to call it. "She doesn't get sick, Jim—just ups and dies. That's Author's Disease.

So my contribution was that little Eva would be cast as a post-teen-ager, small enough to wear a tot's clothes and go to heaven in Act III, but actually quite a sexpot. I knew, of course, that before we got done with it she would wind up as Field's daughter and look exactly like Poppy, but at least I didn't make her like that. So, I was introduced to Fields, he in his car, an open roadster, in which he had a girl I won't name, as she may still be living, a girl in her 20s, though Fields was now close to 50— though not Carlotta Monti who wrote the book about him. Then, for the rest of that summer, Fields and I would talk, at my apartment on East 19th Street, and then, perhaps around 10 o'clock, walk around to Goodman's apartment, on 10th Street, to pick up the girl, and also for an hour or so of talk. I quickly found out that on story, on plot, on structure, Fields drew a complete blank—and in fact, could hardly make himself get his mind on it. He thought in terms of gags, which followed a set pattern: annoyances, of one kind or another. In "Million Dollar Legs," as president of Klopstokia, he was constantly being interrupted, at Cabinet meetings, by a member who had to sneeze. Paramount hired Joe Sneeze for the job, and the moments while Fields, his white-gloved hands opening and closing, waited for Joe to complete the project, were funny—I still remember them.

Then there was Kadoola-Kadoola, as he called it, I never knew why. In this, halfway through "Poppy," he would come out with a skeleton cello, sit down with it after putting his silk hat on the floor, and start "Pop Goes The Weasel." But he would barely play three notes before the silk hat would start to roll, and continue around the back of his chair, to stop on the other side. He would put it in place again, again, again, and have to stop again. That was the whole sketch, but it was sheer delight, and I don't know anyone who ever figured out how he did it—how he made the silk hat roll, I mean, on cue, in exactly the right way. Even Red Skelton, who did the impersonation of Fields, never tried to do this, and perhaps doesn't know how it was done.

And, of course, there was the celebrated interrupting of the dentist sketch in Earl Carroll's Vanities. In this, the whole thing consisted of Fields, as a dentist, using all sorts of improbable instruments, trying to locate the mouth of a patient who had a gigantic beard. But his assistant, Miss Dorothy Knapp, came on the set one night and touched a flat on her way in. "It began to fall," said Fields, "and I caught it with one hand, pushing it back in place. When I knew they had it backstage I had a look at them and they didn't look good." "Them," or "they," with Fields, were always the audience. "So," he went on, "I dusted my hands together, and told them: "They don't build these houses the way they used to build them." The roar that this got is still remembered. "So," he went on, "after the blackout, Carroll came running back, telling me: 'Bill, I got to have it, I got to, I got to—got to have that laugh every night.' " So Fields was willing, but the stagehands, it turned out, were not. It was absolutely against the rules for a performer to touch a set, unless, of course, by honest accident, and any retake was out of the question. But Carroll was obdurate, so they fixed it up that Miss Kanpp wouldn't touch the flat but would *seem* to touch it, while a stage hand gave it a push; that then, by means of a rope attached to a hook screwed in to a cross-piece, another stage hand would catch it as it fell, and that a third stagehand would pull it back. By this series of strategems, the laugh was retained in the show and the day, or call it the night, was saved.

In the hours we would spend at Goodman's, Fields told many more stories, all of the same kind, once speaking of "that pest of a woman, always with something to tell you, who hangs on and digs her chin in your shoulder." I was startled but then realized this was a completely original conception, that he wasn't cribbing from "Alice in Wonderland," and in fact, had probably never heard of "Alice in Wonderland," or Lewis Carroll. But these harassments were only a part of the talks that went on at my place, before we would walk over to Goodman's. Often he would get off on something that had happened that day, and have to tell me about it. Once, he was struck by the harangue of a rubber he had had at the turkish bath he patronized, and sat there reciting it, working on himself, kneading his leg, as he did, and becoming so wrapped up in his tale as to be transformed. Actually, I sat there staring at him, asking myself "Is that *Fields*?" He didn't look like himself at all, but exactly like a rubber. And I remembered things I had read, for example about Coquelin, the celebrated French actor, and how *"Son visage, s'a change,"* and so on—how his face became different with every part that he played. It was that way with Fields, and I woke up that night to the realization I was beholding one of the great actors of all time.

Goodman, when I'd see him alone, was satisfied with the progress I was making on my end, so when Fields would come, I could lean back, let him talk, and enjoy something memorable. But all things come to an end, and so it turned out with him. Paramount got into the act, with an offer he couldn't refuse, and so he had to back out of Goodman's venture. He did so with obvious regret, and before leaving for Hollywood, gave us a little dinner at a speak in the 40s—an Italian place that he frequented, that had fairly good wine, for this, of course, was in the middle of Prohibition. The Goodmans, Phil, Lily, his wife, and Ruth, whom I've already mentioned, and I were the guests—the girl wasn't with him that night. We had hardly sat down when the proprietor's son, a boy of perhaps 10, "that nauseous brat," as Ruth always called him, planted himself before Fields and piped: "Hi, Big-Nose."

"Hi," said Fields.

That was all, or would have been all, except that a waiter heard and Judased to the proprietor. So, this tall Italian, white with rage, breathing through his nose, appeared from nowhere, seized the boy by the arm, and dragged him back out of sight. Then, to his shrieks, we would hear the hairbrush coming down, or whatever was being used. Fields leaned close to me, and half under his breath, mumbled: "Jim, that's all for my benefit. What kind of imagination is it that thinks I will get pleasure, or satisfaction, or whatever I'm supposed to get, at hearing a boy punished? I have a big nose, and I suppose to him it's a fact of life like the Grand Canyon or Niagara Falls or some other natural wonder, and so. . . ."

He went on, while the spanking went on, but I was within inches of the nose, and for the first time had a good look at it. And I suddenly became aware there was something wrong with it. It was just the least bit lumpy, as though it was not sound tissue. Then I knew this nose had once been frozen, and that's why it looked as it did. I thought of Bill Dukenfield, the boy who had to sleep in the stable, and there practiced his juggling, and what must have happened one bitterly cold night. Compassion for him swept over me—why? I'm not sure I know. At $5,000 a week, which was what Goodman said he would get in Hollywood, he needed no compassion from me. Just the same it was how I felt.

But that night there was more. The proprietor appeared pretty soon, leading the boy by the arm. "I'm sorry, Mr. Fields," came the snuffing apology. "I didn't mean it, honest I didn't."

"Come here, son," said Fields, ignoring the father. And then, for 20 minutes this man, already celebrated for his line: "The man who hates dogs and small boys can't be *all* bad;" gave a show for this small boy, which, had it been put on film, would have been played over and over and over for years. In addition to being a juggler, he was also a master magician, and he made half dollars come out of the boy's nose, letting him keep the half dollars. He stuck toothpicks into the dinner rolls and made them dance on the table. He came up with a yapping dog between the boy's feet then, and went tearing into the boy's pocket when the dog took refuge there, finally fishing him out, a two-inch thing of red flannel, and letting the boy keep him, too. It went on and on, with the boy utterly entranced, Ruth utterly disgusted, and Lily, Phil and I, fascinated.

So it turns out, that in spite of McGargie's pomposity, his cynical viewpoint on life, that Fields himself had a heart of gold. Well, so be it—but I saw the scene with the boy. And it occurs to me that this heart of gold may have more to do than might at first be suspected, with the greenness of *his* legend, here now 30 years later.

Vincent Sargent Lawrence
(*The Screen Writer*, January 1946)

Various writers have become legends in Hollywood, such as Frances Marion, Charles Brackett, and Robert Hopkins among the living, and Jeanie Macpherson, Tom Geraghty, Bill McGuire, and Grover Jones among those no longer with us; but no writer that I know of has become so fantastic an epic, the subject of anecdotes that take such long hours in the telling, as this Vincent Lawrence who has just died. Incredibly enough, most of the anecdotes are true, and yet, in spite of the bizarre personal qualities that begot them, he was one of the most valued writers in the business, and the reason for his value was one of the clearest, coldest, hardest minds that ever faced a confused, divided, and desperate story conference and got order where only chaos had been. He was a screwball, but the screwball wins ball games.

Lest, in case you didn't know him, you still season the tales you have heard with several pounds of salt, let me tell you that none of the tales do real justice to the actuality. In his saga, the fact always dwarfed the apocrypha. If you heard he was ignorant, multiply by seven and you will still be short of how ignorant he was. At all things not worth knowing, such as the number of times Cobb went from first to third on a bunt, how many times Dempsey floored Willard at Toledo, how many points Alabama scored in the Rose Bowl game of 1926, he was encyclopedic, and his testimony needed no further checking. At things of a more substantial kind, regarded by man as having value to the human intellect, he was an utter zero. If a point came up, let us say in the realm of history, something like the Battle of Balaklava and its date, it would be most surprising if he placed it on the right continent and in the right century; indeed, to be wholly candid about it, it would be completely most astonishing if he had ever heard of the Battle of Balaklava, or the Cimean War, or Tennyson. To his friend, the late William Harris, Jr., who complained that the Lawrence 1, 2, & 3 were nothing but the old Aristotelean Beginning, Middle, and End, he exclaimed, irritatedly: "Well General, who the hell was Aristotle, and who did he lick?"

If you heard of his profligacy with money, multiply by seven times seventeen, and you may have some slight comprehension of it. Once, rehearsing a show, he and Harris grabbed a bite in a corner drugstore. Said Harris: "The check for the two of us was 67¢, and the girl would have been quite pleased with the 33¢ that would have been left if he had given her a buck. He gave her $5 and walked out. She was scared to death, for all that spelled to her was a company spotter, and I'm sure she didn't sleep for a week expecting the axe. Things like that make no sense, but he did them, and he wasn't living if he didn't do them." If you asked him to dinner, before you were done with it he had handed your favorite captain, the one who smiles so pleasantly when you five-spot him now and then, a $20 bill, for doing him some never-to-be-forgotten favor like getting him a package of cigarettes. For people in need his generosity was incredible. Once, hearing me talk of a writer I hoped to get a job for, on a Pasadena newspaper, he cut in on me brusquely with: "Job, hell, sure you'll get him a job—sometime. What he needs, here now tonight, is dough." And so help me, ten minutes later we arrived at the door of this man he had never seen, and slipped a note under the door, with a $50 bill in it. And in my own case, the thing sometimes went into four figures. My first novel, The Postman Always Rings Twice, is dedicated to him, in part because of encouragement, in part because of technical help, but in part also because he lent me the money to eat on while I was writing it, and he felt I rated steak, not beans.

If you heard he drank, multiply by 100,000, or 1,000,000, and you will still, probably, be a little short. He drank and drank and drank. He drank enough to float the battleship Maine. He made Honest John Barlocorn's acquaintance quite early in life, and they must have hit it off beautifully for a time, because he went on the wagon at 24 and stayed on it for 18 long years. Then, coming to Hollywood, he began to slip off it, and presently alcohol was the great problem of his life. He licked it, but of course in his own special, peculiar idiotic way, the hard way, as we say nowadays. Charles Jackson took it on the chin until the craving left him, and at last the problem was liquidated. Lawrence would take it on the chin for five days, until the craving had become torture; then, Saturday having arrived, he would enter the Lakeside Club and be served six martinis on one tray, by a waiter who didn't have to be told, but knew what to do and came running. Then would ensue a brief respite, the found weekend, whose only result was to whip craving to an intolerable pitch. Then, drawn, sombre, and grim, he would sweat out another five days, get his work done, add thousands to the take of some movie, and Saturday start all over again. He did this for sixteen years. Of suffering, in consequence of it, he probably had more than most men ever dream of.

If you heard of his pantomimed act—the Ball Game—I would simply quit multiplying, for this was beyond mathematics, whether in this world or out of it. For I have seen the ball game, many times; let me repeat, with these eyes I have seen it. I have also seen the Poker Game, as played by Mr. Bert Williams in the Ziegfeld Follies, and I found the Ball Game greater art. For while the Poker Game had pathos, and profound and nourishing humors, the Ball Game had pain, to say nothing of blood and sweat and tears; it tore you, that that poor slug out there on the mound, giving his all, should get such betrayals, from his fielders, the umpire, above all his catcher. And, mind you, this was no set piece, as Mr. Williams' was, cooked up and needled for your high entertainment. It was but a phase of absent-mindedness, a mere concomitant of cerebration, a discharge of nervous energy, something to be doing with his hands, as some men pitch half dollars in the air and catch them, and other men doodle scratch pads. It had an eerie, other-wordly effect on Hollywood when it first was seen here, for it was a Hollywood still fresh on the imbecilites of the silent picture, and pretty convinced that if any man but be crazy enough, he must, post hoc, propter hoc, prima facie, and ipso facto, be a genius. Thus the ball game, probably more than any other factor, rounded out the legend, put vine leaves in its hair, clothed and anointed it for immortality.

And yet, on the mound or off it, off the wagon or under it, he worked steadily from his arrival here until he died, got out scores of pictures, and most of those who employed him, since they hired him back time and again, showed that they felt he earned the prodigious sums they paid him. He was happiest, I think, with Louis D. Lighton, and I think regarded Test Pilot, done with him, as his best picture. But he worked for many producers, and I have yet to meet one who did not fall under his spell, and I have met one or two who not only fell under his spell, but acquired his peculiar way of talking, with its constant sprinkling of "lad" and "pal," which was nothing but Broadway (acquired from George M. Cohan) superimposed on his native Boston. And I have yet to meet one who had not profited, no matter how long the script took, or caused his company to profit from Lawrence's uncanny gifts with a script. Well, on what were those gifts founded? First, an exhaustive study of the theatre, begun in his days as a playwright in New York, whom George Jean Nathan called "the first high comedy writer of the American stage." It is an institution full of saws and precepts, most of them furnished by ham actors and practically all of them false. Lawrence took nothing on faith. He studied writing, acting, production, and most of all he studied that foundation of all theatre, the audience. This vast fund of information, which he added to constantly, was focused on whatever needed fixing, and lent him a perspicacity that few writers, and still fewer producers could match.

But at the center of this knowledge lay a conviction, partly instinctive but buttressed by study, that the love story was the foundation of everything, and that to enter the love story you must come in by the front door, and not climb in through a window. This seems obvious enough now, this beginning of the main relationship, but it didn't then. It was expounded to a Hollywood that took a summer-park view of the problem, and that hadn't suspected that this perfunctory notion of technique might have something to do with the trouble it was then having at the boxoffice. Until Lawrence got here, it was thought sufficient to send the lovers, as soon as they met, for a little trip to Coney Island and a quick montage in the chute-the-chutes, the roller coaster, the ferris wheel, and the merry-go-round. As they entered the Tunnel of Love, as boy got that look on his face and leaned close to girl, they dissolved and the trick was regarded as done. Lawrence wouldn't have it. There had to be, he insisted, a "love rack," an episode on which we entered the love story. In it, he said, not only the characters but the audience as well, must feel their discovery of each other, and the thing couldn't be phoney. He wouldn't have a manufactured love rack, or a remembered love rack, or a stolen love rack. It had to involve real verses, specially composed for his occasion, and until it was there, he refused to consider the rest of the "1," as he called it, or the catastrophic "2" which was Aristotle's Middle, or the "3" of the denoument, which was Aristotle's End.

This was his big contribution to moving pictures. He was not, of course, the first to write love stories, but he was the first out there, I think, to articulate the philosophy of the love story into the intellectual whole, so that now we know, or think we know, what we are doing. Personally, my debt to him must go farther than that, for the core of his thinking is also the core of my novels; if ever a man had an intellectual parent, at least so far as this narrative part of my work is concerned, I must acknowledge such a relationship with Lawrence. And in closing this little tribute, I might say I have the most indescribably lost feeling doing it. I have hardly written the symbol, —o—, which closes all my stories, in the last twenty years, without wondering what Lawrence was going to think of it. That such a speculation can no longer enter my mind is, believe me, something I shall be a long time getting used to.

Thornton
(Unpublished: Written in the 1970s)

In June of 1929 I attended a luncheon at some yacht club in New Haven, Conn., for the Class of 1884, Yale University, of which my father was a member, and which was holding its 45th reunion. To say I wanted to go would be the misstatement of the century. Such things bore me to death, and I have the greatest difficulty being agreeable through the endless grinning, chattering, and hand shaking they always involve. But Papa's invitation had the color of a summons, and I went, running up from New York, where I was headquartered. I had a wonderful time. For it turned out that another son of '84 was Thornton Wilder, and that a daughter was his sister Miss Isabel. Why they took a shine to me I never found out, as that time I wasn't too well known, but they seemed to and the three of us played it funny—to the unconcealed dismay of their father, Amos Wilder, and mine, James W. Cain, both of whom believed in Character, Human Values, God Country, and Yale and Football—but with distinct understanding it's not whether you win that counts, but How You Play the Game. What Thornton, Miss Isabel, and I believed in was obviously nothing at all, with smartcracks.

Their conversation naturally revolved on *The Bridge of San Luis* Rey to some extent. It was then out no more than a year and had come, so they said, just in the nick of time, so they'd been able to give their mother "a Christian burial," as Thornton called it. I got the idea the funeral had been a dilly, even for New Haven, whose ceremonies for deceased Yale presidents set quite a standard, for gaudiness if not for taste. To all this their father listened with a smile that seemed a bit strained. Watching him, I noted that his features, a bit short in the nose and thick in the chin, formed the face of a tenor, and so in fact it turned out. Some time later, when I reported the day to my mother, she came up with the news that he'd sung in her quartet, in the days when she'd lived in New Haven, before she married my father. Find my mother, and you'd find a male quartet not too far away. In Annapolis, where she moved as a bride, the quartet would be invited to the parties she was invited to, as smart renditions of "Come Where My Love Lies Dreaming," "Kentucky Babe," "Drink to Me Only," and other songs of that era, with coloratoura embellishment, were well worth the extra ham sandwiches—though it must be said that a male quartet has an appetite that must be seen to be believed, and even then it strains credulity.

The next time I saw Thornton was perhaps ten years later, and Miss Isabel wasn't with him. It was at Alec Dean's apartment in the Devon, a New York hotel where I was staying too, though by then my home was in Hollywood. And what had brought me to New York was to work on a play of mine with Alec, to get in shape for production at a summer theatre he had, at Cohasset, Mass., out on the Cape, a venture he ran as a sideline to his main job, which was head of the Drama Department at Yale. It turned out that Thornton had a play too, one about to go into rehearsal, and when he dropped in on Alec, a close friend from the Yale connection, Alec rang me and asked me up, and of course I was only too glad to go. The talk that day wasn't about my play at all, but about Thornton's, which it turned out he meant to do in an odd kind of way that Alec wholly disapproved of, with a stepladder the only prop, people sitting on their own graves, and a stage manager walking around, explaining this state of affairs. Alec, in patient words of one syllable, explained to Thornton why you couldn't do things like that, why they don't work, can't work, and won't work. And what struck me as odd was Thornton's reaction to this kindly advice. He listened with the utmost good humor and utter immovability—he meant to do his play the way he meant to do it, that was plain to be seen. When he left, Alec shook his head and more in sorrow than anger, observed: "You can't tell him anything—he was born bull-headed, and there's nothing to do about it. Well, when that thing flops he'll learn his lesson—perhaps. Even then I'm not sure that he will." The name of the play was "Our Town" and it made theatrical history, done exactly as Thornton said he was going to do it.

The next time I saw him, Miss Isabel was there. It was at an apartment house on Franklin Avenue in Hollywood, where they'd been staying in connection with the picture version of "Our Town," to which he contributed advice free gratis, to the bewilderment of the picture business, which never heard of anything like that. Of course, the papers carried his arrival, and I called him up at once, to ask him up to the house, but for some reason they couldn't come. But then some weeks later he rang me, to ask me down the next day, with Elina, my little Finnish wife, at cocktail time. After querying her, I accepted, but at once warned her: "For God's sake, be careful what you put on—this is their big pay-back stinkaroo, for everyone who's entertained them while they've been here, and even for those who tried to and couldn't, like us." I reminded her of the Parker-Campbell bash, a little intimate thing for 800 guests that we had attended. "And this guy," I said, "is much more important then Dorothy ever was, so everyone's going to be there, the biggest fish in this sea."

So she put on a smart suit that she had, dark blue as I recall, and I put a grass-green special I'd had made by MacIntosh, my tailor on Hollywood Boulevard, in anticipation of an invitation that never came, to a garden party at the Chateau Elysee, which was across the street from the place the Wilders were staying at. It was of Rajah silk, with little white darts in it—oh I was really turned out. So, promptly at four o'clock, we drove down, but at once things didn't look right. No lanterns were out in the patio, or cars up and down Franklin, or anything to indicate big goings on. We went in, had ourselves announced and went up. We were the only guests.

Elina was enchanted.

So perhaps I had better pause for a moment, to tell what Thornton was like, and what Miss Isabel was like, too. He was of medium size, and in early middle age at that time, almost as old as I was, but seemingly much younger. There was something collegiate about him—but not student collegiate or professional collegiate. Rather, I would call him tutorial collegiate, the eternal instructor in the English Department, who helps the boys with their problems and monitors the monthly tests, but not in a snoopy way. Miss Isabel was very goodlooking, rather younger than he was, medium-sized too, but gay, gracious, and magnetic in manner. The two of them obviously were close.

But about his work, the two other times I had seen him, he had taken an aw-shucks, just-hit-it-lucky approach, not in any way solemn. But this afternoon that mask dropped off, and he became for an hour the professional he had to be, to do the things he had done. I was caught off balance, naturally, by the difference between what I expected and what I encountered when I got there, and when he asked me what I was up to, I reached for a book I had had in mind, quite vaguely in mind actually, about incest in West Virginia, about mountain people there, whom I knew very well, and about Pappy's lech for his daughter, a thing that happens quite often. He was interested at once, and O.K.'d the theme unreservedly. Then he went on: "Those nineteenth century novelists knew all about it, Jim. They were pros who made a science of their art, and of course a business of it. But, with that approach, they knew that incest, handled head-on, was just a little too good. So they shaded it: Instead of Pappy leching, it was a louse of an uncle who did. That way they got incest's livid quality, without its slimy actuality. "And so on and so on for quite some time, turning into a man I had never seen, a pro of a pro among pros, in contrast with his jocular amateur he pretended to be.

Elina, on the way, home, kept talking about their breeding as shown by their manners. Lapsing into the German we had spoken when she couldn't speak any English and I couldn't speak any Finnish, she kept calling Thornton "ein Herr," and Miss Isabel "ganz eine Dame." But I kept thinking about incest and what I could do with it, from the angle he had talked about. And so, when I finally got around to writing the book, I did it the way he had said. My leading character slept up with the girl, wholly believing she was his daughter with her believing it too, only to find out near the end that she's not his daughter at all, but the daughter of his wife's lover—all this proved by a birthmark that threaded its way through the story. But then he wakes up to the fact that though he's free to marry this girl and live happily forever afterward, he has killed the one person who can prove it, especially to the daughter's satisfaction. Titled *The Butterfly* from the birthmark, it came off fairly well, and became my second biggest hit, especially in translation, coming out as "La Mariposa" in Spanish, "La Farfalla" in Italian, "Der Schmetterling" in German, and other titles in still other languages.

So, years go by, and last summer, to check what I had that I could wear in hot weather, I opened a clothing bag and found myself looking at a suit I had no recollection of ever having seen before—a grass-green thing of silk, very handsome and utterly improbable. After lifting it out and looking it over, I concluded the cleaner must have made a mistake and delivered the wrong suit. In search of a clue as to whom it might belong to, I examined it carefully and found it was very old—so old it had button closure if you know what I mean. Then at last I turned down the inside pocket, and saw "MacIntosh, Hollywood Boulevard." Only then did it all come back, the reason I had had it made, and the one occasion on which I had worn it. Still, a suit is a suit is a suit, and I took it to Sam Bobrow, a very good tailor I know, to have the buttons replaced by a zipper, and the trousers shortened, partly to conform to present-day style, and partly so I could wear them with a belt, in place of the galluses Hollywood favors.

And then, by a fantastic coincidence, there was Thornton's picture in the paper, and it turned out he was in town, in Washington, that is, just down the road from me, in connection with the production of "The Skin of Our Teeth" at the Kennedy Center. I picked up the phone to find out where he was, so I could ask him and Miss Isabel to dinner, and then suddenly put the phone down, as I crossed my mind how amusing it might be if I showed up in the same old suit, which I didn't think he'd remember, but which I thought would give him a laugh, and with an inscribed copy of *The Butterfly* that he could keep. I arranged that we'd go to the Olney Inn, a very swank place in the country, where they do things quite nicely for me, and in all ways was setting things up to begin where we'd left off. But when I called to find out where he was, he and Miss Isabel had left. And then a few days ago, there was his picture again, with the jolting news he was dead.

Well, a long tale, and a pointless one, no doubt. However, reflecting back on it, I decided that was reality the way he looked at things. *The Bridge of San Luis Rey*, as I read it, was a quest for point, for the meaning of it all, for the divine plan that explained the fall of a bridge in Peru, that caused the death of five people. But at the end it is perfectly clear that there was no point to it all, or divine plan, or anything of that kind. Thornton, I would say, was himself all the point that is needed: a rich, delightful human being, well deserving the fallen arches he got, or at least that I heard he got, from toting the money each Monday, to the bank in two heavy suitcases, that he took in from "Hello Dolly." God Bless Thornton, wherever he is now. God bless "Dolly." God bless us all!

Lana
(*Modern Screen*, April, 1946)

When Carey Wilson of Metro called up one day with the news that he had Lana Turner to play in my "Postman Always Rings Twice," I was not only pleased but elated. For you may think of Lana as a glamour girl—the type that brings nothing but her own flaming personality to the screen. And you can't be blamed at all, for leave us face it, she is a tasty dish. I didn't think of her that way, at least not after that week at the studio last winter when I had to run a number of her pictures one after the other, not only once but many times. This is a murderous test for an actress, but I didn't tire of Lana because I began to notice something. She moved me. Whatever she did, I *felt* something. Then, in "Ziegfeld Girl," I noticed the deft way she played a pretty little rumpot. She didn't go overboard with it. She wasn't monotonous with it. She didn't fail to get vividness into it. So you realized that the girl's trouble was not only booze, but a profound and terrible crack-up inside. Not only did Lana arouse pity in me for this little sinner, but she made such interesting shadings between tight, lit, high, stinko, bloto and stiff, that I became fascinated with her. And suddenly it dawned on me; this is no new glamour girl at all, in spite of her lovely face; this is an actress of the very first competence, one to watch, and watch with sober respect.

So when Carey told me she would do my story, I knew my character Cora was going to get the works. And then later, when it had all turned out so beautifully and I found I was to meet her, I was quite excited, as you may imagine.

I hadn't been in Romanoff's five minutes before I got my first surprise, a most agreeable one. Promptly at four o'clock, splitting the minute in half, she showed up. Now punctuality makes more friends than wit, but you don't quite expect it of picture stars meeting writers for afternoon tea.

My next surprise was her height. On the screen, she seems to me petite. No doubt this is because all things in perfect proportion, whether the

Parthenon Frank Sinatra's voice, or a woman's figure, always seem a little smaller than they really are. Her actual height is 5 feet, 3 one-half inches, which is medium, although with her slimness, high heels and everything, she's tall.

Next there is her total effect, which is much quieter, simpler, and more subdued than I would have thought from her pictures. When I mentioned this she laughed and said: "That glow you say I have—maybe it is just an act." She has little of the pert, rapid manner that you might expect from her acting style. She is inclined to be serious, and to speak in a considered, careful way, frequently using the "played line," as they call it on the stage. I don't mean she acts when she talks to you. But she becomes intense, and makes every effort to make you feel what she is saying to you. Yet her face is always animated with a real sparkle; expressions flit across it with the rapidity of shadows and light on water. She has never acquired a broad A, and there is nothing about her speech that suggests the stage, screen or radio.

Yet of course I was curious as to why she had wanted to play in my story. When a woman goes romantic over a hobo, then helps him kill her husband, you couldn't exactly call her "sympathetic." So I asked her what had attracted her to Cora. "Her honesty,' said Lana.

I almost choked on my tea. "Honesty! Are you kidding?"

"Look," said Lana, "Cora didn't pretend to herself. She knew she was a punk, and that what she was going to do about it was wrong. But she wanted something out of life. She wanted something she could never get if she went along in the same old rut."

"And what did she want?" I asked.

"Respectability!"

"I've often wondered if my readers could believe that."

"I believe it. It's what made Cora so human. She'd kill a man so she could have a little piece of property away out in the hills, a lunchroom, some cabins, and a filling station. Then she'd be something. That's what she said. Well that's so silly you can't help feeling sorry for her. But a lot of things people do don't make any sense, and when she was so honest with herself about it, I wanted to play her. And I loved the chances I had to show her when she was human just like anybody else. There she was—just a woman in love, doing things for a man, feeling the way other people feel, even if she *had* killed somebody."

Well, there's Cora in a nutshell. Lana understood her better than I did. And I wrote the book! The hunch I'd had about Lana was completely justified. She's more than a glamour girl. She's an actress, When she played Cora, she *was* Cora. I think she's going to make a hit of that "Postman" book yet!

An American Author's Authority
(*The Screen Writer*, July, 1946)

It would be difficult to exaggerate the plight of the American writer, or of any writer whose works are sold in the United States, today. If he is a dramatist, he has, it is true, at least the appearance of a favorable status. The conditions of his work compel him to live in New York, or spend considerable time there, so that he meets others of his trade, and with them takes steps for his own protection: he can coordinate with the theatrical unions, also most active in New York; for many years, as a matter of fact, he has done this, so that the Dramatists' Guild is probably the strongest, and has operated in the most satisfactory way, of all the four guilds comprising the Authors' League. But what has brought him trade victories often brings him aesthetic disaster.

Part of his organizational success is due to the fact that he doesn't deal with the big, formidable corporations that other writers face, but with individual producers, most of them temperamentally peculiar, so that collectively they are weak and relatively easy to handle. But this very whacky, fly-by-night, here-today-gone-tomorrow quality that makes them poor adversaries also makes them poor entrepreneurs. They rarely have money, and if they do, are reluctant to put it into plays; the whole Broadway stage is a jumble of producers who might better have been fight managers, angels, and angels' blondes, with the playwright, as often as not, expected to jell this mess into a rehearsal date, and then turn around and direct the show. The writer for the stage is favorably situated only if he has a hit on his hands and it is a question of what share of that hit he can now manage to keep. But if he has only a script on his hands, and it is a question of his chances for a production that will exploit it successfully, all that can be said is it is a matter of luck.

If he writes for magazines, he hasn't even the appearance of a favorable status. He is faced with all sorts of insulting rules, arbitrarily imposed on him by editors; he may offer his work to only one magazine at a time, else have all copies of it returned to him unread. For this the pretense is made that consideration of the work takes time, and must not be hurried by nervousness over a rival's interest. The purpose actually is to deprive him of a competitive market, and eliminate the one factor that might operate toward reasonable promptness. He is compelled to yield to the magazine a senseless catalogue of rights, of no use to it, but of considerable value to himself, on the pretext that it must "protect itself" until after publication, when they will be returned to him, a promise usually broken.

If he writes books, his situation is even worse. Here again, the publishers demand rights there is no reason they should have: abridgement rights, reprint rights, foreign rights, and serial rights, to name only those which are claimed by practically all publishers, and there are not three who will not accept, if they can get away with it, the picture rights, and a share of the picture money. From those of his rights which they control, they take 50% of the revenue, although they give him no service except that customarily given by an agent, and often bungle the exploitation with an incompetence few agents would be guilty of. His royalties they retain for six, eight or twelve months after they are earned, regarding them not as money held in trust, but as funds subject to all ordinary commercial risks, so that if they fail in business he is merely one more creditor. In that case, not only does he not get his money, but he sees his rights disappear in the wreckage too, so that many a book, like Miss Frances Marion's excellent How to Write and Sell Film Stories, simply goes into a deep freeze that has no end under present laws.

Here, too, he faces a conspiracy against him similar in all important respects to the conspiracy of the magazine editors. Up to a certain point, the corporate interest with which he deals blackjack each other, play tricks on each other, strive in various ways to out-do each other, but when the line of the vested interest is reached, they stick together with a touching unanimity. The publishers assert that they too must "protect themselves" in a madly spinning world, and that they are entitled to 50% of the reprint, foreign, abridgement, picture and sometimes the serial rights, because exploitation of these rights cuts in on their regular sales. Not one word of this is true. Appearance of a book in Reader's Digest does not hurt their sales, but stimulates them, which is also the case with reprint, foreign, and serial publication, while the increase that results from the appearance of a picture based on it is prodigious.

And when it comes to Book Clubs, of whose revenue they also take half, the claim that these cut in on their sales becomes simply grotesque, for their beneficient effect on business is legendary. Did any club ever pick a book because of something contributed by the publisher? Regarded simply as an investment, has a publisher yet contributed as much in cash to manufacture, promote, and distribute a book as the author contributes in maintaining himself while writing it? The Book Clubs encouraged this split because at first they encountered opposition from the publishers, and they dissolved that opposition by a bribe. But it was a bribe at the expense of the writer, who was all hot for clubs, for the occasional jackpot they would give him, and willing to close his eyes to the blue chip that went to the house. All claims made by publishers for half of these by-products, as they are often called, are phoney. They get away with the gyp simply because on this issue they encircle the writer with a completely unified front. There is no place he can turn to get his book published without giving up these rights which should belong to him.

If he writes for radio, his situation is still worse. Here, he is expected to assist large ventures in promotion, giving his best thought to what will help his sponsor, his agency, and his network. But not one of these rewards him with the least recognition of his effort, or with any right, share, or interest in the material he produces. It is in this field that the "unexploited right" is such a crying evil, where great corporations own rights and "just sit on them," as the saying goes. And often deals that could be of great profit to writers, especially when picture companies would be quite willing to pay for the use of celebrated programs, are made on a gratis basis simply because it never occurred to anybody concerned with them that the writer was entitled to anything.

But if he deals with picture companies, he is probably the worst off of all. Here, by established custom, he is compelled to part with his property forever, often for sums so small they are grotesque in comparison with the amount made out of it by the company that buys it, and then to stand by and see it remade time after time, without participation of any kind in the perpetual bonanza that he has created. Also by established custom, he often finds such potential profitable rights as he has managed to keep spoiled by the practices of the picture companies, as for example the radio rights, which he could exploit when the book is "hot," but which are usually kept for two years as part of the picture deal, and in that time cool off until they are of no value.

And if he works for the studios, as well as sells them material, what he faces is fantastic. He owns not one dot or comma of what he writes; he must even certify, in some instances, that the studios are the "authors" of his work, and it has even happened that these gifted sons of the State of Delaware have taken picture scripts so written and attempted to produce them as stage plays. In most instances he must sign a contract, if he is to get a contract at all, which binds him for five years, but binds the company for only six months. And for this dubious security he must given an option in perpetuity on any original work he produces during the life of his contract, as a result of the "check-back" clause which all these contracts carry. He may, he is told, elect a "lay-off" period, during which he may write works of his own. Naturally his employers, being very proud of him, and feeling a great interest in everything he does, want "first call" on his work. But if, when he has written it, they do not accept it at his price, and he then gets an offer somewhere else, unless the new offer is greater than the amount he asked of them, he is compelled to give them forty-eight hours to meet the new bid, and if they do meet it, to sell to them. It is argued that this means nothing, since "they all do it," and thus know, when dealing with a contract writer, that they have his home studio to bear in mind. If it means nothing, why do they all do it? And why do they cling to it with a tenacity that has to be seen to be believed? It means they can check their bets until the last call has been made, and then call or stay out as they like. It means the writer must quote a price before he has any idea what strength his book will develop when offered to the public, or what his play will do on the stage, while they needn't bid until the market has fully disclosed itself. And on top of all this, there is the sorry matter of credit.

In other fields, his name is supposed to mean something, but in pictures, even though it be his story that is being told and his script that is telling it, his credit will be inconspicuous, with no allusion to him in the publicity and almost none in advertising. Hard fighting has brought some improvement in this situation, but not much. In no branch of the business can you have a picture until you have a script, and yet, in a business that manufactures glory as a baker manufactures bread, there is none so poor as will weave a writer's chaplet, or even put a dandelion in his buttonhole.

Yet in spite of the foregoing, his worst persecutor is not the magazines, the publishers, the radio, or the picture companies. This honor is reserved for the United States Government. Other fields of endeavor, represented at Washington by formidable lobbies, receive reasonably fair treatment there, and some of them special coddling. The farmer is treated with gentle deference, as is the organized laborer, the manufacturer, the exporter, the flyer. But the writer, represented by nobody, gets no discernible breaks. And recently, in the Clifford Goldsmith case, the United States courts abolished his claim to any ponderable interest in his property, and left him the one man in the country not permitted to keep anything except a bare fraction of what he gets for it, although God knows it takes him just as much work to produce it as it takes anyone else, and at least as much talent.

The case was the one in which the Court of Appeals for the Second Circuit upheld the Treasury Department in its decision to discontinue its original practice of treating picture rights as a capital asset, and taxing the proceeds as such. Instead, it proceeded to tax them as straight income, at a much higher rate. Judge Chase, speaking for the court, held that there had been no sale, of a capital asset or otherwise, when Goldsmith sold the rights to his play, for a copyright was not "separable." It was one piece, this judge held, and the most that could be said for the transaction was that it was a license, as such taxable as income just as royalties would be. Judge Learned Hand concurred with Judge Chase, but for different reasons, and wrote an opinion with which Judge Swan concurred. Picture rights, he said, could "for most purposes" be called "property," and their disposal a "sale." However, it is "stock in trade," or "whatever else is normally included in an inventory." Thus picture rights are "in the ordinary course of business" to a writer, and as such taxable as "ordinary income."

It is hard to take these opinions seriously as law, and one can only conclude that the court was determined to uphold the Treasury in squeezing taxes out of the writer, and willing to use quibbles of whatever was necessary to reach the intended result. It will be most difficult to convince a writer that his works are merely "stock in trade," as Judges Hand and Swan so affably put it, just so many kegs of nails to be rolled over the counter and rung up on the cash register. What he creates is not "stock in trade" but property, and he knows that he has just so many of these ova in his belly, and indeed he is never sure that the latest one he produced will not be his last; it is a special, peculiar and heart-breaking business, wherein one work, done at great labor, time, and expense, may bring almost no return, while another, done with comparative ease, may be a gold mine, and may, more importantly, be the only gold mine this writer ever sees. And any big picture sale, even with top writers, is so unusual that it may be repeated only once or twice during their lives.

When this court, then, with one judge citing a quibble involving sale or license, the other two dismissing literary works as so much "stock in trade," for all practical purposes prohibited writers from enjoying the fruits of their toil, one can only say that a travesty on justice was entered on the record, and that our situation approaches the desperate. And just to complete the picture of what the federal tax gatherer does to the writer, we may note that while his work is not property so long as he lives, it becomes property as soon as he dies, and the appraisers slap arbitrary valuations on it, so that the widow, before she can cash so much as a $5 royalty check, has to put up gigantic sums in inheritance taxes, perhaps greater than any amount she will ever get from his literary works, which can easily slip into oblivion with his death.

But if one set of courts in the East have been abolishing all but a fraction of the writer's property another in the West have been extinguishing his title to even the small remnant he has left. The important cases, so far as infringement of copyright is concerned, are tried in the District Court at Los Angeles, for it is here that most moving picture cases originate, and it is the moving picture cases which involve large sums of money. As a rule, they are assigned to the Hon. Leon Yankwich, for the reason, apparently, that he takes great pride in being a literary expert. It would do violence to the truth to say he is not. He has read everything from pulp classics to Greek classics, and can discuss in the minutest detail stories, plays and novels whose very titles the average writer would find difficult to identify. Again, as one who has his origins in Europe, he has that reverence for literature which so many Europeans have, and so many Americans lack. Writers, to him, if not infra-divine, seem definitely ultra-human, and his personal courtesy to them is invariably marked. Yet this very notion of them gives him a bias that is utterly disastrous to their professional interest. For when they become merely human, and want their money, and perhaps accuse a colleague of becoming all-too-human, and committing a little piracy, he seems to fall victim to an acute, irritated disillusionment, and begins inventing fine-spun and far-fetched law for the benefit of the defendant. He has never, as a matter of actual record, given a verdict for the plaintiff. Members of the Los Angeles bar now advise clients NOT to sue in plagiarism cases. They believe, as they often put it, that a case cannot be won before Judge Yankwich "without 149 pages of carbon copy with typographical errors." For all practical purposes there is no federal copyright in the City of Los Angeles. Literary works may be stolen with perfect impunity, and in fact are stolen oftener than is commonly realized, for the picture companies make it a practice not to sue each other.

Stalking through the foregoing, casting his shadow over the whole dismal tale, is a villain, and it's the same villain whether the question be magazines, publishers, theaters, movies, radio, bureaucrats or courts: The writer has but one formidable enemy, and that is himself; like Jurgen, he lives in a tent of his own creation. It would put a much better face on the matter if it could be said that practices have grown up around him so malignantly that he is the victim of circumstances beyond his control. But, allowing for the conspiracies he faces, and the extraordinary attitude the Government takes toward him, this would not really be true. It would be hard to imagine a profession where practice carries so little weight as it does in writing. The grim, sorry fact which the writer must face, if he hopes to improve his situation, is that the practice is born with each deal as he makes it. The contract governs the case. Unless fraud is present, it determines all issues that arise.

As in the old law of prize, where evidence came solely from the capture itself, every pertinent fact in a writer's case will be found in his contract. It will do him no good to cite Jack London's contract, or point out that Winchell Smith had the benefit of certain practices that permitted him to get rich, which he is denied the benefit of. This would be so much chatter, if a court would listen to it at all. If Jack London had a good contract, or Winchell Smith saw a few angles, it was simply because they were smart guys who made smart deals. The law begins at the opening "whereas" and it ends at "author sign here." No special rules have been made which favor the party of the second part. No tricks, except determination on one side and supineness on the other, have been played. It is right there on the table, six pages in a neat blue cover. And if we sign it as is, it is strictly and only our fault.

We don't have to sign, but we do sign. Why? Because we are writers and have certain characteristics that make it grotesquely easy to pull the wool over our eyes, to flatter us, to cajole us, to organize against us, and then to deal with us separately. To begin with, we secretly think Judge Yankwich is right, and that we are very, very special beings. Of course, we call it "artists," but we try to improve on God, so it cuts up to about the same thing in the end. Unfortunately, we have most of the defects peculiar to gods and few of their virtues, if any. We have a furious, jealous intolerance of all other gods; and indeed, each of us thinks himself the only God and holds all other gods to be phonies, and their follower's heretics. A gang of plumbers can sew up a city with extortionist regulations and hang together like wolves. But anybody who has tried to get their writers to act as a unit on the simplest matter knows what the difficulties are.

Another godlike trait is our illusion of invulnerability. It is almost impossible to get through our heads the fact that we are in any particular trouble, or that there is any reason we should do something about it. And still another is our illusion of infallibility. We feel we know everything and when a publisher, explaining some monstrous swindle, says "it is customary," rather than go to a lawyer, or to another writer, or in any way admit that we don't know whether it's "customary" or not, we abjectly surrender whatever he wants, rarely taking even so much trouble about it as our wives would take over a questionable item in the monthly grocery bill. Only writers who have sweated out the bitter Gethsemane of the "option on two more books" can know the dreadful consequences of light acceptance of what purports to be "customary." And even when formed into guilds so that we have the appearance of organization, we actually achieve only the sketchiest cohesion.

For a century other laborers, having no Jovian complexes, have found the means, through strikes, lobbies, litigation, etc. to make vast gains in their status. Represented by big, strong, able men, they deal with corporate oppression and better their lot. Writers, however, have yet to develop anything describable as force. They call no strikes, hold no parades, intimidate no legislators. The four Guilds maintain correspondence, but there is no central body to steer their activities. They are still under the delusion that some over-worked "executive secretary" can attend to everything that needs attention, and that an unpaid president, elected on the basis of personal popularity, is all that is needed in the way of direction at the top.

The total score, after years of meeting, palavering, passing resolutions, and having the annual fight, is about as small as it would be possible to imagine. If, in the various guilds, the returning veteran has raised a noisy clamor, denouncing inaction, and demanding something be done, the conditions he complains of are typical of our trade. We lack force, we lack power, we lack results. Where we are at is precisely nowhere. Our gay, gaudy frigate sails on a literary Salton Sea, whose elevation is—249 feet 6 inches.

What is the remedy, if there is one? It is hereby submitted that the key to the whole question is the copyright, correctly described by Judge Chase as a monopoly for a period of years, under which the holder, for a consideration permits this, that, or the other kind of exploitation, these restricted assignments having acquired the name of "rights." Now it shouldn't be true, but it is true, that the writer knows almost nothing about copyright, and is probably incapable of learning anything about it; if, in the 3,000 years since Homer, he still is ignorant, as a rule, even of HOW to copyright, it would seem indicated that he should admit he's not the type and flunk the test. But is there anything to prevent him from letting one central authority, under control of his guilds, take over this whole matter, become the repository of his copyright, lease the various "rights" arising from it for his benefit, and never let one right get away from him for permanent possession, during the whole life of the copyright?

What is advocated here is an American Author's Authority, an AAA to operate like the musicians' ASCAP—or more accurately, the SWPA, which does not include publishers—and fill in the hiatus visible in the scope of the existing guilds. For while these, in their various ways, deal with wages, hours, and working conditions, as labor unions do and concern themselves with other things that can be grouped under the heading opportunity, or advantage, none of them deal in any effective way with his rights.

Yet his copyright, that precious, elusive thing from which all other rights spring, is the foundation of every business in which writing figures: theatre, magazine, book, radio, pictures, television. It is the one gimmick which gives promise at last of endowing the writer with something describable as power. If we shall conceive the thing launched it would work like this: The writer will send all works to the Authority to be copyrighted in its name for his benefit. The authority will then say, "We shall copyright for assignment no works except from writers who have become members of the proper guild." This will take care of the outlaw contributor who became so menacing to ASCAP at the time of its fight with the radio studios. It will also say we shall lease no rights except to lessors who comply with the basic agreements of the guilds. The Screen Writers' Guild and the Radio Writers' Guild will say, "We shall permit our writers to work on no material not leased through the Authority," and this will compel every writer in the country hoping for picture or magazine sale to send his work to the Authority for copyright before the magazines or publishers get it.

This is a most important point, for magazines copyright in their own name, and in such a fight as the Authority would face, the question of who gets there first, of who holds this scrap of paper, is of the essence. The Authors' Guild will say to the magazines and the publishers, "We will not permit our members to dispose of any material to you except they copyright first through the Authority," and the Dramatists' will say the same to the producers.

Now here, it is manifest, if the Guilds only stick together and act tough, is a potential source of incalculable strength. For the Authority, naturally, is not going to perform this service, this intricate job of keeping track of contracts, titles, the status of each copyright in accurately maintained files, for nothing. It will charge a fee, and it will assess this fee, not against writers, but against the lessors who obtain the material. If we assume this is 1% of the purchase price, and that it handles $25,000,000 worth of materials a year, its revenue would be $250,000, and for the first time the writer would have funds to take up certain matters that cry for attention.

First, there is the matter of a new copyright law, the present one being full of holes and flaws, its provisions not even extending to the radio, television, or the talking picture. Next there is the matter of a regularly maintained lobby in Washington, and of periodic lobbies in Sacramento, Springfield, and Albany, these being the places where most legislation affecting him is passed. Next, there is the matter of vigorous, aggressive prosecution of the writers' collective case in the courts, which would involve a discontinuation, on the part of the Authority, of the guilds' general policy of avoiding lawsuits if they can. The Authority, to be effective, must expect lawsuits, not only those brought against it, but those it will bring against the great corporate conspiracies noted above. The opportunity for improvement of the writer's status in this direction is prodigious. To advert, once more, to the decision in the Goldsmith case: if a copyright is not separable, as Judge Chase says, and there is no "sale" when picture rights are disposed of, what about these "rights" that picture companies, radio studios, magazines and book publishers are sitting on? Do they exist? Have these somewhat predatory interests, in their eagerness to rook the writer, built up a vast structure made of shadows, that can be made to vanish with smart legal action, and leave the writer once more with the properties he was so shamefully stripped of? Who knows?

Courts, like Talleyrand, usually feel it their duty to take sides with the strong in their struggle with the weak, but if there is so much as 1% of a chance that this vast victory can be won, we certainly should have the means, in sufficiently big dimension, to fight for it.

And finally there is the matter of the individual writer's case when he is the victim of infringement. The point here is that the Authority would itself be the holder of copyright, and would come in as the plaintiff, and not merely appear as amicus curiae, as the Authors' League did in the Goldsmith case; so that instead of a tiny, forlorn, ineffectual suit brought by one lone writer, a smashing, relentless legal action would be started, backed by careful, professional collection of evidence, and dependable, impressive witnesses.

Our purview would include every right that a writer can claim, from his right to be taxed as fairly as other citizens are, to his right to share the wealth produced by his own property, to his right to a competitive market, to his right to join such organizations as he chooses, to his right of free speech, to any other rights that are just. It would in no sense be agential, or ever concern itself with deals, or with prices. It would not be geared to do so, and if it attempted to do so it would probably be in trouble under the federal statutes. This is a field for agents, and its policy would be to cooperate with agents, in the belief they do a great service to the writer. But if, as often happens, a studio barred an agent, it would come piling in with the cut-out open, to enforce the writer's right to a representative of his own choosing.

Nor would the Authority concern itself with wages, hours, working conditions, royalties, fees, or any of the matters best dealt with by the guilds. But on any question of rights, as for example the failure of a magazine, a publisher, a radio station, or a picture company to live up to its contract, it would take over, to enforce the agreement the guild had made. Eventually, on the question of the writer's right to security, it would envisage the levy of a straight tax on all corporations with which the writer deals, based on their audited gross, in order to maintain a pool out of which member writers would receive, according to their rating, a sum every year, or perhaps an annuity. This, of course, is in the future, for the Authority must become very strong before it can attempt such a thing. The immediate problem is what we do now, and it does seem that if the four guilds will take the power that awaits them, a massively powerful organization is possible in a very short time, with a $1,000,000 kitty and a full-time tough mugg at the head of it.

It would be hard to say which will drive at it hardest, the magazine, the publishers, the radio stations, or the picture companies. But the situation is favorable wherever one looks. Naturally radio stations are limited in number, but there never was a time when new blood could get into business in other fields more easily, whether to start a new magazine, a new publishing house, or an independent picture company, or when more capital was available for these ventures. In Hollywood, particularly, the independent producers are quite hospitable to the idea of licensing material, instead of buying it outright, for this simplifies certain tax problems. When the Sale of Original Material Committee of the Screen Writers' Guild reported in favor of this system, it was thought radical; within a short time it was being accepted on all sides as the way the thing will be done. What the independents will accept the majors must agree to. Our chances, through diverting material to new outfits that will come to terms, are extraordinarily good. But we must have a united front. That, turned against us, has been our undoing. Turned the other way, it can permit us to win.

Who's Who in America
Preface to the 50th Anniversary Edition,
(Published in 1948)

Institutions, if they be actual and not merely nominal, will be found, I think, to possess some element, some simple, pregnant aspect, easily comprehensible to the popular imagination, which sets them off from other members of their class and gives them special status. Harvard University, certainly regarded as a thing apart, is the oldest college we have, and thus arouses reverence in the average mind, which probably doesn't know that it is also the richest, and certainly doesn't care that it is possibly, as some think, the wackiest. The late Caruso, not greatly surpassing various contemporaries in style, repertoire, or beauty of voice, could nevertheless sing louder than anybody on earth, and so passed into legend, along with Dan Patch, Babe Ruth and other living wonders. And Who's Who in America, though a gospel, a heresy, and a raging polemic in one, and thus potentially suspect, is at the same time a Dun, a Bradstreet, a social register and a hall of fame, all merged into a grand consolidated national glory highway, and thus unique in the eyes of the American people—this in spite of its frantic denials that it is any such thing, and the ironic agreement of its critics, that it certainly is not.

It didn't seek, and doesn't seek, this role, to that extent its asseverations are true; but this is merely one more instance of the difference between what is aimed at and what is hit. The original idea, as conceived by the late A.N. Marquis, who founded it in 1897, was simply that it be a source of exact information to be supplied by the subjects themselves, for the use of schools, libraries, newspapers, and scholars, about people likely to be frequent objects of inquiry. For a title, it is well known, of course, that he adapted to his purposes the title of the English "Who's Who," which had been published since 1848. What is not so well known is that this book, except for its title, bore almost no resemblance to the book Mr. Marquis had in mind. Until then, the English Who's Who was simply a handbook of official dignitaries, bearing more than a passing resemblance to the Social Register, the Royal Blue Book, and parts of the Statesman's Year Book, with no attempt at biography at all. Indeed, for most of the people it listed, there was little of a biographical nature to tell except their clubs, recreations, and degree of consanguinity with some noble lord; for the main point about them was their position, whereas Mr. Marquis was concerned, and indeed the whole American social scheme forced him to be concerned, with achievement. It is interesting to note that when his innovation prompted the English publishers to have a whirl at biography too, the change gained scant praise, so little that the change was regarded as a failure, and the editor responsible for it lost his job. Once accepted, though, it couldn't be discarded and crept steadily into the policy of the English book until even what a man had done began to take precedence over what he had been borne to. Of course, Mr. Marquis tried to standardize achievement as well as he could, so as to dissociate it from his personal opinion. Above a certain rank, in various fields of endeavor, such as the judiciary, the military, the Government, the academic faculty, and the like, the subject was listed ex officio. If he was an Army officer of specified rank or higher it made no difference whether he was a hero or not, whether Grant had relieved him at Cold Harbor, whether McKinley liked him: If he was of that general rank he was included in, if not, out. Industry, the liberal arts and the learned professions had to be considered on an individual basis, since they did not, and do not, make rank a systematic matter, but here eminence in the main was a guide, and since it was easily ascertainable, selections were not difficult.

And yet, back of all this, in spite of the impersonality which Mr. Marquis imposed on himself, judgments had been passed, comparisons made, citical standards raised. If he explained that all Federal judges were in, regardless of what law schools they had been graduated from or which Presidents had appointed them, there would be those to demand by what right a judge assumed to be of more importance than the owner of a 30,000-acre ranch, or why playwrights, as a class, apparently took precedence over wholesale grocers, or admirals over contractors. Without his knowing it, there lurked in this stubby, red-bound book, which presently came off the presses with some 8,000 biographies listed, the elements of a storm which goes on, though eased by sensible changes and prestige that time has conferred, quite briskly to this day.

However, there was little indication, from the reception accorded volume 1, of the controversies that would ensue later. It was reviewed, and in the main favorably, and the sales permitted Mr. Marquis to go ahead with volume 2, his plan being to bring out a new edition every 2 years; but it was not, so far as inspection of old newspaper files shows, very hot news. And it doesn't seem to have occurred to many people that anything unusual in the way of a reference book had made its appearance. For one thing, the county history, or book of sketches in which persons of prominence were written up for some trifling sum like $150, were what the country was accustomed to in the way of brief biography, and while Mr. Marquis said no sketch in his book could be paid for, many assumed that this needn't be taken too literally; such statements, indeed, were in no way unusual in that era, even in patent-medicine advertising, but it was usually found that a quid pro quo, a contribution to a worthy cause, could be discovered somewhere along the line, for a little looking. Little by little, however, through hearsay and repetition and personal testimony, it began to seep into popular consciousness that the Marquis statement was true: You couldn't in the case of this book buy in. Then a great many Americans began to ask: "If you can't buy in, but at the same time you are in, what is the answer?" It wasn't long before they said it: "You are a success." The next step, as soon as popular consciousness began to stir editorial consciousness, was that the book did become hot news, but of a peculiar kind. For, in addition to national and international apsects, it had city, state and even county aspects; it became as Gen. W. S. Hancock said of the tariff, "a local issue," and for much the same reason: it touched, directly and separately, every community in the land, for there was hardly one of them who didn't have somebody in it, only some lawyer who had got himself appointed to an official body which carried exofficio listing for its members. Thus, as each new volume appeared, all papers carried page 1 stories about it, with lists of local boys who had made good, and special attention to new boys in the freshman class. Then the editorial writers took over, airing countless opinions about it, some of them favorable, others not. Among those against was Mr. H. L. Mencken, and his biennial remarks on the subject first, in the Smart Set and, later, in the American Mercury, were awaited by all, and by none more eagerly, it was said, than the staff of Who's Who in Amercia themselves.

Opinion, as it appears in American newspapers, need not be taken too seriously, for lying back of it is the fact that an editor is always up against it for something to write about, and finds it easier as a rule, as well as more entertaining, to knock than to boost. Thus many complaints were captious and some were waggish. Yet in the early years there runs through these criticisms a fairly consistent vein; the book gave far too much space, it was said, to obscure clerics, do-gooders, and professors in small universities, and too little to hustlers, comedians, and similar celebrities, really in the news. It may be conceded, I think, that this complaint was more than slightly founded on fact. Mr. Marquis, though I never knew him, had the reputation of being a godly man; his picture, as I look at it now, suggests more a bishop of one of the Protestant faiths than a lay publisher of books. And he constantly proved, by the policies he adotped, that he was profoundly impressed by education and the deference due to educators. From the beginning, the advertisements of schools, colleges, and universities were the only ones he would accept, this rule being still in force, so that an American, when he opens the English Who's Who and finds all sorts of blurbs, notices and appeals scattered through it, and even stamped in gold on the cover, gets a bit of a jolt.

And it must be conceded he was almost incredibly indifferent to stage, screen, and the other lighted arts. It was the limited interest shown in these fields, I think, which really annoyed commentators most, as the omissions were glaring. And yet now, I think it can be argued that this very austerity, whether by luck or some profound sagacity that guided most things Mr. Marquis attempted, had much to do with the position the book occupies today. For it is almost impossible to picture such a work, dedicated to the cafe society of the early 1900s, as commending the confidence of intellectuals, and this confidence it had to have if it was to win general acceptance. Later, when rock-ribbed repute had been attained, would be time enough for broadening in places that had been too narrow. As a matter of fact, this liberalizing of the book has long since taken place. Mr. Wheeler Sammons, when he bought out Mr. Marquis in 1926, did not, so far as I know, make any radical changes. But he is a man of somewhat different temperament, more hospitable to the sophistications of life, and given to more contacts, so that he is probably in wider contact with his country than was his predecessor. He is said to maintain an organization, a set of advisors scattered all over, which makes it unlikely that any important subject be left out, and almost impossible that some inappropriate subject get in. Inappropriate subjects, from all one hears, are perhaps his chief grief. They lay siege to him in droves, by wire, by mail, by personal visit and by importunities of their friends, trying to get themselves listed. It is surprising, however, how few downright absurdities have been placed on the roll.

The Samons innovations are in no way dramatic, but they should be pondered by all who edit reference books, for they are corrective of the special ills that afflict reference books. The first, apart from the changes already noted, is the indication, in a clear, simple way, of the pronunciation of names about which there can be any doubt. To those who have struggled through musical reviews which assume familiarity with the most obscure titles, historical treaties which allude to forgotten personages without explaining who they were, or Britannica articles which quote, without translation, long passages of Latin—to all who have been annoyed by such phony pretensions of contributors, this gesture toward common sense is most refreshing. Often, due for lunch with some visiting fireman, one looks into Who's Who in America for information about him, and it is indeed most helpful, if he has some trick way of pronouncing his name, to know this in advance. And anyway, since names are often so arbitrarily pronounced, it is pleasant to be sure.

The second is the listing, begun some 10 years ago, of the subject's children, in addition to his marriages. This, as the effects accrue year after year and find their way into Who Was Who, will prove of enormous help to the American scholar, and not only lighten his labors but improve his work. As things stand now, information as to the descendents of some character of history is often maddeningly difficult to get, simply because the editors of reference books did not think to instruct their contributors, most of whom have the data at their fingertips, to include it. Such categories, for example, as our military families are not commonly the subject of easily located studies; their members flare into prominence briefly, then are little heard of until the next war, and articles about them are more concerned with military exploits than with sons, daughters, or in-laws. Seeking the kin of some general, one would give almost anything for a book that would list them definitely and quickly. Yet most books do not. The English Who's Who, careless at best on the question of marriage, is a complete blank on the subject of children: "1s, 3d." is its idea of treating the subject; that "s" and "d's" might have names is a possibility nobody apparently thinks of. The Dictionary of American Biography, to take an instance on our own side of the water, is a complete wash-out in this respect. The subjects' marriages it often mentions but rarely in such fashion that one can be sure the subject is fully covered. Children figure in such remarks as, "A daughter, Clara, has written a memoir, My Father and Reconstruction," but as to whether Clara was an only child or had brothers and sisters one is usually left in the dark. The Sammons contribution, if it goes no further than Who's Who in America, will do much to relieve this state of affairs; if it is imitated, as it should be, it could have a considerable effect on American biography.

Sharing Mr. Marquis' interest in education, and concerned over practical methods of promoting it, Mr. Sammons instituted, in 1938, Who's Who in America biennial citations for educational philanthropy. This, like the book itself, is something of a local issue too, for the terms of the award are so devised that it will not become the exclusive possession of a few rich men giving to a few rich colleges. For the amount of the award is considered in relation to the amount of endowment held by the college which gets it, sot hat small donors to small colleges are as likely to be recognized as large ones to larger places, and in point of fact many have been so recognized. Indeed, one can assume that such a citation, whose effect is likely to be considerable, can have the result of channeling money into places where it is really needed, rather than encouraging it to pile up in places where there is a great deal of it already.

In the course of an ordinary writing day, one consults the World Almanac at least once, the Brittanica three times, the Webster Unabridged Dictionary six, but Who's Who in America, in my own case anyway, is thumbed every hour on the hour. This addiction, this habit of settling endless things, from the spelling of a name to the title of a song, by a quick look-see at an appropriate entry goes back to my childhood, when I made the acquaintance of volume 1 in the year 1901, in my father's study at Annapolis, during a summer when I was supposed to be boning square root as a preliminary to a special promotion in school, but actually spent most of my time with this fascinating book, which told all about Roosevelt and Sampson and Schley and Dewey and McKinley and Bryan and other worthies of the era, as well as George W. Cable and James Whitcomb Riley, Joel Chandler Harris, and others lying closer to my heart, and transformed them from fabulous newspaper figures into flesh-and-blood human beings. This early association, long known to Mr. Sammons, is the reason for his suggestion that I contribute a preface—that and the circumstance that I am one of a brief list of persons mentioned both in Who's Who in America and Who Was Who in America.

My education, thus derived in no small part from these pages, has been invariably my entertainment too. I know of no book so endlessly absorbing as this, so full of surprises, so suitable to sporadic peeping or hour-long poring; if you are a stranger to it, I congratulate you, for many pleasant hours lie ahead, an adventure in self-improvement, though one, I am afraid, which is habit forming. It seems odd, as I make ready to wish it well on its second half century, to reflect that I shall not be here to see it make port at the hundred-year mark, and that Mr. Sammons won't, and that most of those now associated with it won't. But so great is its usefulness, so great its vitality, so profound its hold on the country, that I think we are safe in assuming that it will dock, on schedule, with full cargo. Bon voyage, then, red frigate of fortune, and may the passengers of the future match the distinction of those of the past, and of now.

That Which I Should Have Done I Did Not Do—Dammit All
(*The Washington Post*, May, 1976)

Of course, I look like a boy, talk like a boy, and act like a boy, but actually am into my eighties, and inevitably reflect now and then on the things that might have been and now never will be—the great expectations which won't come to pass. One of these, a special heartbreak now that it's rubbed out forever, was the plan I had for some years, of taking H.L. Mencken to see Will Mahoney. Mencken I imagine you've heard of, Mahoney perhaps you haven't. He was a dancer and teller of stories, one of which I can still recall. A young man, it seemed, went to his mother and told her: "Pop's getting married again—he said to tell you, and watch the look on your face." "Oh," said his mother, "I bet it's something to see. But you go back to him now, and tell him all those years he supported a child, meaning you, he thought was his but wasn't—and watch the look on *his* face." But the dancing was truly something, or as Hollywood calls it, out of this world. For example, he would tell a joke while leaning against the proscenium arch at Stage Left, and then start for Stage Center, but lose his balance and start to fall. He would fall and fall and fall, passing Stage Center, and keep straight on, still falling. Only after arriving at Stage Right would he complete his fall, after staggering and tottering and stumbling, finally collapsing in a heap against the other side of the proscenium arch.

All during this, the audience would hold its breath, then break into a roar of applause, at once a tribute to special skill and to the odd kind of originality that could think such an idea up. His whole act was full of things like that, and of marvelous dancing mixed in. But the climax of it was what I wanted Mencken to see. He would mount a thing like a xylophone, but one built so he could play it by dancing on it. Then, with his feet he would play The Stars and Stripes Forever, while firecrackers popped out of his toes. It was truly fantastic, and had the quality of madness. When I told Mencken about it, his face crinkled up in that Mephistophelian grin that he had, and he roared, assuring me that whatever he had on hand, in the way of engagements or plans, would be set aside for a trip to the theatre to see this incomparable show, "which will be an inspiration to me, one I promise you not to miss."

And then, on a winter day twenty years ago, came the news that Mencken was gone. I attended the funeral, of course, or the moment without words that served in lieu of a funeral, and afterward left my car on Hollins Street while Hamilton Owens, I, and two or three others, rode in Frank Kent's car for lunch at Marconi's, and to tilt a glass in Mencken's honor. On the way in I happened to remember my grand project, and Frank Kent shook his head. "If I ever heard of a show that was his kind of show, that would have been it," he said. "I would personally have given five dollars to hear what he would have said about it." So, at Marconi's, Mr. Brooks served us our glass, Hamilton Owens recited a toast, and we drank it.

Another grand project I had was a story I cooked up, that I wanted to offer Jack Benny. In it, Mr. Benny would have been incorporating his laundry, and need a reference for some reason—especially one going back to the days before he entered show business. Not being able to think of one, he would go to the public library, to consult the geographical locator of *Who's Who in America*—the breakdown it used to put out, of its subject listed by place of residence. Happily, he would find his man, one living near Waukegan, and quite prominent, to judge by his data. Mr. Benny would persuade himself he knew this magnifico, list him in his papers and also write him direct, recalling himself as Benjamin Kubelsky, and hoping, in case inquiry came, for a favorable report.

In my story, he was to mail both papers and letter, sure his man could hardly refuse, whether he actually placed him or not, and giving the thing no concern. But then one day Rochester came in to announce "a guy's out there, Mr. Benny—walking up and down." Mr. Benny would look and tell Rochester: "Well, there's no law against it."

"And no reason for it, either," Rochester would say. "Especially for how he looks at this house."

Then would come telephone calls, with a mysterious voice asking if this was the Jack Benny who wrote to a certain party asking for letters of recommendation," Mr. Benny would answer, but before he could say any more the phone would go click, the dial tone would buzz in, and he would realize his caller had hung up.

Then two mysterious men would come, with questions decidely unpleasant. Then the Post Office Department would get in it, with an inspector paying a call, and really putting the probe in. At last, Mr. Benny would find out he had written a man who didn't exist, a human booby-trap, invented by Who's Who in America to catch unethical Who's Whos, who pretend to do their own research, but actually steal it off others. So of course, if a bio sketch of this man appeared in some other Who's Who, it would be prima facie evidence of theft. I had got on his trail when for some reason I never learned, I was on Who's Who in America's "Council," and naturally heard a few things that most people don't. I thought there was merriment in the idea, if I could just meet Mr. Benny and lay it out for him. How to do this I didn't quite know, but thought George Burns a beginning. I had known Mr. Burns in Hollywood, and when he blew a song I happened to know, I wrote him about it, enclosing the words he couldn't remember. He answered very pleasantly, and that seemed an auspicious beginning—he might invite me over, if I happened to be in Hollywood, and I could take it from there. Then came the news Mr. Benny was gone. Apart from my grand scheme, I felt a sadness indescribable. If he was the funniest comedian of his time I have no faintest idea—but he was the one I loved. His passing was a blow, and it still verges on the incredible. He was a part of life, and as such somehow eternal— or at least seemed to be.

Another of my grand projects concerned W.C. Fields, and came about in a cockeyed way. I had been sent for, as they say, by Paramount to do a script on

The Great Gatsby, which they owned. I wasn't too much interested, as Gatsby is a very bad book, and eventually, when it was made a short time ago, resulted in a very, very bad picture. Also, I was up to my ears on a thing of my own, that was giving me all kinds of trouble—a book about the Big Depression, that I got the idea of when I lived in Burbank and would be held up sometimes by a freight, when driving out there from Hollywood. While waiting for it to pull out I would see heads, hundreds of them, of boys on top of those box cars, with nothing to eat and no place to go that night but the top of those box cars—knowing all the time, what they didn't know yet but would find out, that they'd be thrown off a few miles up the line, in some horrible field, perhaps out in the rain. So, I meant to take a boy and let the Depression happen to him. But Depressions don't grow on trees—if you're doing a book about one you have to go out and get it. So, I was in the middle of that, and as my friend Vincent Lawrence used to say: "Once you start rolling that snowball, lad, you got to roll it. You go off and leave it, when you come back it'll be just a wet spot on the lawn."

Still, Paramount was Paramount, so I went over to talk to a roomful of executives, most of them old friends. I set up conditions that didn't sit well, as they rated Gatsby better than I did, and weren't too keen about my ideas, one of which, for example, being that once in the course of the picture Gatsby would have to be shown as what Fitzgerald said he was; a bootlegger, big, ruthless, and successful. So, we got to wrangling, as most story conferees do. But then, as most story conferees also do, we got off the subject, and began talking about Fields. And here, I really went to town, criticizing the way he was handled. I explained I had known Fields very well when I lived in New York, having worked with him all one summer on an idea he had for a picture, that Philip Goodman was to produce and that I was selected to write. Goodman, father of Ruth Goodman Goetz, the playwright, was at that time big on Broadway, and had one curious achievement to his credit: He was the one who persuaded Fields he could talk. Until Goodman came into his life, Fields played in pantomime, mainly as a juggler, never saying anything. But Goodman thought he could talk, and set out to persuade him. Fields was very doubtful, but when Goodman came up with a script that was going around, agreed to give it a try. Between them they cooked up Eustace McGargle, the character Fields played the rest of his life, and the rest was theatrical history. The name of the show was Poppy, and Fields, from being a well-paid eccentric, became one of Broadway's big stars.

So then Goodman got the idea of producing a picture, and Fields knew about what. He would be proprietor of a Tom Show, as it was called, an Uncle Tom's Cabin company, touring the small towns, and so he and I settled down to try and cook up an outline. But we were always being interrupted—by Fields. Whatever we talked about seemed to remind him of something, and endlessly he could enchant me, with some anecdote about what had happened to him that day. And as these anecdotes piled one on top of the other, I little by little realized, that here was a very great actor, not only a gag comedian. I wasn't the only one. One afternoon in Hollywood Charles Laughton showed up at my house, a grin on his face, a Hollywood shirt with sleeves cut off at the elbows, white flannel trousers, and white shoes, to tell me what he had done in connection with the part he was tagged for at Metro, as Micawber in David Copperfield, that he had felt he was wrong for, and that he had persuaded the studio Fields was right for. He had just put the thing over, and when he came in he began talking about Fields and what a great actor he was, seeming greatly surprised I knew about this, and knew Fields. Micawber was distinctly a triumph, Fields proving he could do such a part, and vindicating Laughton.

So I went to town with my friends at our story conference, criticizing the way Fields was being harmed or mishandled, as I complained. I said: "You've got one of the great actors of all time and what do you do about it? You handle him as though he were Laurel and Hardy, or Harpo Marx, or Victor Moore. Why don't you wake up, once in a while? This guy is big—and you handle him small." And so on and on, for quite some time. When I shoot my mouth off I shoot it, I might explain. Tact isn't one of my virtues.

But presently I realized I wasn't getting the reaction I would have expected. They kept staring at me once they realized I knew Fields as well as I said, occasionally looking at each other, in a somewhat baffling way. Then Bill Wright, an old friend, said: "You think we don't know that?"

". . . Well?" I said. "Do you?"

"Yeah, we know it, you know it, and everyone knows it—but Fields. So all you've got to do is sell him and you got a job the rest of your life—or his life, as the case may be. Twenty-five hundred a week at least. So, you fell into something, Jim, go to it: Sell Fields and the job is yours. I'll ring you later today to confirm."

They seemed to mean business, if I did, so I had to think the thing over. I confess that being a nursemaid to Fields, which was what the job would add up to, however, didn't appeal to me, even at $2500 a week, which wasn't hay, and isn't hay now. Also, there was the Depression I was working on, which was giving me more and more trouble. Still, the honor of being the one to steer Fields into something big, simply would give me no peace. I resigned myself to it, that I had it to do. So, to move from the general into the particular, I decided it called for a concrete project, one I could dangle before him, as bait, to get him to change his approach. I hit on the idea of a remake, over at Metro, of the John Lee Mahin script of Treasure Island, with Fields playing Long John Silver, the part Wallace Beery had done, and whatever boy seemed indicated, playing the Jackie Cooper part.

I felt I was getting somewhere.

The Depression began giving less trouble.

Then W. C. Fields died.

I had other big dreams, of things I wanted to do, but these are enough for one day. I once wanted to be a singer, but that blew up too.

A Lance For Hollywood
(New Theater—London-March-April 1947)

I get the impression, from a letter the editors have written me, inviting me to survey things cinematic from the point of view of an American picture writer, that they expect me to be somewhat caustic at the expense of Hollywood. They seem to think that the picture writer, intellectually considered, is several cuts above his employers, and must therefore take some special attitude, perhaps one of complete cynicism, to adjust this difference and arrive at a *modus operandi* that will permit him to do his work. If this is the idea, and it is an idea commonly held in England and many parts of the United States, I am sorry, but I shall have to disappoint.

While there may be an occasional mental giant among the writers who overshadows the executive faculty, there are some tolerably informed men among the producers too, and it would be wholly false to suppose that one group dwells on an intellectual plane much higher than the other. In general, the producers know their job, and if the writer has grievances, most of them are not aesthetic and those that are tend to get ironed out with the years, as various favourable factors make themselves felt.

I should make it clear at the outset that picture writing has its serious aesthetic drawbacks, most of them irremediable. There is to begin with the grim and not easily altered fact that the picture writer does not own his product.

This, unquestionably does bring on a frame of mind which tends to take the cash and let the credit go. And yet, allowing for a good many things, the writer gets pretty fair understanding here in Hollywood, much more understanding than he appears to get in other places, particularly England; A Hollywood writer works under a "producer," a salaried employee of a big corporation. The writer checks in for work. The first morning may be wholly personal, for he and the producer are probably old friends, and if the story comes up at all it is usually for a brief mention before lunch. But in the afternoon both of them get down to brass tacks. Phone calls are cut off, so they may be uninterrupted, and marching up and down on opposite sides of the producer's office, they go over the story, novel, play, or whatever it is, that is to be adapted.

The writer, tends to bring up faults, for he is the one that has to get it on paper, and bad spots worry him. Here are some typical bad spots that often need fixing:

1. Uncinematic background. Experience has taught that squalor, however meritorious on the printed page, doesn't do well when photographed.

2. Uncinematic characters. Say what you will, the story must be acted by human beings, some of them already under contract, and most of them familiar to the public, which even knows the taboos associated with them, such as the one which forbids some celebrated child actress to be kissed by a boy. Or the characters may be drunks, hopheads, of midgets, which large sections of the public find objectionable.

3. Objectionable situations, usually have to do with sex.

4. Weak action.

5. Love story trouble.

Of the five, the first four present as a rule only routine difficulty, and only the last is important; that is uninspired solutions of the first four could get by, as the saying is, and not cause the picture to lose, but faulty handling of No. 5 could have the most ghastly consequences at the box office. Indeed, one of the first things an experienced picture writer does is have his secretary do a "breakdown" of the love scenes in the material to be adapted, with the number of pages devoted to each, a brutal, bookkeeper's test, but one that reveals more than you might think. If the total looks skimpy to him, or for some other reason unsatisfactory, he so informs the producer, and *gets instant response*. For both of them know the love story is *the* story. It is the coal in the bunkers from which everything else, the emotion, the comedy, the illusion of speed, is generated; and the time is past when the producer, irritated with technicalities, commanded the writer to go upstairs and write it anyway.

So, grimly, regretfully, but resignedly, this new type of producer listens to what his writer tells him, and they start the laborious business of finding out what the trouble is. Whatever it is, it is gone into fundamentally, and I would like to make clear, for the benefit of those who assume such weird things about Hollywood, that neither producer nor writer resorts consciously to slick cinematic tricks. Slick, cinematic tricks, we may concede without argument, are resorted to constantly in Hollywood, but not in the good pictures, not in the big $2,500,000 superdupers that are really expected to please a wide public. Tricks are for the B's, and there is no surer way to get a B rating than to begin using them.

Nor is there any conscious reach for sex. For Hollywood, not only the successful part of Hollywood, but the little independents and horse-opera studios as well, long ago found that sex, if she is to make the trip, must always go as a stowaway. If emotion is abroad, there is sex, tucked away under a lifeboat. But if emotion misses the boat, and sex comes abroad on her ticket then the fine brave liner turns into a riverboat. I mean, the whole industry out here knows there is one sure way to make an expensive production look like a cheap burlesque show, and that is to make deliberate lunge at sex.

Now it is right here, if I may put my two-cents' worth into this mighty effort to revitalize English pictures, that the average English picture goes to pieces. It is not, let me say at once, that the average English picture hasn't a great deal of merit. Its acting is distinguished, verging on inspired; its direction is good, though often blurred in the department of accenting; and while its editing, or cutting as it is called, is usually bad, it is not bad enough to be decisive. Yet some factor makes it unacceptable, not to the critics, who usually praise it, but to the great human, 100 per cent British public that the British picture must reach before it can be counted as reaching anybody at all. Let me stress this point. The last time I was in England, which was in 1939, I inquired and looked and hunted, trying to find a theatre that showed all English movies, yet at the end of a week's trudging the best I could find was a place near my hotel which showed one English newsreel. Practically everybody in England, if you go by the bookings, and there is little else to go by, likes Hollywood movies, and almost nobody likes English movies.

The decisive factor, I believe, and many out here in Hollywood believe, is the failure of the British picture writer, with the help of his producer, to solve this problem that lies at the centre of every script: the love story. English pictures simply do not have love story, or enough love story. I can think of no exception to this statement, and I have seen a great many English pictures. Somewhere along the line the English nation which handles aesthetic matters, decided to be quite casual about love. Any open emotion became distinctly bad form, and matter of factness a sort of cult. Now this certainly has charm, on one condition. If we know that under the calm great volcanoes are smouldering, then it is pretty terrific. But if under the calm there is nothing but more calm, then we have only a set of very hollow people betraying their complete futility.

Well, I don't see any futility in the English people, but I see a complete futility in the English movie, for what the English producer has done is mistake the appearance for the substance, and depicted a world so false and so dull that even its own public cannot stomach it.

I don't know if what Hollywood does is worth while, but I do know that what it does is what people like, and have some suspicion that what is liked is what has life in it, i.e., what is good. Hollywood does a love story. And if this makes you smile, I must ask you, in all seriousness; what is so funny, all of a sudden, about this thing called love? The last I heard of it, it was responsible for the perpetuation of the human race. If sex were all, a system of concubinage would do it nicely, and the human race would disappear, as it has in fact begun to disappear in all civilizations where sex became overly important and concubinage became the style. I am talking about what impels one man to marry one woman and settle down with her and have children and pursue happiness. I am talking about what, to a professional writer of tales, is the greatest intellectual challenge he knows: the opportunity to examine this massive fact that supports the human race, to depict its surge and hunger and hope and drive, and do so with a relentless acceptance of the principles by which it moves, and with an opportunity to make other human beings feel about it what he feels about it. And I must say that when the English picture industry assumes that volcanoes have become obsolete, I am completely bewildered. Here they are, at this late date, after appropriating millions for the venture, making the same old mistakes and producing the same old flops. *Caesar and Cleopatra,* written by one man more celebrated for his brains than his loins, and *Henry V,* written by another more celebrated for his word than for his brains and loins combined are just two more out of the same old barrel. Permit me to tip the English picture business off to something: love story is tough. It is hard to write. You can't just order up a lot of Egyptian scenery and a couple of expensive actors, or do a production job in applied boobology masquerading as history, and expect to get away with it. You really have to contrive and work and sweat and get something fresh. That way all the critics will laugh at you and your effort to outdo Hollywood. But the people will buy tickets, because the people love each other, and they haven't heard of this casual thing yet. And when you do this, instead of Hollywood owning Piccadilly, you'll own it.

Well, this started out to be a little item about Hollywood writers, and it turns out to be a betrayal of a vast trade secret, worth at least $150,000,000 to the British picture producers, if they take the trouble to read it. They ought to do what their ambassador has recently done here, in Iowa, of all places: go out and find out what people are really like. If they find one human being who got here by any other method except the good old-fashioned love system, they can send me the bill. I'll pay the whole $150,000,000 somehow.

Americana My Foot
(The Washington Post, October 31, 1977)

In the closing days of the last century, when I was a boy, and you, I imagine, weren't yet a gleam in your romantic father's eye, all barbershops had a sign in the window: CHIROPODIST. And sure enough, when you went in there the gentleman was waiting for you in the shoe-shine assembly, which of course wasn't used for shines except on Saturday afternoons.

It consisted of a high seat, topside, with footrests in front of it, and a low seat in front of the footrests, on which the chiropodist sat. He helped you up to the high seat, and when you had put a foot on one of the rests, helped you off with your shoe and stocking. Then, carefully, so as not to cause pain, he swabbed off your corn, put a compress on to soften it, then began slicing at it with his scalpel, which he intermittently whetted on a stone.

Very quickly, he had the corn completely circled and undercut, then lifted it out. In the center of where it had been was a soft white pip which he took out with his tweezers. Left was a pink hole, to which he applied a dressing and an adhesive-tape bandage, then he gave your trousers a tweak, to let you know he was done, and helped you on with your stocking and shoe.

The charge, which I don't expect you to believe, but I swear is true, as I know from personal experience, having paid it often enough, was 25 cents, the quarter part of a dollar.

Now obviously, for this right to make a living at that moderate charge, a great many people had to have corns, and a great many did. So many did that the chiropodist became a standard American institution so familiar to all that he was the subject of a skit by John Bunny, the leading motion picture comedian of the era, who milked him, as they say, for laughs. One may take exception to Mr. Bunny on the score of taste, for some of the business he put in was quite raw, but it can't be denied that it delighted audiences all over the world, and that it dealt with what, to them, was a completely familiar personage.

So why did so many people have corns? Because it was an era which associated small feet with gentility, and of course if you had small feet, to prove you had small feet you had to wear small shoes. That the shoes hurt, that they didn't fit, was completely disregarded, or accepted as one of the hazards of life, and actually it was assumed that any pair of new shoes had to be "broken in" as it was called, and often, when a man bought a pair, he had a relative, or employee, or debtor "break them in for him," wearing the shoes two or three weeks, until, in theory at least, they were comfortable to his feet. And then suddenly nobody had corns. They just disappeared from the scene. Why?

The U.S. Army got into the act, that's why. It can't use soldiers with corns, and so it had the bright idea, toward the end of 1918, with the First World War going on and soldiers needed to fight it, of putting shoes on the soldiers that were big enough—usually to the soldiers that were big enough—usually to the soldiers' great dismay. I remember when I came in for my shoes, the quartermaster sargeant dropped a pair of brogans on the floor in front of me that simply struck me as funny. They were of what seemed to be raw cowhide, but made with the smooth part inside, the rough part out. When I put them on I burst out laughing. "Sergeant," I said, "I'm sorry to inform you but a pair of cockroaches could run a race without bumping, between these shoes and my foot."

"Okay," he said. "I'll take the gray, you take the black. I'll give you even money—what do you say to $5?"

"I say I want other shoes."

"You don't get them. You're taking these or standing a court."

"I don't like no court."

"Then—"

"I'm taking the shoes?"

"That's it. Now you've got it."

"They look more like beer kegs."

"Something wrong with beer?"

"Not that I know of."

"Okay then—dismissed."

"wore the shoes to France, and all corns dropped off.

So what about now? I called the Podiatry Associates and found things haven't changed much. People still have corns, in addition have buniens and malformations of various kinds, especially women, from wearing the kind of shoes that throw their weight on the ball of their foot, which is not natural for them, and bulge their insteps up. Some years ago, it seems, men began wearing extra high boots but found them so uncomfortable they switched back to sensible shoes of the kind they'd been wearing since they abandoned the too-small shotes of the 1800s.

One point, though, I think should be made. The podiatrist no longer charges the 25 cents the old-time chiropodist charged. His bill will be a bit more.